Routledge Revivals

The Chinese Classic Novels

First published in 1988, this reissue is an important work in the field of national literary exchange. Declared by American Library Association in its Choice publication one of the ten best reference works of 1988, the volume has survived global change - politically, socially, economically, religiously, aesthetically - to promote cultural dialogue between China and the West.

Equally to be observed is accelerating demand, especially in academic institutions, for global cultural exchange through national literatures. How can we of the English-speaking world, for example, adequately understand and converse with our Chinese counterparts without some appreciation of their culture, notably of Confucian and Taoist roles in their history as reflected in their literature?

Overall, a pioneering work whose reissue will be welcomed by both scholars and general readers alike.

The Chinese Classic Novels
An Annotated Bibliography of Chiefly English-Language Studies

Margaret Berry

First published in 1988
by Garland Publishing, Inc.

This edition first published in 2011 by Routledge
2 Park Square, Milton Park, Abingdon, Oxon, OX14 4RN

Simultaneously published in the USA and Canada
by Routledge
270 Madison Avenue, New York, NY 10016

Routledge is an imprint of the Taylor & Francis Group, an informa business

© 1988 Margaret Berry

All rights reserved. No part of this book may be reprinted or reproduced or utilised in any form or by any electronic, mechanical, or other means, now known or hereafter invented, including photocopying and recording, or in any information storage or retrieval system, without permission in writing from the publishers.

Publisher's Note
The publisher has gone to great lengths to ensure the quality of this reprint but points out that some imperfections in the original copies may be apparent.

Disclaimer
The publisher has made every effort to trace copyright holders and welcomes correspondence from those they have been unable to contact.

A Library of Congress record exists under ISBN: 0824066332

ISBN 13: 978-0-415-59524-7 (hbk)
ISBN 13: 978-0-203-83247-9 (ebk)
ISBN 13: 978-0-415-60979-1 (pbk)

THE CHINESE CLASSIC NOVELS

GARLAND REFERENCE LIBRARY
OF THE HUMANITIES
(Vol. 775)

THE CHINESE CLASSIC NOVELS
An Annotated Bibliography of Chiefly English-language Studies

Margaret Berry

GARLAND PUBLISHING, INC. • NEW YORK & LONDON
1988

© 1988 Margaret Berry
All rights reserved

Library of Congress Cataloging-in-Publication Data

Berry, Margaret, 1918–
   The Chinese classic novels: an annotated bibliography of chiefly English-language studies / Margaret Berry.
   p.   cm. — (Garland reference library of the humanities; v. 775)
   Includes indexes.
   ISBN 0-8240-6633-2 (alk. paper)
   1. Chinese fiction—Bibliography.   I. Title.   II. Series.
Z3108.L5B47   1988   [PL2415]   016.8951'3'008—dc19
88-4816   CIP

Printed on acid-free, 250-year-life paper
Manufactured in the United States of America

To Duan-mu Hong-liang

scholar, artist, critic, author, humanist, and

master of HUNG-LOU MENG

who greeted me in Beijing

with words of K'ung Fu-tse:

"Is it not a pleasure to have friends come from afar?"

CONTENTS

Foreword	ix
Preface and Acknowledgments	xiii
Useful Terms and Dynastic Dates	xv

Chapter I
General Introduction ... 1
General Sources (designated A): a) Databases ... 9
    b) Bibliographies ... 9
    c) Specific Works ... 11

Chapter II
THE ROMANCE OF THE THREE KINGDOMS (SAN-KUO-CHIH YEN-I)
Introduction ... 65
Sources (designated B): a) Translations ... 71
    b) Studies ... 74

Chapter III
THE WATER MARGIN (SHUI-HU CHUAN)
Introduction ... 91
Sources (designated C): a) Translations ... 98
    b) Studies ... 103

Chapter IV
MONKEY, or JOURNEY TO THE WEST (HSI-YU CHI)
Introduction ... 127
Sources (designated D): a) Translations ... 134
    b) Studies ... 137

Chapter V
THE GOLDEN LOTUS (CHIN P'ING MEI)
Introduction ... 163
Sources (designated E): a) Translations ... 169
    b) Studies ... 171

Chapter VI
THE SCHOLARS (JU-LIN WAI-SHIH)
Introduction ... 191
Sources (designated F): a) Translations ... 197
    b) Studies ... 200

Chapter VII
THE DREAM OF THE RED CHAMBER (HUNG-LOU MENG)
Introduction ... 215
Sources (designated G): a) Translations ... 226
    b) Studies ... 231

Author Index ... **281**
Title Index ... **289**

FOREWORD

It is just the right time for the appearance in the West of THE CHINESE CLASSIC NOVELS: AN ANNOTATED BIBLIOGRAPHY OF CHIEFLY ENGLISH-LANGUAGE STUDIES by a scholar who has for three decades studied and taught Chinese traditional literature. Today, as China undergoes an unparalleled time of opening to the outside world, that world urgently needs to understand the nation whose history and culture go back three thousand years. What better way than through its classical literature, especially the novel? Johann Wolfgang von Goethe read these works in translation and his appreciation for them deeply impressed his European followers.

Indeed, the best way to know a nation's social customs and understand its attitudes and actions is through its literature. Only this reading can convey a vivid picture of its national reality and the wave of its history. I myself know a little of the United States through the novels of Washington Irving, Mark Twain, Jack London, Ernest Hemingway, and others. In Twain's work, for example, I have learned about the Mississippi river and life along its shores. In Chinese classic novels Westerners can know of the living Yangtse and its sister Yellow River, about people living in the two great valleys, and about their inner worlds.

THE CHINESE CLASSIC NOVELS bridges a chasm between China and the English-speaking West; it offers a key to doors locked by language and other cultural barriers. Marco Polo's footprints have been engraved on the Logouqiao Bridge as well as on gold bricks of the Emperor's Audience Hall. Yet the explorer's first knowledge of Yuan China rested on translations. This ANNOTATED BIBLIOGRAPHY points out another kind of Logouqiao Bridge, across which journeys can be made.

I sincerely hope that the reading of translated Chinese classic novels will surge in the future so as to reveal to hosts of Western readers the beauty, clarity, and humanity of Chinese literature.

This work offers a key to open China's doors culturally.

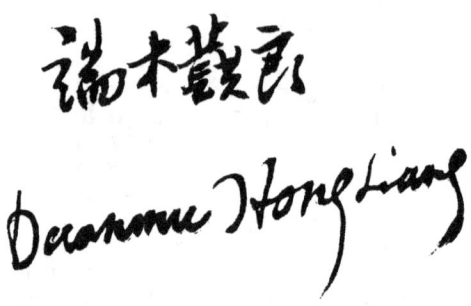

Duan-mu Hong-liang (pen name, Cao Jingping) is a native of Chang Tu County in Liaoning Province, China. He entered Tianjin's Nankai Middle School in 1928, joined the Northern Leftwing Writers' League in Beijing in 1932 and, after an examination, was admitted into Qing Hua University's history department. There, serving on QING HUA WEEKLY's editorial committee, he set up a postbox under the pseudonym "Xin Ren" to receive progressive newspapers, and periodicals from home and abroad. In fall 1933, as the Leftwing Writers' League met trouble, Duan-mu ran away to Tianjin to write his novel KERQIN BANNER PRAIRIE. In 1935 he returned to Beijing to take part in the December 9 Movement, afterwards going to Shanghai where he wrote another novel, THE SEA OF THE EARTH, and short stories which appeared in noted magazines such as LITERATURE, WRITERS, and MAINSTREAM before publication in one volume, HATRED.

FOREWORD

In 1938, Duan-mu, now married to writer Xiao Hong, went to Chongqing, invited by Sun Hanbing, Fudan University's Dean of Studies, to edit ABSTRACT SUPPLEMENT and act as University Professor of Information. Unable, for health reasons, to accept his later appointment as literature professor, he and Xiao went to Hong Kong, where he supervised THE GREAT LITERATURE AND ART SERIES and founded the monthly TIME-LITERATURE. Following the outbreak of the Pacific War and Xiao's death, Duan-mu retired to Guilin; there, from 1942 to 1948, he produced the novels THE YANGTSE RIVER and SIDELIGHTS OF CHONQING, afterwards returning to Hong Kong.

On the eve of the founding of the People's Republic of China, Duan-mu returned to Beijing to help set up the Beijing Federation of Literature and Art Circles, becoming Vice Secretary General. Presently he serves as a council member of the China Writers' Association, as vice president of the Beijing Writers' Association, as adviser of the HUNG-LOU MENG and Smedley-Snow-Strong Societies, and as member of the International PEN. In recent years he has published collections of prose, RECENT WORKS OF DUAN-MU HONG-LIANG and FEATHERS OF THE FIREBIRD, as well as the first two volumes of his novel TS'AO HSUEH CH'IN. Currently he devotes himself to the third and final volume of this work.

PREFACE

This bibliography is created primarily for teachers who, without competence in Chinese, choose to know and to teach as much as they can about Chinese literature. Unhappy with the general exclusion in this country of Chinese classics, literary and vernacular, from introductory, survey, genre, and comparative courses, they venture to find the best possible translations of the finest works and their soundest explications and to use them unstintingly for personal and professional pleasure and profit. Pioneers though they find themselves, their gains outweigh their risks by far, and to them these chapters are especially addressed.

Yet this target audience does not exclude others: comparativists who refuse to remain ignorant of what may profitably be known in translation; historians and social scientists who want to learn from literary depiction of historical and contemporary eras; lovers of literature generally; even specialists who delight in quick and comfortable reviews.

The six novels at the heart of this enterprise, all completed between 1600-1800, are, by critical consensus and in C.T. Hsia's words, "historic landmarks" in the development of the Chinese novel. To them critics turn for prototypes of the historical novel, the adventure romance, the long supernatural tale, the Juvenalian account of bourgeois manners and morals, the autobiographical satire, the novel of psychological realism. To some of us it may come as a surprise that even among scholars the Chinese novel has been the subject of serious published studies in English for little more than a quarter of a century. Even the most famous and popular novel, HUNG-LOU MENG (DREAM OF THE RED CHAMBER) had no English book-length studies until the 1960s when two were produced.

With few exceptions the books, articles, monographs, and dissertations here listed have been individually handled, read, evaluated, and abstracted. Problems have been concerned less with the readings than with the codifying of transliterations and variant titles and characters' names as they appear in different versions of the same work. My not very satisfying decision has been, where possible, to prefer the Wade-Giles system to pin-yin (a newer system) and to exercise flexibility in the matter of titles and names, permitting them to appear in Chinese and/or English as seems convenient in a given context. Despite efforts at consistency of style in these matters, circumstances constantly arose to frustrate that intent.

Of the four hundred or so works annotated in this volume, about five percent, in French or German, are included as reminders of world interest in Chinese literature and as points of comparison this writer has found enlightening.

After a preliminary survey of the rise and development of the novel form in China, an introductory bibliography lists databases useful in literary research, specific bibliographies, and general historical and critical studies. In a chronological treatment of the novels according to estimated date of composition, each succeeding chapter first discusses the narrative itself and the body of English-language commentary and criticism concerning it, with special attention to recurring and controversial problems. Following these considerations appear lists of annotated translations and thereafter of annotated individual studies, usually but not always descriptive rather than normative.

Extended notes have been given for articles deemed of special importance to the target audience. Chapters are lettered in sequence but numbered autonomously, and indices provide separate author and title lists.

I wish to acknowledge John Carroll University's generous support in providing time and means to complete this project, librarian Brother William J. Balconi's indefatigable and indispensable aid in procuring materials, faculty secretary Jean Belin's patient and tireless preparation of camera-ready copy, and editor Phyllis Korper's always available direction and encouragement. Thanks also to George

PREFACE

Erikson of the Santa Barbara Press, Santa Barbara, California, for permission to reprint the poem "To Kuo Mo-jo, November 17, 1961" as translated by Ma Wen-yee from SNOW GLISTENS ON THE GREAT WALL, 1986. I cannot, finally, let the opportunity slip of acknowledging the long and loving support of my many brothers and sisters, each of whom has, in his or her own special way, contributed to whatever success this work may have.

Useful Terms

ch'uan ch'i — short, classical-language tales originating in the T'ang Dynasty

five-elements — a cosmological theory that five metaphysical forces or modes (represented by wood, fire, earth, metal, and water) dominate or control time periods in fixed succession, and, by analogy, all aspects of the divine and natural worlds (e.g. animals, grains, organs, colors, directions, virtues, planets, officers, and historical reigns)

hsiao-shuo — a Han Dynasty term for trivial expression, which, by Ch'ing times, had come to mean non-historical short stories and novels

hua-pen — a Sung Dynasty term for the vernacular short story, also used at times to designate storytellers' prompt books

kung-an — crime-and-detection vernacular fiction, often involving court cases

pien-wen — Buddhist stories sacred and secular (often intimately related to pictures), most dating from the eighth through the tenth centuries and associated with manuscript findings in the Tun-huang Caves

pi-chi — brief, casual jottings

p'ing-hua   vernacular narratives dealing with an historical period rather than with a single individual

pin-yin   an international transliteration code devised to supersede the Wade-Giles system

tao (the Way)   the underlying principle, the basic, undivided unity in which all contradictions and distinctions are ultimately resolved (Taoist); the underlying principle in which moral and cosmic order are one (Confucian)

yen-i   a fictionized historical narrative remaining, in the large, faithful to historical records

yin-yang   the principle of complementary opposites, ever transforming into each other

Some Important Dynasties

Han Dynasty (202 B.C.-A.D. 220)

[Time of Troubles (220-609)
   Includes the Period of the Three Kingdoms (220-280)]

T'ang Dynasty (618-906)

Sung Dynasty (960-1279)
   Includes the Northern Sung Dynasty (960-1127)
            the Southern Sung Dynasty (1127-1279)

Yuan (Mongol) Dynasty (1260-1368)

Ming Dynasty (1368-1644)
   Includes the Wan-li Period (1573-1620)

Ch'ing (Manchu) Dynasty (1644-1912)
   Includes the K'ang-hsi Period (1661-1722)
            the Yung-chung Period (1723-1736)
            the Ch'ien-lung Period (1736-1796)

The Chinese Classic Novels

CHAPTER ONE

General Introduction

Depending on one's definition of fiction, the novel form can in any country be traced to the dawn of its art. Narrowing the concept to imaginative non-metrical narrative, one can still track it to a nation's earliest sustained prose. Unsurprisingly, then, the Chinese novel's distant antecedents include consciously fictive elements in pre-dynastic classics: the SHU CHING (BOOK OF HISTORY), for example; the CH'UN CH'IU (SPRING AND AUTUMN CHRONICLES); the ANALECTS; the BOOK OF MENCIUS; the TSO CHUAN COMMENTARY; or the BOOK OF CHUANG-TSE, and, later, the SHIH CHI (RECORDS OF THE HISTORIAN), compiled by Han Grand Historians Ssu-ma T'an and his more famous son Ssu-ma Ch'ien.

But in these works history, philosophy, and ethics are central, fiction but a maid. Not until the T'ang Dynasty (618-906) does prose fiction, in the ch'uan ch'i literary tales, emerge as an independent form centered on consciously shaped imaginative material. Written by scholars in classical language and a simple, moving style, ch'uan ch'i would soon at times merge with vernacular prose.

That vernacular prose, however, received its greatest impetus from Buddhist oral and written storytelling rising alongside ch'uan ch'i. Hundreds of pien-wen, Buddhist tales often with accompanying pictures and usually of religious import, are listed in the 30,000 Chinese manuscripts dating from the fifth through the thirteenth centuries found in Unit 16 of the frescoed Caves of the Thousand Buddhas. These were recovered when, in 1900, Sir Aurel Stein opened the Tun-huang archaeological complex between China and Central Asia near the end of the Great Wall. Combining religious zeal and sectarian talent, the pien-wen exhibit numerous narrative techniques preparing the way for the novel: devices for creating suspense, underscoring dialogue, arousing laughter, exciting wonder, including song and recitation as in chantefable and drum-accompanied performances.

But if salvation of souls was pien-wen's original goal, it did not for long so remain. Secular tales and domestic intrigue quickly found expression in the new medium. By Sung times (960-1279) Buddhism had waned, but not its storytelling art, now the special province of leisured middle classes in burgeoning urban districts, demanding entertainment. In amusement centers great and small, however, in city, town, and country, wherever people wanted to be amused and maybe in the process improved, storytellers' guilds flourished. Some masters of the art wrote down plot notes providing a ground for inexhaustible improvisation, transitional cues, stock phrases to refresh their memories. Their introductions demanded dialogue, comedy, a song or two; breaks (to become novel chapter divisions) had to be provided for refreshment, money collection, and exhortation to attend the next session. Such matters required memoranda booklets called hua-pen, some of which developed their own unity and independence as reading material and became, as it were, novelettes. These hua-pen, with Yuan p'ing-hua (vernacular/simple-classical tales of an historical era rather than of individuals), became the immediate forebears of the novel form.

Inevitably, as narrative variety grew—historical, supernatural, realistic, religious—clusters of stories focused on the same person or event; cycles were developed. The novel was at hand, but not to be realized before absorption of Yuan dramatic techniques.

Mongols of the Yuan Dynasty (1260-1368), enamored by superior Chinese culture, especially its vernacular literature, had chosen drama as their favored form. Upon it, until then in official disfavor, and upon its theaters and performances they lavished unprecedented patronage. Drama, for its part, drew from history and fiction, whether single episodes, clusters of tales, or well-rounded cycles of events. All novelists being at heart dramatists, stage presentation could not but enrich storytellers' developing powers of suspenseful narrative and vivid characterization.

With the Ming Dynasty (1368-1644) arrived the full-fledged Chinese novel, a shaping of many episodes, developed

GENERAL INTRODUCTION 3

perhaps in storytelling and drama, into a coherent whole. First to excel in the genre was the fourteenth-century SAN-KUO-CHIH YEN-I (ROMANCE OF THE THREE KINGDOMS), recounting events during the fall of the Han Dynasty (202 B.C.-A.D. 220) and its turbulent aftermath and relying, not on vernacular texts, but on historical documents. In dominantly literary language, its contents are described as seven-tenths historical, three-tenths fiction.

SAN-KUO had dealt with dynasty-building; other yen-i treated the process of national stabilization or dynastic succession and increasingly relied upon vernacular rather than classical Chinese. Eventually and perhaps inevitably there arose the pseudohistorical novel, more properly called the romantic adventure novel, of which the greatest is the sixteenth-century SHUI-HU CHUAN (THE WATER MARGIN). Claims of this work to historicity lay chiefly in the bandit hero's name and in a vaguely formulated twelfth-century setting. Other such novels rose out of an author's need to conceal identities, to find a suitable context for a story or theme, sometimes for the convenience of an easily defined setting. As well as providing the writer with a recognized past, "history" could supply other literary needs, including respectability, and authors were not remiss in availing themselves of so rich an opportunity.

Besides historical and pseudohistorical novels, others, less esteemed because less reliant on China's known past, were the hsiao-shuo (a Han expression for trivial or undignified writing, which developed into a comprehensive term for short stories and non-historical novels) covering at first, vernacular narratives of manners, brothels, scholar-and-beauty romance, knight errantry, pornography, crime and detection, and moral and satirical allegory. The most famous collections of these forerunners of the realistic, non-historical novel appear in three volumes of editor Feng Meng-lung (1574-1646).

By the end of the Ming Dynasty (1368-1644) the supernatural novel HSI-YU CHI (MONKEY, or JOURNEY TO THE WEST), with its realistic implications for everyday life and its easily detected satire on religious institutions, had captivated the hearts of thousands of Chinese readers by its imaginative flamboyance, vivid characterization, and high comedy. CHIN P'ING MEI, the first novel of manners and domestic realism, had stunned them with its powerful satire on personal, familial, professional, and political corruption, seen from bourgeois perspective.

Despite literati rejection of hsiao-shuo (popular fiction) from the category of works distinguished as "literature," many scholars and bureaucrats not only read and enjoyed these works, but often, anonymity assured, themselves wrote and disseminated them. With the expansion of printing and publishing and increasing urban middle-class taste for novels came demand for newer, more experimental approaches to the art of long fiction.

The eighteenth century, with its troubled consolidation of the Manchu Dynasty (1644-1912) and the growing dominance of novel over short story, saw new forms arise, including two of China's greatest novels. JU-LIN WAI-SHIH (THE SCHOLARS), written in exclusively vernacular but simple and dignified style, is China's first known autobiographical novel, an embittered satire against corrupt social institutions, especially the examination system, depriving the idealist Confucian of noble public service and self-fulfillment therein. Greatest of all China's novels, HUNG-LOU MENG or THE DREAM OF THE RED CHAMBER, (also, in the Hawkes-Minford translation, known as SHIH T'OU CHI or THE STORY OF THE STONE) stands, with GENJI MONOGATARI, RECHERCHE DU TEMPS PERDU, and MIDDLEMARCH, as a world classic of psychological realism. But HUNG-LOU MENG is, too, a novel of manners, a family saga, a pageant of eighteenth-century Chinese society, a tragic triangular love affair, an autobiography, an allegory against Manchu domination, a novel of initiation and apprenticeship--all these and more.

Authorship of classic Chinese novels presents numerous problems. Some of these spring from evolutionary and composite composition; others from exigencies spawned by official disdain for the theory and practice of fiction. Scholars today rigorously question authorship attributions not founded on assuredly contemporary evidence available in extant documents. The attributions persist, nevertheless, and become troublesome as one moves from critic to critic. Rendering the problem more complicated is the fact that not until late Ch'ing times did authorship become a viable economic choice; other incentives than fame and fortune had to inspire a novelist.

GENERAL INTRODUCTION

The six classic Chinese novels, not in all respects typical of their contemporary literatures, nevertheless invite some generalizations about their content and style.

The narratives show an unquenchable thirst for life, an affirmation of the world and zest for experience diametrically opposed to the dark, escapist views of Dravidian-based South-Asian literatures or the nihilism of modern existentialist and absurdist Western writers. No ennui, as C.T. Hsia remarks, or arid cynicism afflicts Chinese characters; no Stranger (as in Camus) or Underground Man (as in Dostoyevsky) appears. Chinese classic novels show, too, insatiable curiosity about individuals, as often as not with self-destructive obsessions, confronting society.

Characteristic devotion to history and pressure to conform to long-established social norms in these novels invariably color events and relationships. All the narratives, with the possible exception of SAN-KUO-CHIH YEN-I, in some degree recognize as an appropriate novel function the criticizing of social and government excess. All are conscious of an overriding moral law and inexorable retribution for wrong. Most use, in Andrew Plaks' terms, complementary bipolarity (yin/yang theory) and multiple periodicity (the five-elements system of correspondences) as structural entities. Rarely do the authors enter a character's mind, instead revealing what they must of hidden motivations and reactions by gesture, symbol, and dialogue.

The most important single content factor is, however, the triple religious dynamic: Confucian, Taoist, and Buddhist. Unstable political and social conditions of Ming and early Ch'ing Dynasties weakened traditional religions; despite the Neo-Confucianism now entrenched in officialdom, syncretism ruled the day. Frequently in the novels some aspect or other of one religion is given disproportionate emphasis, or two or three religions function without conclusive choice. One finds the same novel labeled by different scholars Confucian, Taoist, or Buddhist. In any event, all the religions, each in its own way powered by yin-yang and five-elements correspondences, strive toward harmony. That harmony--beginning with an individual's own faculties, rises through family, state, world, and cosmos--to achieve the Great Harmony, the essential Chinese ideal.

Among the one hundred plus books and articles in the general bibliography certain interests and concerns stand out: 1) The need for a comprehensive, reliable history of Chinese literature, specifically of the Chinese novel. Such a work would, according to scholars here cited, involve both a) external literary history (as the status of literary creation, the development of vernacular vis-à-vis classical literature, censorship, subversiveness, social-economic-political factors, manuscript and print versions and variations, authorship and dating canons, schools, movements, writers, critical history), and b) internal development (as genres, structures, point of view, modes lyric, dramatic, and narrative, verisimilitude, archetypes, language, and other symbol systems).

2) The need for more aesthetic, formalist scholarship in appreciation of the Chinese novel, as compared with past emphasis on historical, textual, sociological, religious, political, autobiographical, and thematic studies.

3) The corresponding need for a poetics of Chinese literature, specifically for the novel. Such an articulation would call on theorists to formulate definitions, neither too broad nor too narrow, of literary genres, critical theories, terms and technical practices, and taxonomies acceptable to diverse literary schools. A number of articles here identify as relative to the novel little known and/or appreciated works and passages of theoretical and applied criticism in the Chinese literary canon.

4) The need, in fact, of a universal poetics in which Chinese theories and practices, critical and creative, would take their place in the body of world literature. For this end critics urge Chinese litterateurs first to clarify and articulate their own nation's insights and achievements, then to integrate their findings with Asian poetics generally, and then, finally, to seek incorporation into a global poetics. Such a procedure might relieve the insecurities of Western scholars who, we are told, have been less than hospitable and courageous about the inclusion of Chinese writings in comparative, critical, and world-literature programs, courses, conferences, journals, and proceedings generally. An incidental but important consideration is the substantial work being accomplished in the field by Taiwanese Chinese as differentiated from the emphatically Marxist theories and practices of the People's Republic. Another is

the need to test the viability of modern Western critical theories--Freudian, formalist, archetypal, existentialist, feminist, structuralist, deconstructionist--in Asian literatures.

5) The need for better understanding of East-West literary relations. Such a goal involves, among other things, new and better translations, with introductions, commentaries, and annotations calculated to ease the transition from one culture to another. It involves, too, cultural exchange at personal, professional, and institutional levels, and accelerated use of media and computer science to urge and facilitate the reading of the great works, especially the novels, they being usually more amenable to translation than other forms. Persuasive articles cited below show, for example, how Western linear and architectonic approaches to fiction complement Chinese spatial and interstitial structuring.

6) The need for inclusion of Chinese literature (the novel) in the disciplines of world, critical, and comparative literatures, especially but not exclusively at the college and university levels. Curriculum shapers, textbook publishers, conference convenors must be alerted to the implied inferiority of an academic project which, aspiring to world perspective, fails to include adequate and appropriate Chinese matter, especially the novel. A Western literary work is inadequately known without the context and comparison supplied by its hemispheric counterpart.

7) A few critics advert to the need for exploration of the feminine presence or lack of it in the creation of Chinese literature, specifically the novels. More than one suggests that imbalances in some novels may be attributed to the lack in China of any institution comparable to Western feminine-oriented medieval and renaissance chivalry or the neo-classical salon.

8) The need to better probe the role of religion/ philosophy in a given work. If we understand these terms as relating to the basic value system on which a novel rests and the ways in which and the reasons for which they are, in the narrative, accepted or rejected, then a grasp of the author's outlook real or presumed, is crucial for fruitful reading. In the sixteenth through the eighteenth centuries, for example, the crystallization of Neo-Confucian thought

and Tung-lin Academy reforms profoundly affected attitudes and therefore behaviors relative to the self, society, nature, and cosmic harmony. These inevitably figure in a novel's plot, setting, characterization, and theme.

9) The need to relate a work to its historical backgrounds, whether, in the case of the classic novels, to the Ming period (1368-1644), a time of recovery from one alien rule, the Yuan Dynasty (1260-1368), and advance toward another, the Ch'ing or Manchu Dynasty (1644-1912), or that last Dynasty itself. Sociologically these periods involve, among other factors, shifts of class perceptions of themselves and of others, a stiffening of female oppression among upper classes concurrently with a loosening of controls in the inferior grades; the intensive growth of cities; increased printing and publication, growing literacy, and inevitable censorship problems--all with important implications for the novel form.

Of the many subjects yet to be addressed by scholars and critics of the classic Chinese novel, one is the presence and role of untamed nature in the topological sense, including flora and fauna, mountains and skies, winds and waves and wilderness generally. In the Japanese masterpiece GENJI MONOGATARI, cats, birds, flowers, insects, glowworms, forest creatures, lakes and stars and luxurious growths of plants, trees, and flowers tumble with apparent abandon into plot, character, and theme. The Chinese classic novel seems --with the exception of considerable amounts of poetry and of the contrived and humanized parks of THE DREAM OF THE RED CHAMBER's Takuanyuan--to be less aware of this aspect of human experience. Even weather plays a lesser role than in many other long narratives. Is this impression accurate? If so, is it due to Confucian devotion to, not to say obsession with, the human?

At any rate we are grateful for the studies so far available. Among the most frequently cited scholars in this introductory chapter and those whose articles have received the lengthiest annotations are John J. Deeney, C.T. Hsia, Ma Yau-woon, William H. Nienhauser, Jr., Andrew H. Plaks, Jaroslav Prusek, Robert E. Hegel, and John C.Y. Wang. Without their rich and diverse research and commentary those of us without competence in Chinese would be beyond measure impoverished in our search for appreciation of the Chinese novel.

GENERAL SOURCES

Databases

A1. BOOK REVIEW INDEX. Corresponds to the printed BOOK REVIEW DIGEST. Important for reviews of translations of Chinese literary works, as well as critical assessments thereof. Available through Dialog and Wilsonline.

A2. DISSERTATION ABSTRACTS ONLINE. Definitive listing of current and historical dissertations on all subject areas in United-States (and some international) institutions. Available through Dialog.

A3. HUMANITIES INDEX (from February 1984). Indexes some 300 English-language periodicals in the United States and abroad. Specializes in literature. Available through Wilsonline.

A4. KNOWLEDGE INDEX. A special reduced-rate Dialog service enabling access to data bases at night and on weekends, when libraries may be closed.

A5. MLA ONLINE. Corresponds to the Modern Language Association International Bibliographies. Offers supercoded descriptors to facilitate research. Available through Dialog.

Bibliographies

A6. Davidson, Martha. A LIST OF PUBLISHED TRANSLATIONS FROM CHINESE INTO ENGLISH, FRENCH, AND GERMAN. Ann Arbor, Michigan: J.W. Edwards Company, 1952.

Fifteen thousand entries of pre-World War II writings on Poetry (Volume I) and [other] Literature (Volume II). Self-styled a "tentative publication," and superseded by Yuan's 1958 CHINA IN WESTERN LITERATURE.

A7. De Bary, William Theodore, ed. A GUIDE TO ORIENTAL CLASSICS. New York: Columbia University Press, 1964.

As companion to APPROACHES TO ORIENTAL CLASSICS, has for over two decades served as vade mecum to non-specialist world-literature teachers. Discussion questions after each unit: seven for Islam, 22 for China, 10 for Japan.

A8. Deeney, John J. "Chinese-English Comparative Literature Bibliography: A Pedagogical Arrangement of Sources in English." TAMKANG REVIEW 12 (Summer 1982): 333-404.

A well-ordered, comprehensive updating of resources indispensable to a field of growing interest and concern.

A9. Deeney, John J. "Comparative Literature and China: A Bibliographical Review of Materials in English." CHINA AND THE WEST: COMPARATIVE LITERATURE STUDIES. Eds. William Tay, Chou Ying-hsiung, and Yuan Heh-hsiang. Hong Kong: Chinese University Press, 1980. Pages 287-301.

A succinct, authoritative listing to the late 1970s of bibliographies and general works, periodicals, proceedings (periodic conferences), books and dissertation indices for Chinese-Western literary relations.

A10. Li Tien-yi. CHINESE FICTION: A BIBLIOGRAPHY OF BOOKS AND ARTICLES IN CHINESE AND ENGLISH. New Haven: Yale University Far Eastern Publications, 1968.

For specialists in Chinese language. Entries include Chinese characters, romanization according to Wade-Giles, and English translation. No annotations.

A11. Li Tien-yi. THE HISTORY OF CHINESE LITERATURE: A SELECTED BIBLIOGRAPHY. Second Edition. New Haven: Yale University Far Eastern Publications, 1970.

For experts in Chinese language and literature.

A12. Yang, Winston L.Y., Peter Li, and Nathan K. Mao. CLASSICAL CHINESE FICTION: A GUIDE TO ITS STUDY AND APPRECIATION. ESSAYS AND BIBLIOGRAPHIES. Boston: G.K. Hall Publishers, 1978.

An indispensable reference work for all students of Chinese fiction, early or late, long or short, literary or vernacular. Views fiction broadly, beginning with anecdotes, myths, legends, fictional biographies and histories from ancient China through the novels of late Ch'ing, i.e. about 1900, but specializes in Ming and Ch'ing long narrative. Offers in Part I nine essays: early fictional writing; the literary tale; the colloquial story; THE ROMANCE OF THE THREE KINGDOMS and THE WATER MARGIN; CHIN P'ING MEI and the PRAYER MAT OF FLESH; MONKEY and FLOWERS IN THE MIRROR; THE SCHOLARS; DREAM OF THE RED CHAMBER; and THE TRAVELS OF LAO TS'AN and STRANGE HAPPENINGS IN THE LAST TWENTY YEARS.

Provides in Part II 1) bibliographies of general sources, including Chinese-Western comparative studies, and 2) periods, major works, and minor works not yet generally recognized by non-specialists. Addressed to both generalists and specialists. Well but unobtrusively documented in an exceptionally attractive format.

A13. Yuan Tung-li. CHINA IN WESTERN LITERATURE: A CONTINUATION OF CORDIER'S BIBLIOTECA SINICA. New Haven: Yale University Far Eastern Publications, 1958.

Restricted to books and monographs 1921-1957 in English, French, German, and Portuguese. In one of 28 categories covers poetry, plays, and novels. Lists Western novels about China, writings on Pearl Buck, and works suitable for juveniles.

Specific Works

A14. Adkins, Curtis Peter, and Winston L.Y. Yang, eds. CRITICAL ESSAYS ON CHINESE FICTION. Hong Kong: Chinese University of Hong Kong, 1980.

Honors Ohio State University sinologist Li Tien-yi on his 65th birthday by 10 essays chiefly, but not exclusively, on Ming/Ch'ing fiction. Calls attention to the short time in which translations of Chinese classical literature have been available in the West (about 100 years) and the even shorter time (about 40 years) in which translations of Chinese fiction and Western critiques thereof have been cultivated.

Explores T'ang narrative experiments with point of view, verisimilitude, speech presentation, and social criticism; archetypal criticism a la Frazer-Jung-Campbell-Raglan-Frye applied to early Chinese fiction, notably T'ang <u>ch'uan ch'i</u> (literary tales of the marvelous); literary transformation of historical figures, such as those in SAN-KUO CHIH YEN-I (ROMANCE OF THE THREE KINGDOMS), and establishment of an historical narrative form unique in world literature (<u>yen-i</u>); author Lo Kuan-chung; lesser known novels SUI SHIH I-WEN (1633) and SUI T'ANG YEN-I (1675), author Li Yu (1611-1680?); myth and psychology in HUNG LOU MENG (DREAM OF THE RED CHAMBER); co-incidence and timeliness in the same novel as signaled by the grammar; Ch'ing (Manchu) censorship of novels on political rather than aesthetic/moral grounds; imaginative literature as the only way effectively to handle colossal amounts of historical data.

Concludes that Chinese fiction is a major literary form of international importance calling for vastly increased scholarly exertion.

A15. Aldridge, A. Owen. "Comparative Literature East and West: An Appraisal of the Tamkang Conference." YEARBOOK OF COMPARATIVE AND GENERAL LITERATURE, 21 (1972): 65-70.

A report on Taiwan's first International Conference on Comparative Literature, treating 1) China-West literary relations, 2) China-other Eastern countries literary relations, 3) application of Western literary theories and methods to Chinese literature, 4) problems in analogical studies (rapprochement), and 5) issues in translation.

Highlights controversy about 1) Chin Shih-hsiang's characterization of Chinese literary genius as essentially lyric versus Western perceived preference for epic and dramatic centering, 2) the propriety of John Y.H. Hu's analysis of THE LUTE SONG in terms of Aristo-

GENERAL SOURCES 13

telian norms and Lily C. Winters' use of psychoanalytic theory to link LI SAO (ENCOUNTERING SORROW) with English Romantic poetry, 3) the preference of many East Asians for Western fiction in translation rather than their native creations, 4) study of LI SAO as a venture in allegorical quest similar to that in Spenser's FAERIE QUEENE, and of THE RIVERSIDE PAVILION (a thirteenth-century Chinese play) as an analogue of Shaw's CANDIDE, 5) Ezra Pound and the Orient, and 6) Voltaire's cult of China.

Concludes that conference deficiencies in content, concreteness, and conclusions were handsomely compensated by the overcoming of insularity.

A16. Bauer, Wolfgang. CHINA AND THE SEARCH FOR HAPPINESS: RECURRING THEMES IN FOUR THOUSAND YEARS OF CHINESE CULTURAL HISTORY. Tr. Michael Shaw. New York: Seabury Press, 1976.

Chinese intellectual history from ancient times to the 1970s, sprinkled with useful East-West and ancient-modern tables of comparisons. Little sustained reference to Chinese fiction. Emphasis on changing Chinese ideals of man and society.

A17. Berry, Margaret. "The Meeting of the Twain: Japanese and Greek." PEGASUS OVER ASIA: VENTURES IN EAST-WEST LITERARY ANALYSIS. Hong Kong: Asian Research Service, 1980. Pages 17-30.

Applies selected Western (Greek) norms to a Japanese work, Murasaki Shikibu's GENJI MONOGATARI, and Japanese norms to a Western (English) work, Walter Pater's MARIUS THE EPICUREAN, to test their viability. Finds valid a qualified application to GENJI of *mimesis*, *hamartia*, *arete*, and *nemesis*; none for *hubris*; and an invigorating new role for *catharsis*, i.e. the purging, not of pity and terror, but of dullness and insensitivity. Conversely, finds the Japanese *mono no aware*, sensitivity to the beauty and passingness of things, eminently applicable to MARIUS; as also *sabi*, the beauty in the weatheredness of things; *yugen*, the mysterious, profound stillness beyond formal perfection; and *miyabi*, refined, courtly sensibility. Suggests *en* (charm) and *okashi* (subtle delight or amusement) as other concepts that might be tested. Proposes as a step toward achievement of a universal poetics more such exercises bringing together Eastern and Western literary concepts so as to learn what in them may be shared and what is strictly local.

A18.   Berry, Margaret. PEGASUS OVER ASIA: VENTURES IN EAST-WEST LITERARY ANALYSIS. Hong Kong: Asian Research Service, 1980.

Thirteen essays exploring the relations of subject matter, characterization, themes, and basic philosophic and literary assumptions of paired East-West works. Uses the Chinese novel in a study of literature and national identity, and in a three-way comparison of the ideal youths of English, Japanese, and Chinese classic novels.

A19.   Birch, Cyril, ed. STUDIES IN CHINESE LITERARY GENRES. Berkeley: University of California Press, 1974.

Eleven essays by eminent Sinologist literati on selected genres. An exertion toward the as-yet-to-be-produced adequate history of Chinese literature, a work which must depend largely on understanding of the genres--their definition, evolution, scope, and effects. Diverse approaches according to scholars' choices: In fiction Prusek seeks to understand the influence of urban growth on novel composition; C.T. Hsia analyzes the newly-identified form of the military romance.

A20.   Birch, Cyril, and Robert Hegel. "Studies of Ming Literature: Observations on the State of the Art." MING STUDIES 2 (Spring 1976): 25-30.

Notes heavy imbalances in Ming studies as revealed in the MING BIOGRAPHICAL DICTIONARY. Regrets the division of traditional Chinese literature into elite and popular, as scholars of classical Chinese have tended to stop short of Ming, while vernacular specialists have devoted themselves almost exclusively to fiction and drama, neglecting poetry and non-fiction prose. With the MBD further illuminates the extent to which vernacular works derive from classical texts or tales often written by identifiable men of letters. Points out that choice of the vernacular is now seen to have rested, not on necessity, but on literary effectiveness. Suggests need for more and better translations, not only of unknown and/or neglected works, but, as well, of certain classics, notably SAN-KUO-CHIH YEN-I (THE ROMANCE OF THE THREE KINGDOMS).

A21. Bishop, John L. "Some Limitations of Chinese Fiction." STUDIES IN CHINESE LITERATURE. Ed. John L. Bishop. Cambridge: Harvard University Press, 1965. Pages 237-247.

A comparison of fiction's diverse development in China and in the West. Sees likenesses in lower-class audience appeal without interest in classical tradition, and in an earthy, sensational, and sensuous rather than an intellectual, restrained, and contemplative style. Marks differences deriving from Chinese puritanical morality, anachronistic materials, and stylistic conventions. Suggests that the limitation of psychological analysis in Chinese fiction (with the celebrated exception of HUNG LOU MENG) arises from the absence of an aristocratic-feminine tradition in Chinese literary circles comparable with that supplied by Mme. de La Fayette and Mlle. de Scudery in France and Murasaki Shikibu in Japan.

A22. Buck, Pearl S. "China in the Mirror of Her Fiction." PACIFIC AFFAIRS 3 (February 1930): 155-164.

A classic treatment of the contrast between China's Great Tradition of exalted ethics and philosophy as embodied in the Classics and canonical Commentaries, and its Little Tradition, actual-life thought and behavior of flesh-and-blood humans. Argues that Chinese fiction, denigrated by the literati, conveys their reality; and that short stories and novels alone exhibit the sturdy picaresque romanticism and earthy sexual relations that historically have never ceased to challenge Confucian virtues and proprieties.

A23. Buck, Pearl S. THE CHINESE NOVEL (Nobel Lecture). London: Macmillan Company, 1939.

A 1938 Nobel-Prize lecture dated in its views and one-sided in its sympathies. Declares authoritatively that the novel was produced solely by the common people, for the common people, and without taint of conscious art--views challenged by scholars today (see A94). Presents conventional and politically biased views of the major novels and brief synopses of several others.

A24. Buck, Pearl S.   EAST AND WEST AND THE NOVEL and SOURCES OF THE EARLY CHINESE NOVEL. Peiping: North China Union Language School, 1932.

Uses origins, structure and form, and meaning and purpose to contrast the English and the Chinese novel traditions. Finds virtue in (to Westerners) the seeming formlessness and anonymity of Chinese fiction. Identifies a persistent romanticism of content (supernaturalism and anticipation of fate) and realistic method in robust and straightforward action and conversation. Points to a prevailing omniscient point of view and to a moralism often a mere throwing in of sops of proverbial ethical wisdom to render secular concerns more palatable to traditionalists.

A25. Cevasco, G.A. "Pearl Buck and the Chinese Novel." ASIA STUDIES 5 (1967): 437-450.

Defends Pearl Buck (1892-1973) against critics who charge her with deficient aesthetic form, shallow characterization, pedestrian language, falsity to Chinese social psychology, and a simplicity innocent of archetypes, symbols, the sub-conscious, the unconscious, interior monologue, and stream-of-consciousness. Of the 80-odd books and hundreds of articles and short stories, dominantly about modern Chinese life, chooses THE GOOD EARTH as the best, summarizes its plot, and analyzes it for qualities which won for the author the 1938 Nobel Prize for Literature. Traces Buck's life and writing career, emphasizing the first 32 years of her life spent in China with her missionary parents, and the influence of that milieu on her ways of thought and writing style. Barely mentions Buck's translations, even ALL MEN ARE BROTHERS (SHUI-HU CHUAN), and sheds no light on Chinese fiction *per se*.

GENERAL SOURCES   17

A26. Chang, H.C. ed. CHINESE LITERATURE. Three volumes.
      New York: Columbia University Press, 1973.

      Stories and plays prefaced by a meaty and colorful
      survey of the development of Chinese fiction and drama.
      Attributes their burgeoning in the Sung Dynasty (960-
      1279) to the growth of cities, occasioned by expanding
      domestic and foreign trade, and ensuing demand for
      popular entertainment. Surveys the fairgrounds,
      booths, sheds and halls (some held thousands of specta-
      tors); eight varieties of amusement (story-telling
      being the favorite); temple productions; and staging
      built before palace gates—all in the Sung Golden Age
      of Entertainment and Patronage.

      In the storyteller's art sees the beginnings of the
      novel and its various genres. Classifies their matter
      and form as a) chiang-shih, about colorful historical
      characters, in a ponderous and lofty chronicle style
      marked by archaisms and debased-classical declamation,
      providing gist for the later SAN-KUO-CHIH YEN-I
      (ROMANCE OF THE THREE KINGDOMS); b) shu-ching, Bud-
      dhist tales of casuistry, using highly symbolic and
      imaginative imagery, propounding doctrines such as
      inspired Tripitaka's adventures, and anticipating HSI-
      YU CHI (MONKEY, or JOURNEY TO THE WEST); and, finally,
      c) hsiao-shuo, single-sitting stories without text or
      central hero, stringing out episodes marked by wit,
      invention, variety, and ingenious use of song and
      dance (often as a kind of Greek chorus); development
      of numerous matters—as evil spirits, amorous female
      ghosts, romance, law courts with spinoff sword- and
      cudgel-skits, immortals, magicians, and "Dick Whitting-
      ton" success stories. Follows the slow development of
      hsiao-shuo into story clusters about a single charac-
      ter until finally a master would arise to shape the
      larger and more homogeneous into novels—this in Ming
      and Ch'ing Dynasties.

      Describes fourteenth/fifteenth-century writers' guilds
      engaged in collecting, editing, revising, and synthe-
      sizing narrative materials. Relates developments to
      the elegant, classical T'ang ch'uan ch'i. Analyzes
      the major classic novels: a) SHUI-HU CHUAN (THE WATER
      MARGIN), with its banquet-seating structure; b) HUNG-
      LOU MENG (DREAM OF THE RED CHAMBER), with its story-

teller's paraphernalia of suspenseful verse breaks at chapter ends, displaying the author's best and worst; its digressive insert pieces for showing traditional lore; and its ritual beginning to facilitate the author's assumption of the storyteller's role; and c) JU-LIN WAI-SHI (THE SCHOLARS), with its specious fidelity to historical usage and its subtle undermining of such techniques by a deadly satire in the very mode designed to prevent it, language marked by brevity, restraint, detachment, and solemn forms of speech.

A27. Ch'en Shou-yi. CHINESE LITERATURE: A HISTORICAL INTRODUCTION. New York: Ronald Press, 1961.

The first attempt at a truly comprehensive and detailed history of Chinese literature. Lacking footnotes and bibliography as well as the last quarter-century of scholarship, nevertheless provides a unified, cohesive, and useful reference. Not completely superseded by the less complete, more aesthetically oriented and more scholarly work of Liu Wu-chi.

A28. Cheng, Gek Nai. LATE CH'ING VIEWS ON FICTION. Palo Alto, California: Stanford University, 1982. An unpublished dissertation.

Accredits Western political novels through Japanese intermediaries with important influence on Ch'ing theories of fiction, dominantly pragmatic, propagandistic, journalistic, and public, as China began its study of fiction as an important critical and theoretical discipline. Surveys in Part I late Ch'ing political and intellectual climate as well as Shanghai publishing and journalistic ventures instigating new literary developments. Traces fiction criticism in traditional China, focusing on such fundamental concerns as the function and subject matter of fiction; the relation of writer and work; techniques of form, structure, characterization, and language; the roles of reader and critic; similarities in and differences between Chinese and Western fiction; the contributions of Schopenhauer, Hegel, and other Europeans to Chinese literary thought; and, finally, specific late Ch'ing views on fiction as significant both aesthetically and historically. Provides in Part

II, translations of late Ch'ing essays on fiction criticism.

A29. Chi Ch'ui-lang. "The Concepts of Classicism and Romanticism: Through Applications to Chinese Literature." TAMKANG REVIEW 3 (1973): 235-251.

Insists that, the protean character of the term "romanticism" notwithstanding, Chinese literature discloses identifiable Romantic movements in content and form. Reviews the term's meaning and history in contradistinction to Classicism and its more rigorous and narrow development as Neoclassicism. Attributes Classicism's dominance to Confucian insistence that the arts primarily subserve public and moral ends, aesthetics being assigned an ancillary role. Calls Liu Hsieh (465-522) the foremost theorist of Chinese classicism, comparing his views with those of English Neoclassicist Alexander Pope (1688-1744).

Uses Liu Ta-chieh's monumental history of Chinese literature (1941) to review the following "romantic" periods: 1) late Southern Chou, in which appeared the CH'U TZ'U anthology and the legendary Ch'u Yuan; 2) the Wei and Chin Dynasties between the post-Han Time of Troubles and the rise of Sui and T'ang, a time when in the popular mind Taoism and Buddhism prevailed over Confucianism; 3) early eighth-century T'ang, when the Wang-Wei school of painters and poets developed, on the one hand, a Wordsworthian relation with nature and peasants, and, on the other, a Byronic passion for the turbulent and sublime, and when the most gifted and representative of Chinese Romantic poets, hedonist and iconoclast Li Po, cultivated Taoist and chivalric ways of life; 4) late Ming, inspired by the subjectivism and emotionalism of Wang Yang-ming (1472-1529), which rejected current mechanical imitation and fettering rules; and, finally, 5) the twentieth century, following Hu Shih's 1916 literary revolution which, rejecting the past, focused on contemporary models, vernacular language, and emotional confrontation.

Despite these five often short-lived Romantic movements, concludes that, under China's romantic veneer, lies much that is classical, realistic, and firmly bound with the past, as witness the present determination to make literature serve, not primarily aesthetic, but public, political, and moral ends.

A30. Clark, Richard C. "Approaches to a History of Chinese Literature: Bibliographical Spectrum and Review Article." REVIEW OF NATIONAL LITERATURES 6 (1975): 128-156.

Despite post-1930 attempts of English, Russian, German, and French scholars, concludes that the herculean task of writing a definitive history of Chinese literature is yet to be accomplished. Judges the 1949 Margoulies HISTOIRE most useful and insightful; Ch'en Shou-yi's 1961 CHINESE LITERATURE: A HISTORICAL INTRODUCTION only a noble pioneer work, devoid of documentation; Lai Ming's 1964 identification of four striking patterns (consensus on the great periods and outstanding authors, Buddhist influence, popular origins of genres, and close connection with music) helpful; and Birch's 1974 clarification of divergent East-West concepts of literature important. Proposes, finally, that the very nature of Chinese characters (composite ideograms and phonograms) helps explain the absence of epic and tragic visions from the traditional educated Chinese mind, while lyric vision flourished there, a phenomenon reversed in Western aesthetics.

A31. Dawson, Raymond, ed. THE LEGACY OF CHINA. Oxford: The Clarendon Press, 1964.

A latecomer to the Oxford University series, begun in 1921 with THE LEGACY OF GREECE to facilitate more cosmopolitan views among humanists by surveying a nation's major achievements in philosophy and religion, literature, art, science, and the art of government. Gives literature the most extensive treatment, as being, not the most important, but the most difficult subject to treat briefly. Attends to the "three literatures": classical (literary), oral (vernacular), and the written vernacular. Looks at the influence on fiction and drama of the physical development of the Chinese city. Discusses each of the six major classic novels.

A32. De Bary, William Theodore, ed. APPROACHES TO THE ORIENTAL CLASSICS. New York and London: Columbia University Press, 1966.

Proceedings of a 1958 Columbia University conference. Besides general statements on the role of Asian literatures in American higher education, includes specific studies of the Confucian ANALECTS, the LOTUS SUTRA, and Chinese narrative. Argues that appreciation of the Chinese novel depends less on specialist knowledge of the country and more on close reading of great Western novels and the capacity to relate such works to personal experience.

A33. De Bary, William Theodore, ed. SELF AND SOCIETY IN MING THOUGHT. New York: Columbia University Press, 1970.

Among its dozen studies offers none dealing with Ming fiction, a curious omission, despite inclusion of C.T. Hsia's study of T'ang Hsien-tsu, a major literary playwright. Refers once, in De Bary's "Individualism and Humanitarianism in Late Ming Thought," to SHUI-HU CHUAN (THE WATER MARGIN) as, in the eyes of thinker-writer Li Chih, with other similar vernacular works, "justified, not merely as harmless diversions, but as exemplifications of heroic virtue in the common man and indeed as serious works of importance even to government." Finds, in the same essay, similarity of tone in some Li-Chih writing to the irony and absurdity in Wu Ch'eng-en's HSI-YU CHI (MONKEY, or JOURNEY TO THE WEST), though Wu's gentleness and compassion become in Li Chih bitterness and disillusion.

A34. Deeney, John J. "Chinese-English Literary Relations." TAMKANG REVIEW 1 (October 1970): 105-139.

Follows up a previous article on comparative literature involving China. In <u>Problems and Questions</u> touches on the fresh objectivity possible to a comparativist of a different culture; suspension of disbelief relative to alien philosophies and religions; the use of contrast rather than comparison, and differentness rather than similarity; the absence of the epic form in China; whether Western techniques help or hinder the Chinese writer; and exchange of symbols between disparate cultures. In Topics includes the translators' creative versus their imitative tasks; literary allusions and the imperative of multiplied quality-renditions of Chinese works into English and vice versa; literary influences and indebtedness; and thematology, seen as a fascinating and quickly rewarding aspect of comparative studies. Finally, in Pedagogy considers motivation, resources, and attitudes. Provides invaluable annotated bibliographic aids.

A35. Deeney, John J. CHINESE-WESTERN COMPARATIVE-LITERATURE THEORY AND STRATEGY. Hong Kong: Chinese University Press, 1981.

Based on a series of papers presented at the 1979 Hong Kong Conference on East-West Comparative Literature. In four papers treats adaptation of Western critical methods to Eastern texts; in three others, applies these principles to specific works.

A36. Deeney, John J. "Comparative Literature Studies in Taiwan." TAMKANG REVIEW 1 (1970): 119-145.

Reviews problems, questions, topics, and tasks in the assimilation of Chinese writing into world comparative literature, viewing Taiwan as an especially advantageous place to study China's cultural heritage. Recommends seeking variety rather than unity, and distinguishing historical and contextual from aesthetic approaches. In this respect points to identity of aim between Chinese philosophy and Chinese art (harmony of individuals within themselves, with their society, and with the universe), and the disparity of method between Taoist and Confucian artists and thinkers--factors basic to assessments of Chinese literature, alone or in comparison. Deplores the lack of an acceptable methodology for West-East comparative literature, despite development of a considerable bibliography. Calls for a comprehensive, world-inclusive, standardized glossary of literary terms cognizant of diverse meanings in different eras, in the same era, in different countries, in the same country, in the same writer, and in various genres and arts. Warns that such an effort sails a precarious course between the too narrow and the too general definition.

A37. Deeney, John J. "Comparative Literature: West and/or East?" TAMKANG REVIEW 4 (October 1973): 157-166.

Denounces the intolerance, insensitivity, arrogance, and Eurocentrism of the 1973 Seventh Congress of International Comparative Literature held in Canada. Urges Chinese scholars to build up their own theories and methodology before seeking place with Western comparativists. Sees three urgent Western needs in effecting the exchange: a) realization of limitations by way of cultural ignorance; b) modification of modes of literary thought by inclusion of Chinese concepts, standards, forms, and particular works--as, for example, the lu-shih (regulated verse), perhaps superior to the sonnet, and Liu Hsieh's WEN-SHIN (THE LITERARY MIND AND THE CARVING OF DRAGONS), a masterpiece of impressionism; and c) need to master specific Chinese cultural contributions: its exaltation, for example, of the sage giving counsel instead of the armed epic hero, and Chinese projection of ecstasis rather than mimesis as the governing literary principle.

A38. Deeney, John J. "Some Reflections on the History of Comparative Literature in China." TAMKANG REVIEW 6 (October 1975/April 1976): 219-228.

Reviews comparative-literature developments in Taiwan, Hong Kong, and China, beginning with Western advocates A. Owen Aldridge of COMPARATIVE LITERATURE STUDIES, Horst Frenz of the International Comparative Literature Association, Harry Levin of Harvard's Greek-Latin program, and Rene Etiemble of a well-known challenge to Western hegemony in the field. Recognizes Taiwan's doctoral program in comparative literature (from 1971), its TAMKANG REVIEW and LITERARY MONTHLY, devoted to comparative studies, its National Comparative Literature Association, and its frustrating experience with a Eurocentrism indifferent to or condescending towards Asian literatures.

Finds at the University of Hong Kong and the Chinese University of Hong Kong a tendency to focus excessively on China, despite commitment to the teaching of foreign languages and literatures. Approves Yuan Heh-hsiang's challenge of the whole conceptual and methodological bias of Western premises, his insistence that basic cultural differences are vastly more numerous and weighty than any similarities, and that only rigorous scholarship can bridge the gap. Commends Chinese University of Hong Kong's RENDITIONS, a Chinese-English translation magazine, and its new series of book-length renderings. Finds little to date (1978) achieved on the mainland despite intense interest in Western literary practice following the May 4th Movement (1918-1923). Sees Taiwan's Second International Comparative Conference on Literary Theory and Criticism East and West as offering hope for new progress in the field.

Recommends, among other advices, that 1) the West implement its proposal to include Asian productions in its comparative-literature exertions, 2) that Asian countries consolidate within each and among themselves their own concepts, theories, and praxis, so as to attain a clear voice and recognizable and strong identities, 3) that scholars, if they mean to work effectively, master, not only the language, but the entire target culture, 4) that native and foreign scholars share their expertise, 5) that conferences exercise more rigor in paper and discussion standards, and 6) that Mandarin, with simultaneous translation as needed, function as the official language of East-West conferences held in the East.

A39. Eberhard, Wolfram. GUILT AND SIN IN TRADITIONAL CHINA. Berkeley: University of California Press, 1967.

Illuminates the moral lives of the Chinese by discussion of norms and motivations in terms of shame, i.e. public humiliation, seen as the basic Chinese moral sanction, and guilt, i.e. inner judgment, characteristic of the West. Limits illustration to short fictional forms, but suggests application to Chinese novels. Discusses both scholars' and moralists' evaluations of sin and shame in four categories: sexual, social, property-related, and religion-related. Closes with exemplary material on the sin of suicide.

A40. Eide, Elisabeth. "Ibsen's Nora and Chinese Interpretation of Female Emancipation." MODERN CHINESE LITERATURE IN ITS SOCIAL CONTEXT. Ed. G. Oran Malmqvist.

Stockholm: G.O. Malmqvist Publisher, 1977. Pages 140-151.

Attributes Ibsen's strong influence in twentieth-century China, not to his dramaturgical reforms, but rather to his social ideas, notably his insistence on personal independence and individual fulfillment. Finds that Chinese novels based in part on A DOLL'S HOUSE are less concerned with women's plight per se than with individual emancipation for men and women alike from oppressive social norms. Insists, nevertheless, that individual fulfillment in the Chinese milieu is perceived solely as a means for the promotion of a better society, as in THE LADY FROM THE SEA (author unnamed), Mao Dun's HONG (RAINBOW), and Ba Jin's JIA (THE FAMILY). Observes that all the writers, Ibsen included, stress education, the severing of ties with the past, and the restructuring of marriage as crucial to the new society.

A41. Eoyang, Eugene. "The Immediate Audience: Oral Narration in Chinese Fiction." CRITICAL ESSAYS ON CHINESE FICTION. Ed. William H. Nienhauser, Jr. Hong Kong: Chinese University of Hong Kong Press, 1976.

Argues the necessity for perceiving both oral and aural aspects of literature, especially but not exclusively in Chinese narrative. Points out the historical disadvantage to Chinese culture of the long maintained gap between its literary (classical) language and its vernacular, bridged somewhat by development of a third medium, the written vernacular. Draws examples from stories in the Tun-huang manuscripts of eighth- and ninth-century China and from the later HSI-YU CHI (MONKEY, or JOURNEY TO THE WEST) and HUNG-LOU MENG (DREAM OF THE RED CHAMBER). A corrective to excessively literary perspectives.

A42. Fan Ning. "Ming Dynasty Fiction." CHINESE LITERATURE 7 (1980): 64-73.

Basic facts about the rise of Ming fiction, its contents and kinds, and detailed analyses of the four major novels as to sources, themes, plots, characters, style, and overall significance. No new insights or information. Generous exemplary material.

A43. Feng Yuan-chun. A SHORT HISTORY OF CLASSICAL CHINESE LITERATURE. Trs. Yang Hsien-yi and Gladys Yang. Peking: Foreign Languages Press, 1958.

A simple, brief, readable, chronological mini-history, enriched by illustrations from oracle bones and sacred bronzes of the earliest times, to the calligraphy, woodcuts, and paintings of later dynasties.

A44. Feuerwerker, Mei Yi-tse. "The Chinese Novel." APPROACHES TO THE ORIENTAL CLASSICS. Ed. William Theodore de Bary. New York and London: Columbia University Press, 1959. Pages 171-185.

Presents the novel as the form that best survives translation,m providing not only story, cultural interaction, and thematic interest, but also insight into particular and universal problems of individuals and society. Views the Chinese novel as essentially subversive, arriving at the end of China's great civilization and portraying the collapse of traditional values in times of cultural breakdown and social dissolution. Applies this view to the traditional novels. In a statement refuted by subsequent scholars, says that, because of its despised position among Confucian literati, the Chinese novel had no art and no critical theory and only in the twentieth century has been taken seriously.

A45. Fitzgerald, C.P. "The Chinese Novel as a Subversive Form." MEANJIN QUARTERLY 10 (Spring 1951): 259-266.

Presents the classic Chinese novels as, with the exception of SAN-KUO-CHIH YEN-I, vehicles of protest against the establishment. Sees rejection of the classical language and choice of pai hua, current speech, for the extended narrative as horrifying to scholars and teachers, who thereupon introduced a censorship only aggravating storytellers' determination to expose political, social, and domestic failures, and to undermine Confucian beliefs on which they claimed to rest. Observes that, while twentieth-century China chose to glorify the novels for their attack an old institutions, the same novels today remain important links with the vanished imperial world, whose ideas, art, and atmosphere they have immortalized.

A46. Frankel, Hans H. "The Chinese Novel: A Confrontation of Critical Approaches to Chinese and Western Novels." LITERATURE EAST AND WEST 8 (Winter 1964): 2-5.

Written on the occasion of MLA's first inclusion of Chinese literature in its annual meeting, stresses the need to bring China out of its isolation and into the circle of world literature. Focuses on the six major classic Chinese novels. Recalls that late development and suspicion as to moral and aesthetic value marked the novel's rise in the West as in China, but that non-aesthetic and non-literary considerations have continued to dominate Chinese criticism of the form. Proposes that some Western concepts can usefully be applied to the Chinese novel: e.g. Kayser's categories of Geschehnisroman (historical, focusing on a sequence of events), Figurenroman (featuring an individual's development), and Raumroman (treating a segment of the world at a certain time and place). Sees SAN-KUO-CHIH YEN-I (THE THREE KINGDOMS) as an example of the first, and CHIN P'ING MEI (THE GOLDEN LOTUS) and HUNG-LOU MENG (DREAM OF THE RED CHAMBER) as examples of the third. Denies to China a novel of the second type, because China "does not recognize ... the growth and development of personality [in the Western sense]," seeing in individuals only "a fixed pattern that merely unfolds in the course of a human life." Poses also the problem of the contemporaneity of persons and events in purported historical narratives and commends China's persisting use of different stylistic levels in the same work, a technique allegedly lost in modern Western narrative. Pleads for development of universally accepted concepts, theories, and practices applicable to the novel.

A47. Giles, Herbert A. A HISTORY OF CHINESE LITERATURE. New York: Grove Press, 1958.

Originally published in 1923, purports to offer the first attempt in any language to develop a history of Chinese literature. Ranges over 2500 years to modern times, covering topics such as the first writing, Ch'in dynasty book-burning, Confucian, Taoist, and Buddhist classics, the invention of block-printing, and the origins of the theater. Discusses literary forms--novel, poetry, scientific documents--in their historical cultural contexts. Includes some outdated and erroneous data and faulty interpretation, especially relative to the classic novels.

A48. Goodrich, L. Carrington, and Chaoying Fang, eds. DICTIONARY OF MING BIOGRAPHY 1368-1644. Two volumes. New York: Columbia University Press, 1976.

Substantial articles (with bibliographies) by eminent scholars. Includes illustrations, maps, charts, glossary, and indices.

A49. Hawkes, David. "An Introductory Note." THE LEGACY OF CHINA. Ed. Raymond Dawson. London: Clarendon Press, 1964. Pages 80-90.

Concentrates on radical twentieth-century changes in Chinese literature, beginning with the 1919 literary revolution and the manifestoes of Hu Shih and Ch'en Tu-hsiu demanding ideological and linguistic change to allow China to enter the modern world. From Confucian emphasis on the past and on the humanities, observes the new orientation toward the present and the future and the bringing of science and technology to the educational fore. Linguistically notes the movement from elitist classical Chinese, empowering the bureaucracy and obstructing scientific progress, to the 1922 government mandate for educational institutions to replace classical Chinese with the vernacular.

Warns that Western based comparative literature, obsessed with Aristotelian norms and genres, must open its views to Eastern norms and genres--each hemisphere modifying the other--if a universal poetics is to be attained. Identifies as major differences a) the absence in most Chinese literature of religious inspiration, its secularity, b) the persisting state patron-

age of Chinese literature through the ages and the
intense value attached to learning and the arts, as
evidenced by the enormous array of its encyclopedias
(a form originating in China and not excelled in the
number and substance of its productions), and c) the
antiquity and venerableness of its classical literature.

A50. Hegel, Robert E. "Heavens and Hells in Chinese Fic-
tional Dreams." PSYCHOSINOLOGY: THE UNIVERSE OF
DREAMS IN CHINESE CULTURE. Ed. Carolyn T. Brown.
Washington, D.C.: Woodrow Wilson International
Center for Scholars, 1987. Pages 1-14.

Demonstrates the dependence of dreams in early Chinese
vernacular fiction on classical, historical, and
imaginative sources, notably in effecting communication with celestial and infernal regions and beings;
in generally but not exclusively reenforcing the
Confucian ethic, especially relative to the individual's essentially social being; in the implication of
the body-mind continuum; and in the projection of
social-political commentary. Traces dream origins to
characters' and authors' feelings and to their need to
be instructed in heaven's will. For exemplary material draws on SHUI-HU CHUAN, HSI-YU CHI, and HUNG-LOU
MENG.

A51. Hegel, Robert E. THE NOVEL IN SEVENTEENTH-CENTURY
CHINA. New York: Columbia University Press, 1981.

Covers the century between the catastrophic 1589
Peking earthquake under the Mings and the consolidation of Ch'ing power in the 1690s. Forgoes study of
the major novels in favor of minor classics deserving,
the author believes, of systematic study. Uses varied
critical approaches to extend insight into the power
and complexity of the Chinese novel tradition. Following an overview of cultural ambience, shifting at this
time from indigenous Ming to outlander Mongolian
governance, examines novelists' relation to current
political events and related suffering. Looks at
specific works to correlate context and themes, characterization and structure. Finally, relates the novels
to the overall developing Chinese tradition and
assesses their influence on later works. Indexes

literary sources and textual histories and, for individual chapters, provides generous annotations and bibliographies.

A52. Hegel, Robert E., and Richard C. Hessney. EXPRESSIONS OF SELF IN CHINESE LITERATURE. New York: Columbia University Press, 1985.

Explores ego-consciousness in Chinese poetry and criticism, drama and fiction. Concludes that the Chinese Self is mostly defined as duty to sovereigns, family, and friends, though one writer sees individualism vis-à-vis social role exemplified in the maids and other servants of HUNG LOU MENG (DREAM OF THE RED CHAMBER), G93.

A53. Hightower, James R. "Chinese Literature in the Context of World Literature." COMPARATIVE LITERATURE 5 (1953): 117-124.

Sees Chinese literature as occupying an important place among national literatures for its enormous time range, over 3,000 years; its variety of genres, lacking only tragedy and epic; its arguable supremacy in the mass of its high-quality lyric, notably in T'ang and Sung Dynasties; its several great novels, yielding to none in scope, subtlety of character portrayal, and elaborate plot. Contrasts Europe's rapid change from the parent Latin to the vernaculars and China's persistence in maintaining two distinct streams, literary (classical) and written vernacular.

Suggests that chronology be set aside in favor of other conditions of comparison, as, for example, background factors in China's flourishing thirteenth-century drama and Europe's in sixteenth and seventeenth centuries. Notes that China's greatest dramas center on romantic love, as in HSI-HSIANG CHI (THE ROMANCE OF THE WESTERN CHAMBER), a theme disdained by literati. Suggests that comparativists should pursue in Europe-China pairings analogous movements such as romanticism and classicism, seeking constants and variables in forms, works, tropes, and devices.

A54. Hightower, James R. "Individualism in Chinese Literature." JOURNAL OF THE HISTORY OF IDEAS 22 (1961): 159-168.

Examines Chinese writings for examples of individualism in a society so strongly committed to conformity that deviates are referred to as bandits. Allows that toleration extends to Taoist recluses, presumably engrossed in self-cultivation, yoga, or alchemical searches for immortality, and to public servants who refuse to serve corrupt rulers. Shows by extended poetical analysis the strong impersonality of most Chinese literature. Contrasts with this attitude Ch'u Yuan's LI SAO (ENCOUNTERING SORROW), China's first long narrative poem and one of its greatest, which, besides being intensely personal, deliberately violates standard practice in form, length, absence of musical setting, and relation of poet to poem. Sees the author's conflict resolved, not through suicide by drowning as suggested by the Dragon-Boat Festival, but by dedication to the Taoist pursuit of immortality.

Proposes as a second example of individualism Ssu-ma Ch'ien, an honest man in a decadent society, who, to fulfill his mission as Grand Historian, submits to the socially disapproved castration rather than commit suicide, considered the more honorable way to satisfy justice, and who defends his action even as, in the biographies, he tells of other men who have defied social opinion. Declares the fourth-century collection of anecdotes SHIH-SHUO HSIN-YU (VERSIONS OF CURRENT STORIES) the best source for spectacular examples of eccentricity. Among the poets cites Li Po as practitioner and at times advocate of individualism.

In vernacular literatures, especially the novels, sees SAN-KUO-CHIH YEN-I (ROMANCE OF THE THREE KINGDOMS) as having only one example of individualism, Lu Ta, the generous comic ruffian; HSI-YU CHI (MONKEY) as offering in its raffish hero a genuine loner; HUNG LOU MENG (DREAM OF THE RED CHAMBER), as demonstrating the bad end of rebel Pao-yu, its "willful, effete, and sentimental hero"; and in JU-LIN WAI-SHIH (THE SCHOLARS) outstanding eccentrics from all walks of life, who reject the examination system and disdain social sanctions.

On the whole sees Chinese literature as approving individualism only in safely historical cases and regarding it as too politically chancey for writers often to glorify.

A55. Hightower, James R. TOPICS IN CHINESE LITERATURE: OUTLINES AND BIBLIOGRAPHIES. Cambridge: Harvard University Press, 1965. (First printed in 1950, revised in 1953.)

Intended for students, therefore marked with special directness, clarity, succinctness, and simplicity. Offers 17 outlines, of which two deal with literary and vernacular genres: the first chiefly tracing stages in the evolution of the form; the second summarizing each of the major novels as to overall significance, language, time, place, circumstances of composition, special merits, and recognized weaknesses. A still-useful resource despite its age and several ensuant decades of meaty and abundant scholarship.

A56. Hou, Sharon. "Women's Literature." THE INDIANA COMPANION TO TRADITIONAL CHINESE LITERATURE. Ed. William H. Nienhauser, Jr., and others. Bloomington: Indiana University Press, 1986. Pages 175-192.

Surveys the literary achievement of Chinese women over the centuries against a background of extraordinary discrimination due, not only to a patriarchal social system, but also to a Confucianism which, while less rigorous in early times, under Neo-Confucianism became rigidly anti-feminist. Treats women's economic dependency, political powerlessness, and oppressive manipulation. Details social usages including, from Sung times and for upper-class women at least, foot-binding, a custom disabling the victim and physically barring her from the outside world; and denial to her of education, female talent and learning being perceived as not only unbecoming, but as actual signs of depravity.

Even in upper-class families observes that female education, while including music, painting, chess, calligraphy, and poetry, stressed domestic arts--sewing, weaving, embroidery, household supervision--these enabling a woman to fulfill her three major duties: performing household tasks, ministering to the needs and comforts of her husband and her elders, and bearing and raising children. Designates as the goal of such education the supreme Chinese good, the continuance of the family line, an end assured by faithful performance of ancestral worship, rites legitimately performed only by males. Notes that textbooks for female education consisted of biographies of admirable women, each exemplifying a virtue proper to her sex, and theoretical explications of the virtues, accompanying conduct rules for daily life. Marks the irony of the fact that excessive stress on Confucian sexual morality resulted in intensified prostitution, a profession in which women, already depraved, might freely and publicly exercise their talents for learning, song, dance, poetry, and other forms of entertainment.

Among the great novels notes only Wu Ching-tzu's JU-LIN WAI-SHIH as portraying women who speak up for their rights and argue for love, respect, and near-equality in marriage; Li Ju-chen's lesser known CHING-HUA YUAN (FLOWERS IN THE MIRROR) as offering imperial examinations for women, and, in a section called A Kingdom of Women, reversing sexual roles. Identifies specific women writers and their works, listing as greatest Li Ch'ing-chao and Chu Shu-chen, both of the Sung Dynasty. Summarizes in four statements: 1) Deficiency of education caused women's writing to be less scholarly than men's. 2) They wrote generally in the literary rather than in the vernacular language. 3) They produced subjective and sensual content rather than social critique. 4) They excelled in poetry rather than in fiction or drama.

A57. Hsia, C.T. THE CLASSIC CHINESE NOVEL: A CRITICAL INTRODUCTION. New York and London: Columbia University Press, 1968.

An important and readable work written mainly before 1966 for specialists and non-specialists alike. Features a comprehensive history of the novel in its divergent manifestations. Relates structure, style, characters, and episodes to moral and philosophic themes. Generous excerpts, often newly translated, for comparative study of different versions. Useful bibliography to 1966 and detailed indexing.

A58. Hsia, C.T. "The Military Romana: A Genre of Chinese Fiction." STUDIES IN CHINESE LITERARY GENRES. Ed. Cyril Birch. Berkeley: University of California Press, 1974. Pages 339-390.

Differentiates the popular-chronicle historical novel, with its greater fidelity to fact and realism as exemplified by SAN-KUO-CHIH YEN-I (THE THREE KINGDOMS), from the military romance, with its augmented fantastical and magic elements and its kinship with Taoist lore as seen in SHUI-HU CHUAN (THE WATER MARGIN). In characterization sees the military romance as conventional in treating the hero's astral origins, exceptional birth and infancy, human or celestial masters, initial public ordeal, token magic implement or sword, sworn brotherhood, and persecution by envious villains. Often portrays the emperor as weak-willed and soft-eared, though commanding the hero's loyalty. Analyzes in detail many novels wherein women warriors, passionate lovers, and proficient soldiers alter public and personal destinies. Calls attention to Ming and Ch'ing novels seldom if ever referred to in current critical literature.

A59. Hummel, Arthur W. EMINENT CHINESE OF THE CH'ING PERIOD 1644-1912. Washington, D.C.: Government Printing Office, 1943-44.

Provides useful accounts, not only of the novelists, but also of persons closely associated with them and with their works.

A60. Hwang Mei-shu. "Is There Tragedy in Chinese Drama? An Experimental Look at an Old Problem." TAMKANG REVIEW 10 (1979): 211-226.

Proposes that even by Aristotelian norms and contrary to popular belief, Chinese dramatists produced genuine tragedy, as in TOU-O YUAN, compared with ANTIGONE; THE ORPHAN OF CHAO, compared with MEDEA; THE PEACOCK FLIES SOUTHEAST, compared with ROMEO AND JULIET; PA-WAY AND HIS LADY, compared with AJAX. Fails to grasp the profounder view of tragedy as grave human waste occasioned by a) hubris and hamartia, b) the gods or the Establishment, and/or c) Necessity, Destiny, Fate, the Stars (an amoral, arational, and inaccessible absolute governing human affairs). Omits, too, the dilemma of the Greeks, responsible for the powerful tension of their drama--the clash between their belief, on the one hand, in universal order and justice, and, on the other, blatant evidence to the contrary in much of human life and experience.

A61. Idema, Wilt Lukas. CHINESE VERNACULAR FICTION: THE FORMATIVE PERIOD. Leiden: E.J. Brill Company, 1974.

Examines the origins of vernacular fiction (novel and short story), acknowledging Hanan's yeoman work on the subject and arriving at these conclusions: 1) that no link exists between professional storytelling and the origins of vernacular fiction; 2) that consumers of fiction, highly diversified between literary and high-class persons and those of lower class with only moderate literacy, amounted to no more than 5% of the reading public, these with relatively few books to read; 3) that critics must distinguish between a story per se and its vernacular-fiction version; 4) that "the storyteller's manner," not a leftover from a recent past, was a late and deliberate artistic choice marking a new fictional development; 5) that novels and short stories were generally derived from plays, and not vice versa; 6) that vernacular fiction cannot be used as a source for Sung social history. Concentrates on the nature and role of hua-pen (vernacular short story) and p'ing-hua (an all-prose narrative on an historical theme) in Chinese novel- and short-story development. Suffers from lack of an index.

A62. Jor Chi-keung. "Chinese-English Comparative Literature Studies: Historical Survey of Publications in English." TAMKANG REVIEW 12 (Fall 1981): 85-91.

A brief, exciting, and challenging survey of English-language activities, periodicals, and studies, addressed to students of Chinese-English comparative literature, with particular appeal for generalists. From its earliest writing sample (1838) to the (at the time) latest conference (Hong Kong 1982), notes the trend toward increasing variety of approaches and sophistication of materials, as well as accelerating involvement of comparativists like Levin, Aldridge, and Guillen. Calls attention to related meetings, triennially at the University of Indiana, quadrennially at the University of Taipei, occasionally at the Hong Kong Universities, and annually at the MLA Conference. Cites the TAMKANG REVIEW (since 1970) and RENDITIONS: A CHINESE-ENGLISH TRANSLATION MAGAZINE (since 1973) as notable publications in the field, to which may be added LITERATURE EAST AND WEST (1953-1980, with hope of revival). For China's place in world literature refers to Hightower's 1952 essay in COMPARATIVE LITERATURE and Hawkes' 1964 assessment in Dawson's THE LEGACY OF CHINA.

A63. Kaltenmark, Odile. CHINESE LITERATURE. New York: Walker and Company, 1964.

A lucid and meaty short history originally produced in 1948. Focuses, in the end, on "The Literary Revolution," events and non-events following the 1949 Communist takeover. A handy, succinct reference for review of the historical, philosophical, and literary contexts out of which the Chinese novel emerges.

A64. Kao, George, ed. CHINESE WIT AND HUMOR. New York: Sterling Publishing Company, 1974. (First published in 1946.)

Anthologizes passages of wit and humor from Confucius and Mencius to Lin Yu-tang. In Section II, "The Humor of the Picaresque," offers selections from each of the six major novels. Attractive presentation, well chosen selections, pithy introductions.

A65. Knechtges, David R., and Stephen Owen. "General Principles for a History of Chinese Literature." CHINESE LITERATURE: ESSAYS, ARTICLES, REVIEWS 1 (1979): 49-53.

Traces the history of current efforts to create a comprehensive and detailed history of Chinese literature comparable to the CAMBRIDGE HISTORY OF CHINA or to the OXFORD HISTORY OF ENGLISH LITERATURE. Describes the 1975 opening conference for implementation of this aim in Issaquah, Washington, with University of Washington's Knechtges and Yale's Stephen Owen (now at Harvard) as co-editors. Lists as general considerations a) factual and descriptive matter; b) norms and conventions of presentation; and c) hypotheses about change and development in periods and authors. Specifies as <u>historical context</u> 1) dating of authors, movements, periods, works; 2) social backgrounds; 3) relation of literature to contemporary intellectual theory; 4) historical writer-groupings, and 5) what was read; as <u>literary-historical context</u> a) the specific literary age or period and the changes therein and b) specific authors and their literary development.

Refers to debates about matters of evaluation (whether by tradition or for other stated reasons) and in matters of terminology (whether to coin new terms, use Western terms redefined, or Chinese terms expanded). Envisions 10 years to complete all volumes, including old Chinese poetry, old Chinese prose, poetry Han to T'ang, T'ang poetry, Sung poetry, classical prose T'ang through Ch'ing, literary theory and criticism, poetry Yuan through Ch'ing, vernacular fiction, drama, and twentieth-century literature.

A66. Lai Ming. A HISTORY OF CHINESE LITERATURE. Pref. Lin Yutang. New York: Capricorn Books, 1966.

Stresses the Communist view of literature as a tool of social and economic reform. Traces the journey of Chinese narrative from "effete" intellectualism ridden with "questionable moral cliches" to fertile, joyous, imaginative products of the "great common people" of China. Within this stricture offers vivid if at times dogmatic accounts of real and reputed major authors and their chief works.

A67. LeFevere, Andre. "Western Hermeneutics and Concepts of Chinese Literary Theory." TAMKANG REVIEW 6 (1976): 159-168.

Believes that Western litterateurs can profitably share certain Chinese literary concepts and practices, notably Chinese preference for a hermeneutics of "teaching the Way," using technical analysis only as an aid. Recalls that Chinese theory sees the work, not as an aesthetic object to be grasped in its full historical reality, but as a vehicle of intercommunication between the author's mind and the reader's, a conversation resulting ideally in modified behavior.

Calls attention to the Chinese view of literature as a rule-governed activity, with genre as a major system among others--prosody, imagery, figures of speech, cultural context. Argues that, imaginatively and flexibly used, rules maximize the possibilities of intercommunication and validate metacreations like translation, performance, and imitation. Insists, finally, on the evil of excessive literary nationalism and on the benefit of comparative study of culturally disparate nations and their products.

A68. Lidin, Olaf G. "Harmony With Nature in Chinese Theory and Opposition to Nature in Western Theory." JOURNAL OF INTERCULTURAL STUDIES 1 (1974): 5-9.

Reviews major facets of the classical Chinese worldview: the harmony of heaven (divinity), earth (nature), and man under the aegis of tao (the divine principle of being and becoming); yin-yang complementarity; divination and the I CHING (THE BOOK OF CHANGES); the five-elements theory and its subordinate systems, all, components in an essentially harmonious process. With these views contrasts Western belief in the inferiority of nature and in the Judaeo-Christian mission to subdue and conquer it, to act as adversary to it in a world progressing, not by harmonious cooperation, but by conflict. Observes the replacement of the religious sanction, after the Age of Enlightenment, with the imperatives of Science and Technology. Charges the Maoist regime with deserting its heritage of trust in cosmic harmony and adopting Western destructive ethics. Sees in post-Maoist China a return to the native tradition.

A69. Liu Hsieh. THE LITERARY MIND AND THE CARVING OF DRAGONS. Tr. Vincent Y.C. Shih. New York: Columbia University Press, 1959.

An annotated translation of a 1500-year-old classic on literary theory and criticism, worthy to be considered alongside even older such documents from Greece and

India. After viewing comparable passages from pre-T'ang and pre-Han dynasties, Shih's lengthy introduction shows the influence of Liu Hsieh's work through the centuries, even to 1950, on Chinese literary concepts and praxis.

A70. Liu, James J.Y. THE CHINESE KNIGHT-ERRANT. Chicago: University of Chicago Press, 1967.

Elucidates an ancient and persisting Chinese tradition, a practicing knight-errantry. Defines knights as roamers over the countryside righting wrongs by force and exhibiting a sense of justice, loyalty to friends, courage, and impetuosity. Differentiates Chinese from Western chivalry in social classism, religious affiliation, and romantic love. Reads in the Chinese chivalric code a spirit of revolt and non-conformity to feudal usage in high contrast to Western knights' support of feudal society. Of the major novels sees only SHUI-HU CHUAN as having significant knightly content, but with this element superbly presented.

A71. Liu, James J.Y. CHINESE THEORIES OF LITERATURE. Chicago: University of Chicago Press, 1975.

Proposes 1) to facilitate and contribute to development of an eventual universal theory of literature, 2) to serve students of Chinese literature, and 3) to pave the way for a more adequate synthesis of Chinese and Western critical views geared toward practical criticism. Adapts M.H. Abrams' four-part critical design in THE MIRROR AND THE LAMP (1958) to Chinese purposes and, in separate chapters, focuses on metaphysical, deterministic, expressive, technical, aesthetic, pragmatic, and synthesizing aspects of theoretical problems.

A72. Liu, James J.Y. ESSENTIALS OF CHINESE LITERARY ART. North Scituate, Massachusetts: Duxbury Press, 1979.

An undergraduate, non-specialist text presenting highlights in Chinese literary development and summary critiques of SAN-KUO-CHIH YEN-I (THE ROMANCE OF THE THREE KINGDOMS), SHUI-HU CHUAN (THE WATER MARGIN or

ALL MEN ARE BROTHERS), HSI-YU CHI (MONKEY), and HUNG-LOU MENG (DREAM OF THE RED CHAMBER).

A73. Liu Ts'un-yan. THE AUTHORSHIP OF THE FENG SHEN YEN-I. Volume I of BUDDHIST AND TAOIST INFLUENCES ON CHINESE NOVELS. Wiesbaden: Kommissionsverlag Otto Harrassowitz, 1962.

A highly technical work addressed to specialists in the late Ming novel. Little direct relevance to the six major classics.

A74. Liu Ts'un-yan, ed. CHINESE MIDDLEBROW FICTION: FROM THE CH'ING AND EARLY REPUBLICAN ERAS. Hong Kong: Chinese University Press, 1984. (Distributed by the University of Washington Press.)

A fascinating, unique, and unindexed collection of translations, commentaries, and illustrations, offering seven late Ch'ing and early-Republican novels thematically unified by concubines, courtesans, and singsong girls. Considers these works traditional but a cut below the novels generally acknowledged as great. Argues that not until the 1919 May 4th Movement were the great Ming and Ch'ing novels rescued from literati disdain, opprobrium, and moral condemnation. Valuable for social backgrounds and for occasional comparisons between middlebrow and more prestigious works in the field. Includes translations, in whole or in part, of P'u Sing-ling's MARRIAGE AS RETRIBUTION, Han Pang-ch'ing's SINGSONG GIRLS OF SHANGHAI, Tseng P'u's A FLOWER IN A SINFUL SEA, H.P. Tseng's MY FATHER'S LITERARY JOURNEY, Chang Hen-shui's FATE IN TEARS AND LAUGHTER, Li Po-yuan's MODERN TIMES, and Wu Wo-yao's BIZARRE HAPPENINGS EYEWITNESSED IN TWO DECADES.

A75. Liu Wu-chi. AN INTRODUCTION TO CHINESE LITERATURE. Bloomington: Indiana University Press, 1967.

A product of the 1960's surging interest in Chinese fiction and drama. Considers the Classics, other historical and philosophical literature, and the forms and schools of poetry and non-fiction prose. Uses these traditions as preamble and context for the author's major interests, fiction and, more notably, drama. Generous and newly translated excerpts.

A76. Liu Wu-chi. "Moral and Aesthetic Values in Chinese
Literature: An Historical Survey." TAMKANG REVIEW
1 (1970): 3-13.

A pleasant if undistinguished survey of the historical
development of Chinese literature, seen as leaning at
any given time to either rigorous Confucian or lax
Taoist norms. Notes that, when a balance is struck
between moral and aesthetic motivations, as in T'ang
poetry, Yuan drama, or Ming/Ch'ing fiction, masterpieces are born. Displays faulty understanding of
Western intellectual history during and after the
Middle Ages.

A77. Lo Chin-t'ang. "The Changing Attitude Toward Chinese
Fiction." CHINESE CULTURE 9 (March 1968): 34-51.

An extraordinary, loosely-linked succession of chrono-
logically arranged passages from Chinese classics and
ongoing literature showing attitudinal changes of
Chinese writers and critics from scorn for fiction,
hsiao-shuo, as the enemy of truth to, in late Ch'ing,
enthusiastic recognition of its moral power and humanizing effect. A reservoir of analects and anecdotes
for scholars and other lovers of Chinese literature,
especially in its fictional forms.

A78. Lu Hsun. A BRIEF HISTORY OF CHINESE FICTION. Tr.
Yang Hsien-yi and Gladys Yang. Peking: Foreign
Languages Press, 1954.

The first significant attempt to produce a history of
Chinese fiction, authored by China's best known modern
writer (1881-1936). From pre-Han anecdotes to sophisticated Ch'ing productions, traces the origins, birth,
and evolution, and interprets and evaluates specific
works of a form today challenging its sister genres--
poetry, history, moral philosophy--for importance in
national development. Not even objections of later
scholars--1) Lu's undue disparagement of minor works
(Hsia), 2) his failure to separate mythology and fiction (Y.W. Ma), 3) his confusion of the two types of
hua-pen, fictional and historic (Andre Levy), 4) his
questionable dating of YEN TAN-TZU (Ma) and 5) his
inadequate appreciation of characterization in SAN-

KUO-CHIH YEN-I--cancels the zest, readability, and authenticity of this text as translated by the Yangs.

A79. Lynn, R.J. CHINESE LITERATURE. Canberra: Australian National University Press, 1979.

A badly organized potpourri of unexamined secondary sources with obvious errors and no annotation of entries.

A80. Ma Yau-woon. "The Beginnings of Professional Storytelling in China: A Critique of Current Theories and Evidence." ETUDES HISTOIRE ET DE LITTERATURE CHINOISES OFFERTES AU PROFESSEUR JAROSLAV PRUSEK. Paris: Bibliotheque de l'Institut des Hautes Etudes Chinoises, 1976. Pages 227-237.

Attacks the over-enthusiasm of some scholars for proving the existence of very early professional storytelling (pre-eleventh century), confusing speculation with information. Blames four myths for the fallacies: 1) belief that a prominent literary tradition must have a long history, 2) identification of mere narrative with professional storytelling, 3) application of modern connotations to terms like hsiao-shuo occurring in pre-Sung texts, 4) acceptance of pien-wen narrative as the immediate predecessor of Sung storytelling, without differentiating the essential singing dimension of pien-wen as contrasted with colloquial discourse in hua-pen.

A81. Ma Yau-woon. "The Chinese Historical Novel: An Outline of Themes and Contexts." JOURNAL OF ASIAN STUDIES 34 (1975): 277-293.

Distinguishes the true historical novel, exemplified by the SAN-KUO-CHIH YEN-I (THE THREE KINGDOMS), which treats events of the post-Han struggle among Wei, Shu, and Wu contenders, from purported historical novels like SHUI-HU CHUAN (THE WATER MARGIN), a Robin Hoodesque fabrication of events and personages. Defines yen-i as a blending of actuality and imagination in a respectful recreation of a core of historical events. Demonstrates the wide and confusing misuse of the term for disparate productions. Classifies China's long historical narratives according to their subject matter as dynasty-building, stabilizing, or chronicling. Notes that in each the emperor is spared direct or harsh criticism, blame being shunted onto councilors or villains, a technique raising doubts about historical figures' being given their due.

Remarks the prevailing role of a heavenly providence guiding and governing events, even raising up villains to effect punishment and vengeance for potentates' misdeeds. Shows how a) villains of dynasty-building novels, however tricky, inexorable, or Machiavellian, are never outright demons, but, like Ts'ao Ts'ao of SAN-KUO, by their grand scale, style, determination, and sensitivity believable human beings, whereas national-security plots blacken bad guys beyond credibility; and b) how heroes of both struggles fail their missions, reflecting tragic national degeneracy and a sense of historic fatality and heroic limitation. Traces the power of the dynastic-chronicling novels in projecting, despite structural weakness due to the quantity of material, a real sense of history and the patterns of disorder wrought by treacherous and self-serving ministers, nobles, and commoners.

Points out that Western historical novels, à la Scott, rely on carefully researched holistic reconstruction of an era and seldom center on a major historical figure, whereas their Chinese counterparts emphasize particular events and personages and readily focus on major historical characters. Sees the latter in this respect closer to Shakespeare than to Scott. Finally, discusses the supernatural element in Chinese historical novels, often deprecated by Westerners as digressive, unsophisticated, and inappropriate. Declares that, though some works do exaggerate and distort events, the best employ the supernatural as central to plot development and as functional rather than decorative. Cites SAN-KUO's famous Battle of the Red Cliff, wherein Chu-ko Liang exerts power over climatic elements and thus symbolically indicates the finality of the Providential decree and the frequent dependence of earthly affairs on forces beyond human ken or control.

A82. Ma, Yau Woon. "Fiction." INDIANA COMPANION TO TRADITIONAL CHINESE LITERATURE. Eds. William H. Nienhauser, Jr., and others. Bloomington, Indiana: Indiana University Press, 1986.

Tracing the origin and development of Chinese fiction, chides those who see in early Chinese historical, mythological, and philosophical narrative the beginnings of the form, and, worse, loosely apply key terms with limited intent to broadly unrelated productions. Insists that fiction, here defined as conscious creation of imaginative reality, begins with the Six Dynasties (post-Han) period and the gradual development of subforms including pi-chi (jottings), ch'uan ch'i (classical-language tales), pien-wen (Buddhist stories, chiefly known from the Tun-huang cave findings), hua-pen (vernacular stories used by professional storytellers), kung-an (crime and detection narratives), and p'ing-hua (vernacular story commentaries on historical periods).

Of these forms, most of which use the literary language, finds hua-pen the major formal antecedent of the novel by reason of its chiefly vernacular language, its stock phrases, interpolated verse, and linking devices between storyteller sessions (religiously used as chapter divisions by virtually all Ming and Ch'ing novelists because of the Chinese conformist spirit and respect for tradition). Dismisses as unfounded attributions of authorship of SAN-KUO-CHIH YEN-I and SHUI-HU CHUAN and suggests composite authorship involving enlargement, condensation, and combination. Finds acceptable Wu Ch'eng-en's authorship (as compiler-recreator-editor) of HSI-YU CHI (MONKEY).

Identifies the Wan-li period (1573-1620) of the Ming Dynasty as the golden age of vernacular fiction, a time in which the novel challenged the story for preeminence and gained in liveliness and directness as, in these qualities, the story form abated; a time, also, in which lavish illustration figured largely in textual presentation and development. Faults Sun K'ai-ti's classification of novel types as inadequate and in large part arbitrary, especially in lumping together a vast quantity of undifferentiated fiction as historical, and also by listing these works by content instead of by date of composition.

Argues that the time is not yet ripe for full classification of the novel, that the notion of historical novel ought to exclude works not centering on a body of verifiable facts, and that included works might usefully be sorted as dynasty-building, dynasty-securing, and dynasty-chronicling. In late Ch'ing fiction notes the break from historical emphasis to contemporary materials associated with political, social, intellectual, and aesthetic issues in a rapidly changing society. Laments lack of effective fiction criticism, while explaining that, as a depreciated form in a Confucian milieu, it had no guidelines for excellence comparable with those long since developed for poetry and drama. Recalls that financial rewards were often contingent on pseudonyms and/or a veneer of morality. Attaches much importance to the serialization of novels in the increasingly prestigious newspaper and magazine market.

Urges that, for development of a healthy fiction, both creation and criticism steer clear of politics and that research focus on specific problems of historical, textual, generic, formalistic, aesthetic, structural, thematic, and/or contextual importance.

A83. Maeno Naoaki. "The Origin of Fiction in China." ACTA ASIATICA 16 (1969): 27-50.

Concentrates on the mythic antecedents of the novel form, beginning with early fourth-century Kan Pao's SOU-SHEN-CHI (STORIES OF SPIRITS AND DEITIES). Notes that, whereas Western fiction traces its genesis back to myth through the intermediary epic, China has had few myths and no systematic mythology like the celestial and netherworld spheres of Greece, Rome, or Japan. Observes, further, that the sparse myths introducing some Chinese histories are there only to provide certain rational elements to be incorporated into the histories, an attitude in line with Confucian refusal to discuss spirits, deities, and supernatural worlds.

Argues, nevertheless, that China's small reservoir of myths, mostly evocative of fear and uneasiness (as goddess Nu-wa, with her snake body, or Hsi-wang-mu, originally a leopard-tailed, tiger-toothed demon), inspired storytellers to exploit persistent popular interest in tales of the marvelous. Cites Confucian classic CH'UN CH'IU (SPRING AND AUTUMN CHRONICLES) for instances of myths recounted by courtiers so as a) to suggest noble lineage and a hierarchy of deities worshipped by their various tribes; b) to endorse the position of Official Recorder, responsible for memorizing names, deeds, and pedigrees of deities; and c) to divide lords and ministers into those practicing divination and consulting oracles and shamans, and those like Confucius making their own decisions and assuming responsibility apart from gods' directives. Analyzes Ch'u Yuan's LI SAO as ancient myth doubling for the poet's own odyssey, and similar stories recounted by Mencius, Han Fei-tze, and Ssu-ma Ch'ien.

Concludes that Kan Pao gathered all such mythic fragments and in SOU-SHEN-CHI presents them, not, as alleged, for religious edification, but to please and satisfy popular curiosity about goings-on in transcendental worlds.

A84. Mei, Y.P. "Man and Nature in Chinese Literature." CONFERENCE ON ORIENTAL-WESTERN LITERARY RELATIONS. Eds. Horst Frenz and G.L. Anderson. Chapel Hill: University of North Carolina Press, 1953. Pages 163-173.

Calls Chinese literature probably the richest in the world in content and volume, attributing to it an extraordinary and symphonic unity of pattern, significance, and spirit. Reviews T'ang-Dynasty revolt against excessive and slavish convention and its bifurcation into Confucian "message-vehicle" writing and Taoist "free-spirited" literary expressionism. Quotes eighth-century Han Yu's castigation of Taoist and Buddhist distortions of the concept of tao, while, on their part, Taoist followers of Chuang-tze persisted in seeking reality through spontaneity, suggestiveness, and spiritual understanding found, not in reason, but in perfect naturalness.

Reconciles moralist and aesthetic views by focusing on the similarity of Taoist shen (spirituality) and Mencian ch'i, (boundless breath, a quasi-mystical concept). Traces alternations between dual situations:

on the one hand conveying truth and freedom of expression in times of peace, prosperity, and stability; and, on the other, doing the same in times of chaos and frustration. Relates Chinese nature poetry to Sung landscape painting.

A85. Mei, Y.P. "Man and Nature in Chinese Philosophy." CONFERENCE ON ORIENTAL-WESTERN LITERARY RELATIONS. Eds. Horst Frenz and G.L. Anderson. Chapel Hill: University of North Carolina Press, 1953. Pages 173-183.

Identifies as dominant three principles in Chinese philosophy: emphasis on man, appreciation of nature, and profound awareness of affinity between the two. Shows how, in the national search for perfection, the sage-king functions as teacher and guide, projecting the eightfold path of the GREAT LEARNING: investigation, knowledge, sincerity, rectification of mind, and cultivation of the person, the family, the state, and the world. Follows the sage's belief that, applied to human government, this path can lead to the ideal state, to world peace, and to cosmic harmony. Cites eleventh-century Chang Tsai's famous WESTERN INSCRIPTION as the epitome of the Neo-Confucian world view. Reviews Lu Hsun's arguments against this posture in favor of human opposition to and mastery of nature, a position favored by Mei. Suggests that the old orthodoxy tragically retarded Chinese scientific development. Perceives, finally, that Chinese humanism and naturalism are faithfully portrayed in its literature.

A86. Miller, Lucien. "Allegory and Personality in Modern Chinese Literary Criticism." TAMKANG REVIEW 9 (1979): 379-405.

Citing Fletcher, Strelka, Frye, Bateson, Falk, and Krieger, presents literary criticism as a form of allegory, in which language carries a major meaning below the surface wording. Concludes that this idea elucidates Chinese criticism, notably that of Chou Tso-jen (1885-1966) and Wang Kuo-wei (1877-1927). Proposes that such dual meaning, sometimes reenforcing and sometimes antagonistic, arises from the conscious or unconscious interplay of the persona (public, official, authorized, objective voice) and the person (the private, subjective, anti-systematic view).

Identifies ethical and moral allegory as primordial and powerful forces in fashioning both personae, as exemplified a) in early readings of the romantic songs of the SHIH CHING (BOOK OF POETRY) as prince-prime minister political relationships; b) in Confucian and Neo-Confucian insistence on literature as the vehicle of the Way; and c) in modern readings of DREAM OF THE RED CHAMBER as political allegory, a dirge to the fallen Ming Dynasty, or socialist realism; or MONKEY as Marxist dialectic.

Reads Chou Tso-jen's criticism as essentially personal and subjective, inimical to ideological bias. Identifies a major shift in Chou's thought as he turned away from his early view of literature as a moral agent to a conviction of its uselessness for anything but relaxation. Analyzes an early essay "Humane Literature" for its rejection of almost all the Chinese literary canon (Confucian and Taoist writings, as well as drama, supernatural tales, and pornography) as inhumane, and its praise of "humane attitudes" (first understood in the English Renaissance and the Protestant Reformation) concerning male-female equality and marriages of love. Shows how such views led to praise of Ibsen's DOLL'S HOUSE, Tolstoy's ANNA KARENINA, and Hardy's TESS OF THE D'URBERVILLES and to condemnation of Tagore (for his exaggerations of female chastity, as in suttee) and Dostoyevsky (for actions and events unfounded in real human emotions and strength). Marks that in and out of Chou's arguments intrude objections of the persona, the voice of objectivity and officialdom.

Calls Wang Kuo-wei's 1904 "A Critical Essay on DREAM OF THE RED CHAMBER" for its philosophical insight and historical awareness a vital development in modern Chinese criticism. Views its author as the first Chinese comparatist in East-West literary relations and the source of modern Chinese aesthetics. Traces Wang's blending of Schopenhauerian ideas (on the aesthetics of pessimism, the ethics of suicide, Longinus on the Sublime, and Aristotelian tragedy) with Buddhist views of reality. Follows his search for a literary examplar of his world view in DREAM OF THE RED CHAMBER and his creation of a persona intent on a truth and objectivity which will nevertheless feed his private needs.

Shows how Wang a) adopts Schopenhauer's life philosophy and his concept of the hero as the achiever of lifelessness or will-lessness; b) repudiates readings of the novel as political allegory and/or autobiography; and c) conceives of it instead as Schopenhaurian tragedy whose characters, avidly craving life, end in poignant suffering. Develops Wang's belief that tragedy thus liberates the reader from the will to live, purges him of fear and dread, and so unites aesthetic with moral value. Remarks the irony of the essay's concluding analysis of Schopenhauer's views, declaring that individual will-lessness is but another form of self-seeking pleasure, as impossible as selflessness.

A87. Min Ze. "Realism in Chinese Classical Literature." CHINESE LITERATURE 5 (1981): 113-116.

A brief and confused attempt to explore the history of realism in Chinese literature. Often incomplete and inadequate, with badly placed definition of terms, poor organization, and blurred literary theory and practice.

A88. Munro, Donald. "Other Values, Other Assumptions: The Self and Social Order in China, Past and Present." THE CONCEPT OF MAN IN EARLY CHINA. Stanford: Stanford University Press, 1969.

An authoritative analysis of Confucian and Taoist postures toward an ancient Chinese ideal: the natural equality of men. Makes no direct application to literature, specifically the novel, but provides a firm philosophic base for analysis of literary themes, events, and characters. Notes the importance to both schools of the behavioral implications of belief, in contrast with Western emphasis merely on a tenet's logical validity. Cites Confucian belief that human equality lies in the evaluating mind common to all, so that an individual's use of that mind will determine his merit, ergo his place in the political/economic hierarchy.

For Taoists--opposing man's centrality in the universe and promoting the consciousness of permanence amid change--observes that the principle of human equality rests on the cosmic, eternal element (<u>tao</u>) present in all men and in all things; that men are called, then, not to increase differences among themselves by Confucian striving for excellence, but, rather, by passivity (<u>wu-wei</u>) precisely to diminish differences and move toward an undifferentiated One.

A89. Nienhauser, William H., Jr., ed. CRITICAL ESSAYS ON CHINESE LITERATURE. Hong Kong: Chinese University of Hong Kong, 1976.

Twelve essays of literary analysis, none on a major work of fiction, honoring Indiana University scholar and teacher Liu Wu-chi. Covers formal elements, thematic development, reader-work relations, dream and daemonic in traditional Chinese literature, biographical significance, generic evolution, and intellectual and bibliographical backgrounds. A book for specialists.

A90. Nienhauser, William H., Jr., and others, eds. THE INDIANA COMPANION TO TRADITIONAL CHINESE LITERATURE. Bloomington: Indiana University Press, 1986.

Like the OXFORD COMPANION TO ENGLISH LITERATURE on which it is modeled, features the most generally useful information: in Part I, essays on Confucian and Buddhist literature, drama, fiction, literary criticism, poetry, popular literature, prose, rhetoric, and Taoist and women's literatures; and, in Part II, name and title identifications and subject discussions. In journal-list, general bibliography, and dynastic tables uses unobtrusive Chinese characters and romanizations. An indispensable literary tool.

A91. Plaks, Andrew H., ed. CHINESE NARRATIVE: CRITICAL AND THEORETICAL ESSAYS. Princeton: Princeton University Press, 1977.

A major contribution toward a literary (vs. historical) understanding of Chinese fiction, especially the novel, resulting from a landmark 1974 conference assembling key scholars. In an early, middle, late (through Ch'ing) structure, joins critical theory to specific applications, including two analyses of the rarely treated (in English) JU-LIN WAI-SHIH (THE SCHOLARS). Concludes with the editor's effort to construe from its fiction and history a comprehensive critical theory for Chinese novels. Considers six areas: 1) definitions, in the Chinese context, of narrative categories; 2) generic and non-generic sub-divisions; 3) variations in narrative rhetorical stance; 4) patterns of narrative structure; 5) characterization; and 6) relations between textual patterns and the meaning of the narrative.

A92. Plaks, Andrew H. "Full Length Hsiao-shuo and the Western Novel: A Generic Appraisal." NEW ASIA ACADEMIC BULLETIN 1 (1978): 163-196.

Despite differences in structure, characterization, and literary history, links the Chinese novel with its Western sister in basic respects: 1) Both arise out of contemporary social and economic developments. 2) Both offer realistic representation either in subject and/or treatment, a style leading to problematic aspects of life and character. 3) These aspects generate irony as the genre's central mode. 4) The irony arises from broader intellectual issues in the contemporary world. 5) These issues are essentially critical, a searching for accommodation between prevailing cultural norms and need for change. Argues that popularization of Sung Neo-Confucianism and concurrent social and economic change ripened China for development of the novel genre some centuries before similar changes in sixteenth- and seventeenth-century Europe prepared the way for the first great Western novels.

A93. Plaks, Andrew H. "Issues in Chinese Narrative Theory in the Perspective of the Western Tradition." PTL: A JOURNAL FOR DESCRIPTIVE POETICS AND THEORY 2 (1977): 339-366.

A94. Plaks, Andrew H. "The Problem of Structure in Chinese Narrative." TAMKANG REVIEW 6 (1976): 439-440.

Explores with unusual depth and clarity the issue of "unified" versus "episodic" narrative structure. Attributes Western stress on integrated overall design to 1) the favored status of the myth, 2) an Aristotelian norm intended for relatively short forms, and 3) Western philosophical emphasis on temporal rather than spatial modes.

Finds the cohesion of Chinese narrative in interrelated and overlapping categories (interstitial rather than architectonic structure) derived from the Chinese view of existence as cyclical recurrence governed by complementary bipolarity (as in yin-yang) and multiple periodicity (as in the five-agents theory and its table of 64 correspondences generated to cover all human situations).

Illustrates the operation of these codes as unifiers in Chinese novels, not in neat patterns, but in overlapping axes and cycles of existential change "crossing each other at different angles and at varying intervals of alternation." Points also to acceleration and retardation strategies for balancing opposites: peace and turbulence, joy and sorrow, prosperity and decline, life and death.

To the charge of insufficient action in Chinese narrative responds that, not lack of action or development, but totalization of action, the overseeing of the temporal flux, dispenses with a clear sense of kinetic direction and creates a kind of motionlessness. Names formal relations as China's answer to Western modes of action as the key to artistic unity. Notes that Chinese narrative ends long after the climax because of a parabola form requiring dispersion time to equal that of gathering and because of the cyclical logic in which the decline is never final or absolute, but only descent into a state where new life and form begin even before the old has gone.

Concludes that the unity of Chinese narrative is that of internal cohesion, patterns of recurrence, intended to totalize human experience within a cyclical view of history.

A95. Plaks, Andrew H. "Towards a Critical Theory of Chinese Narrative." CHINESE NARRATIVE: CRITICAL AND THEORETICAL ESSAYS. Princeton: Princeton University Press, 1977.

See A91.

A96. Prusek, Jaroslav. CHINESE HISTORY AND LITERATURE: COLLECTION OF STUDIES. Holland: D. Reidel Publishers, 1970.

Offers subjective and Marxist readings of traditional and vernacular writings, laced with scholarly references, Northeast-Asia residential experience, and background as a Czechoslovakian scholar. Thoughtful and arguable positions contrasting basic qualities of the Chinese mind with those of the Western mind, and Chinese concepts of history and epic with those of classical Greece. Sometimes in English, at others in French, presents 10 lectures probing aspects of classical Chinese writings; 10 others of vernacular literature. Among the novels allows a full chapter only to the SHUI-HU CHUAN. Rich in studies of early Chinese vernacular fiction, storytellers' art, and the rise of the cities as a factor in literary development.

A97. Prusek, Jaroslav. "History and Epics in China and in the West." DIOGENES 42 (1963): 20-43.

A substantive if tendentious treatment of the relation of literary genres—epic (and by extension the novel) and lyric—to the mode of a nation's historiography, a relation expressive of cultural identity. Sees Western (Greek) historiography as a distortion of facts and of truth by its imposition of continuous-flow narrative and integrative homogeneity by theme or subject on documentary material. Attributes this treatment to Western demand for an aesthetic pleasure in history similar to that provided by the epic. (Unaccountably omits reference to British historian Thomas Babington Macaulay's theory and practice.)

With this usage contrasts Chinese history which, fearful of distortion, bending, and fictionizing of truth, demands a more objective method. Cites the categorizing and systematizing of all materials (as dynasty lists, annals, chronologies, treatises, family records, speeches, biographies) as data strictly separated from interpretive, judgmental, and moral commentary intended for human improvement. Observes that this history proper (documentary data) thus provides authentic material for political and moral discussion.

Marks, further, that Chinese and Western history differ in focus according to the genres from which, respectively, they are derived. Chinese lyric and history alike eschew the particular, the individual, the exceptional and unrepeatable in favor of the general, the typical, the norm, the representative in a loose chain of details, events, or materials, creating a general impression, a feeling rather than a concrete, specific reality--a lyric effect. Contrastingly, notes that Western history focuses on the individual, particular, and unrepeatable in epic style. Relates these observations to modern Chinese novels, which continue to neglect individualistic romantic heroes, preferring groups of people caught up in great social movements or forces.

Finally, charges Burton Watson (in SSU-MA CH'IEN, GRAND HISTORIAN OF CHINA) with serious misreading of sources in his allegation that Ssu-ma had no conception of general history outside individual biography.

A98. Prusek, Jaroslav. "The Importance of Tradition in Chinese Literature." ARCHIV ORIENTALNI 26 (1958): 212-223.

Demonstrates that popular as well as classic Chinese literature hews largely to the line of maintaining traditional structures and techniques, each within its own métier, seeking only to perfect the patterns and sharpen the details. Attributes change to writers of lowered social status, often fallen bureaucrats or victims of fortune, who, mobilizing their talents against political and social decadence, established the novel as the favored form of the greatest writers of the Ch'ing Dynasty (1644-1912). Considers that even in this situation the writers clung to recognized conventional forms--as, in the case of the novel, episodic shaping and epic elements mingling with the more integrated and lyrical usages of classical productions. For modern China recommends a criticism based, not on the writers' personalities, as in the past, but on features such as genre development and methods of work.

A99. Rickett, Adele, ed. CHINESE APPROACHES TO LITERATURE FROM CONFUCIUS TO LIANG CH'I-CH'AO. Princeton: Princeton University Press, 1978.

Nine papers from a 1970 St. Croix, Virgin Islands, conference on Chinese literary criticism, sponsored by the American Council of Learned Societies Committee on Studies in Chinese Civilization. Explores the problems of 1) "closed circuitry" or unwarranted assumptions by writers of critics' familiarity with layers of previous documents, 2) the scattered form, as in notes and letters, of much Chinese theory and criticism, and 3) the variant semantics of key terminologies. Calls attention to the complicating factor of poet-critics' dual roles and the related emphasis on the Confucian view of literature as educative rather than aesthetic, and, finally, to the relationship between the writer and external nature. Identifies as the main principles of practical criticism the setting forth of truth in both human and non-human realism and simplicity in rhetoric. Sees curiosity about the creative process as a persistent concern, especially as related to other dynamic forces in the universe.

A100. Rickett, Adele. "The Personality of the Chinese Critic." YEARBOOK OF COMPARATIVE CRITICISM 6 (1973): 111-134.

Concentrates on poetic criticism in China, stressing the classical norms of genre, imitation of the ancients, rules, stress of typical rather than individual, and moral-political formative (and reformative) power and intent. Notes the advantages and disadvantages for the poet-critic (generally the same) in addressing a homogeneous group of learned bureaucrats like himself. Suggests that systematic neglect of the aesthetic dimension results partly from this inbreeding and partly from overstress on the circumstances of composition. Points out a) the paucity of book-length critical studies, and the scattering of critical dicta in short comments, personal letters, prefaces, and colophons; b) the blending of Confucian this-worldly practicality with Taoist/Buddhist transcendental searchings; and c) differences between Chinese critical theory and that of the West. Probably of little use to the generalist student of Chinese fiction.

A101. Rickett, Adele. "Technical Terms in Chinese Literary Criticism." LITERATURE EAST AND WEST 12 (1968): 14-47.

In discussing the critical term hsing-ch'u (inspiration and interest) as applied to poetry, elucidates the Taoist idea that words may point to but not contain an ultimate meaning or truth: "The purpose of words is to explain the symbol, but once the symbols have been grasped, the words may be forgotten." Proposes that hsing-ch'u encouraged the great T'ang poets to discard rigidity of form and compulsory use of allusions.

A102. Ruhlmann, Robert. "Traditional Heroes in Chinese Popular Fiction" THE CONFUCIAN PERSUASION. Ed. Arthur Wright. Stanford: Stanford University Press, 1960.

Argues that social historians of China have need to explore its fiction as a means of penetrating the mythic veil cast over the country's past by official historians. Analyzes fictional heroes of the major novels for a) their historic and mythic components; b) their relation to the feelings and thoughts of the masses, virtually unrepresented in official literature; c) oral elements in a fictional hero's evolution; d) the six major subject matters of oral narration (ghosts and the supernatural; Buddhist miracle tales; daily life and love; crime and detection; feats of strength and courage; and historical tales of great men); e) storytellers' guilds and specializations, usually anti-Confucian; f) stereotyping of roles; and g) transcendence of the golden-mean ideal. Identifies as three kinds of hero 1) the Swordsman, brave, good-natured, impetuous, uninhibited; 2) the Scholar, knowledgeable, wise, disciplined, resourceful, eloquent; and 3) the Prince, mandated by Heaven, unspectacular in action, and prudent in his choice of Scholar and Swordsman attendants.

A103. Schultz, William. "Chinese Literature and Twayne's World Authors Series: A Status Report." CHINESE LITERATURE: ESSAYS, ARTICLES, REVIEWS 1 (1979): 215-217.

Reviews the already published 20-odd volumes devoted to Chinese authors, those in progress, and others planned for the immediate future. Of classic-novel authors, lists as published or planned only Timothy Wong's WU CHING-TZU (1978). Spells out the Twayne plan of providing for non-specialist readers (defined as intelligent lay persons, beginning students of Chinese literature, and comparativists) critical and analytic studies of important writers past and present. Describes the content of the typical Twayne biography as life and career chronology, the larger literary and historical context, and the subject's influence on later trends and developments.

A104. Wang Hsi-yen. "Characterization Through the Depiction of Externals." CHINESE LITERATURE 7 (July 1964): 58-93.

Dissects methods of characterization in China's major classic novels (except HSI-YU CHI and CHIN P'ING MEI), including appearance, conversation, action, and behavior under conflict and struggle.

A105. Wang, John C.Y. "The Cyclical View of Life and Meaning in the Traditional Chinese Novel." ETUDES HISTOIRE ET DE LITTERATURE CHINOISES OFFERTES AU PROFESSEUR JAROSLAV PRUSEK. Paris: Institut des Hautes Etudes Chinoises, 1976. Pages 275-299.

Applies to six major classic novels the Chinese belief that human life, inexorably conditioned by time, moves in cycles, flowing and returning, waxing and waning. Notes that authors' responses to this belief largely determine the structure and tone of their works: those of Taoist persuasion accepting the inevitable and willing to do nothing about it; Confucianists exerting themselves in their short time to live worthily and thus leave example and good name to posterity; Buddhists resolving to escape it all by techniques of transcendence and liberation.

Sees SAN-KUO-CHIH YEN-I (ROMANCE OF THE THREE KINGDOMS) and SHUI-HU CHUAN (THE WATER MARGIN) as dominantly Confucian; HSI-YU CHI (MONKEY) as chiefly Taoist, with Buddhist overtones; and CHIN P'ING MEI (GOLDEN LOTUS) and HUNG-LOU MENG (DREAM OF THE RED CHAMBER) as ambivalent mixtures of Buddhism and Confucianism. Concludes by applying to Chinese fiction Nicholas Berdyaev's three basic categories of time and history and finding that only one--cosmic time--has much relevance, linear and existential time seldom figuring substantially in the actions of Chinese novels.

A106. Wang, John C.Y. "M.H. Abrams' Four Artistic Coordinates and Fiction Criticism in Traditional China." LITERATURE EAST AND WEST 16 (1972): 997-1012.

Treats of Abrams' four elements (work, artist, universe, audience) only in the last two pages, applying them to notable Chinese critics according to their kind, degree, and combination of emphasis among the four. Marks how sixteenth-century Li Chih, author of "On the Mind of the Child," focuses on the creator's psyche; seventeenth-century Chin Sheng-t'an on the work itself; his contemporary, Feng Meng-lung, on reader/audience reaction; and early twentieth-century Hsiang Mo-hsi on the universe imitated by art. Traces from the sixteenth century the growing legitimacy and respectability of vernacular fiction, as critics find in the free expression and power to move of works like SHUI-HU CHUAN a form consonant with Chinese moral earnestness.

Sees Chin Sheng-t'an as the most literary and influential of the pioneers, noting his remarks about negative capability and empathic power, and his list of fifteen *fa* (techniques) in SHUI-HU, among them, recurrent images, satire, contrast, suspense, and comic relief. Notes turn-of-the-century (1900) emphasis on fiction as the most powerful force for social change and reform as, in the past, the classics had operated to atrophy social, political, and economic institutions, points cogently argued by Liang Ch'i-ch'ao. Views nineteenth-century introduction of Western works as, despite poor selection and deficient translation, a dominantly healthy phenomenon, opening Chinese eyes to new possibilities in subject matter and technique, means quickly explored by writers; for example, by Wang Kuo-wei, whose famous essay on HUNG-LOU MENG largely relies on Schopenhauer's dicta on tragedy.

A107. Wang, John C.Y. "The Nature of Chinese Narrative: A Preliminary Statement on Methodology." TAMKANG REVIEW 6 (1976): 229-245.

For purposes of comparative literature proposes a narrative model applicable to all cultures: a pattern of sequential events characterized by followability (suspense), linear and multi-dimensional perspectives, and the indispensable components of story, character, point of view, and meaning. Observes that stories move more or less from equilibrium to loss of it, then to recognition of the loss and search for and reestablishment of it; that Chinese narrative has preferred as subject matter men-men rather than men-women bonding; has exploited dream matter; has encouraged uninhibited expression of emotion; and has depicted static rather than dynamic characters because of its concern for the essential and abiding rather than the particular and changing detail. Further characterizes traditional Chinese narrative as relying less on dialogue, action, and psychological penetration (mind-reading) than on authorial descriptions and other-character comment (a celebrated exception being HUNG LOU MENG).

Remarks Chinese predilection for indirection, for dependence less on details in themselves than on their powers of suggestion, and their almost invariable choice of third-person point of view, the I-narrator being rare, as too direct and intimate for Chinese taste. Distinguishes the simple, objective, reportorial, matter-of fact <u>histor</u> of classical Chinese narrative from the omniscient third-person emerging in the long-winded, more personal, referential work of the storyteller using the vernacular. Finds that the meaning, the purport of a work as realized in the text, rests in complex, often clashing relationships among author, narrator, characters, and audience; and that, whereas the meaning of a narrative is also its theme, it may (but need not) be distinguished from the subject-matter of a story, while always implying the author's specific attitude toward that subject matter.

A108.   Wang Pi-tuan Huang. "Utopian Imagination in Traditional Chinese Fiction." Madison: University of Wisconsin, 1981. An unpublished dissertation.

Demonstrates that Chinese utopian writers have offered no detailed constructive plans for an ideal society and typically exhibit, in their search for natural simplicity, a Taoist flight from responsibility. Categorizes the genre into dream stories, satires, and cave narratives. Includes among its detailed studies HUNG LOU MENG (THE DREAM OF THE RED CHAMBER). Observes in the Western-influenced twentieth century an accelerating tendency on the part of Chinese utopianists to concentrate on social ends.

A109.   Witke, Charles. "Western Analogues to Chinese Literary Archetypes." TAMKANG REVIEW 10 (1980): 309-317.

Discusses Andrew Plaks' position that two archetypal patterns, complementary bipolarity and multiple periodicity, dominate Chinese allegory, as in HUNG LOU MENG, whereas Western allegory rests squarely on the inexorable unilinearity of universal history--in other words, that the Chinese vision of reality is essentially spatial, whereas Western writers propose a dominantly temporal view. Challenges Plaks' exclusion of the two archetypes from Western allegory, showing in Greek and Roman literary traditions rich examples of both. Attributes diminishment of these dimensions to the sudden hegemony of Judaeo-Christian culture, with its overemphasis on linear history. In the growing mass of East-West comparative studies, cautions against exclusivisity in applications of literary norms, notably in those traditions, as in the West, of extraordinary complexity and diversity.

A110.   Wivell, Charles. "Problems of Teaching Chinese Literature in a Comparative Literature Program." JOURNAL OF CHINESE LANGUAGE TEACHERS ASSOCIATION 9 (February 1974): 13-19.

Finds interpretive and structural methods most helpful, relying upon the best available translations and a few incisive articles from specialist journals. Acknowledges limitations due mostly to translation, but insists on the possibility of usefully analyzing motifs, themes, plot lines, and to a large extent characterization. Recommends prior to the reading of the great novels a review of themes frequent in world literature: quest, visits to paradise and to the netherworld, heroes, lovers, ghosts, detectives, folktales, hagiography, and romance as a basis for seeking Eastern parallels. Specifically applies the journey motif to various short stories and offers three levels of structure: a) overt plot and theme, b) literary allusions, and c) patterns of verbal imagery and action.

A111. Wong Yoon-wah. "The Parallelism Between Aristotle and Two Chinese Novelists: Principles of Criticism." TAMKANG REVIEW 6 (1976): 465-480.

Uses the seventeenth-century JOU P'U T'UAN (THE PRAYER MAT OF FLESH) and the eighteenth-century HUNG LOU MENG (DREAM OF THE RED CHAMBER) to establish the essential identity of the "Chinese principle of catharsis" with the famous Aristotelian norm. Contrasts Plato's opposition to tragedy for its excessive cultivation of the emotions and ensuant psychic anarchy with the Aristotelian and Chinese notion of tragedy's salutary effect in discharging bodily and psychic excess. Applies to both novels Aristotle's description of disaster as being more powerfully cathartic when family members clash. Likens the erotic novel's purging effect to that of tragedy. Sees as crucial cathartic points <u>peripeteia</u>, <u>epiphaneia</u>, and <u>agon</u>. Points out the medical origins and implications of the term <u>catharsis</u>.

A112. Wright, Arthur F., ed. THE CONFUCIAN PERSUASION. Stanford: Stanford University Press, 1960.

Symposium papers focusing on 1) the effect of Confucianism on individual lives and on the evolution of social institutions, and 2) the pattern of growth and change in the tradition as it adapted to shifting needs through 25 centuries. In the chapter on traditional heroes in popular fiction shows how the characterizations follow Confucian elements in the theory of painting, with special reference to kings and emperors, scholars, swordsmen, and composite types. Gives attention to all the major classic novels.

A113. Yang, Winston L.Y. "Classical Chinese Fiction in the West: 1960-1980." RENDITIONS 13 (Spring 1980): 40-55.

An important summary of recent developments, contemporary trends, present problems (including teaching and research), and future prospects in bringing Chinese fiction to the West. Points out current gains in more direct, faithful, and complete translations; anthology and journal production; study and interpretation generic, thematic, textual, biographical, historic, and comparative; and multiplied learning programs. Urges more study of the kind and degree of use in China of Western literary theories, models, and standards; the kind and degree of applicability in the West of Chinese theories, criticism, and unique features and background; approaches to translation, whether in the direction of greater readability or greater textual fidelity; control of bibliography; and promotion of all types of publications. Cites Plaks' work as exemplary accommodation of Eastern and Western theory and practice.

A114. Yang, Winston, L.Y. "Western Critical and Comparative Approaches to the Study of Traditional Chinese Fiction." PROCEEDINGS OF THE SEVENTH CONGRESS OF THE INTERNATIONAL COMPARATIVE LITERATURE ASSOCIATION. Stuttgart: Bieber Publishers, 1979. Pages 681-686.

A115. Yang, Winston, L.Y., and Curtis Adkins, eds. CRITICAL ESSAYS ON CHINESE FICTION. Seattle: University of Washington Press, 1981.

See A14.

A116. Yeo Song-nian. "The Problem of 'Sentimental Fallacy' in Chinese Literary Criticism." TAMKANG REVIEW 6 (1976): 341-356.

Presents poetic theories of Chinese literary criticism with frequent reference to analogous Western thought.

Stresses the stimulus-response pattern as productive of overemphasis, not on the subject matter, but on the poet's feelings, in such a way as to validate these feelings chiefly by reference to the poet's morality, high or low. Curiously omits reference to Ruskinian thought on the matter. Gives no attention to fiction.

A117. Yieh Ch'ing-ping. "Conservatism and Originality in Chinese Literature." TAMKANG REVIEW 6 (October 1976): 99-108.

Discusses the perennial clash of chai-tao (stress on the didactic function of literature) and yien-chi (stress on literature as the emotional expression of purposeful thought) in Chinese literary development, with specific reference to Six-Dynasties poetry and parallel prose, and to Sung Dynasty tz'u. Suggests that insofar as emotions are construed as inevitably linked to morality, a third, freer mode of creation is needed. No attention given to fiction.

A118. Yu, Anthony C. "Problems and Prospects in Chinese-Western Literary Relations." YEARBOOK OF COMPARATIVE AND GENERAL LITERATURE 23 (1974): 47-53.

A useful prospectus of principles and methodologies for developing East-West comparative-literature studies. Postulates that, without genetic and linguistic cultural relations, the two literatures nevertheless share norms such as inventive transformation of sources, growth and attenuation of genres, migration of themes and topoi, and evolving roles of mythological and historical figures. Summarizes literary exchanges of modern times involving both temporal and spatial dimensions. Calls for serious cross-hemispheric exertions in translation, interpretation, and criticism.

CHAPTER TWO

SAN-KUO-CHIH YEN-I (THE ROMANCE OF THE THREE KINGDOMS)

"Empires wax and wane; states cleave asunder and coalesce." So opens the early Ch'ing version of SAN-KUO-CHIH YEN-I (THE ROMANCE OF THE THREE KINGDOMS). A refinement of the lost original, this recension has, for over 300 years, been accepted as the novel's standard version.

Yet not all scholars agree that the-rise-and-fall-of-kingdoms is the novel's central theme. Some read it, instead, as a study of overreaching ambition; others as a sardonic reflection on obsessive politicism, destructive of jen, human-heartedness, best-loved of Confucian virtues. Still others identify the core of the novel as its observation of the law of retribution inexorably governing human affairs, or, again, as ironic deflation of popular stereotypes and romantic views.

Yet whatever the interpretation, this long, unified narrative, classified by its author (often but never definitively identified as Lo Kuan-chung c1330-1400) as yen-i, is almost universally acknowledged as China's first great novel, worthy to stand with more famous world classics in the historical mode.

Literally, an explanation in the popular style, and, consentually, historical narrative or romance, yen-i is, by its particular blend of the real and the imaginative, unique. Described by Ch'ing commentator Chang Hsueh-ch'ang as "seven-tenths history and three-tenths fiction," it remains remarkably true to actual events and their dramatis personae as recorded by late third-century historian Ch'en Shou and his fifth-century counterpart P'ei Sung-chih. More than one critic suggests that while, in the matter of using history to focus on great historical figures and crucial historical events, SAN-KUO's author differs strikingly from English historical romanticist Walter Scott (1771-1832), he (the Chinese author), by the same token, strongly resembles dramatist William Shakespeare (1564-1616).

In any case, to mark its greater dignity and its independence of oral storytelling traditions, the 1522 yen-i pointedly omits such raconteur devices as an opening historical survey (though Mao Tsung-kang later provided a brief preamble serving a similar purpose); a storytelling title; reliance on magic and superstition (though some episodes refer briefly to such practices); and fanciful embroidering of events.

The enormous and never-ending popularity of SAN-KUO, following its 1522 publication, inevitably resulted in the takeover of the term yen-i for fictions with little if any basis in history. While forgoing the term itself, another sixteenth-century novel, SHUI-HU CHUAN (THE WATER MARGIN), so successfully camouflaged its romantic adventures as history that Ming publishers habitually bracketed it with SAN-KUO-CHIH YEN-I.

But whether historic or pseudohistoric, both kinds of novels exploited the chivalric ideal of mounted warrior-heroes serving a great leader and his cause, rescuing the oppressed, and redressing wrong. Unlike Western chivalry, founded on religion, romantic love, idealized femininity, and support of the establishment, Chinese chivalry looked for reality and rational behavior, embraced the sworn brotherhood as its chief emotional attachment, and sought human rather than divine rewards. Novels of dynasty-building or conserving or chronicling like SAN-KUO-CHIH YEN-I, however, like their Western counterparts, perceived as the proper chivalric goal the defense of the establishment and/or the restoration of a fallen social order. Romantic-adventure novels like SHUI-HU CHUAN, on the other hand, pursued justice for the oppressed and the destruction of institutions interfering with that ideal.

The story of SAN-KUO-CHIH YEN-I covers about a century, from the last decades of the Han Dynasty (202 B.C.-A.D. 220) to China's temporary reunification under Emperor Tsin in 280. It follows the political and military struggles of three rulers vying for takeover of the Han kingdom before and following the death of its last, young and inef-

SAN-KUO-CHIH YEN-I (THE ROMANCE OF THE THREE KINGDOMS) 67

fective emperor: a) Ts'ao Ts'ao of Wei in North China's Yellow-River plains; b) Sun Ch'uan of Wu in the East, along the lower Yangtse valley; and c) generally regarded as the legitimate Han successor, Liu Pei of Shu in the Southwest's upper Yangtse valley.

The evolution of the novel is not easy to trace. One scenario envisions Sung and Yuan storytellers--whether in oral or written media--as steadily cheapening historical events and persons by invention or accretion of fantastical episodes marked by cheap sensationalism pandering to popular taste. Such efforts culminated in an outrageous Yuan p'ing hua (popular historical tale) about the post-Han Time of Troubles, having little if any connection with the novel. Another views enormously popular Yuan dramas about Three-Kingdoms affairs and earlier shadow and puppet plays and chantefables as further distorting characters and events.

The most believable account of SAN-KUO's origins credits a single author of late Yuan or early Ming times with stripping the story of undesirable accretions and providing a unified and authentic account of the Three-Kingdoms Period with just enough fictional elaboration to revitalize events and make history throb with human passion and heroic deeds. English historian Thomas Babington Macaulay (1800-1859) held comparable views as he set about writing his HISTORY OF ENGLAND, seeking to make that literary form read like fiction.

Written in a combination of simple-classical and dignified-colloquial language, the original novel, produced perhaps in late Yuan or early Ming times, was, seemingly, copied a number of times before its first known publication in 1522 (bearing a preface dated 1494), referred to as the hung-chih version. Over 20 (known) variant editions of this work appeared in rapid succession during the following century.

In early Ch'ing times Mao Lun and his more famous son Mao Tsung-kang (fl. 1660) undertook a thorough revision of the hung-chih version of SAN-KUO-CHIH YEN-I, modeling their emendations on Chin Sheng-t'an's reshaping of SHUI-HU CHUAN. Their revision sought a) to bring the stories closer to historical truth, while (unfairly) exalting Liu Pei and denigrating Ts'ao Ts'ao; b) to add a few interesting episodes or passages, while deleting others thought repetitious or dull; c) to rearrange the text, opting for a 120- rather than a 240-chapter division; and d) to remove superfluous wording and refine the language.

Besides revising and editing the work, Mao Tsung-kang provided a valuable commentary and perceptive interlinear glosses illuminating personalities and stylistic techniques. His contributions in these matters rank with those of Chin Sheng-t'an for SHUI-HU CHUAN and Chang Chu-p'o for CHIN P'ING-MEI. HUNG-LOU MENG's (THE DREAM OF THE RED CHAMBER's) famous commentator and interlinear annotator, Chih-yen Chai, would, of course, join the illustrious group in the following century.

The earliest of the four Ming masterpieces of the novel, SAN-KUO shares in the characteristics marking the emergence of the genre at that time as a new and successful form in Chinese literature. As defined by Andrew H. Plaks (to whose writings I am indebted for much of the following analysis), the genre involves "self-conscious manipulation of structural and textual patterns in the depiction of figures and events ... governed by a normative stance of irony."

Like its sister novels, SAN-KUO exhibits an architectonics involving a) a prologue (abbreviated in SAN-KUO) indicative of the metaphysical principle(s) dominating the tale; b) 10- or 12-chapter chuans marking off significant divisions; c) a parabolalike structure tracing the gradual gathering and grouping of characters and, following the apogee of action (here the Battle of the Red Cliff), the dissolution of the mission and dispersion of participants; d) an ending pointed toward vacuity, futility, or emptiness; e) contrastive pairings and groupings; f) numbered sequences of events; g) complex schemes of spatial and temporal organization, often involving binary polarity (yin/yang) and multiple periodicity (five-elements theory and its system of correspondences); and h) consciously contrived compositional devices like the interweaving of narrative detail, "figural density" (overlapping patterns of recurrent narrative units), and techniques of acceleration and retardation.

Yet, more important than specific matters of structural and textual sophistication, the basic, indispensable requirement of the sixteenth-century Ming novel is, according to Plaks, its ironic view of life, the clash between reader-expectation of stereotyped persons and events conformable to popular storytelling and drama, and the reality of life and human nature.

"Things are not what they seem." The beloved Liu Pei appears kind, gentle, noble; he is, too, a vengeful, blundering fool. Ts'ao Ts'ao, abhorred in folk imagination as a consummate Machiavel, shows himself, to be sure, ambitious, ruthless, cruel, duplicitous; he is, also, a brooding scholar and a poet capable of humanity and magnanimity. The Chu-ko canonized in popular imagination for wisdom and rectitude historically functioned as a Confucian Legalist. The superbly courageous Kuan-yu exhibits haughty, childishly vain, conceited, even stupid behavior.

Yet the end result of the author's ironic view is neither blind acceptance of what cannot be changed or bitter cynicism. It is, rather, a raising of profound questions about sworn brotherhood, about human motivation, about virtue itself--i, for example, righteousness. How is it to be realized in complex situations where right and wrong inextricably intermingle? How to be practiced when duties clash? How accommodate sworn-brotherhood loyalty and duties to family, sovereign, and state?

In keeping with the ironic reversal of simplistic popular characterizations created by and perpetuated in popular literature, the tone of SAN-KUO is perceived by critics as remarkably free from the overt moralism of most traditional Chinese literature, both classical and popular, in both stories and plays (though in some vernacular works scholars increasingly question its sincerity). SAN-KUO, on the other hand, though exploring ethical concepts and problems, leaves judgment to its readers.

While most scholars perceive SAN-KUO as basically expressive of a Confucian world view, two other perspectives lie await, like actors in the wings, for their moments on stage. Taoism, for example, punctuates the narrative, whether in Ts'ao Ts'ao's dark broodings or in Chu-ko's sad reflections as he resists Lui Pei's pressures to leave his farms and involve himself in public struggle (one thinks of Ulysses' demurral on being drafted for the Trojan Wars). Legalism, on the other hand, with its pragmatic concern for centralized control and its reliance on law and its sanctions rather than on ethics as the safeguard of economic and political affairs, must be considered the aegis for certain attitudes and decisions. Thus Chu-ko's historical reality as a Legalist administrator finds congenial Taoist amoralism (in the Confucian sense) and its notion of the ruler as presider over, rather than active participant in, a system of self-sustaining rules and regulations.

Because of its greater emphasis on factual history and its aim to avoid imaginative excess, poetry plays a lesser role in SAN-KUO than in the other novels. Still, it is there: in the couplets substituted by Mao Tsung-kang for original titles and in his borrowings from sixteenth-century poets to replace "doggerel" verses he disdained; above all, in authentic selections from the much praised second/third-century poetry of Ts'ao Ts'ao himself.

Among the most popular and beloved passages of SAN-KUO-CHIH YEN-I is the Peach-Orchard sworn-brotherhood pact, to end only in the deaths of Liu Pei, Kuan Yu, and Chang Fei. Another is the momentous and crucial eight-chapter description of the climactic Battle of the Red Cliff. One critic, however, finds that episode overwritten and prefers the less fictionalized Kuan-tu battle, wherein the confrontation between Ts'ao Ts'ao's armies and those of Yuan Shou provides material "fit for Greek tragedy," people "caught in the web of a weighty historical event fraught with deep human significance."

The popularity of SAN-KUO, rivaled through the centuries only by SHUI-HU CHUAN, rested partly on its power to instruct grownups and children about their historical heritage. It lay, too, in its inspiration for patriots and plotters in times of dissension and unrest, and in the model it provided for sworn brotherhood, perpetuated in secret societies and clan organizations unto this day.

SAN-KUO was, in addition, a glory to the literary world, not fully perceived as such until centuries later. Then critics honored its pioneer break with academic and stereotyped models; its purifying of the folk language from vulgarities and its development of a plain but discriminating vocabulary; its severe reduction of magical, super-natural, and superstitious elements, so important to other popular entertainment; and, finally, its creation of a new and unique historical genre, the yen-i.

SAN-KUO-CHIH YEN-I (THE ROMANCE OF THE THREE KINGDOMS) 71

Mention must be made here of the achievement of C.H. Brewitt-Taylor, whose courageous pioneer translation (1925) has not yet, after 60-odd years, been entirely superseded, though English-language readers of Chinese novels look forward to early publication of the new, complete translation proposed by Moss Roberts of New York University. His 1976 partial translation, entitled THREE KINGDOMS: CHINA's EPIC DRAMA and covering about one-fourth of SAN-KUO, has from scholar and laic alike won praise.

In addition to a new, definitive translation of SAN-KUO-CHIH YEN-I on the order of Anthony Yu's 1977-1983 JOURNEY TO THE WEST (HSI-YU CHI), more English language studies are needed on the formal, aesthetic, strictly literary aspects of SAN-KUO. To this end Plaks and others (among them, Ma Yau-woon, Paul W. Kroll, C.T. Hsia, Winston L.Y. Yang, Edward Buote, and Andrew Lo) have opened avenues filled with suggestions: How, for example, do binary polarity (yin-yang) and multiple periodicity (five-elements theory and system of correspondences) enter into the structural design? To what extent, if at all, can Western notions of <u>hubris</u>, <u>hamartia</u>, and <u>catharsis</u> illuminate characters and episodes?

Teasing suggestions have been made about a likeness of SAN-KUO's treatment of history to that of Shakespeare. Can this notion be spelled out? Is it true that the West has no significant work describable as yen-i? What is the posture of the work toward women, and what does that posture say about the times and about the author? To what extent, if at all, are themes, characters, events, and aesthetic methodology of SAN-KUO-CHIH YEN-I echoed in twentieth-century Chinese literature?

Translations

B1. Brewitt-Taylor, C.H., Tr. ROMANCE OF THE THREE KINGDOMS (SAN-KUO-CHIH YEN-I). Two volumes. Rutland, Vermont: Charles E. Tuttle Company, 1983. (Ninth reprinting since 1959. Originally published in Shanghai in 1925.)

A generally unabridged, highly readable 120-chapter translation of China's earliest or near earliest novel, called by Roy Andrew Miller "one of the world's major works of fiction, a vast but coherent and amazingly well constructed historical romance." In Miller's introduction describes historical backgrounds, methods of accretion and collection of materials, and major characters. Defines as central theme, not the famous opening sentence, "Empires wax and wane; states cleave asunder and coalesce," but the nature of human ambition.

B2. Chai Ch'u, and Winberg Chai, trs. and eds. "SAN-KUO-CHIH YEN-I (ROMANCE OF THE THREE KINGDOMS)." A TREASURY OF CHINESE LITERATURE: A NEW PROSE ANTHOLOGY INCLUDING FICTION AND DRAMA. New York: Appleton-Century, 1965. Pages 192-209.

Discusses, in the introduction, the putative authorship of Lo Kuan-chung; the third-century source, Ch'en Shou's history; the 1494 earliest edition with its 24 books in 10 sections, each headed by a seven-word verse; and textual changes thereafter. Considers the novel great for its "rich content, brilliant plot construction, and remarkable characterization." Sees as central thrust rulers' power struggles carried on by skilled generals in stirring battles. As excerpts presents the Prelude and Chapter One, detailing Han-contender Liu Pei's Peach-Orchard compact with sworn brothers, and Chapter 46, introducing the famous Battle of the Red Cliff.

B3. Cheung Yik-mau, tr. ROMANCE OF THE THREE KINGDOMS. Hong Kong: Cheung Publishers, 1972. Chapters 43-50.

B4. Chu Y.S., tr. ROMANCE OF THE THREE KINGDOMS. Hong Kong: Kuan-chih shu-chu, 1965.

Several episodes.

B5. Fang, Achilles, tr. THE CHRONICLE OF THE THREE KINGDOMS. Two volumes. Cambridge: Harvard University Press, 1962-1965.

A translation of Chapters 69-78 of the monumental TZU CHIH T'UNG CHIEN (COMPREHENSIVE MIRROR FOR AID IN GOVERNMENT) by Ssu-ma Kuang (1019-1068). Called by

SAN-KUO-CHIH YEN-I (THE ROMANCE OF THE THREE KINGDOMS) 73

critics the second greatest national history of China, covering 493 B.C.-A.D. 959 (the first being, presumably, the work of Grand Historian Ssu-ma Ch'ien [c145-c185 B.C.]). Offers a reasonably objective account of the Three-Kingdoms Era, based on Ch'en Shou's third-century account and P'ei Sung-chih's fifth-century compendium of earlier sources. Offers material apt for comparison with the fictionized account in SAN-KUO-CHIH YEN-I. Notes the Confucian aim of the work "to give object lessons to sovereigns who want to bring about good government."

Presents, in these chapters from the COMPREHENSIVE MIRROR, the last days and death of the historical Ts'ao Ts'ao (155-220) and relevant speeches and writings. Describes the recension and rearrangement of parts of the work effected by Chu Hsi (1130-1200), first great formulator of Neo-Confucianism, for his own didactic purposes, a fact leading Andrew Lo to suggest that source-seekers for SAN-KUO-CHIH YEN-I would do well to consult Chu Hsi's work.

B6. Kuhn, Franz, tr. DIE SCHWURBRUDER VON PFIRSICHGARTEN: ROMAN AUS DEM ALTEN CHINA. Kohn and Berline: Kiepenheuer and Witsch, 1953.

A German adaptation rather than translation of the novel.

B7. Nghiem Toan, and Louis Ricaud, trs. LES TROIS ROYAUMES. Three volumes. Intro. Robert Ruhlmann. Saigon: Societe des Etudes Indochinoises, 1960-1963.

Offers in unwieldy tomes the complete text in translation, preceded by a substantive introduction and augmented by extensive background notes. Enlivens the narrative by generous illustrations and, at chapter heads, Mao Tsung-kang's commentaries, dating from about 1600.

B8. Parker, Z.Q., tr. "The Story of the Three Kingdoms: The Battle of the Red Cliff." CHINA JOURNAL 3 (1925): 250-430, 308-316, 367-373, 426-430.

Four episodes: Liu Pei's alliance with Sun Ch'uan; his meeting with Chow Yu; Kung-ming and Chow Yu's counterplotting against the enemy; and their conference about stirring up the southeast wind.

B9. Roberts, Moss, tr. THREE KINGDOMS: CHINA'S EPIC DRAMA. New York: Pantheon Books, 1976.

Concentrates on Chapters 20-85 of the original 120, using summary bridges, condensations, and splices--in all, covering about one-fourth of the original. Enriches the narrative by full-page illustrations drawn from early Ch'ing woodblocks and later Ch'ing editions; by four large maps placed at strategic points; and by a meaty introduction to historical backgrounds, including the role of the secret society, the Yellow Scarves. Points out moral dilemmas posed by clashing loyalties, the law of retribution flashing through events, and ironies arising therefrom. Remarks, finally, the sparing use of magic and the supernatural.

B10. Yang Hsien-yi and Gladys Yang, trs. "The Battle of the Red Cliff." CHINESE LITERATURE 1 (January 1962): 40-90 and 2 (February 1963): 21-61.

Presents, in the Yangs' crystalline prose, marked by pithy description, concise, pointed dialogue, and charming full- or half-page illustrations, the eight important chapters known as the Battle of the Red Cliff.

Studies

B11. Balazs, Etienne. "Political Philosophy and Social Crisis at the End of the Han Dynasty." CHINESE CIVILIZATION AND BUREAUCRACY: VARIATIONS ON A THEME. Ed. Arthur F. Wright. New Haven: Yale University Press, 1964. Pages 187-225.

Analyzes the life and works of three philosophers representing and inspiring developments during the Han-Dynasty decline and its bloody aftermath: 1) Wang Fu, Confucian eremite, seeking restoration of class order among peasants, craftsmen, and merchants in a natural economy; 2) Ts'ui Shih, Legalist, proposing systematic governmental rewards and punishments as the only way to social health; and 3) viewed as most attractive of the three, T'ung Chung-ch'ang, Taoist counselor of Ts'ao Ts'ao. Reviews Ts'ui's eight political principles blending cynical authoritarianism, Taoist poetry, and revolt against tradition as groundwork for social regeneration. Elucidates the intellectual atmosphere in which the historic and heroic deeds of the ROMANCE OF THE THREE KINGDOMS transpired.

B12. Balazs, Etienne. "Two Songs by Ts'ao Ts'ao." CHINESE CIVILIZATION AND BUREAUCRACY, VARIATIONS ON A THEME. Ed. Arthur F. Wright. New Haven: Yale University Press, 1964. Pages 173-186.

Illuminates the character of Ts'ao Ts'ao as a hero/villain "wrapped in history, poetry, and legend," a man of manifold contradictions and innumerable roles: successful military commander, expert strategist, Machiavellian usurper, wise founder of a dynasty, and one of China's greatest poets. Reviews turbulent events and movements of the age: the struggles of an effete nobility and corrupt bureaucracy against greedy eunuchs, a smoldering peasantry organized under the Yellow-Turbans banner hoisted by the Chang brothers, and clashing Confucian, Taoist, and Legalist philosophies--to no one of which Ts'ao fully subscribed.

Associates Ts'ao as poet with Ch'u Yuan and the SONGS OF THE SOUTH (both possibly fourth century B.C.) and with Taoist feel for nature and freedom and pessimism about social organization. From two dozen surviving poems selects two songs "on the air CH'IU-HU (MULBERRY TREE IN THE BALK)" for explication, carefully placing the poems in the context of Ts'ao's Szechuan campaign against Chang Lu in spring 215. (See Chapter Four's Introduction.)

B13. Brown, Carolyn Thompson. THE TREATMENT OF TS'AO TS'AO IN CHINESE VERNACULAR LITERATURE. Ithaca, New York: Cornell University, 1968. An unpublished Master's thesis.

Traces differences between the historical Ts'ao Ts'ao and his portrayal in selected Yuan and early Ming dramas and in the novel SAN-KUO-CHIH YEN-I.

B14. Buote, Edward I. CHU-KO LIANG AND THE KINGDOM OF SHU-HAN. Chicago: University of Chicago, 1968. An unpublished dissertation.

Studies the life, work, and character of Chu-ko (182-234), prime minister and commander-in-chief of Liu Pei, leader of Shu contenders for the Han succession. Concludes that Chu-ko historically exhibited extraordinary talent and integrity so as to epitomize the Confucian chun-tse or Superior Man. Traces his military campaigns and governmental career before demonstrating the development of the Chu-ko legend in folk tale, drama, and "the famous historical romance" SAN-KUO-CHIH YEN-I.

B15. Ch'en Ming-sheng. "On THE ROMANCE OF THE THREE KINGDOMS." CHINESE LITERATURE 2 (February 1962): 62-69.

Reviews the basic history of SAN-KUO-CHIH YEN-I, beginning from Ch'en Shou's third-century history and P'ei Sung-chih's later annotated version of it, through fifth-century anecdotal development. Continues with T'ang and Sung legendary accretions, Yuan chantefables and operatic plays, and Ming storytellers' and promptbook productions. Refers to the famous earliest-known unified version of the stories (1494) as Lo Kuan-chung's, to Li Tso-wu's sixteenth-century annotated revision, and, finally, to Mao Tsung-kang's newly revised and rigorously pruned seventeenth-century edition, today's standard version.

Describes the basic and partisan-presented contest between just and kindly Liu Pei of Shu (Han), villainous Ts'ao Ts'ao of Wei, and ineffectual Sun Ch'uan of Wu. Writes in detail of the powerful eight-chapter Battle of the Red Cliff. Praises the novel's characterizations as well as its narrative power, noting the historical influence of the work and its wide regard as a textbook on life in feudal China.

B16. Crump, James I, Jr. "P'ing-hua and the Early History of the SAN-KUO-CHIH." JOURNAL OF THE AMERICAN ORIENTAL SOCIETY 71 (October-December 1951): 249-256.

Declares the formation-history of SAN-KUO-CHIH YEN-I a muddle, some elements of which can be clarified by backtracing its p'ing-hua components from the 1494 edition. Imputes egregious error to Prusek's description of p'ing-hua as plain narrative, mostly without poetry (A96). Demonstrates that all known p'ing-hua (historical narratives with elaborate tables of contents and/or lavishly illustrated titles) contain yung-shih, didactic historical poems, at first titled by place names and later by time indicators. Shows how these creations, mostly doggerel, from being merely didactic verses for teaching history and its moral implications, came to function as structural units borrowed from known poets, notably T'ang versifiers Hu Tseng and Chou T'an, to link narrative episodes. Remarks the steadily decreasing inclusion of the poems in post-1494 editions and attributes this change to the aesthetic inferiority of the yung-shih.

B17. Fitzgerald, C.P. "The Chinese Novel as a Subversive Force." MEANJIN QUARTERLY 10 (Spring 1951): 259-266.

Shows how this earliest of the great novels supported the establishment and had as its purpose to demonstrate that a united empire tends to disintegrate and a divided one to unite in a strong central government. Deplores establishment blindness in condemning the work because of its breach with the past in using pai-hua (colloquial language) instead of traditional literary, classical Chinese. Finds the consequence in the proliferation thereafter of anti-establishment vernacular writing.

B18. Grousset, Rene. "The Three Kingdoms." THE RISE AND SPLENDOUR OF THE CHINESE EMPIRE. Trs. Anthony Watson-Gandy and Terence Gordon. Berkeley: University of California Press, 1970 (eighth printing). Pages 96-103.

A straight but colorful historical account of events constituting the matter of China's first and greatest historical romance.

B19. Hanan, Patrick. "The Development of Fiction and Drama." THE LEGACY OF CHINA. Ed. Raymond Dawson. London: Clarendon Press, 1964. Pages 126-127.

After discussing the applicability of the term epic relative to Chinese literature, concludes that the fourteenth-century novel SAN-KUO-CHIH YEN-I, reputedly by Lo Kuan-chung, offers an epiclike compilation of heroic tales generally faithful to historical accounts, developed through the centuries by story and drama, and merged into one long work, marked by a terseness and plainness different from the full and expressive manner of the pseudo-historical SHUI-HU CHUAN. Notes the emergence from a horde of characters of the three great protagonists contending for the Han succession in (and after) the declining years of the dynasty, 202-260: Liu Pei of Shu, whom Lo defends as the legitimate scion; Sun Ch'uan of Wu; and consummate villain Ts'ao Ts'ao of Wei.

Concludes that the sworn-brotherhood ideal supersedes other allegiances, and that uxoriousness or even devotion to one's mother occasions at times a hero's fall and disgrace. Points out that, as the novel progresses, characters develop a degree of complexity: obsessed with desire for avenging a sworn brother's death, Liu blunders fatally; honest Chang Fei precipitates violence; righteous Kuan Yu struggles with moral dilemmas; Chu-ko Liang functions as both scholar-hermit and magician-strategist; above all, Ts'ao Ts'ao, a brooding Machiavel, shows glimmers of magnanimity.

B20. Hightower, James R. TOPICS IN CHINESE LITERATURE: OUTLINES AND BIBLIOGRAPHIES. Cambridge: Harvard University Press, 1965. Page 104.

Identifies the language and style of SAN-KUO as both simple literary and dignified colloquial.

B21. Hsia, C.T. "THE ROMANCE OF THE THREE KINGDOMS." THE CLASSIC CHINESE NOVEL: A CRITICAL INTRODUCTION.

SAN-KUO-CHIH YEN-I (THE ROMANCE OF THE THREE KINGDOMS) 79

    New York: Columbia University Press, 1968. Pages 34-74.

    Focuses on the compiler-author's restraint in altering historical dimensions of characters to suit the new narrative form yen-i, in contrast with the supernaturalism and folklorism rampant in contemporary p'ing-hua versions of the stories. Finds conscious intent to create a dialogue of sardonic commentary on men immersed in politics to the detriment of their humanity. See A57.

B22. Idema, Wilt Lukas. "The SAN-KUO-CHIH YEN-I." CHINESE VERNACULAR FICTION: THE FORMATIVE PERIOD. Leiden: E.J. Brill Company, 1974. Pages 102-106.

    After reviewing the life and legend of Lo Kuan-chung, demonstrates the reputed author's removal from his work of any connection with popular oral literature; his cultivation of simple literary Chinese, wen-yen; his omission of the usual opening historical summary; his choice of a non-storytelling title, yen-i (exposition of the meaning). Points out that only after SAN-KUO was the storyteller's manner assumed by authors, for whom it was not a residual phenomenon but a deliberately chosen artistic convention.

B23. Irwin, Richard Gregg. THE EVOLUTION OF A NOVEL: SHUI-HU CHUAN. Cambridge: Harvard University Press, 1953.

    See C32.

B24. Irwin, Richard Gregg. "THE WATER MARGIN REVISITED." T'OUNG PAO 48 (1966): 393-415.

    See C33.

B25. Kaltenmark, Odile. CHINESE LITERATURE. Tr. Anne Marie Geoghegan. New York: Walker and Company, 1964 (revision of the 1948 original). Page 116.

    Despite the novel's "poor construction," notes its great popular appeal and, for the lower classes, its educational value.

B26. Kroll, Paul William. PORTRAITS OF TS'AO TS'AO: LITERARY STUDIES OF THE MAN AND THE MYTH. Ann Arbor: University of Michigan Microfilms, 1981.

Considers under four rubrics Ts'ao Ts'ao (155-220), China's great late-Han leader and complex human being, chief villain of SAN-KUO-CHIH YEN-I: 1) the official man, as revealed by his contemporaries and by his own public writings, including a lengthy autobiographical edict (given in full) and other proclamations; 2) the poet, as reflected in his 21 poems using new and experimental techniques; 3) the fictional man, reflected in third-century and, later, T'ang, Sung, and Yuan accounts, and, finally, the SAN-KUO-CHIH YEN-I (AN ELABORATION ON THE TREATISE OF THE THREE STATES); and 4) the dramatic man, chiefly as depicted in five tsa-chu Yuan plays.

Finds that fictional and dramatic characterizations falsify and grossly underestimate the historical character, portraying him as merely duplicitous, inept, and cruel, whereas the true Ts'ao balanced his pride and ambition by continued loyalty to the Han emperor, maintaining for him the unity of Northern China during the turbulent Chien-an Period (189-220); by sensitivity to the sorrows and yearnings of the common troops; by his patronage of learning and the arts and the establishing of village schools and, for his own estate, a coterie of scholars; by his careful education of his sons, one of whom became the most noted poet of his time, another the most learned of China's emperors and the pioneer of its literary-criticism genre.

Stresses that, in choosing public officials, Ts'ao repeatedly called for talent and practical ability as prior to Confucian human-heartedness (jen) and righteousness (i); and that, in directing the new poetics emergent from sterile academic forms, he demanded talent, imagination, and even individualism. Traces the more benign interpretations of Ts'ao to Wang Ch'en's WEI-SHU (255) and vilifications chiefly to the anonymous TS'AO MAN CHUAN of about the same time, reinforced by Yuan dramas and by the fourteenth-century SAN-KUO-CHIH P'ING-HUA. Also points out that the smearing and blackening may have resulted from the exigencies of storytelling itself, constrained as it was to produce stereotypical good and evil characters. A must book for students of China's first and probably greatest novel in the historical genre.

B27. Lai Ming. A HISTORY OF CHINESE LITERATURE. New York: Capricorn Books, 1966. Pages 284-287.

Accepts Lo Kuan-chung's authorship of SAN-KUO-CHIH YEN-I and his language as half-vernacular and half-classical. Cites the Confucian classic SHIH CHING (THE BOOK OF POETRY) as a source, enumerates Mao Tsung-kang's seventeenth-century revisions, and provides a one-page summary of the plot.

B28. Li, Peter. "Narrative Patterns in SAN-KUO and SHUI-HU." CHINESE NARRATIVE: CRITICAL AND PHILOSOPHICAL ESSAYS. Ed. Andrew H. Plaks. Princeton: Princeton University Press, 1978. Pages 73-84.

Against much modern, though not older, criticism, argues that SAN-KUO exhibits a substantial, if weak, overall organization and a structural unity based on a conflict-resolution model (point of contention, confrontation, open conflict, and resolution) and carried through in four major conflict situations. Sees, on the other hand, strong internal organization in three intermeshing lines of action involving Ts'ao Ts'ao's 11 career steps, Liu Pei's 14, and Sun Ch'uan's seven. Demonstrates numerous and intricate linkings of these story lines within a six-part narrative division identified by Mao Tsung-kang. Contrasts the weak overall and strong internal structures of SAN-KUO with the converse in SHUI-HU CHUAN.

B29. Liu Ts'un-yan. "Lo Kuan-chung and His Historical Romances." CRITICAL ESSAYS ON CHINESE FICTION. Eds. Winston L.Y. Yang and Curtis P. Adkins. Hong Kong: Chinese University Press, 1980. Pages 85-114.

From analyses of diction, syntax, and thought concludes that the fourteenth-century author of popular fiction and drama had little to do with the production of the works known today as SAN-KUO-CHIH YEN-I and

SHUI-HU CHUAN, although portions of an early version of the latter were written by him.

B30. Liu Wu-chi. "The Novel as Folk Epic." AN INTRODUCTION TO CHINESE LITERATURE. Bloomington: Indiana University Press, 1966. Pages 195-212.

Stresses the novel's enormous popularity and its tremendous influence historically on the Chinese people as a crystallization of their love for the past, for historical continuity, and for imaginative and idealized recreations of their heroes. Compares the sixteenth-century novel with its fourteenth-century p'ing-hua predecessor. Calling SAN-KUO seven-tenths history and three-tenths fiction, elaborates on the characterizations, biased toward Shu-Han protagonists and against their enemies, notably Wei-prince Ts'ao Ts'ao, but achieving, nevertheless, intriguing complexity of portrayal. Devotes three pages to Chu-ko Liang, scholar, statesman, diplomat, and master military strategist for Shu-prince Liu Pei.

B31. Lo, Andrew Hing-bun. "SAN-KUO-CHIH YEN-I." THE INDIANA COMPANION TO TRADITIONAL CHINESE LITERATURE. Eds. William H. Nienhauser, Jr., and others. Bloomington: Indiana University Press, 1986. Pages 668-671.

Suggests that SAN-KUO-CHIH YEN-I, probably completed in late Yuan times (fourteenth century), perhaps by Lo Kuan-chung, did not originally derive from p'ing-hua (historical tales), but, perhaps, from Chu Hsi's twelfth-century treatise MIRROR FOR AID IN GOVERNMENT. Calls attention to numerous similarities in the works and to one striking difference--that the treatise directs moral interpretation, whereas the novel leaves such conclusions to the reader. Cites SAN-KUO's frequent use of i (righteousness), not to judge persons and events, but rather to explore the word's semantics, its changing meanings in different situations.

Discusses the novel's "standard version," shaped by seventeenth-century Mao Lun and his son, who tightened and refined the language, abbreviated documents, added some anecdotes, omitted others, and, in short, thor-

oughly revised the original. Calls the novel, with
the possible exception of SHUI-HU CHUAN, the most
influential Chinese novel, invoked even today by
secret societies and clan organizations. Notes focus
on Chu-ko's wisdom, Hua T'o's professional skill,
Ts'ao Ts'ao's Machiavellianism, Kuan Yu's divine
patronage in war--above all, on the friendship,
brotherhood, and loyalty of the favored contenders.

B32. Lo, Andrew Hing-bun. "SAN-KUO-CHI YEN-I and SHUI-HU-
CHUAN in the Context of Historiography: An Interpretive Study." Princeton: Princeton University, 1981.
An unpublished dissertation.

Relates the two novels and historiography in terms of
intent, especially moral aim. Finds both novels more
exploratory than hortatory in reference to the virtue
of i (righteousness, honor, integrity), as it is woven
into the stories' fabric. Concludes with a reconsideration of the historical novel in relation to the vision of the novelist.

B33. Lu Hsun. A BRIEF HISTORY OF CHINESE FICTION. Trs.
Yang Hsien-yi and Gladys Yang. Peking: Foreign
Languages Press, 1959. Pages 163-173.

Reviews, in this pioneer literary history compiled
from the author's lecture notes, early publications,
and revisions of the 1920s, a) the 97 years (A.D.
184-280) covered in SAN-KUO-CHIH YEN-I, stressing
Ch'en Shou's third-century history of the times; b) an
undatable 24-book, 240-chapter first version; and c)
the 70-chapter, much altered production, edited by Mao
Tsung-kang in emulation of Chin Sheng-t'an's work on
SHUI-HU CHUAN.

B34. Ma, Yau-Woon. "Chinese Historical Novels: An Outline
of Themes and Contexts." JOURNAL OF ASIAN STUDIES
34 (February 1975): 277-294.

Attempts to open up new vistas for Chinese literary
history and criticism by concentrating on the earliest
novel genre to gain recognition among literary critics, the historical novel. Defines and differentiates
terms like yen-i, showing misconceptions in current
translations of such terms. Among the 154 true histor-

ical novels identified in 1957 by Sun K'ai-ti, selects three major themes: dynasty-building, national security, and dynastic chronicle, each with strengths and weaknesses vis-à-vis literary art and historical accuracy.

Attributes the popularity of the narratives, not to escapist desires, but to a profound consciousness of national continuity and heritage and the need for reinforcing political morality. Calls attention to the tendency of historiographers to glorify the successful and disparage their failed adversaries, however worthy, a propensity with regrettable consequences for literature as well as for history. Urges careful assessment of the so-called excessive use of the supernatural, arguing that the propriety of such elements depends on their role in thematic development and contextual integrity.

In characterization finds Western analogues, not in Scott and his followers, but in Shakespeare's history plays and in Hegel's world-historical individuals, at once makers and products of evolutionary forces.

B35. Ma Yau-Woon. "Lo Kuan-chung." THE INDIANA COMPANION TO TRADITIONAL CHINESE LITERATURE. Eds. William H. Nienhauser, Jr., and others. Bloomington: Indiana University Press, 1986. Pages 594-597.

Rejects conventional acceptance of Lo as author of SAN-KUO-CHIH YEN-I, considering the evidence highly questionable, even the 1422 REGISTRY of Chia Chung-Ming identifying Lo as poet and playwright (but not fictionist), and even though all extant early copies of the novel bear Lo's name as author. Regards the processes of professional storytelling, communal transmission, cyclical evolution, and radical editorializing as too complicated for final authorship judgment at this time. Recommends consideration of Lo Kuan-chung as merely a minor playwright with three dramas to his name.

B36. McLaren, Anne Elizabeth. MING CHANTEFABLE AND THE EARLY CHINESE NOVEL. Canberra: Australian National University, 1983. An unpublished dissertation.

Contends that the 1967 discovery of 11 fifteenth-century chantefables in a tomb near Shanghai produced three almost certainly influential in the development of the early Chinese novel, notably SAN-KUO-CHIH YEN-I. Points to chantefable prose-song narrative, prologues, narrator impersonation, and storyteller patter, including audience questioning, as indications of influence on organized long fiction. Argues that the chantefable model moved the Chinese historical novel away from the restrictive norms of popular works like hua-pen and p'ing hua.

B37. McNaughton, William. "The Chinese Novel and Modern Western Historismus." CRITICAL ESSAYS ON CHINESE FICTION. Eds. Winston L.Y. Yang and Curtis P. Adkins. Hong Kong: The Chinese University, 1980.

Recommends that Western writers of the new history-turned-novel genre (as Truman Capote's COLD BLOOD and William Styron's THE CONFESSIONS OF NAT TURNER) use Chinese yen-i for models.

B38. Miller, Roy Andrew. "Introduction." ROMANCE OF THE THREE KINGDOMS. Tr. C.H. Brewitt-Taylor. Two volumes. Rutland, Vermont: Charles Tuttle Company, 1959. I: v-vii.

See B1.

B39. Plaks, Andrew H. THE FOUR MASTERWORKS OF THE MING NOVEL: SSU TA CH'I-SHU. Princeton: Princeton University Press, 1987.

An important book by a scholar noted for pioneer work in literary analysis of Chinese fiction. Points out that the fullest recensions of these works "represent a sophisticated new genre [the novel] of Chinese prose fiction arising in the late Ming dynasty, especially in the sixteenth-century ... and reflect the values and intellectual concerns of literati of the period." [Arriving too late for personalized review in this bibliography, the book is sure to be a landmark in studies of SAN-KUO-CHIH YEN-I (ROMANCE OF THE THREE KINGDOMS), SHUI-HU CHUAN (THE WATER MARGIN), HSI-YU CHI (MONKEY, or JOURNEY TO THE WEST), and CHIN P'ING MEI (THE GOLDEN LOTUS).]

B40. Plaks, Andrew H. "SHUI-HU CHUAN and the Sixteenth-century Novel Form." CHINESE LITERATURE: ESSAYS, ARTICLES, REVIEWS 2 (January 1980): 3-53.

Shows how SAN-KUO-CHIH YEN-I exhibits the same essential marks of the newly emerging novel form as its sister masterpieces of the Ming period: 1) a high degree of conscious attention to structural design, 2) controlled manipulation of narrative detail and complex interweaving of recurrent figures to create textual density, 3) finely tuned rhetoric, and, most importantly, 4) the introduction of the ironic mode to exhibit the clash between stereotypical attitudes and characters and the realities of history and human nature. See C48.

B41. Prusek, Jaroslav. "History and Epics in China and in the West: A Study of Differences in Conception of the Human State." DIOGENES 42 (Summer 1963): 20-43.

See A97.

B42. Ruhlmann, Robert. "Traditional Heroes in Popular Chinese Fiction." THE CONFUCIAN PERSUASION. Ed. Arthur Wright. Stanford: Stanford University Press, 1960. Pages 141-176.

See A102.

B43. Steinen, Diether von den. "Poems of Ts'ao Ts'ao." MONUMENTA SERICA 4 (1939-40): 78-100.

Pours new light on the strength, complexity, genius, and humanity of a Chinese leader much besmeared by history and to some extent by SAN-KUO-CHIH YEN-I. By testimony of disinterested contemporaries delineates Ts'ao as a lover of learning, a devotee of the classics, and a lyricist who set his poems to wind and chord instruments. From the 20 extant poems derives moving glimpses of a creative spirit who wrote, not because an educated gentleman should, but because he passionately needed to express his reflections and emotions. Further regards the poems as interesting deviations from Chinese propensity to keep its art in a jade tower apart from life.

Attributes the neglect of Ts'ao's poetry to his innovative spirit. Takes the poems (all yueh fu, poems set to well-known tunes) one at a time, identifying the occasion, often more exciting and sensational than fictional events, like his father's death at the hands of political enemies. Annotates each line for its art, especially its allusions. An enlightening exercise in Chinese poetry in translation, accompanied by a brief bibliography of editions of Ts'ao's works.

B44. Surh, Olga. "SONS, SHUI-HU CHUAN, and SAN-KUO-CHIH YEN-I." THE CHINA CRITIC 11 (October 31, 1935): 107-109.

See C52.

B45. Wang Hsi-yen. "Characterization Through the Depiction of Externals." CHINESE LITERATURE 7 (July 1964): 85-93.

Stresses Chinese emphasis on external detail to effect characterization. For appearance, in SAN-KUO-CHIH, cites the descriptions of sworn brothers Liu Pei, Kuan Yu, and Chang Fei, showing, for example, how unusually large ears, eyes, and arms indicate imperial status, and splendid garments a person of authority; for conversation, Liu Pei's attempts to persuade hermit Chu-ko to join the outlaw band; for behavior in conflict, the actions of the warrior contenders for the Han succession.

B46. Wang, John C.Y. "The Cyclical View of Life and Meaning in the Traditional Chinese Novel." In ETUDES D'HISTOIRE ET DE LITTERATURE CHINOISES OFFERTES AU PROFESSEUR JAROSLAV PRUSEK. Paris: Institut des Hautes Etudes Chinoises, 1976. Pages 275-301.

See A105.

B47. Yang, Winston, L.Y. "The Literary Transformation of Historical Figures in the SAN-KUO-CHIH YEN-I." CRITICAL ESSAYS ON CHINESE FICTION. Eds. Winston

L.Y Yang and Curtis P. Adkins. Hong Kong: Chinese
University of Hong Kong, 1980. Pages 47-84.

Shows how the putative author of SAN-KUO, Lo Kuan-
chung, diverged from his main source, the third-century SAN-KUO CHIH, in glorifying Liu Pei of Shu as the
legitimate and heroic heir to the Han Kingdom and vili-
fying Ts'ao Ts'ao of Wei as cruel and treacherous,
while retaining for each a degree of moral and professional complexity. Notes the author's similar cos-
metic service on Shu's Chu-ko Liang and Wei's Chou-yu,
while maintaining basic historical truth, including
popular reports of Chu-ko's supernatural and magic
feats.

Explains Lo's use of sources other than the SAN-KUO
CHIH, notably fifth-century P'ei Sung-chih's commentary, and varied mythic, legendary, and folk accounts
used to dramatize rather than to falsify historic
events and personages. Likens the work as a whole to
Chinese scroll painting, with only a single episode
and a few characters visible at any one time. Finds
it analogous, not to Western epic per se, but rather
to medieval cyclical romance.

Differentiates, however, the subject matter: the Western individualized and romanticized knight hero, engaged in concerns of love, religion, and death as
defined by chivalry; and, in the Chinese counterpart,
the realistic and rationalized accounts of a brotherhood insensitive to romantic love and even to family
relations. Stresses the uniqueness in world literature of the yen-i form, with its particular blend of
history and fiction.

B48. Yang, Winston L.Y. "Lo Kuan-chung." DICTIONARY OF
MING BIOGRAPHY 1368-1644. Two volumes. Eds. L.
Carrington Goodrich and Chaoying Fang. New York:
Columbia University Press, 1976. I: 978-980.

Traces arguments pro and con for the life and career
of an author for whom the sole contemporary reference
is Chia Chung-ming's 1422 REGISTRY referring to Lo as
poet and playwright (not as historical romanticist)
and as a lonely and peculiar man whom Chia had last
seen 60 years before his writing. Concurs with Roy

Andrew Miller in viewing Lo as probably a disappointed and rejected scholar-official who, to escape depression, turned to writing yen-i, but questions a Ming account involving the author in a Yuan rebellion.

Of the many works attributed to Lo, declares the impossibility of ascertaining authorship of so broad and diverse a collection, whose only shared trait is an interest in history. Sees only SAN-KUO-CHIH YEN-I as having reasonable claim to Lo authorship, despite the long, slow evolution of its narrative; its lesser use of folkloristic elements; and a seeming conscious departure from storytelling traditions. Believes that Lo's primary role in the creation and composition of the finished work is most likely as editor, redactor, compiler, or recreator rather than as original author. Adverts to the enormous influence and appeal of the work in China through the centuries and remarks the extension of that popularity to Japan and Korea.

B49. Yang, Winston L.Y. "ROMANCE OF THE THREE KINGDOMS and THE WATER MARGIN." CLASSICAL CHINESE FICTION: A GUIDE TO ITS STUDY AND APPRECIATION: ESSAYS AND BIBLIOGRAPHIES. Eds. Winston L.Y. Yang, Peter Li, and Nathan K. Mao. Boston: G.K. Hall Publishers, 1978. Pages 39-51.

Proposes three periods in the evolution of the Three-Kingdoms narrative, originally recorded by third-century historian Ch'en Shou and commented on extensively by fifth-century P'ei Sung-chih: a) T'ang oral tales, present in a p'ing hua (plain or commenting narrative of an historical era); b) Ming elaborations of Ch'en's and P'ei's works without dependence on the Ming p'ing-hua, including the narrative attributed to Lo Kuan-chung; and c) the Ch'ing revised edition with the Mao Tsung-kang commentary, now considered standard. Calls attention to the embellishment of the Han loyalist (Shu) characters and the corresponding vilification of opponents like Ts'ao Ts'ao, whom history shows as courageous and at times admirable. Names ambition as central theme, with stress on accidents of time and place as fatal and ironic facets of history, seen with special clarity in powerful death scenes.

Finally, identifies yen-i (popular history) as a genre unique to China, forgoing much of fiction's imaginative power, yet escaping the rigorous limitations of formal history.

B50. Yang, Winston L.Y. THE USE OF SAN-KUO CHIH AS A SOURCE FOR THE SAN-KUO-CHIH YEN-I. Ann Arbor, Michigan: University Microfilms, 1971.

Concludes that SAN-KUO-CHI YEN-I represents a form unique in the literary world, the yen-i or popular narrative chronicle, midway between history proper and the novel. Differentiates yen-i by its basic fidelity to historical fact in personages, events, chronology, geography, cause and effect. Observes, also, its vitalizing and dramatizing of these data with elaborations suggested by folkloristic sources such as storytelling and popular drama as well as by the author's own imagination. Remarks, too, that the author (reputedly Lo Kuan-chung) glorifies Shu leaders, notably Liu Pei and Chu-ko Liang, whom he considers the legitimate Han successors, and correspondingly vilifies Wei and Wu opposition leaders, Ts'ao Ts'ao and Sun Ch'uan--a strategy deemed imperative to preserve the greater truth of good versus evil.

Observes that yen-i differs from Western historical romance by greater emphasis on history than on imagination; by depiction of multiple leading characters and events in a scroll-like unfolding of successive episodes and emotional swellings, each with its individual unity and focus; and by its lesser use of symbol and poetic image. Summarizes SAN-KUO's achievements thus: imparting new vitality to historical fact; instructing the common people in their national evolution; refining and purifying folk speech by elimination of certain vulgarities and by use of a plain and easily understood vocabulary; severely limiting the use of supernatural and superstitious elements; and creating a new literary genre found only in China.

CHAPTER THREE

SHUI-HU CHUAN (THE WATER MARGIN)

To think of SHUI-HU CHUAN (THE WATER MARGIN) is, according to some critics, to think of a picture gallery of twelfth-century China, the late Sung Dynasty. That is to say, that the work abounds in realistic characters and atmosphere, in a social, political and economic milieu marking a declining dynasty shot through with weakness and corruption and increasingly vulnerable to invading Mongols. The intruders would, in the end, as the Yuan Dynasty, control all China, South as well as North.

Yet such a statement overlooks the fact that no women in the narrative occupy central roles. No counterparts of a Wife of Bath or a Prioress appear, as in that other great picture gallery (of fourteenth-century England). And, in fact, more than one critic has included among SHC's deficiencies a pronounced misogyny, possibly part of a profounder will-to-power ready to crush whoever or whatever impedes its climb.

So what is this work for four centuries beloved by the Chinese and perennially influential in their affairs? Is it China's prose epic, counterpart of the ILIAD and the ODYSSEY, or the MAHABHARATA or RAMAYANA? Or chivalric romance, analogous with the cycles of Arthur, Charlemagne, Alexander, and Robin Hood? Or group-picaresque in the mode of Lazarillo de Tormes? Or saga such as medieval North Europe knew?

Perhaps this pseudohistorical work, rejected by yen-i specialists as lacking substantial historicity and likewise denied company with CHIN P'ING MEI as a novel of realistic contemporary fiction, is sui generis, is unique.

Wherein, then, lies the unity of SHUI-HU CHUAN as an artistic work, an aesthetic creation? Again, little critical consensus appears. Yet still we are faced with the <u>de facto</u>, the not-to-be-denied decision of the centuries that SHUI-HU is indeed a master work of literary art.

Of the possibilities posed by scholars for a unifying theme, several stand out. It may be 1) a story of a sworn brotherhood, its organization, cast of characters, activities, and code; or 2) a tracing of the disintegration of the Sung Dynasty by reason of its chief characters' estrangement from a corrupt officialdom, and, at a deeper level, the analogy of Liang Shan as a microworld reflecting the macroworld of the dynasty itself; or 3) a revolutionary encounter in the ongoing class war of poor against rich, of oppressed against privileged; or 4) an ironic commentary on the clash between popular attitudes, ideals, and stereotypes regarding national history, and the actualities of that history and its personae; or 5) an aborted attempt to realize a powerful middle class in Chinese society between its peasantry, on the one hand, and, on the other, its bureaucracy.

Determining a novel's central dynamic requires knowledge of its origins, and here, at every turn, frustration and defeat lie await for the most earnest seeker. Probably we shall never know with certainty how or why or when or by whom the original, the earliest form, of the novel SHC appeared. A late and shoddy thirteenth-century history, HSUAN-HO I-SHIH, briefly names and describes an early twelfth-century Sung Chiang and his outlaw band; concurrently and later, Yuan and Ming stories and dramas about the men proliferate. Then suddenly the scenario jumps to a supposedly complete 100-chapter novel, published about 1550 at the behest of scholar-nobleman Kuo Hsun. Though many subsequent publications claimed to be derived from this first-known version of a lost original, a mere five-chapter segment (51-55) remains today.

But the 1550 novel, by our standards, was not yet "full-fledged." For another century and a half it continued to evolve through a dozen or more editions and revisions, versions and variations, corrections, deletions, and accretions. Some have divided these works into simpler (<u>fan-pen</u>) and fuller (<u>chien-pen</u>) texts and have sought to relate their content and style. Special notice has been given to a 1589 printing of 100 chapters, purportedly copied from the 1550 work, and to a 1614 120-chapter edition, with new stories about anti-insurgent campaigns waged by the reinstated Liang-Shan outlaws on behalf of Emperor Hui-tsung.

Yet none of the above was to become the standard edition of SHUI-HU CHUAN. That status was reserved for the 70 (71 with preface)-chapter version of Soochow commentator and man-of-letters Chin Sheng-t'an (1610-1661), produced in 1641. Besides severe revisions of content and style, including excision of the final 50 chapters of the then favored 120-chapter version, Chin omitted verses he considered inferior, substituting for them others by contemporary poets. Moreover, considering Sung Chiang less than honorable and admirable, he (Chin) in several passages cut him down to size without altogether changing the heroic view of him maintained by other characters and by people of the countryside. Events of the omitted sections are, in Chapter 70, revised and telescoped into a dream in which Sung and his followers envision fatalities ensuant on their renewal of fealty to Emperor Hui-tsung.

More important than Chin's, for the most part effective, emendations of the text, however, are his extensive commentary, a classic of Chinese literary theory and practice, and interlinear glosses elucidating and enriching the text, in general aesthetically. Perhaps because of these important additions, Chin's edition has, for over 300 years, that is, until recently, been accepted as the standard SHUI-HU CHUAN.

The structure of SHC is clearly marked into a first part, dealing with the gradual gathering of the outlaw band and its leaders and their formation into a brotherhood (Chapters 1-70); and a second part, dealing with the outlaws' honorable surrender to Emperor Hui-tsung and their subsequent career as fighters in his service (Chapters 71-120).

One by one, in the early chapters, 108 persons, some volunteers (usually of lower-class or inferior abilities) and others at least partially coerced (usually upper-class or otherwise distinguished), recognizing their original situations as hopeless, throw in their lot with the zealous Sung Chiang and join his heroic and not always altruistic adventures. Besides this elite portion of the fraternity, thousands of dispossessed on the countryside look upon Sung

Chiang as a protector of the poor against the rich and the weak against the powerful, and accordingly pay him allegiance. Of the 108 outlaws with leadership functions, 36 belong to a top-echelon corps. In the climactic Chapter 70 these, with their 72 minor fellows, gather at Mount Liang Shan-p'o to celebrate undying fidelity to Sung Chiang, to each other, and to their quest for a just society.

In the later chapters (71-120 of the 1614 version) events take a reverse and downward turn. Despite fierce and unrelenting objections by Li K'uei, his closest friend and lieutenant, Sung Chiang secretly longs for amnesty with the emperor and reabsorption into the larger society. In the end he, with his company, surrenders to the Establishment, though on terms Sung himself lays down so as to preserve for all, honor and dignity. Ironically Li K'uei's premonitions are fulfilled as, following three successful military campaigns waged by the reinstated warriors against the emperor's enemies, envious court ministers effect their dispersion and, for most, their extirpation in the battle against insurgent Fa Lang and his outlaw band.

Another structural consideration remarks the parabolalike time of gathering, marked chiefly by recruitment and aggression and climaxing in the Mount Liang-Shan banquet, followed by the gradual dispersion and extinction of the group. This structure is seen by Andrew H. Plaks as characteristic of all the great Ming novels. Again, with respect to closer, textual design, the same author suggests extensive use of doublet characters and events subtly contrasting ideal with real behaviors. Such are the two episodes of tiger-killing, in one of which the pugnacious Wu Sung deliberately engages the animal in fight; and, in the other, Li K'uei, bearing his aged and blind mother on his back, is forced into the encounter.

A third analysis sees in the novel concentric circles of meaning, symbolized by the fortress within the valley, circled by mountain peaks, on a lake surrounded by a marsh, within the province of what is now Shantung. Metaphysically the same idea refers to the individual within the family, within the local society, within the state, and within the nation.

Though several critics insist on the structural importance of poems scattered through the novel, their role in the work's construction has not yet been satisfactorily examined. Indubitably, because of the numerous deletions and accretions marking the text's evolution, the task presents almost insuperable difficulties, yet the study could enhance understanding and appreciation of the structural artistry of this unique narrative.

Finally, one author refers to the hybrid nature of the work: halfway between the improvisatory structures of oral storytellers and the conscious artistry of fictionists in writing. The tension between the two modes is seen by the critic as an obstacle to the novel's artistic unity.

As to authorship, it seems that credence can no longer be given for that role to Lo Kuan-chung (late Yuan or early Ming) and/or Shih Nai-an (late Yuan). Evidence supporting the case for these hypothetical authors has been demonstrated slim, perfunctory, and unverifiable. Current critical opinion prefers to think of the authorship as composite and evolving, dating to some unknown germinal original in late Yuan or early Ming times.

Like every other aspect of SHC the question of characterization generates lively controversy. Eulogists perceive the dramatis personae as vivid, individualized, and complex. Another view declares the same personae stereotyped, repetitious, simplistic, and generally unconvincing. How, apart from personal reaction, can one resolve such conflicting judgments?

Help in this area comes chiefly from C.T. Hsia and Andrew Plaks, beginning with the former. In the middle of his diatribe against the savagery and sadism of the Liang-Shan "gang," Hsia declares the general effect of the novel to be an exploration of the dark side of the Chinese character. In this matter he identifies as the most enduringly interesting outlaws Lu Chih-shen, Lin Ch'ung, Yang Chih, Sung Chiang, Wu Sung, Li K'uei, Shih Hsiu, and Yen Ch'ing. For particular attention he selects Li K'uei and Sung Chiang, perceiving them as alter egos representing the profoundest reaches of human consciousness (as, in Joseph Conrad's THE HEART OF DARKNESS, Marlow and Kurtz develop as alternate sides of the one personality). Sung Chiang yearns for the Confucian Great Harmony of emperor and subject and cherishes Liang Shan's pastoral peace and simplicity. Yet he recognizes another, fiercer self, his latent ambitious self, in the unrestrained rages and revenges of Li K'uei, who cannot be reconciled to surrender and to the end defies the emperor.

It remained for Plaks, picking up Hsia's analysis, to lift it to a more metaphysical plane. The central truth about SHC's characterization, Plaks proposes, is the author's ironic intent: to challenge the false and misleading attitudes and stereotypes promoted by popular legend, storytelling, and drama, by exposing the clash between these ideas and the truth about history and historical characters. All this in the light of intellectual issues fermenting in Ming China, notably the nature of the historical process, the meaning of human activity, and the relation of self and society.

Other critics discuss the presence or lack thereof of a tragic element in SHC's characterizations. One, at least, finds tragedy suggested in the farewell scene between the dying Sung Chiang and the Li K'uei he has deliberately poisoned. This extreme measure, to be sure, prevents Li's murdering the emperor; more importantly, it allows consummation of the brotherhood oath. In it the heroes have vowed to die as well as to live and fight together, a theme and a scene closely linking this work with SAN-KUO-CHIH YEN-I.

Finally, analysts of SHC's characterization are quick to point out elements of fun and humor enlivening and enriching this work in a way distinctively Chinese.

No facet of SHC has aroused more controversy than its moral effect. As compared with CHIN P'ING MEI, it is more difficult here to make a case for retribution, for the wages-of-sin-is-death theme. It has, on the contrary, been cogently argued that cruelty, torture, sadism, treachery, lying, and oppression of the weak (despite protestations to the contrary) are in this work associated with heroic figures made to seem admirable and worthy of emulation.

Nor does this view begin with moderns. Already in the early seventeenth-century the novel's most famous and esteemed commentator, Chin Sheng-t'an, had drawn attention to Sung Chiang's hypocrisy and cruelty and his warriors' moral deviations. Taking her cue from Hsia's scathing description of SHC's "gang morality," Bartell likens the work to modern gangster films, highlighting a) the common background of a corrupt society, b) a story in which class-conflict is more important than episodes, c) differences systematically resolved by violence, and d) similarly unconventional attitudes toward women, parents, brotherhood, religion, and material possessions.

To the charge of egregiously offensive morality, if not in all the individuals at least in the band as a whole, other critics have rallied, responding that, in terms of the times, the ill conduct can be understood and forgiven. Catholics, they argue, have done as much in explaining Inquisition torture, and Americans the institution of slavery.

The heroes' code of honor (as defined by themselves, and not by Confucius) embraces truth, filial piety, loyalty to the emperor (though some here default), protection of the poor and oppressed, and absolute loyalty to the brotherhood. Yet the last of these, the friendship bond, so overrides the others as at times to diminish or cancel entirely the most sacred traditional ties of family and sovereign.

SHC is, nevertheless, perceived by most critics as essentially Confucian, its elements of Taoism and Buddhism being considered passing or peripheral. In this regard, it is interesting to note that the declining Sung Dynasty, reversing its earlier attitude, saw at just this period the revival in China of Buddhism under its new, more humanistic form, Pure-Land. At the same time Taoism was developing the concept and cult of a transcendent divinity, "the pure (or Jade) August One." This deity having, for the first time in China, revealed himself to Emperor Hui-tsung, the sovereign thereafter paid constant homage to the newly known divinity and joined his worship to that of Confucian _t'ien_ (heaven) and Buddhist bodhisattvas.

The amalgam renewed interest in the doctrine of the unity of the three teachings (Confucianism, Taoism, and Buddhism), so important in the following centuries. Yet no English-language writings of which I am aware have as yet explored the impact of this principle on SHC.

A major difference in SHC from its eminent predecessor SAN-KUO-CHIH YEN-I is SHC's almost exclusive use of the colloquial language. This preference is seen by some critics as due, not to servile reliance on traditional oral storytelling and drama, but as a conscious choice made by a literary artist or artists for maintenance of lively action and a vivid, conversational effect.

The influence of SHC was, from the beginning, recognized. Emperor after emperor, fearing subversion and intensified banditry, prohibited the publication, dissemination, preserving, and reading of the work. Yet the ongoing proscription is perceived by some as less than serious, especially as compared with the intensity of Communist attitudes.

Following the 1949 establishment of the People's Republic, Mao-tse Tung extravagantly endorsed SHC as an authentic portrayal of an ideal peasant uprising against feudal oppressors. His followers were not slow to parallel the story with Communism's rise and success in China; Sung Chiang was seen as a Mao-prototype. (In fact, no practicing-peasant plays any major role in SHC and no interest is shown in cultivation of the land.) That position came to a screeching halt in 1975 when Mao, suddenly reversing his judgment, attacked the work as a study promoting betrayal of revolutionary ideals. Only with the 1978 changing of the guard did the previous attitude return, and then only in part.

Of great practical importance to readers of Chinese fiction in English is the question of translations. Happily, superseding both Pearl Buck's 1933 ALL MEN ARE BROTHERS and J.H. Jackson's 1937 THE WATER MARGIN, Sidney Shapiro's 1981 OUTLAWS OF THE MARSH offers a complete translation of the first 70 chapters and only slight abridgment of the others. Special notice goes to Richard Gregg Irwin's 1953 pioneer work in textual analysis, THE EVOLUTION OF A CHINESE NOVEL: SHUI-HU CHUAN, and to the monumental research of Andrew H. Plaks embodied in his 1987 THE FOUR MASTERWORKS OF THE MING NOVEL.

Translations

C1. Buck, Pearl, tr. ALL MEN ARE BROTHERS. Two volumes. New York: The John Day Company, 1968 (a reprint of the 1937 revision of the 1933 first edition).

Rejects the literally-translated title WATER MARGIN (for SHUI-HU CHUAN) as meaningless, in favor of a Confucian saying thought fitting for the outlaws of the declining Sung Dynasty: 108 men (36 major and 72 minor), sworn-brotherhood leaders of thousands of disaffected people on the countryside. Idealizes the refugees in their mountain stronghold, Liang Shan-p'o near Shantung, with its beautiful lake and surrounding reedy marsh. Notes the outlaws' origin in an historically real group revered by the common people (the poor and the oppressed) and the maintenance among the outlaws of rigid laws about warfare, conduct, and courtesy. Disavows academic or scholarly aspiration, at the same time proposing as literal a version as possible, even to tolerating lifeless passages, changing only names so as to facilitate Western reading.

Includes in the introduction the text of a 1799 Ch'ing Dynasty law forbidding printing, distribution, and reading of the novel under severe sanctions for all involved (a lax official incurs loss of a year's pay). Garbles the account of authorship squabbles involving Lo Kuan-chung and Shih Nai-an. Of the four notable early-novel versions, varying in number of chapters, chooses the first (70-chapter) as the most spirited and unified and the freest from the seeming attempt of later editors to remove the revolutionary spirit (the outlaws are made to join the Establishment and reverse their roles) and superimpose a moral acceptable to the governing classes.

Provides illustrations from a rare old copy of the work and tailpieces from ancient drawings of weapons like those of the robbers. Declares the work true in spirit, not only to twelfth-century China, but, as well, to the China of today (1933). Notes that "the newest and most exciting party in China, the Communist, has issued a special edition of SHUI-HU CHUAN, calling it the first Communist literature of China, as suitable to this day as to the day it was written."

Concludes that, despite the passing of centuries, the novel is still great and full of humanity.

C2. Buck, Pearl, tr. "The Plot Against the Birthday Convoy." ANTHOLOGY OF CHINESE LITERATURE. Ed. Cyril Birch. New York: Grove Press, 1965.

Chapters 14-16 from Buck's translation of SHUI-HU CHUAN as ALL MEN ARE BROTHERS, chosen for their vivid portraits of Mount Liangshan's good-willed, generous-hearted bandits.

C3. Chai Ch'u, and Winberg Chai, eds. and trs. "SHUI-HU CHUAN (THE STORY OF THE WATER MARGIN)." A TREASURY OF CHINESE LITERATURE: A NEW PROSE ANTHOLOGY INCLUDING FICTION AND DRAMA. New York: Appleton-Century, 1965. Pages 210-215.

In the introduction tentatively accepts Shih Nai-an as author, Lo Kuan-chung as reviser of the 120-chapter version, and editor Chin Sheng-t'an as producer of the 70-chapter version. In the Ming account of 108 outlaws of the Liangshan Marches, led by the historical Sung Chiang during the Northern Sung Dynasty, finds brilliant characterization and exciting scenes. Presents Chapter Three, wherein Lu Chih-shen takes refuge in a Buddhist temple, becomes a monk, and devastates the order of the holy place.

C4. Dars, Jacques. AU BORD DE L'EAU (SHUI-HU CHUAN). Two volumes. Paris: Gallimard Publishers, 1978.

A readable translation of the 92-chapter-plus-epilogue version of SHUI-HU CHUAN, supplemented by Etiemble's foreword examining picaresque and pseudoautobiographical elements of the story. In an extended introduction covers a) the ostensible historical context of Sung personae and events and Five-Dynasties conflicts; b) the evolution of the romance from oral storytelling and drama; c) its social, political, and economic implications; d) the authorial roles of Shih Nai-an and Lo Kuan-chung; and e) contemporary (post-Maoist) revisions of traditional interpretations. Augmented by well-executed maps, generous endnotes for each chapter, glossaries, name-identification lists, and a table of chapter contents.

SHUI-HU CHUAN (THE WATER MARGIN)   101

C5. Dunlop, Geoffrey, tr. (from the German translation of
     Albert Ehrenstein). ROBBERS AND BROTHERS. New
     York: A.A. Knopf Publishers, 1929.

     A recension of SHUI-HU CHUAN, devoid of scholarly
     apparatus and centering on the life and death of poor
     Chinese village schoolmaster Wu Sung. Employs SHUI-HU
     sequences to point out the use of dreams in early
     vernacular fiction to clarify Heaven's will. Includes
     Dunlop's eulogy of Ehrenstein, linking his gifts with
     those of Flaubert, Homer, Voltaire, and Swift.

C6. Jackson, J.H., tr. WATER MARGIN. Two volumes. Shang-
     hai: Commercial Press, 1937.

     In a three-page foreword apologizes for the portrayal
     of thirteenth-century (!) Chinese people as ignorant
     and cruel, but matches the phenomenon with similar
     Western events, as oppressed masses historically
     revolted against cruel overlords. Using the 70-chap-
     ter version, as notable for its excellent style and
     effective editing, proceeds in free-wheeling style
     with judicious textual condensation to delineate the
     heroes of marsh-girded Mount Liang Shan-p'o, as they
     plan and carry out their sieges. In a purportedly
     thirteenth-century introduction and preface attributed
     to Shih Nai-an, details the human and Taoist back-
     grounds out of which the finished novel came.

C7. Kao, George, ed. "The Adventures of the Tattooed
     Monk." CHINESE WIT AND HUMOR. New York: Sterling
     Publishers, 1974. (First published in 1946.)
     Pages 62-97.

     The riotous adventures of a major character among the
     outlaws of Liang Shan-p'o, inspired by a juvenile ver-
     sion called THE TATTOOED MONK RAISING HELL ON THE
     WUTAI MOUNTAIN. Includes a rip-roaring introduction.

C8. Kuhn, Franz, tr. DIE RAUBER VOM LIANG SCHAN MOOR.
     Leipzig: Insel-Verlag, 1934.

     In a sturdy, small, attractive, well-illustrated vol-
     ume, gives the pioneer nearly-complete Western transla-
     tion on which numerous retranslations and recensions

are based. A Nachwort, or Afterword, provides sparse notes on texts and interpretation.

C9. Shapiro, Sidney, tr. OUTLAWS OF THE MARSH (SHUI-HU CHUAN). Two volumes. Bloomington, Indiana: Indiana University Press (in association with the Foreign Languages Press, Beijing), 1981.

Introduces the story of the 100-odd alienated men and women who formed and led an outlaw army of thousands in the final years of Sung emperor Hui Zong's rule (1101-1125). Traces the narrative's evolution through storytelling and drama, acknowledging controversial issues of authorship, manuscript authenticity, variant texts, and dates. Praises the individualizaton of the characters, the integration of episodes, and the intimate portrayal of a people and their society.

Faithfully follows the text of the 70-chapter manuscript, but adds a freer rendering of the final 30 units of the 100-chapter edition, omitting chapter-head poems (doggerel!) and redundant and cumbersome detail. Attributes the seeming modernity of the dialogue to the conservative nature of the Chinese language, spoken as well as written.

Supersedes Pearl Buck's ALL MEN ARE BROTHERS (1933) and J.H. Jackson's WATER MARGIN (1937), but lacks the rich supplementary material (maps, endnotes, glossaries, tables) of Dars' LE BORD DE L'EAU.

C10. Shapiro, Sidney, tr. "Outlaws of the Marshes." CHINESE LITERATURE 12 (December 1959): 3-61: 10 (October 1963): 46-72.

In Chapters Six through Ten covers bureaucrat Lin Chung's ordeal, as he resists persecution of overlords, occasioned by his wife's beauty, and, disguised as a monk cultivating monastery fields, escapes the enemy and at last, in desperation, joins Sung Chiang's outlaw band. In Chapters 14-16 depicts the dark side of Sung officialdom and the fearless battles waged by Lu Chih-shen, Li K'uei, and others of the 108 outlaws of the sworn brotherhood. Despite the mostly fictitious characters and events, points out, in the introduction, the vivid, conversational style, the authentic picture of the times, and the far-reaching influence of the "second best-known and loved" of Chinese classic novels, "an epic of over a million words."

C11. Shih Hung. THE WILD BOAR FOREST (adapted). Illus. Pu Hsiao-huai. Peking: Foreign Languages Press, 1961.

A picture-book for children (and others) from Chapters Seven through Nine of SHUI-HU CHUAN. Traces Lin Chung's exile and ruin, occasioned by an enemy's lust for his beautiful wife, and his consequent joining of the famous outlaw band and its uprising against the oppressive ruling class.

Studies

C12. Alber, Charles J. "A Survey of English Language Criticism of SHUI-HU CHUAN." TSING HUA JOURNAL OF CHINESE STUDIES 7 (1962): 102-118.

Deals with SHUI-HU CHUAN's structure, characterization, and morality. After reviewing major critics' judgments on the novel's design or lack thereof, concludes that its unity lies in the attempt to recreate history with characters less important in themselves than in their voicing of critical attitudes toward social, political, economic, and moral aspects of contemporary society.

Presents contradictory views on characterization, focusing on the contrast between Western psychological probing into characters' minds and motivations, and Chinese refusal to delve into inner selves, relying on other means (gesture, symbol, dialogue) to indicate lacunae between word and thought, appearance and reality. Finds valid Frankel's contrast between the Western theory of personality as individual growth and development and the Chinese view of it as having a fixed pattern of development which, in the course of action, merely unfolds. Disdains Irwin's belief that character portrayal constitutes the major advance in SHC's achievement.

In critical assessment of SHC's morality, finds extremes of praise (all men are brothers) and of condemnation (all men are childish and brutal savages). Believes that Hsia's charge of gang morality and misogyny fails to attend to the author's attitude toward his subjects' behavior, fails also to note current literary conventions and techniques and their relation to the narrative (C28 and C29).

Observes several critics' remarks about the absence of an aristocratic feminine tradition as an impediment to the development of a literature exhibiting what Hsia calls "the agreed upon ideals of humanity." Finally, suggests that critics must decide whether the "heroes" act from self-interest or public-mindedness.

C13.   Bartell, Shirley Miller. "The Chinese Bandit Novel and the American Gangster Film." NEW ORLEANS REVIEW 8 (Winter 1981): 102-105.

Basing her study on the human need and capacity to create forms expressive of observation and intuition, parallels the fourteenth-century SHUI-HU CHUAN (accepting Irwin's judgment that Pearl Buck's ALL MEN ARE BROTHERS provides the most reliable translation) and classic American gangster films LITTLE CAESAR (1930), THE PUBLIC ENEMY (1931); and SCARFACE (1932).

Identifies likenesses in a) theme, a corrupt society producing its own rebels; b) origin, in an historical person; c) overall conflict, as dominant over plot; d) resolution of conflict, by violence; e) similarity of attitudes, toward society, women, parents, brotherhood, religion, and material possessions.

C14.   Chang, H.C., ed. CHINESE LITERATURE. Three volumes. New York: Columbia University Press, 1973. II: 17-21.

Offers, as the clearest example of the coalescence of related subject matters in works of skilled writers, SHUI-HU CHUAN, associated with the names of Shih Naian as compiler and Lo Kuan-chung as editor. Looks at the "banquet position" structure of the novel, based on the Liangshan hierarchy, shown clearly in table arrangements and battle-formation positions. Considers other storytelling devices such as narrative breaks signified by verse and the use of other verse passages enabling a storyteller to embroider his narrative with displays of curious lore and historical remembrances. Parallels two seventeenth-century accounts of the Birthday Gift Convoy (Chapter 16) to illustrate methods of storytellers on the one hand and of storywriters on the other. Shows SHUI-HU CHUAN as halfway between the improvisations of the one and the conscious artistry of the other.

C15. Chao Ching-shen. "Some Recent Studies in SHUI-HU CHUAN or THE STORY OF THE WATER MARGIN." PHILOBIBLON 2 (September 1948): 3-7.

A dated study of certain specialist (Chinese) texts relevant to SHUI-HU CHUAN's a) linguistic interest; b) antecedents in story and drama (107 story titles and over 30 play names are identified); c) the degree of historicity of the characters and differences of characterization between novel and pre-novel drama forms; and d) the site of Liang Shan-p'o, "where the brigands congregated to administer justice on behalf of heaven," here determined to be near Kaifeng, a Sung dynastic capital.

Mentions Lu Erh-kang's SHUI-HU CHUAN AND THE HUNG OR HEAVEN AND EARTH LEAGUE and Sa Meng-wu's SHUI-HU CHUAN AND CHINESE SOCIETY as studies of the novel's social influence, especially in "ennobling" brigandage and making rebellion a moral imperative, positions perennially heartening to Chinese secret societies and their gangster organizations.

C16. Cheang Eng-chew. LI CHIH AS A CRITIC: A CHAPTER OF THE MING INTELLECTUAL HISTORY. Ann Arbor, Michigan: University Microfilms International, 1982.

Reviews the judgment of the noted Ming critic-martyr Li Chih (1527-1602) that the Confucian classics lose their luster in comparison with SHUI-HU CHUAN, the heroes of which Li views, not as hard-core criminals, but as Northern Sung loyalists. After exploring problems of textual authenticity, reviews Li's portrayal of Li K'uei as a living Buddha, Sung Chiang as a somewhat affected but able brigand leader, and Wu Yung as a sharpster in whom Buddhahood is dead. Approves Li's defense of the novel as historical and manners-depicting, and his focus on Lu Chih-sheng, disturbingly true to his nature, and on harum-scarum, simple, sincere, and devoted Li K'uei.

C17. Chesneauz, Jeane. "Modern Relevance of SHUI-HU CHUAN: Its Influence on the Rebel Movement in 19th- and 20th-century China." Tr. Alyce Mackerras. PAPERS ON FAR EASTERN HISTORY (Australian National University) 3 (March 1971): 1-25.

Details the subversive role of SHUI-HU CHUAN in raising and supporting armed rebellion from the sixteenth century. Shows how the novel's editors and commentators were imprisoned, executed, or driven to suicide, and the reading of the work proscribed.

Identifies nineteenth-century secret societies and peasant uprisings which drew upon SHC for titles, ideologies, slogans, and jargon, notably the Taiping Movement, with its goal of universal peace (t'ai p'ing) to be achieved through loyalty, justice (ching-i), and heroic brotherhood, as taught by the Liang Shan-p'o disciples of Sung Chiang.

In Communist culture, as epitomized in Mao Tse-tung's lifelong [but see C45 and the Introduction to this chapter] devotion to Sung Chiang and his cohorts and in his essay CONTRADICTIONS, sees a) imitation of an heroic collectivity pursuing a noble cause, b) constant use of the novel as a story source for writers and dramatists, c) prolific comic-book presentations of the stories to the young, and d) mottoes and allusions of the Great Leap Forward. Analyzes the socially highly-mixed bandit constituency and its strategic geographic placement in a marginal region bordering on several provinces and away from capitals and other centers of repression.

Stresses the non-revolutionary character of the novel, not at all interested in the peasantry as such or the land, and dedicated, rather, to the correction of abuses and the healing of social wounds in an accepted social and political system--ergo the propriety of the band's reconciliation with the emperor in the end, and its ironic deployment in the emperor's cause, the quashing of revolutionaries.

C18. Csongor, B. "A Comparative Analysis of SHUI-HU CHUAN and HSI-YU CHI: The Bounds of the Classic Chinese Novel." ACTA ORIENTALIA 29 (1975): 1-6.

Argues that the two novels basically deny the possibility of individuals' effecting fundamental social change and that the heroes' adventures are wish-dreams, fantasies of picaresque existence which must, in the nature of things, dissolve into the static securities of mandarin bureaucracy and traditional life styles.

Parallels the careers of Sung Chiang and Sun Wu-k'ung (Monkey) in establishing states through armed force in the face of superior powers terrified of them; in finally surrendering to and serving their adversaries; in the supernatural circumstances of their births; and in the anticlimactic nature of later narrative parts.

Differentiates the quasi-historical background of SHUI-HU and the fantastical milieu of HSI-YU CHI; Sung Chiang's passivity and Monkey's frenetic activity; Sung Chiang's gregariousness and Monkey's one-man exertions; and Sung's claim to a heavenly mandate versus Monkey's persistent defiance of the gods in the name of his personal ambitions.

C19. Csongor, B. "On the Popularity of the SHUI-HU CHUAN." ACTA ORIENTALIA 28 (1974): 308-318.

Contends that, fictionized events and personages notwithstanding, the SHUI-HU CHUAN faithfully dramatizes contemporary social tendencies and demands and the atmosphere and dynamics of twelfth-century China. Cites in support of this position the enormous popularity of the work in its own time and later despite repeated suppression.

Stratifies the rebels into its nameless masses, the hsiao lou-o, and its 108 leaders, 36 major and 72 minor, spreading throughout the nation in a tight-knit brotherhood with a rigorous conduct code. Contrasts the unorthodox society with the analogous orthodox mandarin-peasant society, observing that neither mandarins nor (practicing) peasants play any part at all in the SHUI-HU.

Identifies a spectrum of occupations among personae ranging from nobleman to merchant to thief; experts including calligrapher, judge, artilleryman, farrier, seal maker, shipbuilder, tailor, civil engineer, butcher, smith, jailer, executioner, brewer, innkeeper; and a leadership drawn from soldiers, clerks, scholars, monks, landlords, and merchants. In short, identifies a middle class as corporate protagonist in contrast to mandarins or peasants, a new perspective in Chinese literature suggestive of a utopistic vision of a new kind of society. Contrasts Sung Chiang's constant resolve to submit at last to the emperor with the continuing rebellion of Li K'uei, and critics' tendency to accuse Sung of betrayal of the revolutionary masses, though Sung himself spelled out the terms of the surrender.

Regards the Liang Shan-p'o mission as, in the end, a glorious failure, the middle classes not yet being ripe for the change and the government being too inexorably in control. Stresses that the mission was, nevertheless, thoroughly in accord with the Confucian ideal of a fraternity of men led by their ablest.

C20. Csongor, B. "On the Pre-history of the SHUI-HU CHUAN." ACTA ORIENTALIA ACADEMIAE SCIENTIARUM HUNGARICAE 25 (1972): 77-81.

Explores SHUI-HU CHUAN sources, notably HSUAN-HO I-SHIH, focusing on the hierarchy of the 36 leaders. Somewhat advances Irwin's 1957 study.

C21. Fitzgerald, C.P. "The Chinese Novel as a Subversive Force." MEANJIN QUARTERLY 10 (Spring 1951): 259-266.

Identifies in the ostensibly Sung story of an outlawed bandit and his followers a description of the Ming Age in decline. Details reasons for the major characters' exit from conventional life as judgments on an unjust and repressive society.

SHUI-HU CHUAN (THE WATER MARGIN)

C22. Goodrich, L. Carrington. "Shih Nai-an." DICTIONARY OF MING BIOGRAPHY 1368-1644. Eds. L. Carrington Goodrich and Chaoying Fang. Two volumes. New York and London: Columbia University Press, 1976. II: 1204.

Dismisses reports on the fourteenth-century reputed author of SHUI-HU CHUAN, Shih Nai-an, as uncorroborated. Yet believes on the whole that he may well have been the first collector of tales, folklore, prompt books, and twelfth- and thirteenth-century dramas providing materials for the work. Calls attention to the enormous circulation of the narrative, widely considered the greatest of the Ming Period, and, despite its public prohibition from the beginning as inflammatory, its continued production and sale, not only in Chinese, but in Japanese, Korean, Latin, French, German, English, and Russian versions.

C23. Hanan, Patrick. "The Development of Fiction and Drama." THE LEGACY OF CHINA. Ed. Raymond Dawson. London: Clarendon Press, 1964. Pages 129-130.

Contrasts the time-place spaciousness of SAN-KUO with the more restricted purview of SHUI-HU CHUAN, in which no empire hangs in balance and little historical reality controls the compilation of stories about the 108 outlaws of twelfth-century Shantung. Praises the novel for its precise evocation of the physical in armed conflict, sieges, contests of strength, and a memorable tiger fight. Calls particular attention to a times-revealing vignette of a female singer-narrator, whose act is followed by a comic drama.

C24. Hegel, Robert E. "Heavens and Hells in Chinese Fictional Dreams." PSYCHOSINOLOGY: THE UNIVERSE OF DREAMS IN CHINESE CULTURE. Ed. Carolyn T. Brown. Washington, D.C.: Woodrow Wilson International Center for Scholars, 1987. Pages 1-14.

See A50.

C25. Hennessey, William. "HSUAN-HO I-SHIH." THE INDIANA COMPANION TO TRADITIONAL CHINESE LITERATURE. Eds. William H. Nienhauser, Jr., and others. Bloomington: Indiana University Press, 1986. Pages 437-438.

Describes the contents of HSUAN-HO I-SHIH, a history of the decline and fall of the Northern Sung Dynasty, especially under Emperor Hui-tsung (r. 1101-1126). Analyzes views, often considered biased and inaccurate, unflattering to the emperor and to his mistress Li Shih-shih. Points out sections dealing with the exploits of Sung Chiang and his men of the marshes. See D29 (pages 190-208) for further light on the emperor to whom Sung Chiang surrendered honorably and for whom he fought until envious ministers of the court destroyed him (Sung).

C26. Hightower, James R. "Individualism in Chinese Literature." JOURNAL OF THE HISTORY OF IDEAS 22 (1961): 159-168.

See A54.

C27. Hightower, James R. TOPICS IN CHINESE LITERATURE. Cambridge: Harvard University Press, 1965. Page 104.

Identifies SHUI-HU CHUAN's language and style as purely colloquial; the content as a combination of two cycles of bandit stories from, respectively, Shantung and Shansi; the focus on picaresque incident rather than on character; and the frame story as the only unifying element.

C28. Hsia, C.T. "Comparative Approaches to WATER MARGIN." YEARBOOK OF COMPARATIVE AND GENERAL LITERATURE 11 (1962): 121-128.

As antidote to a perceived excessive praise of SHUI-HU CHUAN by undiscriminating critics, attacks the novel's weaknesses: a) development into a mechanical, boring hodgepodge after a vivid, colloquial beginning with a rapid narrative pace and characterization effectively presented through dialogue and action; b) a gang morality pervaded by savagery and sadism; and c) a pronounced misogyny used to heighten "virile heroism."

Cites SAN-KUO-CHIH YEN-I as exemplary historical romance paralleling, not the romanticized fictions of Scott-Tolstoy-Stendhal, but, rather, the Shakespearean chronicle plays. Attributes SHUI-HU CHUAN's conceptual failure to the author's confusion over its form, an anomaly neither fish nor fowl, neither history nor romance, but a false construction alleging the one but carried away by the other. Further, believes that the compiler's imaginative power, promising in the beginning a lively picaresque tale, was seduced by public appetite for historical reenactment. Charges that the work flounders into a morass of unintegrated fictional detail and pseudohistory, leaving to its near-contemporary CHIN P'ING MEI the merit of becoming the first extended prose work consciously to create a world independent of historical personages and events.

Observes, too, that, with few exceptions, the military enterprises lack, on the one hand, the suspense and tension generated in SAN-KUO by precarious balances of power among Wei, Shu, and Wu, and, on the other, the internal dissensions dynamizing a work like MORTE D'ARTHUR. Perceives another structural weakness in the band's alleged commitment to the Will of Heaven and to Justice and Fidelity, and their actual behavior. Lists among their vices self-interest, disregard of decency, lust for aggression and ruthless pursuit of even the least enemy, their forcing recruits "to climb Liangshan," their willingness to murder whole families and innocent children to gain their ends, and their systematic annihilation of villages to sate their craving for revenge.

Contrasts the novel's moral confusion with the stern code of Iceland's NJAL'S SAGA, limited in its use of violence, unequivocal in its stand for peace, order, and justice, sure-keyed in its view of female treachery and vengeance as only part of a larger human nature. Marks, on the other hand, SHUI-HU CHUAN's misogyny, women being presented as totally depraved and as men's worst enemies, the sole safeguard against them being the heroes' radical continence, though it cuts them off from life at its "most complex, most tender, and most devious."

Further contrasts such dehumanized characterization with that of Hsi-men Ch'ing, originally a minor character in SHUI-HU CHUAN, resurrected in CHIN P'ING MEI to a degree of humanity far beyond anything envisioned in the original tale. Points out Hsi's development from carnal infatuation to full-bodied passionate devotion, capable of profound grief and, before his final destruction, evincing a real capacity for love and suffering.

C29. Hsia, C.T. "THE WATER MARGIN." THE CLASSIC CHINESE NOVEL. New York: Columbia University Press, 1968. Pages 75-114.

Rates this sixteenth-century novel as inferior to its famous predecessor SAN-KUO-CHIH YEN-I by reason of lesser realism, historical authenticity, and probing of the darker aspects of the Chinese mind. (For refutation of this view see C37 and C40 below). Details source materials, authorship theories, and competing versions. Stresses the cowardice, acrobatics, sexual puritanism, hearty appetites, craving for vengeance, and gang morality of major characters, while disparaging the importance of the work as, according to Communist critics and interpreters, an anti-government and revolutionary tract.

C30. Hummel, Arthur W. "A Chinese Classic (SHUI-HU CHUAN)." ASIA 34 (1934): 22-25.

Mixes praise for Pearl Buck's gallant attempt to translate the complete (70-chapter) novel for the first time into a Western language with adverse criticism for her changing the original title to one derived from her own fancy. Insists that, despite her noble effort to achieve fidelity to the original and her success in colloquial passages, she fails effectively to render poetic allusion and correct geographic, historical, and literary terminologies. See C35 and C50.

Appends an essay by Nathaniel Peffer acknowledging the probable correctness of Hummel's strictures (Hummel, a sinologist and one-time chief of the Library-of-Congress Orientalia Division), but declares that exactitude in poetic allusion and meticulous correctness in historical, geographic, and linguistic refinements of classical Chinese have but little importance in this novel. Declares that, if not sinologically flawless, the translation is, nevertheless, on every major count artistically correct. Includes seven large illustrations borrowed from a seventeenth-century set of 70, assigned, respectively, to the novel chapters.

C31. Hung Ming-shui. YUAN HUNG-TAO AND THE LATE MING LITERARY AND INTELLECTUAL MOVEMENT. Madison: University of Wisconsin, 1974. An unpublished dissertation.

See E29.

C32. Irwin, Richard Gregg. THE EVOLUTION OF A CHINESE NOVEL: SHUI-HU CHUAN. Cambridge: Harvard University Press, 1953.

Calling SHUI-HU the standard-setter for the Chinese picaresque novel and the progenitor of its romance, traces the work's gradual development from its beginnings in legends about hero Sung Chiang (fl. 1117-1121) to its culmination in the voluminous seventeenth-century novel. Reviews historical and geographical backgrounds before detailing developments associated with oral traditions, earlier and later written texts and publications, and variant versions, sometimes substantially altered in content, political orientation, and/or tone. Underscores the role of seventeenth-century Chin Sheng-t'an in changing the original glorification of the rebels to portrayal of them as, in the end, faithful servants of the Establishment and, by their deaths, atoners of past disloyalties. For a different point of view consult C38.

C33. Irwin, Richard Gregg. "WATER MARGIN Revisited." T'OUNG PAO 48 (1966): 393-415.

A technical analysis of variant manuscripts and editions, based on a 1954 Chinese-produced collation. Leads Irwin to revise certain views projected in his 1953 EVOLUTION OF A CHINESE NOVEL: SHUI-HU CHUAN, notably the earlier editorial attribution of the first extant 120-chapter version with commentary to Li Chih instead of to Yang Ting-chien or Yuan Wu-yai.

C34. Kaltenmark, Odile. CHINESE LITERATURE. Tr. (from the French) Anne-Marie Geoghegan. New York: Walker and Company, 1964 (a revision of the 1948 original). Page 116.

Calls SHUI-HU better written and more imaginative than SAN-KUO-CHIH YEN-I. (Compare with Hsia's views in C28 and C29.)

C35. Kuhn, Franz. "Review of Pearl S. Buck's ALL MEN ARE BROTHERS." ASIA MAJOR 10 (1963): 369-372.

Points out in Buck's translation of SHUI-HU CHUAN as ALL MEN ARE BROTHERS errors relative to geographic, historical, and sociological detail. Refers to Buck as an amateur. Written in German. See C30 and C50.

C36. Lai Ming. A HISTORY OF CHINESE LITERATURE. New York: Capricorn Books, 1966. Pages 291-298.

Assumes Shih Nai-an's authorship and declares the work the first Chinese novel to be written exclusively in the vernacular. Differentiates editor Yang Ting-chien's 120-chapter and the more popular 70-chapter version edited by Chin Sheng-t'an.

C37. Li Hsi-fan. "A Great Novel of Peasant Revolt." CHINESE LITERATURE 12 (1959): 62-71.

Answers to Hsia's charge of indiscriminate and excessive praise lavished on SHUI-HU CHUAN (C28 above) and, not surprisingly, proposes that the greatness of the novel lies in the heroic opposition of peasants to economic and political oppression endemic in Chinese history. Describes the novel as a collective work, arising from a real late-Sung revolt, augmented by popular tales and professional storytelling, composed by educated men into a comprehensive whole, and further enhanced by writers of advanced technical skill. Accepts as compiler-author Shih Nai-an and as editor Lo Kuan-chung.

Concentrates on the life, career, and psychology of Lin Chung, a military officer repeatedly beaten down by rapacious and salacious superiors until finally he must choose between death and resistance. Finds the characterization brilliant, convincing, realistic, and moving by reason of Lin's complexity, combining profound humanity with obsessive timidity, his gradual change under social and political pressures, and an individualism in striking contrast with other characters, notably Wu Sung and Li K'uei.

Imputes the tremendous popularity and continuing political power of the work, not to its adventure stories, but specifically to its historical account of fundamental social incompatabilities.

C38. Li, Peter. "Narrative Patterns in SAN-KUO and SHUI-HU." CHINESE NARRATIVE: CRITICAL AND THEORETICAL ESSAYS. Ed. Andrew H. Plaks. Princeton: Princeton University Press, 1978. Pages 73-84.

Attacking Irwin's judgment that SHUI-HU is merely a collection of tales (C32), cites Chen Chen-to's perception of it as water-tight and close-knit and Hanan's finding of a system of linked plots governed by a superstructure of the assembling of the heroes at Liang Shan-p'o and the consequent birth and death of rebellion. Urges an even stronger unifying device in the conflict-resolution model (point of contention, confrontation, open conflict, and resolution) between righteous fugitives on the one hand and, on the other, corrupt, abusive government forces--this in addition to the strong geographical focus of Mount Liang. As contrasted with SAN-KUO-CHIH YEN-I, sees SHUI-HU's internal structure as rather weak, but its external structure, unified by a combination of elements, as remarkably strong.

C39. Liu Ching-chih. TEN YUAN DRAMAS ON STORIES FROM THE WATER MARGIN. Hong Kong: University of Hong Kong, 1982.

[An anonymous, undated list distributed at a 1987 Asian conference, includes six items as extant complete Ming ch'uan ch'i plays based on SHUI-HU CHUAN (dates are first printings): Li K'ai-hsien's PAO CHIEN CHI (THE PRECIOUS SWORD), 1529; Ch'en Yu-chiao's LING PAO TAO (THE MARVELLOUS SWORD), 1588?; Shen Ching's YI HSIA CHI (THE ALTRUISTIC KNIGHT), before 1607; Hsu Tzu-ch'ang's SHUI HU CHI (WATER MARGIN), 1590?; Lu

Su-fu's YUAN HSIAO NAO (THE LANTERN FESTIVAL DISTURB-
ANCE), 1962 (1640?); and Fan Hsi-che's T'OU CHIA CHI
or YEN LING CHIA (STEELING THE ARMOUR or THE WILD
GOOSE-FEATHER ARMOUR), after the seventeenth century.]

C40. Liu, James J.Y. THE CHINESE KNIGHT-ERRANT. Chicago:
      University of Chicago Press, 1967. Pages 108-116.

Takes issue with Hsia's severe critique of SHUI-HU
CHUAN (C28 and C29) as a tale of pseudohistory and
gang-morality, without artistry or social validity.
After point-by-point rebuttal of Hsia's position, concludes that the work is a masterpiece of its kind, a
novel of Chinese knight-errantry.

C41. Liu Wu-chi. "The Novel as Folk Epic." AN INTRODUC-
      TION TO CHINESE LITERATURE. Bloomington: Univer-
      sity of Indiana Press, 1966. Pages 195-212.

Sees social realism and the revolution of a long-
suffering people against tyranny as keys to the enormous success of this mostly fictional account of Sung-
Yuan transitional years. Praises the novel's portrayal of vast, complex, and multicolored facets of Chinese society, in an epiclike narrative "comparable in
scope and grandeur to the Greek and Indian epics."
Rejects seventeenth-century Chin Sheng-t'an's condemnation of leader Sung Chiang as a hypocritical villain,
seeing him instead as the ideal archrebel, hospitable,
generous, loyal in heart even against the government
he has renounced. Analyzes major characters and collates two tiger-killing episodes to show the author's
skill in differentiating personae. Includes textual
history and authorial speculation.

C42. Lo, Andrew Hing-bun. SAN-KUO-CHIH YEN-I AND SHUI-HU
      CHUAN IN THE CONTEXT OF HISTORIOGRAPHY: AN INTERPRE-
      TIVE STUDY. Princeton: Princeton University, 1981.
      An unpublished dissertation.

Relates the two novels and historiography in terms of
intent, chiefly moral aim. Finds both novels more
exploratory than hortatory in relation to the virtue
of $\underline{i}$ (righteousness, honor, integrity), as woven into
the novels' fabric. Concludes with a reconsideration

of the historical novels in relation to the novelists' visions.

C43. Lu Erh-kang. "SHUI-HU CHUAN and the Hung or Heaven and Earth League." TA-KUNG PAO. Historical and Geographical Weekly Supplement #9.

See C15.

C44. Lu Hsun. A BRIEF HISTORY OF CHINESE FICTION. Trs. Yang Hsien-yi and Gladys Yang. Peking: Foreign Languages Press, 1959. Pages 183-194.

Accounts for six existing editions of SHUI-HU CHUAN, four of them important.

C45. Ma Yau-woon, and Ma Tai-loi. "SHUI-HU CHUAN." INDIANA COMPANION TO TRADITIONAL CHINESE LITERATURE. Eds. William N. Nienhauser, Jr., and others. Bloomington: Indiana University, 1986. Pages 712-718.

Stresses the extraordinary difficulty of determining the best and/or most authentic text of SHUI-HU CHUAN. Concludes that the earliest extant versions of SHC date from the early sixteenth century and that the textual evolution ends in the mid-seventeenth century.

Classes the numerous versions produced over these years as the simpler (chien-pen) and the fuller (fan-pen) texts, with a third "compromised" text lately identified. Of these, declares the early seventeenth-century 71-chapter recension (with commentary and interlinear glosses) by Chin Sheng-t'an the general reader's standard text, though increasing attention is being given the "compromised" 120-chapter reading which restores the 50 chapters omitted, probably for political reasons, by Chin.

Identifies six major sections: 1) the gradual gathering of the characters through a series of heroic episodes, culminating in their asssembly at Liang Shan-p'o (71 chapters); 2) events leading to honorable surrender; 3-6) four campaigns on behalf of the emperor against rebellious groups, the most notorious being that of Fang La.

Finds traditional political censorship of the novel as subversive less serious and interesting than the rapid attitudinal shifts in Communist China, moving from 1) glorification of the work, under Mao-tse Tung's endorsement, as an ideal peasant revolution against feudal oppressors, Sung Chiang being viewed as a Mao prototype, to 2) Mao's sudden and fierce attacks on the novel in 1975 as exemplary (in Sung's amnesty with the emperor) of betrayal of revolutionary ideals, to 3) a partial reinstatement into favor since Mao's demise and the changing of the guard. Lists many "exaggerated claims" for the novel's merit, discusses the role of SHC in the performing arts, and describes the content of several important sequels.

C46. Ogawa, Tamaki. "The Author of the SHUI-HU CHUAN." MONUMENTA SINICA 17 (1958): 312-330.

C47. Plaks, Andrew H. THE FOUR MASTERWORKS OF THE MING NOVEL: SSU TA CH'I-SHU. Princeton: Princeton University Press, 1987.

See B39.

C48. Plaks, Andrew H. "SHUI-HU CHUAN and the Sixteenth-Century Novel Form: An Interpretive Analysis." CHINESE LITERATURE: ESSAYS, ARTICLES, REVIEWS 2 (January 1980): 3-53.

A rehearsal for the currently being printed FOUR MASTERWORKS OF THE MING NOVEL, develops the thesis that the novels share characteristics marking them as a newly emerged genre, the full-fledged Chinese novel. Lists these traits as conscious attention to structural design, manipulation of narrative detail, rhetorical tuning, and, most essentially, the ironic point of view.

Defines this point of view as a revision of sources so as to expose the clash between popular ideas and attitudes and the realities of history and human nature. Believes that the novels, accordingly, raise serious questions reflecting Ming society's intellectual concerns: the historical process, the significance of human activity, and the relation of self to society.

After summary treatments, in the light of his theory, of CHIN P'ING MEI and HSI-YU CHI, analyzes structural elements in SHUI-HU CHUAN. Finds architectonic sophistication in the structuring of a) a prologue to announce metaphysical principles at the heart of the narrative; b) a chuan (division) arrangement of 10/12 chapters per narrative unit; c) a gradual gathering of characters bonded by sworn brotherhood, and a tracing of their activities to a height, followed by as gradual a dissolution of the mission and dispersal of the participants; and d) an aesthetically effective closure in directing affairs toward a Buddhistic feeling of emptiness and futility. Notes a billiard ball effect in the narrative line, as one character advances the action until he runs into another, whereupon a new trajectory begins.

In textual matters shows a) advanced "figural density," i.e. overlapping patterns of recurrence with subtly contrasting nuances suggestive of ironic commentary; b) use of contrastive pairings or nuclear groupings of characters, again to underscore ironic intent; c) binary polarity (yin/yang) and multiple periodicity (five-elements theory and its system of correspondences) used for expanding microcosmic to macrocosmic significance and for raising the particular to the universal; d) self-conscious expansion of rhetorical conventions, e.g. mimesis of colloquial speech, ostensibly inherited from professional storytelling and theater, in reality cunningly chosen for ironic purposes.

Argues that no character can be taken at face value, and that the relationship between leader Sung Liang and his follower Li K'uei steadily functions to reveal exactly those moral deficiencies that constitute the author's meaning. Even so, maintains that, far from being cynical, the author pointedly supplies balancing, positive characters so as to leave only gnawing uncertainty about deeply held beliefs relative to national heroes and their actions, especially in the context of sworn brotherhood. In the end, reverts to "the backdrop of cosmic emptiness out of which the monumental plot emerges and into which it dissolves with the final dispersal and disbanding of the group."

Finally, notes the intellectual ferment of sixteenth-century Ming times as compared with the "unimpressive" fifteenth-century, and the need of scholars to take into account a) the post-Wang Yang-ming "philosophy of the mind"; b) the new idea of the unity of the three teachings (Confucian, Taoist, and Buddhist); and c) the Neo-Confucian rethinking of the relations of the self and the world.

C49. Prusek, Jaroslav. "SHUI-HU CHUAN et son auteur." ARCHIV ORIENTALIA 22 (1954): 632-641. Also in Prusek's CHINESE HISTORY AND LITERATURE: COLLECTION OF STUDIES. Dordrecht, Holland: D. Reidel Publishing Company, 1970.

A lengthy review of Irwin's 1959 THE EVOLUTION OF A CHINESE NOVEL (C32). Charges Irwin with failures of interpretation "un peu trop influencees par l'acribie exageree des savants chinois" and too little enlightened by the "savants eminents de la nouvelle Chine democratique." Predictable views from the brilliant Marxist sinologist.

C50. Steinen, Diether von den. "In Reply to Mr. Franz Kuhn (On Pearl Buck's translation of SHUI-HU)." MONUMENTICA SINICA 2 (1936-1937): 165-166.

Scathing but not very illuminating attack on Franz Kuhn's review of Pearl Buck's ALL MEN ARE BROTHERS (C30 and C35). Calls Kuhn's place-name errors more egregious than Buck's less significant slips.

C51. Sun, Phillip S.Y. "The Seditious Art of THE WATER MARGIN: Misogynists or Desperadoes?" RENDITIONS 1 (Autumn 1973): 99-106.

Studies SHUI-HU CHUAN as a male-chauvinist work, not only centering exclusively on men and on killing, plundering, and other men-associated acts of violence, but "exceedingly cruel" to women, even while expertly delineating a few of them, as crones Grandma Yang and Grandma Yen, drawn "with more vividness and vitality than Juliet's nurse." Cautions that this misogyny is atypical of Chinese literature generally, from the compassion of the Classics for abandoned women to post-Sung romantic dramas and novels wherein heroines

shine, not only for beauty and virtue, but as well for
literary gifts and aptitude for Buddhist disquisition.
Likens the manner to Europe's courtly love milieu.

Attributes THE WATER MARGIN's hostility to women to a
desperado mentality viewing amorous passion as danger-
ous, debilitating, and detrimental to the aims of
sworn brotherhood. Ridicules the "chivalric courtesy"
of Robin Hood's band as totally unrealistic, an artificial and pastoral behavior arousing only laughter
among real social outlaws.

Describes the celibacy ideal among the heroes as a
result, not only of a basic view of women as essentially lascivious, but also of a whitewashing of
reality intended to impress the masses and win male
adherents to the cause. Names this narrative, accordingly, a forerunner of China's propagandistic novels
and suggests that discussion of it as a work of art
ought to deal with the mentality of its authors as
desperadoes and to study their propagandistic techniques.

C52. Surh, Olga. "SONS, SHUI-HU, and SAN-KUO." THE CHINA
CRITIC 11 (October 31, 1935): 107-108.

Exemplifies Western critics' early failure to recognize Chinese principles of literary organization and
their references to the classic novels as formless and
fragmentary. Parallels certain narrative elements in
Pearl Buck's SONS with episodes in SAN-KUO-CHIH YEN-I
and SHUI-HU CHUAN, concluding that, unlike the Chinese
works, Buck's story presents a unified artistic whole.

C53. Venne, Peter. "Pearl Buck's Literary Portrait of
China and the Chinese." FU JEN STUDIES 2 (1968):
71-86.

Scans the life, works, and style of the novelist who,
because of her works on Chinese life, culture, and
character, translated into a dozen languages, holds,
with Mark Twain, the "first place among the most popular American writers abroad." Defends the novels
against charges of a) inaccurate content (Buck's
earliest three decades were immersed in Chinese life
and language); b) a style innocent of myth and arche-

type, stream-of-consciousness and symbolism (her style reflects the life-rhythms of Old China and its love for parallelism free of relatives); c) failure to probe the minds and souls of her characters (she is ever faithful to common strains of humanity); and d) religious and philosophical shallowness (though eschewing sectarian religion, she insists on the religion of kindness, tolerance, helping the suffering, working for justice, and living out the brotherhood of man). Points out Buck's appreciation of Taoist tenets promoting these values and practices.

Sorts the sixteen novels by theme into three groups: a) China at home, including THE GOOD EARTH trilogy (1931-1935), which won Buck the 1938 Nobel Prize for Literature; b) China in conflict with Western civilization, including EASTWIND-WESTWIND (1930), wherein attitudes are reconciled, and THE FIRST WIFE (1933), wherein they are not; and c) the national awakening of China in the war with Japan, including DRAGON SEED (1941), wherein a military conqueror seeks to suppress the people. Unaccountably ignores Buck's famous and ever popular translation of SHUI-HU CHUAN as ALL MEN ARE BROTHERS (1933).

C54. Wang Hsi-yen. "Characterization Through Depiction of Externals." CHINESE LITERATURE 7 (July 1964): 85-93.

Using physical appearance, dialogue, and behavior under contradiction or conflict, shows how Shih Nai-an, reputed author of SHUI-HU CHUAN, relies on external factors rather than on interior analysis (a Western way) to realize his characters. Illustrates this thesis by the opening description of Lu Chih-shen, indicative of power and rectitude; by Li K'uei's conversation against his beloved master, suspected once of sympathy with the enemy and once of kidnapping a young girl; and by long-suffering peasants, rising at last against evil feudal rulers.

C55. Wang Jing. THE MYTHOLOGY OF STONE: A STUDY OF THE INTERTEXTUALITY OF ANCIENT CHINA STONELORE AND THREE CLASSIC NOVELS. Amherst: University of Massachusetts, 1985. An unpublished dissertation.

Uses the composite symbolism of the stone in Chinese folklore to explore its use in SHUI-HU CHUAN, HSI-YU CHI, and HUNG-LOU MENG. Notes how modifications and accretions mark the literary use of the stone symbol.

C56. Wang, John C.Y. CHIN SHENG-T'AN. New York: Twayne Publishers, 1972.

Makes a case for the greatness of the seventeenth-century critic, the emender of SHUI-HU CHUAN, a contemporary of the celebrated Li Chih and the Yuan brothers. Identifies Chin Sheng-t'an as, in morality, an imaginative Confucian and, in literary outlook, a classicist-romanticist. Details his work with SHUI-HU CHUAN, beginning with his three prefaces, continuing through chapter introductions, and culminating with interlinear glosses.

Defends Chin's extensive textual alterations on the grounds of improved consistency, compactness, and vividness, and, relative to his elision of the final 50 chapters, summarizes arguments pro and con. Stresses Chin's marked ambivalence toward the bandits whom, on the one hand, he roundly condemns, and, on the other, treats with sympathy and understanding. Applies this ambiguity to Sung Chiang, denounced as wicked and false, while, through his associates' attitudes and words, shown to be, in fact, faithful and generous.

C57. Wang, John C.Y. "The Cyclical View of Life and Meaning in the Traditional Chinese Novel." In ETUDES D'HISTOIRE ET DE LITTERATURE CHINOISES OFFERTES AU PROFESSEUR JAROSLAV PRUSEK. Paris: Institut des Hautes Etudes Chinoises, 1976.

See A105.

C58. Widmer, Ellen Bradford. THE MARGINS OF THOUGHT: SHUI-HU HOU CHUAN AND THE LITERATURE OF MING LOYALISM. Cambridge: Harvard University Press, 1987.

Studies the most important of the many sequels to SHUI-HU CHUAN, with numerous references to the prototype.

C59. Widmer, Ellen Bradford. SHUI-HU HOU-CHUAN IN THE CONTEXT OF SEVENTEENTH-CENTURY CHINESE FICTION CRITICISM. Cambridge: Harvard University, 1981. An unpublished dissertation.

C60. Wong, Timothy C. "The Virtue of Yi in WATER MARGIN." JOURNAL OF ORIENTAL LITERATURE 7 (May 1966): 49-52.

C61. Wu, Jack. "The Morals of ALL MEN ARE BROTHERS." WESTERN HEMISPHERE REVIEW 17 (Winter 1963): 86-89.

C62. Yang, Winston L.Y., Peter Li, and Nathan K. Mao. "ROMANCE OF THE THREE KINGDOMS and THE WATER MARGIN." CLASSICAL CHINESE FICTION: A GUIDE TO ITS STUDY AND APPRECIATION. ESSAYS AND BIBLIOGRAPHIES. Boston: G.K. Hall Publishers, 1978. Pages 39-51.

Lists as major differences between SHUI-HU CHUAN (THE WATER MARGIN) and SAN-KUO-CHIH YEN-I (ROMANCE OF THE THREE KINGDOMS) 1) the shorter time period covered by SHUI; 2) its more imaginative and fictitious content, without dependence on historical sources; 3) its weaker internal structure (loosely connected cycles, each with a different hero), but more powerful external and overall pattern of conflict and resolution; 4) its concern with outlaws and rebels rather than with princes and generals struggling to uphold or establish dynasties; 5) its rejection of Confucian norms in favor of a more generalized pursuit of righteousness and justice; 6) its more colloquial language and style.

After differentiating the 1614 120-chapter version and editor Chin Sheng-t'an's 1641 70-chapter version with commentary, cites as inherent flaws in the work "authorial digressions, contradictory views, stereotyped personae, sadism, narrative inconsistency, loose structure, and extraneous episodes." Suggests as strengths a few well-developed characters, smooth and expressive colloquial style, exciting episodes, limited dependence on sources, and realistic description of common people--traits epitomized in the episode of Wu Sung's barehanded killing of a tiger.

C63. Yu Yuh-chao. "Chinese Influences on Pearl Buck." TAMKANG REVIEW 11 (1981): 23-41.

After summarizing Buck's life (1892-1973), especially the early years, recounts these major influences on her writing career: four decades of living in China, from her birth (with a few years out for education in America at Randolph-Macon College and Cornell University); childhood playmates and first-language use of Chinese; an old Chinese nurse who enthralled her with native stories, including Taoist and Buddhist tales rich in supernatural, allegorical, parabolic, and animistic detail; and her Confucian-scholar tutor, a Mr. Kung.

Links these experiences with Buck's Western education in history, geography, arithmetic, English, music, art, and nature, imparted by her mother so as to blend with the other learning and produce what Buck called her "mentally bifocal" perspective. Recalls the novelist's early devotion to religious toleration, despite the scandal caused in Miss Jewel's high-school class when Pearl linked Confucius with Our Father in Heaven and viewed the Blessed Virgin as younger sister to her favorite, Goddess-of-Mercy Kuan-yin.

Traces Buck's writing successes from childhood through college and university, and afterwards years spent in a provincial town where husband John Lossing Buck pursued agricultural research and university teaching. Vouches for the superiority of Buck's Asian writings over those dealing with the West.

Attributes to Chinese attitudes toward fiction a) Buck's deprecation of the novelist's art, for which Sinclair Lewis reproved her; b) her defense of the reputed formlessness of the Chinese novel; c) her praise of its flexibility of language in dealing with different situations, and its subordination of style, plot, and purpose to characterization; d) her championing of Chinese romantic realism, exemplified in the humane use of the supernatural.

Concludes by detailing major likenesses between Buck's 1932 novel SONS and SHUI-HU CHUAN, a translation of which, as ALL MEN ARE BROTHERS, she published in the following year.

CHAPTER FOUR

HSI-YU CHI (MONKEY, or JOURNEY TO THE WEST)

How many American Presidents have been poets we do not know. The question has rarely, if ever, been raised. But in traditional China it has been normal for leaders--emperors, governors, generals--to express their feelings in verse, much as English Renaissance gentlemen, we are told, were wont to do.

Not surprisingly, then, Mao-tse Tung (1893-1978), like his illustrious or infamous predecessor Ts'ao Ts'ao of the Three-Kingdoms period, instinctively turned to poetry for release of powerful emotions. The result is a surprisingly good collection of about 50 poems, all in classical meters (for which Mao apologized to Chinese youth, calling his choice regrettable, a hangover from early education). Marking each stage of the leader's revolutionary career, the published verses begin with a love poem to his bride of two years on the occasion of their 1923 forced parting, he to lead insurrectionists, she (eventually) to be executed for treason.

Among the 50 poems, many of which refer to heroes and events of SAN-KUO-CHIH YEN-I (ROMANCE OF THE THREE KINGDOMS), is one attacking Soviet leaders and their current "revisionist" and dictatorial policies. Entitled TO KUO MO-JO (NOVEMBER 17, 1961), the poem for thematic, structural, and textual design rests on a famous episode from HSI-YU CHI (JOURNEY TO THE WEST), depicting one of Monkey's three victories over the White-Bone Demon. This monster, described in Chapter 27, continuously sought to gain immortality by devouring monk Hsuan-tsang's heart. Mao's poem responded to verses of Kuo Mo-jo, a poet-scholar described in Klein-Clark's 1971 BIOGRAPHIC DICTIONARY OF CHINESE COMMUNISM as "the closest thing to a Renaissance man that China has produced this century." Kuo Mo's poem had been prompted by a recent presentation of the opera, THE THREE CLASHES BETWEEN THE GOLDEN MONKEY AND THE WHITE-BONE DEMON. Mao's poem reads:

> Out of a heap of white bones the demon rises
> When a sudden thunderstorm cracks over the land.
> In this tale of struggle between good and evil
> The monk is but a befuddled fool,
> But the demon is evil itself,
> Who brings to mankind
> All the dreaded calamities of his dark world.
> Sensing this danger,
> The Golden Monkey jumps into the fight.
> Swinging his iron rod with all his might,
> He sweeps the Jade Palace clean of evil.
> Today we call for the help of the Golden Monkey
> For the evil mist is again whirling around us.
> (Translated by Ma Wen-yee in
> THE GREAT WALL GLISTENS, 1986)

The poem and its occasion illustrate the ease with which even today Chinese people summon up traditional folk heroes, especially from their novels, and the readiness with which they transform these protagonists into fighters for current causes. Marxist literary theory thus not only dictates the kind of literature to be written; it also reinterprets the classics so as to "rediscover their true meaning," their adumbration of the Communist Revolution.

Hardly less than with SHUI-HU CHUAN, the evolution of JOURNEY offers perplexing problems. While certainty about authorship has yet to be established, critics are almost agreed on Kiangsu's Wu Ch'eng-en (c1506-1582), a scholar-poet-official whose predilection for the strange, the monstrous, the marvelous, the fantastic dates from his early years.

It is, further, accepted that the novel transforms its purported central character, Hsuan-tsang (596-664), from the intelligent, scholarly, wise, and saintly Buddhist monk of history into a nearly helpless, fearful, vain, comfort-loving, somewhat stupid leader. The real Hsuan-tsang of the T'ang Dynasty left, through his disciple Pien-chi, his own account of the 17-year journey to India (629-645) to procure Buddhist sutras for later translation into Chinese. Another disciple, Hui-li, with supplements provided by monk Yen-tsung, expanded that version of actual events and conversations. While the outlines of the histories and the novel are similar, the spirit, tone, and characterization differ enormously.

It was but natural that, when popular imagination began to embroider the account of clerical treks through deserts, forests, and strange and exotic lands, a favorite folklore character, the monkey, should spring to life. As guide and defender of the supposed protagonist he lives in constant danger of his life from monsters, goblins, ghosts, deities, and demons. Thus was born Sun Wu-k'ung, Monkey, who, in subsequent developments, supplanted Hsuan-tsang as the narrative's central character.

Another step of some unknown author's fantasy brought into being the immortal Chu Pa-chieh, Pigsy, who, in comedy and humanity, rivals Falstaff, Caliban, and Mozart's Papageno. Less vivid, though no less crucial in action, are the two other pilgrims, Sha Monk (Sandy) and the White Dragon-horse.

Whatever popular and fictionalized events gathered about the pilgrims, some had by Sung times been realized as art. From Southern Sung (1127-1279) comes a clear antecedent of the novel in a written tale about Hsuan, not yet much transformed but now dependent on Monkey's instructions. From Yuan times (1260-1368) many dramas, including a six-play cycle with 24 acts by Yang Chen-hsin, elaborate the pilgrims' conflicts with fantastical creatures in imaginary settings.

Critics still debate the relation of the 1592 100-chapter edition of the novel, published by T'ang Shih-te and presumably written by Wu Ch'eng-en, and two shorter late Ming manuscripts known, respectively, as Chu and Yang. Still, with the addition of Chapter Nine (about Hsuan's early years), taken from the presumably earlier and certainly more "primitive" (marked by oral storytelling techniques) Chu edition, the 1592 version has remained standard.

HSI-YU CHI has often been viewed as a three-section narrative, following Monkey's early career, Tripitaka's, and the pilgrimage itself. Anthony Yu, however, divides it into five parts: 1) Sun Wu-k'ung's acquisition of magical powers, his rebellion against the gods, and his subsequent taming by Buddha (Chapters 1-7); 2) a heavenly council in which bodhisattva Kuan-yin (Goddess of Mercy) is commissioned by Buddha to find an appropriate person for the Indian mission, and auxiliary pilgrims are introduced (Chapter 8); 3) Hsuan's background and T'ang emperor T'ai Tsung's charging him with the journey (Chapters 9-12); 4) the 81 ordeals decreed by heaven for the redeeming of the pilgrims (all guilty of early moral failures), involving repeated captures and releases usually effected by Monkey's strategems (Chapters 13-97); and 5) the meeting with Buddha, the difficult but triumphant return to China, and, finally, the redeemed pilgrims' installation, with various degrees of beatitude, in the Buddhist paradise (Chapters 98-100).

In classifying HYC, critics name an assortment of genres, including allegory, myth, and satire, and suggest, as well, elements of epic, picaresque, and romance.

As allegory HYC is interpreted by some scholars as a study in the three ways of salvation: Buddhist detachment, Taoist search for immortality (through alchemy, ritual, passivity, and/or oneness with nature), and Confucian reliance on self-cultivation in harmony with social and cosmic ideals. Others see it as a study of religious and/or philosophical emancipation, involving fall from grace into realms of attachment, divisiveness, and vulnerability; and a redemptive journey, advancing through struggle and suffering to a recovered and enriched mental enlightenment.

A psychological variant on this metaphysical interpretation sees Pigsy as id (obsessed with sensual pleasure and avoidance of pain), Monkey as super-ego (reason marked by creativity and ambition), Sandy as ego and reconcilor (an essentially stoic observer), and Tripitaka as Everyman. Finally, Marxists read JOURNEY as an allegory of class warfare in which, as representative of the suffering masses, Monkey defies authorities of heaven, earth, and hell on behalf of his clientele.

Applying canons suggested by Carl Jung, Northrop Frye, Tzvetan Todorov, and Vladimir Propp, myth-pursuing scholars seek archetypes, realities suggesting primordial human situations and events. These point out the novel's beginning with the creation of the world and Monkey's hatching from a stone egg. Continuing, they explore episodes including or suggesting fertility rites, often involving incest, ritual murder, and cannibalism. Such applications, in the case of HYC, inevitably develop a comic dimension, a derision of cults based on gratification without discipline.

Those preferring a comic reading to myth and allegory name satire as the formative energy of the novel. They perceive as the author's major intent the threefold derision of individual excess, bureaucratic ineptitude and corruption, and/or religion-inspired absurdities.

Some critics, however, among them Hu Shih, Lu Hsun, and Liu Wu-chi, dismiss altogether the notions of allegory, myth, and satire as HYC's central dynamic. They, instead, praise the novel as primarily entertainment, filled as it is with adventure, suspense, conflict, scintillating conversation, fantastical creatures and settings, above all comedy and wit. Such readings invoke elements of picaresque and of medieval romance as good storytelling ingredients, and of epic as from time immemorial the people's mode of enjoying leisure time.

But such a reading does not sit well with the more traditional Chinese mind. Besides condemning the Hu-Shih school for ascribing Indian origins to HYC and, without adequate evidence, declaring Wu Ch'eng-en its author, Feng Yuan-chun deplores their reading of HYC as a book of playful humor, without interest in contemporary social and political realities.

By whatever genre HSI-YU CHI is identified, however, or its theme defined, the work radiates an extraordinary and compassionate insight into the human condition that lifts it beyond the merely national. A world masterpiece, it invites comparison with other globally famous works.

Scholars have, accordingly, fruitfully collated MONKEY with other fictions of quest literature: the ODYSSEY, though Ulysses goes towards the real world and the Chinese pilgrims away from it; DON QUIXOTE, though differences appear in master-man relationships; HUCKLEBERRY FINN, though the societies regard contrastingly the juxtapositions of slave and free, talent and status; and PILGRIM'S PROGRESS, with the difference of MONKEY'S enormously more entertaining color and wit.

As parallels for Sun Wu-k'ung, critics are quick to point out, not only archrebels like Satan of PARADISE LOST and Prometheus of Greek legend, but also obsessively ambitious quasi-tragic characters like Faust or the saucily self-assured like Ariel. As for Pigsy--who could miss Prospero's Caliban, or Papageno and Falstaff, those counterparts of Princes Tamino and Hal? One critic declares the Western personae actually less three-dimensional than Chu Pa-chieh, the Pigsy of Wu Ch'eng.

Almost all critics recognize the thematic importance to JOURNEY of the Buddhist HEART SUTRA, at least one critic calling it the central theme. Certainly sentiments from this short work (a prajnaparamita or Wisdom sutra) reappear continuously throughout the novel, especially in Monkey's exhortations to his master at crucial moments in the expedition to remember that "form is emptiness and emptiness is form." That saying from the HEART SUTRA epitomizes sunyata, the ancient Pali term for "emptiness," a doctrine known to Hinayana Buddhists, but developed to capacity by Mahayana-Madhyamika (Middle-Way) Buddhists under second-century Buddhist sage Nagarjuna. Paraphrased to mean the mid-point between nihilism and positivism, nirvana and samsara, the phenomenal and the absolute, this teaching accords with the tone and structure of HSI-YU CHI.

Indeed, structural considerations must include the Plaks formula of complementary bipolarity (yin/yang) and multiple periodicity (the five-elements theory and its table of correspondences). Thus students of the novel should observe the many sets of opposites transforming into each other with cyclic regularity, and identifications of characters and events with given natural elements that reveal both a unified world view and an integral artistic design. Often, within this pattern, poetry functions to underscore structural and textual intent, as well as to provide opportunity for insertion of interesting bodies of lore. In this area caveats are issued to those who would, in the interests of brevity, sacrifice the poetry.

Stylistically, besides the many points already noted --wit and humor, fantastic invention, gusto, sparkling dialogue, suspenseful narrative, jocose but biting satire, HYC features a multileveled and polysemous rhetoric operating on several levels according to characters and events. Finally, because HYC combines dignified vernacular with simple classical Chinese, the work is judged by James Hightower to be in the ch'uan ch'i (literary tales in classical Chinese) tradition established in the T'ang Dynasty.

In the matter of English translations of HSI-YU CHI, Anthony Yu's monumental four-volume JOURNEY TO THE WEST, definitive, complete, and fully annotated, effectively supersedes all others. Completed between 1977-1983, it provides a model for the rendering of Chinese classics into English. In the foreseeable future no other translation seems likely to vie with it, though from Beijing the 1983 first volume of another unabridged version, by W. Jenner, promises, when and if finished, an alternative reading. For those who want or need a shorter, less elaborate edition, Arthur Waley's MONKEY (first published in 1944), with its faithfully translated first 12 chapters and its choice of other passages (reducing 88 chapters to 18) still provides a delightful introduction to this unique work.

At least five English-language book-length studies of HYC have been completed, beginning with Arthur Waley's 1952 THE REAL TRIPITAKA AND OTHER PIECES, based on the seventh-century historical travelogues. In 1970 Glen Dudbridge produced his pioneer textual study, THE HSI-YU CHI: A STUDY OF ANTECEDENTS OF THE SIXTEENTH-CENTURY CHINESE NOVEL; in 1972 James Shu-hsien Fu his THE MYTHIC AND THE COMIC ASPECTS OF THE QUEST: HSI-YU CHI SEEN THROUGH DON QUIXOTE AND HUCKLEBERRY FINN; in 1973 Frederick Brandauer his A CRITICAL STUDY OF HSI-YU PU, an exploration of the expansion of HYC's Chapters 59-61 into an independent work (with implications for the original) by Tung Yueh; in 1976 Alfred Yeh his THE EVOLUTION OF A REBEL: AN INTERPRETATION OF WU CH'ENG-EN'S JOURNEY TO THE WEST; and, finally, in 1981, Nicholas Andrew Koss his THE HSI-YU CHI IN ITS FORMATIVE STAGES: THREE LATE MING EDITIONS.

Besides the names cited above, others deserving of special mention for the light they have shed on JOURNEY are C.T. Hsia, Karl S.Y. Kao, Andrew Plaks, and Francis H.K. So.

Translations

D1. Avenol, Louis, tr. SI YEOU KI, OU, LE VOYAGE EN OCCIDENT. Two volumes. Paris: Editions du Seuil, 1957.

Despite an attractive format, readable style, interesting illustrations, and--except for the omission of the poetry--comprehensiveness of translation, offers a reading, in Yu's judgment, "riddled with errors and mistranslations."

D2. Boner, Georgette, and Maria Nils, trs. MONKEYE PILGERFAHRT, EINE CHINESISCHE LEGENDE. Zurich: Artemis-Verlag, 1946. Based on Waley's translation.

D3. Chai Ch'u, and Winberg Chai, eds. and trs. "HSI-YU CHI (PILGRIMAGE TO THE WESTERN REGIONS)." A TREASURY OF CHINESE LITERATURE: A NEW PROSE ANTHOLOGY INCLUDING FICTION AND DRAMA. New York: Appleton Century, 1965. Pages 216-234.

Examines, in the introduction, the origins of the sixteenth-century historical-fictional story of seventh-century Hsuan-tsang's pilgrimage to Magadha, India. Includes among HSI-YU CHI'S sources T'ang ch'uan ch'i classical stories, Sung hua-pen, a Yuan PILGRIMAGE TO THE WEST, and a Ming work of the same title, as well as specific Buddhist and Taoist legends and innumerable folk tales.

Reviews the novel's three sections, of unequal length: a) the story of Monkey (Sun Wu-k'ung), b) the story of Tripitaka (Hsuan-tsang) and his mission to India, and c) the journey narrative proper, tracing 81 major and minor trials in the quest for Buddhist sutras. Refers to Tung Yueh's seventeenth-century "sequel," HSI-YU PU. Excerpts Chapter 59, events leading to the Battle of the Flaming Mountain, illustrative of Monkey's wisdom and the author's extraordinary imagination, good humor, and humanity.

D4. Chan, Plato, and Christina Chan. THE MAGIC MONKEY. New York: McGraw-Hill Book Company, 1944.

HSI-YU CHI (MONKEY, or JOURNEY TO THE WEST) 135

    Buy two dozen copies of this 50-page illustrated storybook from "an old Chinese legend" by two prodigious youngsters, and distribute them to all the children you know, five to ninety-five.

D5. Herzfeldt, Johanna, tr. DIE PILGERFAHRT NACH DEM WESTEN. Rudolstadt: Greifenverlag, 1962.

    A German adaptation of the WESTERN JOURNEY story.

D6. Hsia, C.T., and Cyril Birch, trs. "The Temptation of Saint Pigsy." ANTHOLOGY OF CHINESE LITERATURE (From early times to the fourteenth century). Ed. Cyril Birch. New York: Grove Publishers, 1972. Pages 68-85.

    Chapter 23 of HSI-YU CHI.

D7. Jenner, W. THE JOURNEY TO THE WEST. Volume I. Peking, 1983.

    Another unabridged readable version of HSI-YU CHI (on the heels of Yu's monumental four-volume work, completed in 1984), enriched by many full-page, colored, late nineteenth-century Chinese lithographs, but lacking the comprehensive, scholarly introduction and endnotes distinguishing Yu's work.

D8. Theiner, George, tr. THE MONKEY KING. Ed. Zdene Novatna. London: Paul Hamlyn, 1964.

    A richly illustrated and invitingly formatted volume, free of scholarly apparatus—a genuine storybook by an ingenious Czech adapter.

D9. Waley, Arthur, tr. "Monkey." MASTERPIECES OF THE ORIENT. Ed. George L. Anderson. New York: W.W. Norton and Company, 1961. Pages 235-254.

    Before presentation of the complete first two chapters of HSI-YU CHI, recalls the language medium (blended dignified vernacular and simple classical). Then reviews the novel's triple content: a) a religious quest for sacred Buddhist scriptures and, by analogy, for salvation; b) a critique of earthly bureaucracy and irrationality; and c) a comedy consistent with serious religious and satirical meanings. Insists on the mixture of satire and folk tale, fictionized history and religious allegory.

D10. Waley, Arthur, tr. MONKEY. New York: John Day, 1944; New York: Grove Press (Evergreen), 1958; Hammondsworth: Penguin Books, 1961.

A readable and reasonably faithful translation of Wu Ch'eng-en's classic, more convenient for general readers than Yu's four-volume, scholarly, complete version. Reviews the factual data of Hsuan-tsang's seventh-century journey to India, the enormous accrual of fantastic legends by the tenth century, and thirteenth-century extensive staging. Notes that abridgments had heretofore tended to keep all episodes while cutting essential dialogue, whereas Waley's version omits many episodes but, with the exception of verse passages, retains all the matter of the selected narratives.

Marvels at the work's combination of beauty with absurdity, profundity with nonsense, in a many-faceted form including folklore, allegory, religion, history, anti-bureaucratic satire, and pure poetry. Identifies Tripitaka as blundering, ordinary man; Monkey as restless, unstable genius; Pigsy as physical appetite and patient brute strength; Sandy as, despite his essential role, ill-defined and colorless.

D11. Wang Chi-chen, tr. "The Monkey King (Chapters 1-8)." CHINESE WIT AND HUMOR. Ed. George Kao. New York: Sterling, 1974. Pages 98-125. Originally published in 1946.

The rib-tickling antics of the Monkey King, selected for wit inspired by Lehr's dictum, "Monkeys are the craziest people."

D12. Yang Hsien-yi, and Gladys Yang. THE FLAMING MOUNTAIN. Peking: Foreign Languages Press, 1958.

Presents Chapters 59-61, showing Monkey's growing wisdom and his championship of the oppressed.

D13. Yang Hsien-yi, and Gladys Yang, trs. "Pilgrimage to the West: Chapter 27." CHINESE LITERATURE 5 (1966): 101-117.

In the Yangs' impeccable English offers a new reading of Chapter 27 of HSI-YU CHI, describing Sun Wu-k'ung's (Monkey's) meeting with and triumph over the White Bone Demon. Refers to a translation of three other chapters in CHINESE LITERATURE 1 (1961).

D14. Yu, Anthony C., ed. and tr. JOURNEY TO THE WEST. Four volumes. Chicago: University of Chicago Press, 1977-1983.

The first Western unabridged version of HSI-YU CHI, enhanced by a quiet but probing and comprehensive introduction and chapter endnotes generously sprinkled with primary- and secondary-source citations, some in Sanskrit and Pali. Questions final acceptance of Wu Ch'eng-en's authorship, even while finding him the likeliest candidate, and takes issue with Hu Shih and others, including Lu Hsun, who deny to the work religious, philosophical, and/or allegorical significance. For years to come the definitive English translation and edition.

Studies

D15. Brandauer, Frederick P. A CRITICAL STUDY OF THE HSI-YU PU. Stanford: Stanford University Press, 1973.

Based on Campbell's THE HERO WITH A THOUSAND FACES, explores the nature and significance of the late Ming vernacular novel HSI-YU PU, supplement (following the Flaming-Mountain episode of Chapters 59-61) to the more famous HSI-YU CHI and reliant upon that masterpiece for its own coherence.

Traces, in 14 of the 16 chapters, Monkey's dream, filled with weird and terrifying experiences, providing the novelist with two conditions unavailable to his predecessor: a) a realm separate from common and

historical reality, and b) freedom from restrictions
of commonplace logic, so as to invite imaginative
exploration "through vivid imagery and varied symbolism of a highly complex world," i.e. one including
psychological, religious, historical, sociological,
political, and mythic elements.

Following conventional preliminaries relative to date,
authorship, and text, proposes a Wellek-and-Warren
methodology. As materials, calls on language, story,
and theme; as structure, psychological realism functioning in a dream world, social protest functioning
as satire, and collective reflection functioning as
myth, specifically Buddhist myth.

Adverts to Bishop's judgment (A21) that Chinese novels, with the exception of HUNG-LOU MENG, lack significant psychological analysis, and proposes HSI-YU PU as
another notable exception. Among objects of satire,
treated with both Juvenalian savagery and Horatian
suavity, identifies the court, the examination system,
ambition and greed among men, traitors to the country,
and the military establishment.

D16.   Brandauer, Frederick P.   "The HSI-YU PU as an Example
         of Mythmaking in Chinese Fiction."   TAMKANG REVIEW
         6 (April 1975): 99-120.

Analyzes with clarity and depth HSI-YU PU, late Ming
vernacular novel by Tung Yueh (1620-1686), sequel to
HSI-YU CHI. Considers it, in Joseph Campbell's term,
as a monomyth, focusing on Monkey and following a
setting out-initiation-return pattern in the Buddhist
mode of desire-disillusion-enlightenment. Applies
also Jung's two modes of literature: psychological and
(more interesting for Brandauer's purposes) visionary.
Sees the final value of the novel less in its expression of personal maladjustment than in its projection
of a collective unconscious reflecting Chinese confusion, rage, and protest before massive political,
social, and economic ferment in seventeenth-century
China. A memorable study of a work derived from but
dramatically differing from the HSI-YU CHI.

D17.   Chan Ping-leung.   "Chinese Popular Water-god Legends
         and the HSI-YU CHI."   ESSAYS IN CHINESE STUDIES

HSI-YU CHI (MONKEY, or JOURNEY TO THE WEST)

> PRESENTED TO PROFESSOR LO HSIANG-LIN. Hong Kong: Chinese University of Hong Kong, 1970. Pages 299-317.

D18. Chang Ching-erh. "The Structure and Themes of the HSI-YU CHI." TAMKANG REVIEW 11 (1980): 169-188.

Besides identifying HYC's structure as exposition (Chapters 1-12), ascending action (Chapters 13-73), climax (Chapters 74-77), falling action (Chapters 78-98), and denouement (Chapters 99-100), proposes that these divisions are manipulated by means of the five-elements, yin-yang, and tao theories, with emptiness as a major theme and awareness the goal.

Invokes textual evidence to associate Monkey with the unifying forces of metal and fire; Pigsy with wood; Sandy with earth; and Tripitaka with water. Finds in each episode a movement involving mutual production (as water produces wood; wood, fire) and mutual conquest (as water conquers fire; fire, metal) and moving through three stages--unity, separation, restored unity, in the endless cyclic pattern at the heart of China's view of life and history. Includes useful discussion, in the light of the five-elements theory, of characters' names.

In addition to the self-contained nature of each episode, observes a larger pattern of increasing harmony, trust, and understanding among the characters, and a purging of each one from former sin and from his predominant passion (as Monkey's ambition, Pigsy's sensuality, Tripitaka's weakness) in favor of spiritual awareness of the emptiness of temporal passions and the plenitude of enlightenment. Further regards Monkey as superego or morality-oriented; Sandy as ego or reconcilor; Pigsy as id; and Tripitaka as Everyman.

D19. Chu Rudolph Y. "The Hermit and the Sufferer: Two Different Prototypes in Chinese and Western Literature." TAMKANG REVIEW 6 (1975-1976): 329-340.

See G28.

D20. Csongor, B. "A Comparative Analysis of SHUI-HU CHUAN and HSI-YU CHI: The Bounds of the Classic Chinese Novel." ACTA ORIENTALIA 29 (1975): 1-6.

See C18.

D21. Dudbridge, Glen. THE HSI-YU CHI: A STUDY OF ANTECEDENTS OF THE SIXTEENTH-CENTURY CHINESE NOVEL. Cambridge, England: Cambridge University Press, 1970.

Studies with precision and thoroughness HYC's antecedents, from the historically verifiable records of seventh-century traveler-translator-Buddhist monk Hsuan-tsang, through the 600-year gap to the celebrated thirteenth-century kozanji version of the story and other literary sources, as well as tsa chu drama. Denigrates the tendency popularized by Lu Hsun and his followers to identify too closely the oral storytelling tradition and the hua-pen, not, in Dudbridge's view, prompt books for raconteurs, but literary creations in a more independent sense.

Traces in detail parallels between the Indian Hanumam of RAMAYANA fame and Sun Wu-k'ung (Monkey) of the Chinese novel. In the absence, however, of conclusive evidence that Sung Chinese (and earlier) knew the Indian stories, rejects theories of Hu Shih and others linking the two creations in favor of attaching only a general folkloric significance to the many shared motifs. A major study, indispensable to depth understanding of HSI-YU CHI's origins and development.

D22. Dudbridge, Glen. "The Hundred-Chapter HSI-YU CHI and Its Early Versions." ASIA MAJOR 14 (1966): 141-191.

A technical discussion of a) early editions and manuscripts of HSI-YU CHI, especially the editions known as Yang and Chu, b) Wu Ch'eng-en's alleged authorship (Dudbridge doubts it), and c) the work's dating (the latter part of the sixteenth-century).

D23. Dye, Harriet. "Notes for a Comparison of the ODYSSEY and MONKEY." LITERATURE EAST AND WEST 8 (1964): 14-18.

An illuminating comparison about arguable positions involving MONKEY (comic fairy tale in colloquial prose) and the ODYSSEY (epic tale in high and serious vein). Reads the ODYSSEY as a journey back to the real world, MONKEY as a journey away from it; the epic as bringing divinity down to the human, the fairy tale as using man's divine spark to lift him to the celestial. In Homer sees celebration of the triumph and dignity of human exertions in surmounting obstacles; in the Chinese author, an answering to the thrill of transcending them. Finds the Western hero discovering, exploiting, and subduing nature; the Chinese, as accommodating himself to, then detaching himself from, and at last rising above the natural universe to become a Buddha.

D24. Feuerwerker, Yi-tse Mei. "The Chinese Novel." APPROACHES TO THE ORIENTAL CLASSICS. Ed. William Theodore De Bary. New York: Columbia University Press, 1959. Pages 171-185.

Identifies the work, with its mixture of history, folklore, hagiography, and fantasy, as a Swiftian or Rabelaisian PILGRIM'S PROGRESS, its dangers and obstacles representing humans' inordinate desires and evil impulses. Admires the author's lack of bitterness about human depravity and praises his portrayal of human toughness and resourcefulness as exemplified in the pilgrims' repeated confrontations with agents of destruction.

D25. Fitzgerald, C.P. "The Chinese Novel as a Subversive Force." MEANJIN QUARTERLY 10 (Spring 1951): 259-266.

Reads HSI-YU CHI as a satire on officials and underlings of Chinese government, but offers almost no development or illustration of the idea.

D26. Fu, James Shu-hsien. "The Cyclic Quest." TAMKANG REVIEW 5 (1974): 143-159.

An attempt to compress the author's book-length comparison of HSI-YU CHI with aspects of DON QUIXOTE and HUCKLEBERRY FINN under the rubric of ceaseless quest.

D27.   Fu, James Shu-hsien. THE MYTHIC AND THE COMIC ASPECTS OF THE QUEST: HSI-YU CHI AS SEEN THROUGH DON QUIXOTE AND HUCKLEBERRY FINN. Singapore: Singapore University Press, 1977.

Reviews HSI-YU CHI for a) its Buddhist-Taoist-Confucian allegory; b) historical problems relative to sources, datings, and texts; c) formal design in plot, structure, characters, style, and composition; and d) Marxist revisions of interpretation.

Proceeds to a study of the novel as quest narrative, rich in Jungian archetypes involving dual perspectives between "simple" and "sentimental" life attitudes. To this end compares the Chinese novel with the Cervantes and Twain masterpieces. Identifies as "sentimentalists," i.e. illusion-bound, Tripitaka, the Spanish Duke and Duchess, and Tom Sawyer. Observes two types of "simple" thinkers: a) Monkey, Don Quixote, and Huck, all striving toward an ideal; and b) Pigsy, Sancho, and Jim, settling for the earthy, practical, and possible. Assigns to these groups, respectively, three modes of the comic: sentimental, marked by rigidity; epic, marked by wonder; and pastoral, marked by baseness.

In Chapter One relates the quest theme to the comic styles and to the lyricalization of the narrative, elsewhere shown to be drawn from the pien-wen, Buddhist tales combining chanted verse and prose narrative. In Chapter Two presents the questers as mythic creatures striving for everlasting life and, in the process, transformed from victim to victor to saviors. In Chapter Three observes increasing harmony among the questers as they near their goals. In Chapter Four demonstrates that the end is the beginning, the renewal of perpetual quest. Finally, in Chapter Five dwells on Schlegelian romantic ironies in each work-- loving belief and laughing disbelief.

Incorporates into the discussions wide understanding of Western theories of literature, notably those of

Northrop Frye, and abundant illustration from Western works other than those named in the title. Insists on the centrality of the Mahayana HEART SUTRA and its teaching--"Form is emptiness and emptiness is form,"-- as well as yin-yang and five-elements theories. Examines the complex roles of Kuan-yin and the Jade Emperor.

Perceives the novel's basic pattern as endless metamorphoses in the mythic growth of the Self. Defines the special function of Sandy as the real monk, stoic as a Ch'an (Zen) practitioner ought to be, free from Monkey's ambitions and Pigsy's sensuality, and closest in his negative capability to the author's vision of life well lived.

Places the three novelists among the world's greatest ironists in manifesting the interplay between real and ideal, and between ideal and illusory.

D28. Fu, James Shu-hsien. "Plot and Style of the Quest." TAMKANG REVIEW 4 (October 1973): 79-100.

Links three world classics, DON QUIXOTE, HUCKLEBERRY FINN, and HSI-YU CHI, as quest romances employing a yin/yang structure of opposites transforming into each other in matters of faith/doubt, humor/horror, order/ disorder, nature/civilization, and form/emptiness. For ritual-dream relations borrows from Frye and Frazer; for myth, Malinowski and Jung, always emphasizing the double perspective.

Discerns, nevertheless, three levels of interdependent experience: a) a sentimental (as Cervantes' Duke and Duchess, Twain's Tom, and HSI-YU CHI's Tripitaka); b) the epic (as Quixote, Huck, and Monkey); and c) the pastoral (as Sancho, Jim, and Pigsy). Stresses the role of Mahayana Buddhism, especially as embodied in the HEART SUTRA, for a basic HSI-YU CHI insight: "Form is emptiness and the very emptiness is form."

While failing to note the sect's animadversion to Scripture as the way to salvation, declares Ch'an (Zen) Buddhism the dominant theme of the novel, giving to Chinese aesthetics greater intuitional and perceptive power. Applies the yin/yang principle also to the structure of the novel as midway between oral and written conventions, noting that SHUI-HU CHUAN usually suspends action at a session's end, while HSI-YU CHI chapters are generally (though not always) self-contained narratives. Observes, on the other hand, the novel's use of recurrent exclamations (an oral device for arousing laughter) such as "Great Chief, calamity has come!" whenever Monkey appears to rout the enemy.

D29. Grousset, Rene. THE RISE AND SPLENDOUR OF THE CHINESE EMPIRE. Trs. Anthony Watson-Gandy and Terence Gordon. Berkeley: University of California Press, 1970 (eighth printing). Page 269.

Prefers the straight, vivid travelogue of Hsuan-tsang to Wu Ch'eng-en's narrative, accounted "nothing but fantastic adventures, magic, and sorcery such as one finds in Tibetan tales."

D30. Han, Sherman. "An Anatomy of the Political Satire in HSI-YU CHI." TAMKANG REVIEW 13.3 (Spring 1983): 227-238.

Focuses principally on the relation of the Confucian, Taoist, and Buddhist elements to the political satire.

D31. Hanan, Patrick. "The Development of Fiction and Drama." THE LEGACY OF CHINA. Ed. Raymond Dawson. London: Clarendon Press, 1964. Pages 124-126.

Reviews Wu Ch'eng-en's sixteenth-century story of the overland journey of monk Hsuan-tsang, seeking Buddhist Scriptures in India; his disciple, the subversive, witty, perspicacious, arrogant, mischievous Monkey; Pigsy, carnal but cunning, a Caliban to Monkey's Ariel; and the comic interplay among the three as they encounter assorted ogres, magicians, and sirens. Analyzes the many ironies in the absurd and incompetent performance of the morally earnest monk, lost in a world of amoral creatures and in the antics of his companions, fallen angels seeking a way back to Paradise.

D32. Hightower, James R. TOPICS IN CHINESE LITERATURE. Cambridge: Harvard University Press. Pages 104-105.

Sees Monkey rather than Hsuan-tsang as real protagonist, likens the allegorical narrative to PILGRIM'S PROGRESS, and places the work in the ch'uan ch'i literary tradition.

D33. Hsia, C.T. "Journey to the West." THE CLASSIC CHINESE NOVEL: A CRITICAL INTRODUCTION. New York: Columbia University Press, 1968. Pages 115-164.

Questions the theory of MONKEY's unitary authorship executing Shakespearean magic in transforming multiple sources into a complex and compelling creation. Explores records of a three-faceted and ahistorical metamorphosis of the revered intellectual of history, Hsuan-tsang, into 1) a saintly, mythical monk-leader, 2) a potential Buddha, and 3) an ordinary mortal, an Everyman, subject to all mortal anguish, excess, and error.

Discusses a) Monkey's possible origin in the Hanuman of Indian legend, b) Communist rejection of this view, and c) Monkey's insouciant mixture of roles as spiritual guide-protector, mischief maker, and conveyor of hilarity. Recalls that crazy laughter, after all, has a long history in Asian literature of marking ultimate detachment from the world. The fantastic tale should, Hsia believes, be read as transcending mere political meanings by its triple character as myth, allegory, and comedy. Pigsy is seen as the common man, a Sancho Panza, fulfilling himself in the search for respectable worldly goals.

D34. Hsia, C.T., and T.A. Hsia. "New Perspectives on Two Ming Novels: HSI-YU CHI and HSI-YU PU." WEN-LIN: STUDIES IN THE CHINESE HUMANITIES. Ed. Chow Tse-tsung. Madison: University of Wisconsin Press, 1968. Pages 299-317.

D35. Kaltenmark, Odile. CHINESE LITERATURE. Tr. Anne-Marie Geoghegan. New York: Walker and Company,

1964 (revision of the 1948 original). Pages 75, 106, 117.

Confuses the authorship of Husan-tsang's seventh-century travelogue, but prefers it to the sixteenth-century novel. Perceives the latter as a combination of Taoism and a superficially understood Buddhism.

D36. Kao, Karl S.Y. "An Archetypal Approach to HSI-YU CHI." TAMKANG REVIEW 5 (1974), 63-97.

Another striking use of Western norms to elucidate a Chinese classic. Extends Hsia's hint of HSI-YU CHI's mythical significance in "its rendition of archetypal characters and events" by applying Frye's and Eliade's patterns of analysis. Sees seasonal life cycles as ritual, individualized as dream or fantasy, and, in literary development, parallel to comedy, romance, tragedy, and satire. Cites as examples the Judaeo-Christian bible, Old Testament and New, and Milton's double epic.

Tests the patterns in Part I (Chapters 1-7), recounting Monkey's creation, fall, and redemption; in Part II (Chapters 8-12), similarly rendering Tripitaka's career; and in Part III (Chapters 13-100), covering the 81 Buddhist ordeals and their aftermath. Supplements wide-ranging analyses of these archetypes with generous doses of Eliade's sacred time and place, of Fraser's readings of Greek mythology and Freudian/Jungian expositions thereof, and of Joseph Campbell's quest myth.

D37. Kao, Karl S.Y. "Tung Yueh's HSI-YU PU." WEN-LIN: STUDIES IN CHINESE HUMANITIES. Ed. Chow Tse-tsung. Two volumes. Madison: University of Wisconsin Press, 1985.

Discusses the 16-chapter Ming novelette written as an extension of chapters 59-61 of HSI-YU CHI.

D38. Koss, Nicholas Andrew. THE HSI-YU CHI IN ITS FORMATIVE STAGES: THREE LATE MING EDITIONS. Bloomington: Indiana University, 1981.

Compares the standard Wu Ch'eng-en 1592 100-chapter HSI-YU CHI with two shorter, undated versions, known as Chu and Yang. Concludes that the more literary 1592 version derives in part from the earlier, more primitive Chu rendering, marked by oral storytelling techniques, and that the Yang version (post-1592) drew upon both.

D39. Koss, Nicholas Andrew. "The Relationship of HSI-YU CHI and FENG-SHEN YEN-I." T'OUNG PAO: REVUE INTERNATIONALI DE SINOLOGIE 65 (1979): 143-165.

Uses the 32 poems appearing in both works to conclude that the 100-chapter HSI-YU CHI preceded the 100-chapter FENG-SHEN YEN-I (INVESTITURE OF THE GODS); that the former influenced the latter; and that two sequential authors composed the FENG-SHEN.

D40. Lai Ming. A HISTORY OF CHINESE LITERATURE. New York: Capricorn Books, 1966. Pages 298-107.

Considers HSI-YU CHI more tightly constructed and more engaging than the contemporary SHUI-HU CHUAN. Offers an extensive excerpt notable for its humor, Monkey's confrontation with Buddha as, in company with Lao Tse, he (Monkey) awaits the Jade Emperor's order for his execution.

D41. Liu Ts'un-yan. CHINESE POPULAR FICTION IN TWO LONDON LIBRARIES. Hong Kong: Lung Men Bookstore, 1967. Pages 138-150.

In a study of editions, rare and commonplace, of Chinese popular fiction found in the British Museum and the Royal Asiatic Society of London, discusses, not only dates, authenticity, and publication technicalities, but also exemplary textual problems. Opposing, for example, judgments of Hu Shih and Lu Hsun, establishes the debt of Wu Ch'eng-en's MONKEY to a Ming work, here called TRIPITAKA MASTER'S PILGRIMAGE TO THE WEST.

D42. Liu Ts'un-yan. "The Prototypes of MONKEY (HSI-YU CHI)." T'OUNG PAO 51 (1964): 55-71.

A source study establishing the partial dependence of Wu Ch'eng-en's HSI-YU CHI on a Ming work known as FOUR PILGRIMAGES.

D43. Liu Ts'un-yan. "Wu Ch'eng-en." DICTIONARY OF MING BIOGRAPHY. Two volumes. Eds. L. Carrington Goodrich and Chaoying Fang. New York: Columbia University Press, 1976. II: 1479-1483.

Cautiously accepts Wu's authorship of HSI-YU CHI, though a lengthy editor's note reviews arguments against it. Recalls events of the sixteenth-century poet-prose writer's struggles against poverty and repeated examination failure and his gradual acceptance as scholar, writer, and honored public official. Observes that history lost sight of Wu until Hu Shih's 1923 essay acclaiming him author of HSI-YU CHI and thereby inciting hordes of scholars to revive his name and fame in massive scholarly studies.

D44. Liu Ts'un-yan. "Wu Ch'eng-en: His Life and Career." T'OUNG PAO 53 (1967): 1-97. Also in Leiden, Netherlands: E.J. Brill Company, 1967.

A richly documented but highly speculative account of the gifted sixteenth-century writer named by Lu Hsun and Hu Shih, without conclusive evidence, as the certain author of HSI-YU CHI. Despite excessive detail, provides interesting anecdotal descriptions of contemporary manners and morals and a who's who of sixteenth-century Ming notables.

D45. Liu Wu-chi. "Great Novels by Obscure Writers." AN INTRODUCTION TO CHINESE LITERATURE. Bloomington: Indiana University Press, 1967. Pages 228-246.

Categorizes HSI-YU CHI as a supernatural novel, a blend of folk traditions and the author's imagination, prolific in fantastic creations of infinitely varied gods and demons. Summarizes the plot in three parts: Monkey's early history, Tripitaka's preliminary career, and the main narrative of the monk's ordeals in the journey to and from India with his three animal disciples, Monkey, Pigsy, and Sandy (a fish spirit).

Prefers the interpretation of the novel as primarily good entertainment, filled with wit, humor, variety, and adventure. Acknowledges other readings, however, as a) an allegorical interpretation of China's three major religions, preference being given to Buddhism; b) a depiction of a sociopolitical struggle of people against their oppressors; and c) a good-natured satire against human folly and bureaucratic stupidity.

D46. Lo Chin-t'ang. "Clues Leading to the Discovery of HSI-YU CHI P'ING-HUA." JOURNAL OF ORIENTAL STUDIES 7 (1969), 176-194.

Despite acceptance of certain data now considered questionable (as Wu's authorship and the oral storyteller function of hua-pen), provides an eminently useful analysis of the novel's basic structure, a summary of Hsuan-Tsang's personal history, and an overview of major documents. Names as sources the OLD HISTORY OF T'ANG; Hsuan-tsang's own account as recorded by disciple Pien-chi; a biography of the monk by another disciple, Hui-li; and certain Sung storybooks (hua-pen) and dramas.

Focuses, however, on an ur-collection referred to in several sources and from which excerpts are available, called HSI-YU CHI P'ING HUA. Relates this source to HSI-YU CHI by detailed comparison of the two versions of the wizardry contest between Sun Hsing-che and Po Yen the Magician. Concludes with a diagram tracing the origin and evolution of the story of Hsuan-tsang's famous pilgrimage.

D47. Lu Hsun. A BRIEF HISTORY OF CHINESE FICTION. Trs. Yang Hsien-yi and Gladys Yang. Peking: Foreign Languages Press, 1959. Pages 426-428.

Emphasizes the light-heartedness and humor of a style which makes monsters human and humans monstrous. Disparages didactic and especially religious readings of the novel, proposing instead that "the book was written solely to give pleasure."

D48. Mao Tse-tung. SNOW GLISTENS ON THE GREAT WALL (Mao Tse-tung's poetry). Tr. Ma Wen-yee. Santa Barbara: Santa Barbara Press, 1986.

A complete collection of Mao Tse-tung's poetry, newly translated and annotated and with historical backgrounds provided for individual poems. Reveals Mao's knowledge of and devotion to China's classic novels, especially SAN-KUO-CHIH YEN-I and HSI-YU CHI.

D49. Ota Tatsuo. "A New Study on the Formation of the HSI-YU CHI." ACTA ASIATICA 32 (1977): 96-113.

Follows up Dudbridge's study of the novel's antecedents by condensing eleven articles (by Ota), supplementing findings of the earlier work. Highlights a reputed Southern Sung early version of the story; a Yuan Taoist creation on the same theme edited by Ch'ang-ch'un; a pre-Ming drama, also Taoist, of at least 68 acts; and three Ming variant texts identified respectively as Shih, Yang, and Chu. For specialists in Chinese language.

D50. Plaks, Andrew H. "Allegory in HSI-YU CHI and HUNG-LOU MENG." CHINESE NARRATIVE: CRITICAL AND THEORETICAL ESSAYS. Ed. Andrew H. Plaks. Princeton University Press, 1977. Pages 163-202.

After lengthy review of the nature and history of allegory in the West, concludes that, though no corresponding term exists in traditional Chinese poetics, the practice of allegory is indubitably there; i.e. as a mode of composition rather than a genre per se. Believes that allegory strongly informs much Chinese literature, notably HSI-YU CHI and HUNG-LOU MENG.

Insists that applicability of the term to a work depends upon the author's explicit intent and direction, lacking which some other term must be found: thus SHUI-HU CHUAN cannot be classed as allegory, whereas HSI-YU CHI and HUNG-LOU MENG can, since they explicitly look beyond mimetic surface to philosophical levels of significance.

Differentiates Western from Chinese allegory by world view: the former resting on ontological disjunction (clashing rather than complementary bipolarity), the latter on a conception of a universe with neither beginning nor ending, eschatological nor teleological purpose, "within which all conceivable opposites of sensory and intellectual experience are contained, such that the poles of duality emerge as complementary with the intelligibility of the whole."

Characterizes movement as indispensable to allegory: in the West, goal-oriented and revelation-bound; in China, a shift of elements into larger patterns and cycles of recurrence that, taken as a whole, bear the meaning of the work. Indicates yin/yang and five-elements theories as chief sources of Chinese allegorical organization, and these reducible to the principles of bipolarity (correlative thinking) and multiple periodicity (seasonal or directional considerations). Recommends that both be seen, not as specific formulations requiring completeness of description, but rather as formal relationships of opposites in ceaseless alternation, mutual implication, and overlapping occurrence.

Finds authors' intent signaled by a) suggestive couplets in chapter titles; b) verses at opening, closing, and interspersed positions; c) proverbs and other formulae in dialogue and narration; and d) the actual story. Observes that, as a mode of mimetic narration, a total vision of reality sub specie aeternitatis, allegory offers difficulties involving compromise, uneasiness, and problems ranging from humorous to tragic.

Establishes HSI-YU CHI as an allegory of the mind seeking enlightenment through an abstract journey, endangered by the mind's own propensities to excess, and requiring harmonization with all its sister faculties within the Self represented by Hsuan-tsang. Identifies in the process devices indicating the author's allegorical intent: a) the Heart Sutra with its prajnaparamita wisdom; b) key words often used in introductory, interspersed, and closing positions; c) dialogue and narrative; d) yin/yang, five-elements, and Taoist cinnabar alchemy. Sees all these things conveying, not particularities of a system, but formal relations holding together various terms, each implying all others in the system.

Notes the blending in time of Taoist technique with the ideals of Mahayana or Ch'an salvation and idealist Neo-Confucian self-cultivation as taught by Wang Yang-ming.

D51. Plaks, Andrew H. THE FOUR MASTERWORKS OF THE MING NOVEL: SSU TA CH'I-SHU. Princeton: Princeton University Press, 1987.

See B39.

D52. So, Francis H.K. "Some Rhetorical Conventions of the Verse Sections of HSI-YU CHI." CHINA AND THE WEST: COMPARATIVE LITERATURE STUDIES. Eds. William Tay, Chou Ying-hsiung, and Yuan Heh-hsiang. Hong Kong: Chinese University Press, 1980. Pages 177-194.

Controverting Bishop's complaint about verse in Chinese prose narrative (A21), argues that the technoi pisteis (artistic persuasion) of verse in HSI-YU CHI helps elevate it from mere vernacular novel to masterpiece of multidimensional importance. Demonstrates the work's use of the whole spectrum of Chinese poetry, doggerel included, harmonizing content and form in the colloquial vernacular. In this feat perceives similarity with achievements of Dante and Chaucer, who extended linguistic frontiers of their languages, the one by invention of the dolce stil novo (sweet new style), the other by English adaptation of Machaut's French courtly vernacular.

Differentiates Western dominantly mimetic literary perspective from the more expressive-focused view of Chinese aesthetics. Drawing on Cha Ts'ung's taxonomy of basic hua-pen (Sung prompt-book tales), attributes MONKEY's construction to the sixth and last development: colloquial prose, interspersed with tz'u (irregular verse), shih (regular verse), couplets, and four- and six-character parallel lines of short phrases.

Analyzes the opening poem as an attention-getter suggesting mystical and supernatural, legendary, historical, and human subject matter; affirming a lofty, beautiful, and credible life view; linking the tale with the I CHING (BOOK OF CHANGES) and the SHU CHING (BOOK OF HISTORY), Confucian classics; and, by its language, recognizing the audience as literate but otherwise uneducated.

Presents a second poem, a _fu_, describing Monkey's birthplace (in Latin rhetorical terms: _descriptio_, _pronuntiatio_, _topos_, _exaggeratio_, _dispositio_, _locus amoenus_, _elocutio_, _amplificatio_, _topographia_, _effiguratio_, _conduplicatio_, _ecphrasis_). Sees these devices as panegyric rhetoric preparing for Monkey's first appearance and his status as the novel's hero, and as a statement of geomantic belief in landscape's influence on human destiny.

Offers as a third example another _fu_, an _ecphrasis_ (poetic description of an _objet d'art_ a la Achilles' shield in the ILIAD), serving a) to bring to the fore a hitherto veiled event, b) to show divinity as _deus artifex_; c) to support celestial history, gods' involvement in human affairs and divine destinies bridging Heaven and Earth; and d) the cosmic power of karma--in fine, recapitulating history and intensifying spatial and temporal awareness, the novel's major myth.

Concludes that non-Western literatures share with their Western counterparts basic concern, less with interpretation than with composition and presentation, and that development of artistic universals rests in part on the dimension of rhetoric.

D53. Spence, Jonathan. "The Explorer Who Never Left Home--Arthur Waley." NEW YORK TIMES BOOK REVIEW (October 18, 1970): 32-33.

Reviews with profound appreciation the _tour de force_ that is Arthur Waley's work: translations from the greatest Chinese and Japanese classics by a man (1889-1966) self-taught in Asian languages and innocent of Asian travel. Attributes Waley's phenomenal success to his genius, devotion, and confidence in the power of poetic intuition. Recalls Waley's Bloomsbury associations with Lytton Strachey, E.M. Forster, and Virginia Woolf, and his devotion to the Greek classics, which he often paralleled with the Chinese.

Notes among many Waley translations from the Chinese two volumes of poetry, especially the works of Po-Chui; the ANALECTS of Confucius; the lives of poets Li Po and Yuan Mei: and, above all, the HSI-YU CHI or MONKEY. Praises Ivan Morris' 1970 festchrift of essays honoring Waley by intellectuals, artists, teachers, students, and friends. Concludes with Waley's translation of his favorite Chinese poem, Chang Heng's THE BONES OF CHUANG TZU.

D54. Teele, Roy E. "Arthur Waley." BOOKS ABROAD 43 (1970): 367-368.

Praises Waley's work in poetry and prose, especially his abbreviated version of MONKEY, or JOURNEY TO THE WEST as the more remarkable because Waley was self-taught in the Chinese language, and his style, fresh and lucid, is free from academe.

D55. Waley, Arthur. THE REAL TRIPITAKA AND OTHER PIECES. New York: Macmillan, 1952; Tapei: Mei Ya Publishers, 1972.

A treasury of information, much drawn from the seventh-century account of Hsuan-tsang's travels as remembered by his disciple Hui-li and supplemented by monk Yen-tsung. With some exaggeration and no little dramatic flair, presents the life and career of the Buddhist scholar-saint. Likens Hsuan's epic travels for spiritual ends to those of Aeneas, Arthur, and Cuchulain rather than to those of Marco Polo, Vambery, Augustine, or Aquinas. Follows the monk's geographical route both in leaving China and in penetrating India, emphasizing the relationship with King Harsha and other potentates and monastic debates with Hindu and other partisan religionists.

Attributes to Hsuan the introduction of systematic logic into China, based on famed Indian treatises, notably those dealing with the New Logic of Vasubandhu's disciple Dignaga. Following Hsuan's colorful and exciting return to China, traces his distinguished career as teacher, translator, dialectician, and companion to the great Emperor T'ai Tsung.

Surveys the history of Buddhism in China in this period and the effects on it of the sastras and sutras procured by Hsuan-tsang and translated by him from Sanskrit into Chinese that their wisdom might be accessible to the monks of Ch'ang-an and other strongholds of Buddhist faith.

D56. Wang Jing. THE MYTHOLOGY OF STONE: A STUDY OF THE INTERTEXTUALITY OF ANCIENT CHINA STONELORE AND THREE CLASSIC NOVELS. Amherst: University of Massachusetts, 1985. An unpublished dissertation.

Explores the symbolism of ancient China's stonelore in folk arts and crafts, and then relates these data to the development of stone symbolism in WATER MARGIN, JOURNEY TO THE WEST, and DREAM OF THE RED CHAMBER. Observes the modifications and accretions that accompany the symbol when used as a literary theme.

D57. Wang, John C.Y. "The Cyclical View of Life and Meaning in the Traditional Chinese Novel." IN ETUDES D'HISTOIRE ET DE LITTERATURE CHINOISES OFFERTES AU PROFESSEUR JAROSLAV PRUSEK. Paris: Institut des Hautes Etudes Chinoises, 1976. Pages 275-301.

See A105.

D58. Watters, Thomas, tr. ON YUAN CHWANG'S TRAVELS IN INDIA 629-645 A.D. (As recorded by Pien-chi.) Two volumes. London: 1904-1905.

Gives Hsuan-tsang's own account of the pilgrimage to India as told to his disciple Pien-chi. (A second account by disciple Hui-li is not, so far as we know, available in English translation.)

D59. Wu Tsu-hsiang. "On the PILGRIMAGE TO THE WEST." CHINESE LITERATURE 1 (January 1961): 115-125.

Exemplifies the Marxist tendency to read the classic novels as essentially exposes of feudal corruption and glorification of workers' revolts against the establishment. Describes as tongue-in-cheek condemnation the author's presentation of the three religions, all viewed as vehicles of confused and reactionary upper-class ideas. Interprets the characters' many ordeals as incessant peasant attacks against increasingly oppressive landlords and other power figures. In these clashes, interpreted as bitter satires against gods and saints, sees Monkey's unwilling entrapment in corrupt social and political milieux and his limitations in opposing them.

Insists, nevertheless, on Monkey's superiority to Tripitaka, "the orthodox thought of the ruling class," and to Pigsy, a self-indulgent but good-hearted ally representing small property owners among the peasantry. Analyzes the adventure of the Flaming Mountain (Chapters 59-61) to exemplify the growing wisdom of Monkey, the peasants' heroic representative.

D60. Yang, Winston L.Y., Peter Li, and Nathan K. Mao. "JOURNEY TO THE WEST and FLOWERS IN THE MIRROR." CLASSICAL CHINESE FICTION: A GUIDE TO ITS STUDY AND APPRECIATION. ESSAYS AND BIBLIOGRAPHIES. Boston: G.K. Hall Publishers, 1978. Pages 71-83.

Cites for HSI-YU CHI four possible interpretations: 1) allegorical, relative to the quest for spiritual fulfillment, a kind of PILGRIM'S PROGRESS, though no one of the religions (Taoism, Buddhism, Confucianism) is viewed as free from defect; 2) satire, against social, political, and economic abuses in contemporary affairs; 3) epic, as focusing on heroic deeds of Chinese protagonists but lacking in the hero's withdrawal, return in disguise, and recognition and re-union scenes; and 4) comedy, transcending social, political and economic particulars to look rather at aspects of universal human behavior for entertainment and delight.

Considers the work's limitations to be its overplus of characters, often stereotypical; the repetitiveness of its episodes; and its weak unity. Designates as its strengths wit and humor, fantasy and realism, complex themes and modes of narration, and, most of all, its vivid and subtle characterizations often humanizing gods and demons alike.

D61. Yeh, Alfred Kuang-yao. "The Evolution of a Rebel: An Interpretation of Wu Ch'eng-en's JOURNEY TO THE WEST." FU JEN STUDIES 10 (1976): 19-23.

Identifies SHIH HUA, probably a Sung production, as the earliest extant version of the Pilgrimage story, one which presents Monkey as merely ancillary to central-character Tripitaka, history's holy, intellectual, and brave Hsuan-tsang. In this depiction deviates from Wu Ch'eng-en's sixteenth-century portrayal of the monk as peevish, sanctimonious, and cowardly, a foil to the heroic Monkey.

Divides the latter work into Chapters 1-7, tracing Monkey's origin, his defiance of the Jade Emperor, and final submission to Buddha; Chapters 8-12, presenting Kuan-yin's mission on earth and the reason for Tripitaka's pilgrimage; and Chapters 13-100, detailing the journey to and from India. Sees as hero Monkey, otherwise known as Handsome Monkey King, Sun Wu-k'ang (Aware of Vacuity), Pi Ma Wen (Grand Master of Heavenly Stables), and Great Sage Equal to Heaven--names signifying stages of Monkey's development.

Reviews various readings of the novel as religion, philosophy, politics, good-natured satire, and delightful entertainment. Reflects on Hsia's parallels of Monkey with Western archrebels, notably Faust, with his over-reaching ambition for ultimate knowledge, power, and immortality, and Satan, whose revolt against God appalls no more than Monkey's forays against the Jade Emperor. Links him, most of all, with Prometheus who, in Shelley's poem, triumphs over torture and imprisonment as he wrests from an Old Order a new, idealized, and morally superior world.

D62. Yen, Alsace. "A Technique of Chinese Fiction: Adaptation in the HSI-YU CHI With Focus on Chapter Nine." CHINESE LITERATURE: ESSAYS, ARTS, REVIEWS 1 (1979): 197-213.

Attacks Dudbridge's theory that Chapter Nine of HSI-YU CHI, focusing on Ch'en Kuan-jui, ought to be omitted, as an interpolation with no organic function in the work as a whole (D21). Begins by reviewing the time-honored device of adapting traditional and alien sources for narrative enhancement. Demonstrates the indispensable service of the Ch'en story in establishing the worth, humanity, and divine sanction attributed to Hsuan-tsang in an analogue whose ideas are replayed, not once, but twice in Tripitaka's life.

Recalls a Yuan drama which, though not textually related to the novel, provides a strikingly identical pattern of essential ideas involved in Ch'en's and Hsuan-tsang's stories: prosperity, traveling, attempted murder, return, recognition, life restored, punishment, reunion. Finds such source recasting used to intensify (here, the worthiness of Hsuan-tsang for his mission), multiply (here the application of different phases of the analogue), to dramatize, to stress, and to vary and complicate the plot. An enlightening application of a useful analytic tool.

D63. Yu, Anthony C. "Heroic Verse and Heroic Mission: Dimensions of the Epic in the HSI-YU CHI." JOURNAL OF ASIAN STUDIES 31 (1972): 879-897.

Stresses need for more purely aesthetic and literary appreciation of HSI-YU CHI to complement Ch'ing allegorical readings as Taoist-Buddhist parable; early twentieth-century insistence on historical, authorial, chronological, and textual identifications; and later twentieth-century ideological emphases. Praises Hsia for his attempt, a first, to provide an imaginative and lengthy aesthetic analysis and to establish a poetics for the form, and for his learned comparisons with Western literary works (D33).

Seeks here to interpret the novel as heroic or epic literature. Begins with its plethora of poems, whose varied, vivid, and realistic forms provide both dramatic dialogue furthering the action (a species first perceived in the pien-wen Sung-Yuan manuscripts found in the Tun-huang caves in 1899) and descriptive passages of scenery, battles, and living beings human and non-human. Demonstrates that epic quality radiates from the extraordinary grandeur, energy, and expansiveness of the narrative, its lyric elements being always subordinated to the story line, itself rich with cosmic and comic irony.

In plot construction, remarks the cycle of assault, captivity, and rescue (81 such episodes, nine times nine, a sacred number); and the quest motif, as in GILGAMESH, THE ODYSSEY, and THE AENEID. Above all, argues that the transformation of the noble Tripitaka of history into a weak, pusillanimous, and peevish personality is done 1) to reinforce the idea of mortals' absolute dependence upon supernatural agencies (here externalized in the monk's companions); and 2) to show that the other pilgrims, conversely, acting as divine agents, rely on him for their mission and the occasion for the exercise of their energies.

As another epic element underscores the essentially communal aspects of the Pilgrims' achievements.

D64. Yu, Anthony C. "Narrative Structure and the Problem of Chapter Nine in the HSI-YU CHI." JOURNAL OF ASIAN STUDIES 34 (February 1975): 295-312.

A convincing riposte to Dudbridge's contention that the famous "Ch'en Kuang-jui" chapter is alien in structure and dramatic form to the rest of the novel (D21). Establishes the consonance of this section with the essential features of a popular legend germane to the narrative as a whole and harmonious with its pattern and tone. Reflects the best and most recent scholarship on and interpretation of HYC.

D65. Yu, Anthony C. "On Translating the HSI-YU CHI." THE ART AND PROFESSION OF TRANSLATION. Ed. T.C. Lai. Hong Kong: Hong Kong Translation Society, 1975.

In a paper delivered to the 1975 Asia Foundation Conference on Chinese-English translation, points out practical difficulties encountered in translating the massive HSI-YU CHI. Lists 1) finding in a second language equivalents for the interplay of phonetic and semantic elements in a literary passage, 2) transmitting the meanings of words and passages fraught with esoteric Buddhist and alchemical meanings, 3) projecting relationships founded on yin-yang and five-elements correspondences.

Quoting George Steiner's AFTER BABEL, comments on the fact that a work or passage seemingly untranslatable in one era may--by reason of an access of knowledge and/or experience on the part of the responder--become translatable at another. Because of the author's linguistic virtuosity finds in HYC's rhetoric counterparts to techniques described in classical Western rhetoric, including a) <u>diacope</u>, repetition of a word with one or more words in between, b) <u>anadiplosis</u>, repetition of the last word of a line to begin the next line, and c) <u>epanalepsis</u>, repetition at the end of a line of a word or sound with which it begins. Observes that the problems are most evident in passages of poetry.

Believes that his (Yu's) own purpose to give the most intelligible fidelity to the original may, nevertheless, by reason of his preoccupation with religious and allegorical meanings be vulnerable to a charge of bias. Contends, however, that all translations must be affected by the translator's hermeneutics.

D66. Yu, Anthony C. "Two Literary Examples of Religious Pilgrimage: the COMMEDIA and JOURNEY TO THE WEST." HISTORY OF RELIGIONS 22.3 (February 1983): 202-230.

Interprets JOURNEY TO THE WEST as (like Dante's COMMEDIA) an allegory of the passage from religious and spiritual darkness and deprivation through expiatory and purgatorial ordeals to the height of blessedness. Parallels the rationalist roles of Virgil and Monkey ("the irresistible simian") and the revelatory ones of Beatrice and Kuan-yin (Goddess of Mercy). Explores the nature and history of the pilgrimage as, from the Middle Ages, an important institution, and collates the outer journeys of the two works, vivid in geographical settings and physical confrontations, and inner progressions marking spiritual transformation.

Makes a particular point of the physiological alchemy (transmutation of the base into the noble) constituting, with five-agents cosmology, a major structural device in JOURNEY. Allegorically links these references, rich in Taoist meanings, to the theme of mind-control (Monkey's special province). Sees them as basic, not only to current powerful Neo-Confucian teaching on self-development, but, as well, to the *prajnaparamita* wisdom embodied in the Heart Sutra, central to HYC and to the contemporaneously flourishing Ch'an (Zen) Buddhism.

Concludes that "the readers of both the COMMEDIA and JOURNEY TO THE WEST are fortunate to have in their hands not only marvelously conflated accounts of both journeys but highly entertaining ones, to boot."

CHAPTER FIVE

CHIN P'ING MEI (THE GOLDEN LOTUS)

Liveliest of controversies over the four Ming masterpieces of the novel is that surrounding CHIN P'ING MEI (GOLDEN VASE PLUM or THE GOLDEN LOTUS), named for three of protagonist Hsi-men Ch'ing's six wives. The earliest known reference to this novel is 1592, its earliest known publication 1617. Judgments swing wildly between extreme praise and extreme condemnation of the work's content and form, between pre-1912 political interdiction for subversiveness, and mid-twentieth-century Communist commendation of it as an expose of upper-class and imperial corruption.

Yet even those more literary critics who charge CPM with inconsistencies in point of view, violations of probability, uncontrolled gathering of flimsily related stories, verse gibberish, haphazard realism, and moral and cultural anarchy, even those admit the power of the work. And this power, they concede, resides, not just in sexual explicitness (quantitatively only a small part of the work), but in the whole portrayal of a decadent society nearing dissolution.

The same critics will also admit the pioneer quality of a composition which, for the first time and by the art of a single author (only chapters 53-57 are by a second hand), left aside reliance on historical events real or presumed (as in SAN-KUO-CHIH YEN-I or SHUI-HU CHUAN) and dependence on supernatural fantasy (as in HSI-YU CHI) to focus on realistic portrayals of middle-class men and women struggling for power in a money-mad and sex-obsessed society.

In fact, few deny to CPM the title of China's first novel (in the restricted modern sense of a long, unified, individually and consciously composed prose fiction, with characters recognizable as human beings in a realistic milieu). And beyond this, they will concede the chronological priority of this work to European novels, with the possible exception of DON QUIXOTE (1615), and CPM's rank in time as second only to Murasaki Shikibu's GENJI MONOGATARI (THE TALE OF GENJI), c1010.

Beyond its general and firm identification as a novel boasting (in the opinion of its praisers) a highly unified plot, structural integrity, textual density, extraordinarily vivid and realistic characterization of individuals and of the times, the question arises as to the novel's theme, its statement (if any) about life. Specifically what kind of novel are we dealing with in CHIN P'ING MEI?

Is CPM best described as a novel of moral retribution? Of social and domestic manners? Of psychological realism? A Buddhist/Taoist/Confucian tract on sexual excess? A roman à clef, perhaps, with intent to expose the corruption of the court, using sexual perversion as merely a symbol of larger depravity? Pure pornography? And if one or other genre be named, to what extent do elements of satire, humor, and tragedy enrich and intensify the total effect? These are questions scholars debate in studies listed below.

These analyses, however, go deeper, if possible, that the identifying of form. They search for a basic religious or philosophical dimension orienting the work to some ultimate human value or meaning. For, though CPM purportedly takes place in the last days of the Northern Sung Dynasty (1112-1127), precisely at the time when SHUI-HU CHUAN's Brotherhood of Liang Shan was flourishing, it actually depicts the author's own times--the last half-century of the Ming Dynasty.

Intriguingly, some critics argue for basically Buddhist values in the book; others, for a conservative Confucianism reacting against Ming syncretism, hedonism, and freethinking. Crucial to such judgments are the interpretation of the book's ending, in which, as the wrong-ridden Hui-tsung empire falls, so does the corrupt house of Hsi-men Ch'ing--all its inhabitants dead (often in sordid circumstances) or dispersed among crowds fleeing the Ju-chen (Manchurian) invasions.

Only Hsi-men's first (and legitimate) wife remains, and she, exiled, must observe her teenage son, born on the day of Hsi-men's death years earlier, enter celibate Buddhist monastic life. To Confucianists, for whom a, if not the, supreme moral imperative is the continuance of the family line, such an ending is not salvation; it is tragedy. To Buddhists, of course, it is a realization of principles enunciated in the novel's opening chapter and reiterated throughout the book: the vanity of human wishes, the illusions of the world, the treachery of sexual desire.

Some have speculated that words in the preface to the first (Wan-li) edition attributing the novel to "the scoffing scholar of Lan-ling" link the author's ideas to those of the famous Confucian realist-philosopher Hsun-tse (fl. 298-238 B.C.). Proponent of hardheaded realism, Hsun-tse, like the later, English philosopher Thomas Hobbes (1588-1679), flatly declared human nature evil, all controls artificial, and the movement of moral example ineluctably downward, beginning with the ruler and moving to the lowest classes. If the Lan-ling epithet is substantive and meant to recall Hsun-tse's one-time residence there, it supports a reading of the work as dominantly Confucian (though certainly not of the Mencian kind). Such a reading implies debt not only to Hsun-tse, but also to the TA-HSUEH (THE GREAT LEARNING), a secondary Confucian Classic urging self-cultivation and stressing morality's downward flow from the emperor's example.

Factual knowledge about the author's life might, of course, illuminate speculation as to the book's religious intent, but this help scholars must do without. Besides vague and unsubstantiated conjectures about authorship, nominating, for example, the notoriously eclectic litterateur Wang Shih-chen (1526-1590), folk hero Hsu Wei (1521-1593), and poet-playwright Li K'ai-hsien (1501-1568), nothing of a biography is known to guide religious or philosophical interpretation of the work. Even Yuan Hung-tao (1568-1610), second of the three famous scholar-critic brothers, who in 1592 praised CPM as the equal of SHUI-HU CHUAN and placed both novels on a par with the Classics, did not name the author. Certain identification might have endangered the life of one responsible for a work considered, by the Ming establishment, politically subversive.

Such considerations lead to a closer look at the novel itself, especially at its structure of 100 chapters divided into <u>chuans</u> (10-chapter units, each with a self-contained portion of the story). The first of these, before introducing Hsi-men (whose name means "celebrations at the gate of heaven") and his paramour P'an Chin-lien, discusses the problem of sensuality. The second proceeds to the story of Li P'ing-erh and her relations with Hsi-men, culminating in the birth and, by Chin-lien's machinations, the death of their son.

Halfway through the book Hsi-men acquires from a mysterious foreign monk an aphrodisiac which, ultimately, will cause his death. In watershed Chapters 50-80, the protagonist's worldly and material fortunes continue to rise, even while retribution begins its assault with the deaths of Hsi's infant son and that of the loved P'ing-erh, and with an assortment of inhouse betrayals. Following Hsi-men's gruesome death in Chapter 79, the last two <u>chuans</u> trace the final disintegration of his family and the passage of his estate to a servant, analogous with the passage of Emperor Hui-tsung's rule into Manchurian hands and their establishment of the (ironically named) Chin Dynasty.

Another structural reading sees Chapters 1-10 as introduction; 11-80 as growing degradation, a kind of descent into the archetypal hell; and Chapters 80-100 as regeneration. All these interpretations may be accompanied by binary vertical formations such as cosmic-human, marked by seasonal and festival correspondences; or character-author development and commentary; or domestic-court parallels—or all of these at once.

But if, as Plaks posits, irony is the basic structuring dynamic of the Ming master novels, there must be a sustained and pervasive clash between ideal and real, appearance and reality, anticipation and realization. In this sense the novel emerges as a study contrasting surface meanings of romantic popular songs and dramas set forth in the novel and real-life events transpiring about them. Victoria Cass varies the idea by identifying Hsi-men as an <u>alazon</u> (hubristic character) and his first wife, Wu Yueh-ming, as an <u>eiron</u> (commentator figure).

In any event, almost every discussion of structure includes the roles of yin/yang and five-elements correspondences in providing, not only building elements, but, as well, textual density, i.e. sequential or recurrent patterning. Such devices help explain the difference between Western and Chinese ideas of unity, the one more linear (action focused) and time-concerned, the other more interstitial (relation-focused) and spatial.

The first major analyst of CPM's style was seventeenth-century Chang Chu-p'o. In "twelve introductions, disquisitions, and lists" appended to the so-called C-texts, Chang, according to contemporary critic Ch'en Ssu-hsiang, singlehandedly reversed a hundred years' neglect and misunderstanding of the novel. In "How to Read the CHIN P'ING MEI" Chang stresses the organic unity of the work and the way in which, among other elements, the characters function as parts of a whole.

A major strength, indeed, of CPM is acknowledged to be its characterization. Some complain, to be sure, of a paucity of positive or exemplary personae, yet at least the corrupt characters have a believable mix of virtue and vice. This complexity applies strikingly to the central character, Hsi-men Ch'ing, a typical Ming hustler of the sensationally rising merchant class. His avarice, sensuality, ambition, cruelty, treachery, fraud, and bribery are accompanied by an eerie likability, rising from his cheerfulness in adversity, his unfailing generosity, and his capacity for genuine feeling, as shown at the time of P'ing-erh's death.

Still, there were precedents for male complexity of character: in Ts'ao Ts'ao of SAN-KUO-CHIH YEN-I, for example, with his blend of cruelty and compassion, pragmatism and poetry; and at least in the end of SHUI-HU CHUAN, where Li K'uei and Sung Chiang evince moving, different sides to their characters as they remain faithful to each other unto death. Yet nowhere in novels before CHIN P'ING MEI have scholars found realistic major women characters. In the morally developing Li P'ing-erh and many-sided P'an Chin-lien appear for the first time in the Chinese novel women not unworthy the company of Alisoun the Wife of Bath, or Emma Bovary.

In the matter of style CHIN P'ING MEI is justly famed for its accumulation of realistic detail, domestic and public, so as to win for it the epithet "encyclopedia of

Ming daily life." Wherever money figures—presents, dowries, bribery—every circumstance is included. In domestic affairs the slightest particulars are noted, much of such detail a calculated analogy with bureaucratic life. Even the subtitle, HSI-MEN AND HIS SIX WIVES, is interpreted by some to refer to the six evil ministers of the emperor's court.

Chiefly written in the vernacular, the novel is further marked by lively naturalistic dialogue, usually devoid of flights of imagination or lyrical description, a manner dubbed by adversarial critics "wooden and impersonal." Puns and wordplay abound and, with allusions to and passages from contemporary song and drama, usually function to underscore ironic intent. Blended sarcasm, humor, and pathos thus characterize the tone.

The textual history of CPM, centering on systems referred to as A, B, and C, are complicated and generally of interest only to specialists. The Wan-li or 1617 version, however, is usually considered superior to the Ch'eng-chen (c1628) rendering, with its shortened narrative and diminished verse.

Of the translations, the 1939 Clement Egerton (and subsequent editions, including that of 1972 in which previously Latinized passages are rendered into English), remains the best available. Franz Kuhn's German version is praised by some for a readability fostered by his omission of "tiresome episodes," and Bernard Miall's 1940 recension of the German into English is still available.

The major book-length study of CHIN P'ING MEI is Katherine Carlitz's 1986 THE RHETORIC OF CHIN P'ING MEI, a followup of the author's 1978 THE ROLE OF DRAMA IN CHIN P'ING MEI and of Victoria Cass's 1979 CELEBRATIONS AT THE GATE OF DEATH: SYMBOL AND STRUCTURE IN CHIN P'ING MEI. Other important contributions have been made by Patrick D. Hanan, C.T. Hsia, Paul V. Martinson, Andrew H. Plaks, David Roy (his work on CPM commentator Chang Chu-p'o is indispensable), Peter H. Rushton, and James J. Wrenn.

Translations

E1. THE ADVENTURES OF HSI-MEN CH'ING. New York: The Library of Facetious Lore, 1927.

Privately and anonymously printed in attractive format (750 numbered copies), retells in 18 chapters of simplified English the highlights of the 100-chapter novel. Includes, in the introduction, the famous story of Ming historian Wang Feng-chou's murder of his enemy's son by presenting the titillating book, secretly treated with poison, as a conciliatory gift to the young man who, moistening his fingers to turn the pages, died in convulsions shortly thereafter.

E2. Chai Ch'u and Winberg Chai, eds. and trs. "CHIN P'ING MEI (GOLDEN VASE OF PLUM FLOWERS)." A TREASURY OF CHINESE LITERATURE; A NEW PROSE ANTHOLOGY INCLUDING FICTION AND DRAMA. New York: Appleton-Century, 1965. Pages 235-248.

Dismisses, after identifying, many authorship theories, while pointing up the innovative domestic character of the seventeenth-century 100-chapter Ming novel, as contrasted with its historical and fantastic predecessors. Underscores the tale's moral character as a tragedy of retribution. From its penetrating portrayal of corrupt times presents Chapter One, Hsimen's formation of a Brotherhood to join him in self-indulgence, a takeoff on SHUI-HU CHUAN's opening.

E3. Egerton, Clement. THE GOLDEN LOTUS: A TRANSLATION OF THE CHINESE NOVEL CHIN P'ING MEI. Boston: Routledge and K. Paul, 1972. Two volumes. Earlier editions from New York: Paragon Book Gallery, 1962; London: Routledge, 1939.

Despite its source in a late and inferior version, presents the best translation available in the West. Fifteen years in the making and not purporting to be scholarly, seeks to maintain the "staccato brevity of the original," while in lucid and readable English capturing the spirit of the Chinese narrative. Maintains prose passages largely intact but omits most poems as "gibberish" or "conventional trappings." For a different judgment see E10-12 and E45.

Traces the rise to fortune and later the ruin of a typical merchant family given to extremes of self-indulgence (in this edition uses English for passages previously rendered in Latin). In the introduction denies to the Chinese novel as a whole any "true development of style," a situation attributed to the low prestige of fiction among the learned. Notes, nevertheless, the work's powerful economy in transmitting episodes of detailed ruthlessness, characters of extraordinary complexity, and thematic material working inexorably toward climax and conclusion.

Reviews the story setting in the reign of Sung Emperor Hui-tseng (1100-1126), its authorship, often attributed to Wang Shih-cheng (d. 1590), and prompt censorship meted out to it by the Manchu K'ang-hsi emperor (r. 1662-1722), though about the same time it was translated into the emperor's native language in a version presently considered a literary gem.

E4. Kuhn, Franz, tr. KIN PING MEH, DIE ABEUTEURLICHE GESCHICHTE VON HSI-MEN UND SEINEN SECHS FRAUEN. Leipzig: Insel-Verlag, 1930.

An unchaptered abridgment of considerable interest and easy reading.

E5. Miall, Bernard, tr. CHIN P'ING MEI: THE ADVENTUROUS HISTORY OF HSI-MEN AND HIS SIX WIVES. Intr. Arthur Waley. Two volumes. New York: Putnam, 1940. Reprinted by Capricorn in 1962.

Translates from the Kuhn German version, limited to 47 of the original 100 chapters and lacking many of the mottoes and poems. Provides, in Waley's introduction, the legend of CHIN P'ING MEI's origin in a humble official's desire for vengeance against his father's murderer. Supplements legend with facts about 1) the earliest known references to the work, beginning in 1592; 2) the lacuna between Chapters 53-58 and the inauthentic substitute; 3) the 1687 Manchu interdiction of the work on moral grounds, though subsequently Chang Chu-p'o defended it as the product of filial

CHIN P'ING MEI (THE GOLDEN LOTUS)

piety (a son avenging his father inspired the work); and 4) public demand for the novel, despite censorship continuing until 1912, with surreptitious editions even until the twentieth century often dated 1695.

E6. Miall, Bernard, tr. "Hsi-men and the Gold Lotus." CHINESE WIT AND HUMOR. Ed. George Kao. New York: Sterling Publishing Company, 1974. Pages 126-148.

Suggests that readers of the unexpurgated work may be too busy to look for humor, but that the passage here given is "the keynote passage of the entire book."

E7. Porret, Jean-Pierre, tr. KIN P'ING MEI OU LA MERVEILLEUSE HISTOIRE DE HSI-MEN AVEC SES SIX FEMMES. Traduit du chinois par le Professeur Franz Kuhn. Paris: Guy Le Prat, 1985. (Fourth edition.)

Another recension from the popular German version.

Studies

E8. Bishop, John L. "A Colloquial Short Story in the Novel CHIN P'ING MEI." STUDIES IN CHINESE LITERATURE. Cambridge: Harvard University Press, 1965.

A source and date study accentuating the ingenuity and craftsmanship of CHIN P'ING's author in using a contemporary hsiao-shuo to enrich his tale. Among his stylistic merits lists naturalistic dialogue, accurate domestic detail, and attention to cause-and-effect plotting.

E9. Bryant, Daniel. "Wang Shih-chen." THE INDIANA COMPANION TO TRADITIONAL CHINESE LITERATURE. Eds. William H. Nienhauser, Jr., and others. Bloomington: Indiana University Press, 1986. Pages 1874-1875.

Traces the career of Wang Shih-chen, a literary star of sixteenth-century China, noted for eclectic and prolific production and sometimes associated with the authorship of CHIN P'ING MEI.

E10. Carlitz, Katherine. "Puns and Puzzles in the CHIN P'ING MEI: Chapter 27." T'OUNG PAO: REVUE INTERNATIONALE DE SINOLOGIE 67 (1981): 216-239.

Explicates CHIN P'ING MEI as a satire against persons and institutions repudiating the Confucian ideal of individual self-cultivation for the good of society and for cosmic harmony. Uses linguistic and cultural features of the novel for ironic commentary on the gap between the ideal and the real in both individual and state, as suggested by song and drama allusions, traditional and contemporary, creating structural referents. Sees in puns and other wordplay clustering about clothing, food, musical instruments, weather, celebratory rituals, games, and even the work's title a multileveled code.

Interprets this code to mean that, beyond its literal content, depraved sexuality, with all its attendant ills, symbolizes massive corruption in the political realm. Following the ancient belief that as the ruler so the subject and as the court so the domestic household, casts pervert Hsi-men in the role of emulator of corrupt officials and, within his own household, nauseous model for servants' misbehavior.

Beyond the moral dimension *per se* discerns cosmic laws of what Plaks has called complementary bipolarity (yin/yang) and multiple periodicity (five-elements correspondences). For readers reliant on translation provides insight beyond plot and characterization into the world view of the unknown author, for whom sexuality is but one component and that often symbolic in a comprehensive study of human meaning within social and cosmic milieux.

E11. Carlitz, Katherine. THE RHETORIC OF CHIN P'ING MEI. Bloomington: Indiana University Press, 1986.

Argues that the basic dynamic of CHIN P'ING MEI is Confucianism, specifically as set forth in the secondary classic TA HSUEH (THE GREAT LEARNING), with its emphasis on the ruler's (whether emperor's or householder's) responsibility for the moral character of his constituency and the corollary of his need for self-cultivation. Against Buddhist-Taoist interpretations cites traditional Chinese abhorrence for sterility, loss, and non-involvement in family and state affairs. To this effect remarks use of hundreds of allusions to contemporary fiction and drama and calls attention to the verbal density of the narrative, including puns, puzzles, and revalorization of conventional wisdoms.

Sets forth retribution as a moral marker for ethical offenses originating with the emperor and his court, imitated and played out by Hsi-men and his household, thereafter reenacted in the lower world of servants and other inferiors. Interprets depraved sexuality as a metaphor for general corruption. Analyzes the final two chapters as essentially ironic, a point often missed by general readers and critics alike.

E12. Carlitz, Katherine. THE ROLE OF DRAMA IN THE CHIN P'ING MEI: THE RELATIONSHIP BETWEEN FICTION AND DRAMA AS A GUIDE TO THE VIEWPOINT OF A SIXTEENTH-CENTURY CHINESE NOVEL. Chicago: University of Chicago, 1978. An unpublished dissertation.

An important study confirming Confucianism as the novel's central dynamic by exploration of the ten ch'uan (Southern style) and fifteen tsa-chu (Northern style) dramas figuring prominently in the text. Presents Hsi-men as the epitome of "the last bad ruler," and his household as a microcosm of the current corrupt court, underscoring in both cases the Confucian teaching that as the emperor and the court, so the people and their households.

Insists also on the author's use of the plays, not only to critique the political milieu, but, as well, current dramatic rhetoric. Sees CPM's author as observing in these works an excessive idealism, inadequate to its task of moral instruction, and his calling for a new realism wherein weighty transgression is weightily and finally punished.

Reads familial sexual perversity as symbol, not just of imperial self-indulgence, but also of the political machinations of prime ministers and other court officials. Notes that, contrary to Buddhist readings of

the novel, the retirement of Hsi-men's last surviving
son into a monastery (in the last, the 100th chapter)
does not bespeak hope and new, healthier directions.
Judges the ending, rather, as an appalling statement
of a family's irretrievable fall, sterility, and failure to live on, a Confucian tragedy paralleled by the
concurrent loss of half a kingdom to the declining
Sung empire.

Finally, despite the work's ostensible Sung milieu,
identifies Ming society as the book's real subject,
and a known group of intellectuals (writers, collec-
tors, editors, publishers), eager for renewed social
authenticity and sincerity, as a target audience.
Besides extensive bibliography of primary and secondary sources, includes an invaluable summary of every
10 chapters, an arrangement indicated by crises occurring within those units.

E13. Cass, Victoria Baldwin. CELEBRATIONS AT THE GATE OF
DEATH: SYMBOL AND STRUCTURE IN CHIN P'ING MEI.
University of California, 1979. An unpublished
dissertation.

Taking its cue from the literal meaning of protagonist
Hsi-men Ch'ing's name (celebrations at the gate of
death), treats the novel as a version of Frye's and
Eliade's archetypal journey to death (hell) and re-
birth into life. Or, alternatively, as Propp's
sequence of settings as plot, since in this story-form
characters' functions remain the same from beginning
to end.

Sees Chapters 1-80, dominated by P'an Chin-lien (representing courtship) and Li P'ing-erh (representing consummation), as the progress of corruption--in tragic
modality; and Chapters 81-100, dominated by Ch'un Mei,
as the start of regeneration--in contrasting comic
vein.

Analyzes characters for archetypes, shadow players
(images or versions of a main character), and comic
inversions. Seeks in settings and plot thematic
devices integrating the narrative, exemplified in an
elaborate dissection of the climactic Lantern Festival

in which Hsi-men dies. Confirms the description of the novel as an encyclopedia of Ming daily life.

Evaluates the work as essentially amoral, concerned only with truthful rendering. Omits all reference to Confucianism, barely mentions Taoism, and spares but a paragraph or two to Buddhism. In these aspects contrasts interestingly with the Carlitz study of approximately the same date, projecting the essentially Confucian orientation of CHIN P'ING MEI (E11).

E14. Cass, Victoria Baldwin. "Comparative Essay on Two Novels: CHIN P'ING MEI and ADOLPHE." PHI THETA PAPERS 14 (1977): 20-40.

Tests Frye's theory of tragedy as protagonist isolation from society by self-deception about his value and importance, and, as drama, involving an _alazon_ (a hubris-ridden character) and an _eiron_ (a commentator, a contrasting, socially-integrated persona). Proposes, contrary to Hsia's judgment (E28), that the first 80 and last 20 chapters of CHIN P'ING MEI are not disjointed, but finely integrated, the latter's acceleration reflecting the ominous rapidity of Hsi-men's ascent in every life category except self-awareness. Sees Hsi-men's self-deception echoed in the conduct of P'an Chin-lien (Golden Lotus). In Wu Yueh-niang (Moon Lady), the protagonist's first wife, however, identifies the _eiron_ who, in humiliation and rejection, learns wisdom, accepting human limitations and mortality and by this attitude integrating herself into the true social order.

Despite dramatically different setting, plot, and cast of characters, parallels the Chinese novel with Benjamin Constant's 1816 ADOLPHE, whose lead character, an _alazon_, cultivates this peculiarity, that as diarist he becomes his own judgmental _alter ego_, his own _eiron_, even as Ellenore, his lover, personifies his self-serving vanity.

E15. Cass, Victoria Baldwin. "Revels of a Gaudy Night." CHINESE LITERATURE: ESSAYS, ARTICLES, REVIEWS 4.2 (July 1982): 213-231.

Examines the relation of the Lantern Festival and its imagery--springtime, crowds, lights--to the central theme, construed as the archetypal descent into hell before regeneration. For study of the Lantern Festival in HUNG-LOU MENG see G24.

E16. Chang Su-lee. "Review of CHIN P'ING MEI tr. by Bernard Miall." ASIATIC REVIEW 36 (1940): 616-618.

A mere rehearsal of CPM's plot with no understanding of the insight, appreciation, and even entree into a culture possible through excellent translations, especially of prose fiction.

E17. Chi Ch'iu-lang. "'Fair Needs Foul': Moral Ambiguity in CHIN P'ING MEI." TAMKANG REVIEW 13 (Fall 1982): 71-86.

Seeks to resolve the controversy as to CHIN P'ING MEI's identity, whether a literarily worthless salacious work or a great expose whose explicit sex functions organically within a healthy whole.

Tries to understand the problem in terms of a) Ming intellectual trends, including the challenge to traditional views and Neo-Confucian Wang Yang-ming's focus on individual self-cultivation as means to sagehood, b) point of view, whether judgmental or objective slice-of-life perspective, and c) the author's dual commitment to the irrational, passionate self and Confucian-Buddhist repression of excess; and to a typically Chinese affirmation of life in all its squalor and glory as well as to the self with its thirst for individual fulfillment and drive toward self-destruction.

Contrasts the undifferentiated Chinese view with the more explicitly moral stance of D.H. Lawrence, who emphasized sexuality as a mode of expressing the instinctual and phallic life linking humans to the cosmos and so countering modern civilization's trend toward rationalist mechanization. Notes, further, that Lawrence's lyricism, explications of inner feeling, and omniscience dramatically differ from the panoramic, dramatic presentations of the Chinese author who, by selection of details and skillful manipulation of dialogue, probes with equal power into human dynamics. Attributes CPM's moral ambiguity, further, to the relative lack of exemplary characters and to the parody of the heroic mode of SHUI-HU CHUAN from which its plot was taken.

Concludes by warning that critics with a romantic view of human nature will be turned off by CHIN P'ING MEI's ruthless realism. Recalls that many eminent literary thinkers condemned as mere filth Swift's portrayal of yahoos, while ignoring the compassion that renders GULLIVER'S TRAVELS moral--and such critics will view CPM as only pornography. Believes that another group, however, will pronounce the work great in content and structure as being, not only a novel of manners of sixteenth/seventeenth-century China, but also a profound criticism of life in general, and will accept it unhesitatingly in all its depravity and nobility.

E18. Fastenau, Frauke. DIE FIGUREN DES CHIN P'ING MEI UND DES YU HUAN CHI: VERSUCH EINE THEORIE DES CHINESISCHEN SITTENROMANS. Munshen: Ludwig Maxmilian Universitat, 1971.

Analyzes major and minor characterizations and episodes at two levels--what the characters think and what the author thinks--so as to show YU HUAN CHI (THE JADE NECKLACE) as a significant source in the development of CHIN P'ING MEI as a novel of manners. An item (Fastenau) unaccountably missing from the Carlitz bibliography (E11), though the German study extensively uses the play as an important rhetorical referent.

E19. Feuerwerker, Yi-tse Mei. "The Chinese Novel." APPROACHES TO THE ORIENTAL CLASSICS. Ed. William Theodore De Bary. New York: Columbia University Press, 1959. Pages 171-185.

In view of the amount and explicitness of pornographic content, questions CHIN P'ING MEI's ultimate greatness. Likens it to HUNG-LOU MENG in depiction of actual individuals socially involved in real situations and settings. Finds that CPM's "good" characters are presented as stupid and/or ineffectual and that deep pessimism, even perhaps fatalism or cynicism, diminishes the narrative's final worth.

E20. Fitzgerald, C.P. "The Chinese Novel as a Subversive Force." MEANJIN QUARTERLY 10 (Spring 1951): 259-266.

Declares CHIN P'ING MEI a novel of satire in which despicable domestic characters double for corrupt and decadent public officials and courtly personages. Connects the fall of Hsi-men's family to the concurrent Sung-Dynasty fall. Observes that the analogue holds good as well for the author's Ming Dynasty which, less than a century after the novel's composition, fell to the Manchu regime.

E21. Giles, Herbert A. A HISTORY OF CHINESE LITERATURE. New York: Grove Press, 1923. Page 309.

Calls CHIN P'ING MEI a "marvelous work," with scholar-statesman Wang Shih-chen (1526-1593) as putative author. Identifies it as a seventeenth-century composition covertly satirizing the morals of the K'ang-hsi emperor's court (r. 1662-1722). Describes its style as simple, easy, and close to Peking colloquial; its content as "objectionable," so as to require a translator "with the nerve of a Burton."

E22. Gulik, Robert H. Van. SEXUAL LIFE IN ANCIENT CHINA: A PRELIMINARY SURVEY OF CHINESE SEX AND SOCIETY FROM ABOUT 1500 B.C. TILL A.D. 1644. Leiden: E.J. Brill Publishers, 1974. (First published in 1961.)

Handsomely bound, illustrated, and printed (with Latinized passages) as supplement to the author's 1951 EROTIC COLOUR PRINTS OF THE MING PERIOD. Devotes eight pages _passim_ to CHIN P'ING MEI.

E23. Hanan, Patrick D. "The Development of Fiction and Drama." THE LEGACY OF CHINA. Ed. Raymond Dawson. London: Clarendon Press, 1964. Pages 132-134.

Considers late sixteenth-century CHIN P'ING MEI (THE GOLDEN LOTUS) China's first true novel because of its realistic middle-class characters, merchants and artisans, operating against a background of dramatic social change and conflict, presented in chiefly the vernacular language. Observes the novel's advance in these respects from the heroic patterns of SAN-KUO-CHIH YEN-I and SHUI-HU CHUAN and the mystical supernaturalism of HSI-YU CHI. Remarks, also, that the novel's compositional mode advances from the anecdote-compiling of previous works to the individual extension and development of a short narrative from SHUI-HU's Chapters Four and Five, even while retaining conventions from popular stories, dramas, and songs.

Defends erotic detail as integral to the author's view of the world: an arena where social warfare rages between competitors for power and status in a money-crazed world increasingly dominated by the merchant class and observed by publishers newly aware of increased demand for vernacular literature. Notes the powerful influence of the novel in the last 350 years.

E24. Hanan, Patrick D. "A Landmark of the Chinese Novel." THE FAR EAST: CHINA AND JAPAN. Toronto: University of Toronto Press, 1961.

Denies that CHIN P'ING MEI's extraordinary significance is due to a) its one-man authorship and its lesser dependence on sources; b) its greater fidelity to details of ordinary life and lower-class people; c) its shift from melodramatic incident or plot to characterization, especially of women (here seen for the first time as highly complex and believable), reflecting sixteenth-century woman-dominated popular songs; d) its extreme naturalness of language and relative freedom from the heroic flights of earlier novels; e) its erotic content and style; or f) its expose of social ills.

Proposes, instead, that the distinction of the novel arises from its central content: male striving for status in the business and public worlds by accumulation and manipulation of money; and female striving for it in the household by psychological manipulation and sexual politics. Cites the novel's massive detail regarding money and prices, marital dowries, and bribery as a means of escaping punishment and procuring public office and honor. Relates these matters to the rise of Hsi-men Ch'ing, typical of the meteoric ascent of many hustling Ming merchants from status as barely literate shopkeepers to that of associates of the learned and prestigious.

Examines speech patterns, dialogue, and dress as indices of social caste in a Ming society now acknowledging the merchant class's "spectacular rise to wealth and influence." Concludes that, though "comparison between unrelated literatures is most often a blind alley, useful for orientating oneself, but not worth pursuing to any great degree," CPM may be an exception, as, in Lionel Trilling's concept, essentially concerned with social change and with offering a cross-section of its milieu.

E25. Hanan, Patrick D. "Sources of the CHIN P'ING MEI." ASIA MAJOR (New Series) 10 (1963): 23-67.

With textual evidence, proposes seven sources used by CHIN P'ING MEI's unknown author and examines the influence of each: 1) the novel SHUI-HU CHUAN, 2) the vernacular short story, especially the crime-case story, 3) the erotic short story in literary Chinese, 4) histories of the Sung period and its 5) drama, 6) popular songs, and 7) chantefables.

Declares source-study both critically important and practical in understanding a novel offering, perhaps, China's first example of one man's imagination shaping a great work. Sees the influence of the sources as pervasive, broad (drawing on the whole spectrum of Ming literature)--and often inadequate. Considers this inadequacy as challenging the author's originality, especially in characterization, where, nevertheless, he draws on the methodology of chantefable, song, and drama to achieve revolutionary change in the novel form.

E26. Hanan, Patrick D. "The Text of the CHIN P'ING MEI." ASIA MAJOR (New Series) 9 (1952): 1-57.

Focuses on three systems (A,B,C) of extant editions, establishing the A system as an original, B as an abridgement; and C as differing chiefly in preface, illustration, and annotation. Describes each system

in detail, indicating present text locations. For
discussion of supplied, altered, and missing texts,
examines narrative inconsistencies and linguistic cues.
Besides extant printed editions, discusses others,
thought to be lost, and available manuscripts.

E27. Hightower, James R. TOPICS IN CHINESE LITERATURE.
Cambridge: Harvard University Press, 1965. Page
105.

Defends the actually small pornographic content of
CHIN P'ING MEI as functional within a profoundly moral
context. Sees the work not only as the first novel of
everyday life divorced from historical and legendary
substance, but also as the first to present convincing
women characters. Calls the style wooden and impersonal.

E28. Hsia, C.T. "CHIN P'ING MEI." THE CLASSIC CHINESE
NOVEL. New York: Columbia University Press, 1968.
Pages 165-202.

Denies greatness to the powerful Ming narrative on
grounds of excessive and irrelevant interpolation,
carelessness of detail, sardonic jocularity straining
realistic credibility, cultural anarchy, and contradictory moral and religious assumptions. (See E37, E44,
and E45.) Accepts, nevertheless, the believable complexity of much of this devastating portrayal of human
depravity, never totally devoid of the possibility of
change or the emergence of redemptive love.

E29. Hung Ming-shui. YUAN HUNG-TAO AND THE LATE MING LITER-
ARY AND INTELLECTUAL MOVEMENT. Madison: University
of Wisconsin, 1974. An unpublished dissertation.

A biographical study of Yuan Hung-tao (1568-1610), the
second oldest and most famous of the three sixteenth-
seventeenth-century Yuan brothers, noted for scholarship, poetry, and public service. Recalls Yuan's critical acuity in being the first (known) scholar to
praise CHIN P'ING MEI, proclaiming it in 1606, four
years before its first known printing, a classic equal
to SHUI-HU CHUAN. Provides correspondence and diary

entries valuable to textual as well as to formalist critics.

E30. Kaltenmark, Odile. CHINESE LITERATURE. Tr. Anne-Marie Geoghegan. New York: Walker and Company, 1964 (revision of the 1948 original). Page 118.

Tags CHIN P'ING MEI "licentious and wild," exceeding in these qualities modern Europe's naturalism, yet sees in its crude account of corrupt officials unparalleled realism.

E31. Lai Ming. A HISTORY OF CHINESE LITERATURE. New York: Capricorn Books, 1966. Pages 307-323.

Regards CHIN P'ING MEI as the best Ming novel because of its original creation by one author of a story about contemporary realistic everyday domestic life.

E32. Levy, Andre. "About the Date of the First Edition of the CHIN P'ING MEI." CHINESE LITERATURE: ESSAYS, ARTICLES, REVIEWS 1 (1979): 43-47.

Takes issue with Hanan's speculation about the probability of a lost first-printing of CHIN P'ING MEI in 1610 or 1611, some years before the established printed edition with a preface dated 1617. See E26.

E33. Levy, Howard S. THE HISTORY OF A CURIOUS EROTIC CUSTOM. New York: Walton Rawls Company, 1966.

Approaches the subject of footbinding as one striking example among many of the strange things women of all cultures do to make themselves attractive to men. Devotes one page to the implications for CHIN P'ING MEI: mainly that the abuse, begun and brought to its height in tenth and eleventh centuries, served the double purpose of male erotic excitation and political control.

E34. Liao Chaoyang. "THREE READINGS IN JINPINGMEI." CHINESE LITERATURE: ESSAYS, ARTICLES, REVIEWS 6. 1-2 (July 1984): 77-99.

E35. Liu Wu-chi. "Great Novels by Obscure Writers." AN INTRODUCTION TO CHINESE LITERATURE. Bloomington: Indiana University Press, 1966. Pages 228-246.

Spurns the novel's "unabashed, flagrant pornography," deeming it a major obstacle to the book's acceptance as a masterpiece, but acknowledges the power of its scathing expose of a decadent society. In this sense, apart from "the moral issue," declares it one of China's greatest novels. Notes the amazing realism of the characterizations, executed with blended sarcasm, humor, and pathos.

E36. Lu Hsun. A BRIEF HISTORY OF CHINESE FICTION. Trs. Yang Hsien-yi and Gladys Yang. Peking: Foreign Languages Press, 1959. Pages 232-239. From the author's lecture notes, early publications, and revisions of the 1920s.

Identifies CHIN P'ING MEI as an extraordinarily truthful and penetrating, albeit harsh and bitter, novel of manners about sixteenth-century Chinese society. Notes that the cult of aphrodisiacs reflects widespread beliefs and practices of the time.

E37. Martinson, Paul V. "The CHIN P'ING MEI as Wisdom Literature: A Methodological Essay." MING STUDIES 5 (Fall 1977): 44-56.

Seeking to educe from literature its religious implications, proposes a methodology based on four premises: 1) that, like religion, a literary work rests on a unified world perspective; 2) that descriptive and evaluative analyses must be differentiated; 3) that precision in delineating the critical referent is required; and 4) that the general hermeneutic, differentiated as to meaning and significance, is to be preferred to the local.

Applies the formula to CHIN P'ING MEI, declaring untenable Hsia's description of it as ideologically incoherent and structurally chaotic (E28). Finds binding elements 1) in four religious groupings (Buddhist tales and Taoist rites of passage, magic, and fortunetelling); 2) in motifs of birthdays and promotions;

3) in <u>pao</u>, the principle of reciprocity (giving, receiving, repaying); 4) in the linking of Buddhist narratives of passion and illegitimacy; 5) in Taoist rituals emphasizing yin/yang transformations, basic to the story; and 6) in the Confucian vision of humankind as passionate, social, and moral.

Perceives overarching Buddhist compassion as the finally unifying value, rendering the work hopeful as well as human.

E38. Martinson, Paul V. PAO ORDER AND REDEMPTION: PERSPECTIVES ON CHINESE RELIGION AND SOCIETY BASED ON A STUDY OF THE "CHIN P'ING MEI." Chicago: University of Chicago, 1973. An unpublished dissertation.

Examines CHIN P'ING MEI as vehicle of the religious concept of redemption effected in an order governed by the principle of <u>pao</u>, reciprocity (give-take-repay). First reviews studies of the work as erotic titillation, political satire, Buddhist morality (as in Hsia [E28] and Wu Han), and Confucian filial-revenge composition (as reported in Chang Chu-p'o's late seventeenth-century commentary). Identifies <u>pao</u> (reciprocity) as the central dynamic of Chinese society and religion, construable in both Confucian and Taoist systems, and as a literary technique illuminating the network of social obligations and the role of Eros therein. Probes rituals centered on both living and dead for their significance relative to <u>pao</u> and to associated ideas of retribution, fate, and the gods.

Concludes that redemption, whether in Islam, Christianity, Confucianism, or Buddhism, means arriving at the state of being unobliged, without debt, unowing within the moral community; that is, of achieving total freedom and ultimate harmony by the complete coordination of self with a complex universe.

E39. McMahon, Robert Keith. THE GAP IN THE WALL: CONTAINMENT AND ABANDON IN SEVENTEENTH-CENTURY CHINESE FICTION. Princeton: Princeton University, 1984. An unpublished dissertation.

Explores the social and political subversiveness of Ming fiction, drawing on short stories and novels, among them CHIN P'ING MEI. Shows how the latter's obscenity and eroticism attack excessive restraints and regulations of the time.

E40. Ono Shinobu. "CHIN P'ING MEI: A Critical Study." ACTA ASIATICA 5 (1963): 76-89.

A lucid summary of the earliest references to CHIN P'ING MEI and "the six main (earliest) editions," locations of extant early copies, and their relations to each other and to the source book SHUI-HU CHUAN. Follows the shift of critical status from "a work of comical stories from the street" to "an attack on the conditions of the times," not the purported Sung times, but the author's own Wan-Li Period (1572-1620) of the late Ming Dynasty. Mentions twentieth-century and specifically Communist evaluations, which mix praise for the novel's expose of corruption among the wealthy and blame for its sexual excess.

E41. Plaks, Andrew H. THE FOUR MASTERWORKS OF THE MING NOVEL: SSU TA CH'I-SHU. Princeton: Princeton University Press, 1987.

A major study, unavailable for review at this writing. See B39 and C48.

E42. Plaks, Andrew H. "SHUI-HU CHUAN and the Sixteenth-century Novel Form: An Interpretive Reappraisal." CHINESE LITERATURE: ESSAYS, ARTICLES, REVIEWS 21 (January 1980): 3-53.

Attributes common characteristics to the four master novels of the Ming Dynasty: 1) conscious attention to structural design; 2) controlled manipulation of narrative detail, including the interweaving of recurrent figures (textual density) and finely tuned rhetoric; and 3) a fundamentally ironic revision of popular source materials.

Traces CPM's fidelity to the pattern of a) the 100-chapter work, divided into chuans of five or ten chapters each; b) an introductory chuan placing the story in a cosmic context and announcing certain ethical and/or metaphysical principles central to the story;

c) a gradual gathering of the main characters through the first two-thirds or three-quarters of the novel and their exertions brought to a climax; d) the gradual extinction and/or dispersion of the characters; and e) a closing, aesthetically contrived to echo the opening and often pointing toward a sense of futility or emptiness.

In line with Neo-Confucian teaching based on the Four Classics, especially the TA-HSUEH (THE GREAT LEARNING), underscores the novel's dramatization of the book's central teaching that "as the emperor so the people; as the empire so the household."

E43. Roy, David T. "Chang Chu-p'o's Commentary on the CHIN P'ING MEI." CHINESE NARRATIVE: CRITICAL AND THEORETICAL ESSAYS. Ed. Andrew H. Plaks. Princeton: Princeton University Press, 1978.

Strikingly elucidates the achievement and influence of the seventeenth-century critic who, with contemporary Chin Sheng-t'an (of SHUI-HU CHUAN) and eighteenth-century Chih-yen Chai (of HUNG-LOU MENG) forms a triad of significant literary theorist-critics in traditional China. Adverts to Chang's rejection of authorial and roman-à-clef approaches in favor of strictly literary analyses designed to explore the work's technical achievement and so enlighten other creative writers.

From the prolegomenon to the commentary proper, "How to Read the CHIN P'ING MEI," quotes 11 remarkable passages elucidating the organic unity of the work and the way in which each detail of language, incident, and situation functions within the whole. As constituent elements notes words, names, puns, metaphors, symbols, motifs, themes, poems, songs, jokes, dramatic performances, dialogue, characters, foils, settings, situations, episodes, chapters, sub-plots, and the plot as a whole.

As functions, lists introduction, preparation, prefiguration, prediction, revelation, development, transition, summation, conclusion, characterization, and commentary. As integrating devices, suggests treatment of time, spatial and temporal distribution of characters, juxtaposition or interweaving of parallel or contrasting chapter episodes, dovetailing between individual episodes, incremental repetition of significantly correlated motifs, situations, or episodes, and distribution of contrasting motifs in patterns of periodic alternation.

Remarks Chang's purpose of defending author and work against undeserved calumnies, of illuminating the work's value, and of contributing to literary theory. Stresses the substantial debt of HUNG-LOU MENG, not only to CHIN P'ING MEI, but especially and strikingly to the Chang commentary, the most illuminating critical analysis in depth of any Chinese fiction known to the author and the closest thing we have to a poetics of the Chinese novel. Wishes Chang to be accorded a high place in the history of Chinese literary criticism.

E44. Rushton, Peter Halliday. THE NARRATIVE FORM OF "CHIN P'ING MEI." Stanford: Stanford University, 1979. An unpublished dissertation.

Another rebuttal of Hsia's judgment on CHIN P'ING MEI as a disappointing pornographic novel, marred by digressive and ingeniously placed songs, jokes, and tales Buddhist and mundane; a frequent unseemly mockery and facetiousness; haphazard realism; and an ambivalent religious and moral stance, despite alleged devotion to Buddhist karmic theory (E28). Defends the work on almost every score, attributing to its critic an exclusively Western point of view, especially as regards structure.

Substitutes for beginning-middle-end a bi-level design involving a) cosmic retribution for all morally reprehensible human actions, and b) respect for things as they are at the sheerly human level. Observes the development of this bivalent pattern in a calendrical unfolding of events, including significant seasonal festivities. Notes that particularized and ritual behaviors demand integration, failing which tragedy occurs.

Demonstrates a second organizing principle in shifting equilibria between members of the society, with moments of balance yielding in a kind of chordlike progression to disintegration, at the nadir of which matters return to harmony. Analyzes each major character with depth and precision.

Finally, explores the charge of uninhibited pornography that has shadowed the work, concluding with an appeal to the Neo-Confucian Wang Yang-ming and his school of Mind or Intuition that such an effect depends wholly on individual reader-response: What we see depends on how we think and what we have at heart, in short on who we, as individuals, are.

E45. Satyendra, Indira. "Chapter-opening Mottoes in CHIN P'ING MEI and Scott's THE HEART OF MIDLOTHIAN." An unpublished paper delivered at the 1986 national conference of the College English Association.

Rejects Hsia's suggestions (E28) that the novel would benefit from considerable abridgment, possibly involving elimination of extra-narrative poems, songs, quotations, and chapter-heading mottoes. Argues that since these elements constitute an integral part of the author's rhetoric, damage to the work would ensue. Cites equivalent examples from Western novel literature, especially the works of Walter Scott.

E46. Tay, C.N. "Yuan Hung-tao." Eds. L. Carrington Goodrich and Chaoying Fang. DICTIONARY OF MING BIOGRAPHY 1368-1644. Two volumes. New York: Columbia University Press, 1976. II: 1635-1638.

Reviews the life and career of the second of the three famous Yuan brothers of Kung-an, Hung-tao (1568-1610), who pronounced SHUI-HU CHUAN and CHIN P'ING MEI of equal value with China's ancient classics.

E47. Wang, John C.Y. "The Cyclical View of Life and Meaning in the Traditional Chinese Novel." In ETUDES D'HISTOIRE ET DE LITTERATURE CHINOISES OFFERTES AU PROFESSEUR JAROSLAV PRUSEK. Paris: Institut des Hautes Etudes, 1976. Pages 275-301.

See A105.

E48. Wrenn, James J. A TEXTUAL METHOD AND ITS APPLICATION TO THE TEXTS OF THE CHIN P'ING MEI. New Haven: Yale University, 1964. An unpublished dissertation.

A technical and specialized study establishing 1582 as the earliest and 1596 as the latest date for the completion of CHIN P'ING MEI. Uses three major text-systems (A,B, and C) and two other text-systems known about but lost, for an analysis based on Chinese particles.

E49. Wrenn, James J. "Textual Method in Chinese With Illustrative Examples." T'IEN HSUI MONTHLY (New Series) 6 (1967): 150-199.

E50. Yang, Robert Yi. THE MOON AND THE LEATHER SACK: PARODY IN JIN PING MEI AND JOUPUTUAN. Berkeley: University of California, 1982. An unpublished dissertation.

Articulates the relation of romance, satire, and parody, choosing the last as the essential form of JOUPUTUAN (PRAYER MAT OF FLESH), second to JIN PING MEI as China's most famous erotic novel. Using Apuleius's GOLDEN ASS and Fielding's JOSEPH ANDREWS as touchstones, distinguishes the satiric novel, as JU-LIN WAI-SHIH, from its sister form of parody. Argues that the parodic PRAYER MAT OF FLESH was written 1) to subvert <u>cai-zi jia-ren</u> (handsome scholar-and-beautiful maiden) romance, and 2) to debunk the erotic mode, specifically as it appears in JIN PING MEI, in both its realistic and symbolic dimensions.

E51. Yang, Winston L.Y., Peter Li, and Nathan K. Mao. "CHIN P'ING MEI and PRAYER MAT OF FLESH." CLASSICAL CHINESE FICTION: A GUIDE TO ITS STUDY AND APPRECIATION. ESSAYS AND BIBLIOGRAPHIES. Boston: G.K. Hall Publishers, 1978. Pages 53-69.

Perceives CHIN P'ING MEI (1582-1596) as the first genuine Chinese novel, the first Chinese novel of manners, and the first to treat women characters adequately. Lists as sources Sung vernacular tales such as crime-case stories, literary erotica, histories, plays, popular songs, and <u>chantefables</u>, with their skillful integration of characters and events. Traces CPM's textual history, emphasizing the late seventeenth-century version, with Chang Chu-p'o's commentary and his essay on "How to Read CHIN P'ING MEI." Notes the novel's powerful presentation of Ming society, obsessed with money and status and marked by social mobility, especially a rising merchant class.

In the seeming contradiction between apparently approved erotic passages and rigid charges of immorality immediately following them, notes some critics' bafflement. Concludes that the author's apparent sympathy with sexual need and frustration rests merely on literary borrowings intended to be read as irony, that orthodox Confucianism in fact governs the narrative.

Makes a strong case for rounded characterization, especially in Chin-lien (Golden Lotus)--presented not merely as unfaithful, ruthless, and licentious, but also as sensitive, lonely, troubled, and at times warmhearted; and in protagonist Hsi-men, not merely a vicious and heartless rake, but also at times a sympathetic, generous, and understanding man, capable of profound grief. Includes an excellent plot summary.

E52. Yoshida-Krafft, Barbara. "Wang Shih-chen." DICTIONARY OF MING BIOGRAPHY 1368-1644. Eds. L. Carrington Goodrich and Chaoying Fang. Two volumes. New York: Columbia University Press, 1976. II: 1399-1405.

Refers to "the famous anecdote that he [Wang Shih-chen 1526-1590] authored CHIN P'ING MEI." Attributes such a tale to the extraordinary intellectual, literary, and official achievements of Wang, a devoted Confucian classicist who earnestly studied Buddhism and Taoism. Sees as his highest accomplishment the proclamation that [imaginative] literature is the highest human accomplishment, a dictum encouraging to novelists and dramatists in times of literati persecution.

CHAPTER SIX

JU-LIN WAI-SHIH (UNOFFICIAL HISTORY OF THE LITERATI, or
THE SCHOLARS)

What the unknown author of CHIN P'ING MEI, that "encyclopedia of Ming times," did for the sixteenth century, Wu Ching-Tzu (1701-1754) did for Ch'ing China two hundred years later. That is to say, the eighteenth-century novel JU-LIN WAI-SHIH (UNOFFICIAL HISTORY OF THE LITERATI, or THE SCHOLARS) goes far beyond the presentation of would-be and real scholars and officials. It presents, as well, peasants, shopkeepers, artisans, craftsmen, merchants, actors, bankers, prostitutes, bailiffs, pimps and imposters, saints, and confidence men—in fine, the real-life world, including "a gallery of Chinese womanhood."

More than one critic regrets that this work (completed about 1750 and first published in 1768 and 1779, the first extant edition being 1803) is thought of chiefly as an attack on the examination system, revised and "simplified" in Ming times and thereafter "written in stone" until 1912. In fact, as a comedy of manners the novel satirizes many social evils, with emphasis not only on the evils of bureaucratic testing, but, as well, on discriminations against women and on superstitions derived, ostensibly, from religion and given to futile, revolting, and dehumanizing practices.

As to the examination system, JU-LIN decries it for encouraging rote memory, uncritical thinking, stereotyped writing, false learning, and hypocrisy, not to speak of graver sins of nepotism, graft, favoritism, disloyalty, meanness, and an ambition deleterious to the most sacred duties of family and public life. Thus the ranks of future leaders of the nation are, in the eyes of Wu Ching-tzu and others, poisoned at the root by the obsession with gaining the <u>chin-</u>

shih, the highest examination award, and so winning place in
the bureaucracy and thereafter fame, status, and wealth.

The novel, indeed, raises the perennial question
(cogently argued by John Henry Newman [1801-1890] in his
1873 IDEA OF A UNIVERSITY) as to whether learning is to be
pursued for its own sake or for the rewards of office and
other forms of self-aggrandisement. Wu's answer (concurring
with Newman's) appears in his first chapter, a kind of prologue detailing the career of a fictitious Yuan-dynasty
sage, Wang Mien. This saintly scholar scorned the examinations and, though besought by high authorities, refused
public office. Withdrawn thus from official life, he pursued virtue and learning in an obscure village, undistracted
and uncorrupted by academic competition.

Wang's justification for his way of life, possibly
including his celibacy, lay in the Confucian teaching that
in times of civic peace and health a scholar ought to seek
and carry out the duties of public office. In times of
national corruption, however, he might, blamelessly, and
perhaps ought to withdraw from official life. Such action
protests government evil and at the same time enables
preservation of the individual's integrity as scholar, poet,
and honorable human being.

Such thinking marked Wu's own career. Indeed the
book is known to be autobiographical, including, not only
the author's personal experiences, but, as well, those of
many of his associates, thirty of whom have been identified.

In this respect critics at times raise the question
whether the author's pedigree, his aristocratic and scholarly background, supposedly renounced for a life of poverty,
neglect, ridicule, and disgrace, may in fact have left him
with a residue of hurt pride, defiance, and even snobbish-
ness. Such feelings, a few critics argue, might explain the
venom of Wu's denunciations and his suggestion that most
aspirants for examinations and public office ought really
return to their fields and shops.

On the other hand, JU-LIN carefully distinguishes
two kinds of reprehensible "scholars." Some, sacrificing
moral and intellectual integrity, feverishly pursue success
in the examinations as the sole way to an official career.
Others, affecting disdain for the tests, withdraw from them,

ostensibly to pursue more elegant and refined occupations such as the writing of poetry or the publishing of books, in reality to seek public attention by flaunting eccentricities. This second group of hypocritical and self-serving pseudo-scholars Wu finds more offensive than the first. His castigations recall the preference of Thomas Carlyle (1795-1881) for hustling and serious Philistines to dilettante aristocrats whose sloth and self-indulgence have negated their natural vocation as leaders of society.

But if the matter of the examinations suggests the possibility of sour grapes in Wu Ching-tsu's diatribes, his championship of women's causes does not. Since the inception and institutionalizing of footbinding in the tenth and eleventh centuries, few persons of influence had dared oppose a custom construed to enhance female erotic charm and make women easier to control. The powerful and popular K'ang-hsi (Manchu) emperor (r. 1662-1722) had tried and failed.

Wu used his novel to denounce the inhumane practice, as also concubinage, the ban against widow remarriage, the promotion of widow suicide, the praise of female ignorance as a virtue proper to the sex, construal of woman's duty as total submission to male authority, and restriction of her movements to the home. A memorable anecdote from JU-LIN tells of Wang Yu-hui's widowed daughter who, with her father's encouragement, starves herself to death, and Wang's too-late recognition of his needless loss.

In his own life Wu's relationship with his wife was (for his milieu) extraordinary. Not only loving spouse, she was to him as well friend, counselor, and even, to the merriment of Wu's friends, his companion in entertainments usually reserved for men.

The third major object of Wu's satire was superstition of any kind, especially that involving revolting and unhealthy practices. The more these claimed religion as their sanction, the more hateful they appeared to Wu. He, accordingly, at every opportunity denounced astrology, fortune-telling, geomancy, and traffic with spirits and ghosts.

A fourth object of Wu's satire, less noticed because more subtly presented, was the popular rhetoric of his day, especially among storytellers. His derision of certain exaggerated practices, shared by his great contemporary Ts'ao Hsueh Ch'in, accords with the diminishing importance at this time of short stories as public taste for novels grew.

Of the many "firsts" attributed to Wu Ching-tzu and his work--first novelist to focus on social satire, first to write an autobiographical novel, first to project in it humanitarian concern, first to break sharply from many oral storytelling conventions, and first to display (though he failed to develop) an introspective turn of mind relative to his characters--an especially interesting one is Wu's resting his search for a healthy society on a human rather than a religious rationale.

Certainly the Confucian element, seemingly so strong in the novel (at least one critic, however, denies the preponderance of Confucianism, insisting on the author's noncommittal or at least syncretic position vis-à-vis Taoism and Buddhism) at times implies religious concern. Indeed the great climax of JLWS, occurring at the end of Part Two (Chapter 37), depicts the participation of Tu Shao-ch'ing (the author's fictional self) and his Nanking scholar-friends in the rededication of the renovated ancient Temple of T'ai-po. The whole episode, however, (duplicating an experience from the author's own life, in which he expended a small fortune and strenuous fund-raising exertions), as well as other Confucian passages, easily fits into a "secular" reading.

For the essential meaning of Confucianism, in the eyes of many if not most scholars, is the human-centeredness of this world. Its self-perpetuating and self-governing nature is to be realized through a vast network of human relationships characterized and nourished by righteousness, love of learning, and rituals recalling the virtues of the Ancients and cosmic harmony. The Temple ceremonies, in this reading, reaffirm the principle of human self-reliance and of the power of men to resurrect Confucian ideals when they have fallen or been thrown into desuetude.

One scholar seizes on this truth to contrast the typical traditional Chinese world view, reflected in its literature, with Western traditional insistence on human

JU-LIN WAI-SHIH (THE SCHOLARS) 195

submission to a transcendent Providence governing the world. Critics who call Wu the first novelist to set aside serious consideration of religious elements in the disposition of human affairs are, perhaps, implying that the earlier four great Ming novels drew, in fact, on Buddhism, Taoism, and unorthodox forms of Confucianism for basic explanations of human experience.

Having culled materials for his novel, not only from his own and his associates' experiences, but also from popular storytelling, Wu seems to have completed JLWS four years before his death in 1756, yet he never saw it published. Without access to the lost manuscripts or to vanished editions of 1768 and 1779, scholars today are unable to agree on the original number of chapters. Of the 56 in the 1803 edition, the last is thought a forgery; certain contemporary or near-contemporary sources refer to a 50-chapter original; one editor, in 1888, offered a 60-chapter version; the 1869 55-chapter edition of Chin Ho (a relative of the Wu family) is now considered standard.

Structurally JLWS divides into three sections. Part One (Chapters 1-30) opens with a prologue introducing the Yuan sage-scholar Wang Mien (possibly the author's idealized self) and follows up with the contrasting histories of would-be scholars, officials, and others obsessed with desire for worldly success, fame, status, and wealth. Part Two (Chapters 31-37) tells of Tu Shao-ch'ing (the author's real self as differentiated from his idealized self, possibly expressed in Wang Mien); his cousin Tu Shen-ch'ing, of strikingly different temperament (much as Chen Pao-yu of HUNG-LOU MENG complements Chia Pao-yu); and other Nanking scholars. All these, having helped restore the delapidated T'ai-po Temple, participate in sublime rituals marking its rededication. The exercise results in new hope for the revitalizing of the country's moral, artistic, and intellectual health. Part Three (Chapters 37-55), less unified than the others, offers a group of miscellaneous anecdotes, satiric, didactic, and romantic, and concludes with the impressive postlogue.

In this final chapter a visitor, returning after some years to T'ai-po Temple, finds it in ruins, as if mocking the hopes and aspirations of the noble scholars who years before had rebuilt and rededicated it. Yet, resorting to the city, the visitor finds there four eccentrics who relieve his gloom. These lowly men, refracting the Wang-Mien ideal of the story's opening, exhibit essential intellectual, aesthetic, and moral virtues, without, however, following Wang's example of withdrawal from the world. The most difficult of challenges, the author would seem to say, --maintaining integrity in the midst of temptation--can, in fact, be realized, as, for most people, it must.

Of special interest are the occupations (all among the so-called "noble" Chinese recreations) of the Eccentrics: calligraphy for a homeless man, who finds protection in the temple; painting for a teahouse proprietor; the game of go for a handyman; and lute-playing for a tailor.

Many critics, referring to the work as a mere collection of anecdotes, have denied to JU-LIN WAI-SHIH that unity of design essential to great art. Responding to this charge, the novel's defenders have invoked the familiar unifying image of the scroll, with a gradual pictorial unfolding of a society threatened by corruption in its leadership selection.

Lin Shuan-fu offers instead, as the integrating factor in what he regards as a highly sophisticated structural unity, the principle of li, the ritual ordering of human relationships so as to render harmony possible. Wang Mien is thus interpreted as the personification of li. The anecdotes of Part One illustrate the effects of disregarding li; Part Two, centrally concerned with the Temple, reveals the power of li to awaken noble aspirations; and, finally, Part Three's last chapter shows the four eccentrics who, in spite of mundane surroundings with seductive activities, maintain li. Their success generates hope for the world if it can but regain the knowledge and practice of that which alone makes harmony possible, the practice of li.

A third figure, offered by Lu Hsun, explains the unity of JLWS as similar to that of a patchwork quilt; in it recurrent characters and motifs bring disparate units into a sometimes amazingly rich and harmonious whole.

Despite retention of a few storyteller mannerisms--chapter-opening antithetical couplets, chapter-closing quatrains, and a few formulaic phrases, JLWS does away with the interim songs and verses characteristic of previous novels;

assumes, supposedly for the first time, the omniscient point of view; and, instead of authorial description, uses dramatic devices like dialogue, action, and other-character reports to reveal personality. In the matter of language, its almost pure use of a vernacular free of dialect and slang (reminiscent of William Wordsworth's "selection of language really used by men"), its avoidance of rhetorical flights and purple passages, and its distaste for religious terminologies mark a strong technical advance over previous novel literature.

Apart from individual chapters translated for various periodicals, only one complete Englishing of JU-LIN WAI-SHIH is available: the 1957 translation by Yang Hsien-yi and Gladys Yang, reprinted in New York in 1972 and in Beijing in 1973. Despite the general readability of the Yang work, there is present need for a new, definitively treated, and fully annotated version.

Of the scholars with appreciable contributions to this bibliography, the more notable are C.T. Hsia, revered pioneer analyist; Paul Stanley Ropp, with his book-length study of JLWS's social criticism; and Timothy Chung-tai Wong, with his also lengthy study of JLWS's satire and polemics.

Translations

F1. Chai Ch'u and Winberg Chai, trs. and eds. "JU-LIN WAI-SHIH (UNOFFICIAL HISTORY OF OFFICIALDOM)." A TREASURY OF CHINESE LITERATURE: A NEW PROSE ANTHOLOGY INCLUDING FICTION AND DRAMA. New York: Appleton-Century, 1965. Pages 249-254.

Introduces the translation of Chapter 51 with an essay proclaiming this work first in time and merit to use satire for "a dispassionate picture of the hypocrisy and rottenness of Chinese society in general and of the official world in particular." Sees as central theme scholars' attitudes toward the examination system as virtually the only road to power, wealth, and social prestige, for which they readily sacrifice duty, honor, learning, and loyalty, leaving behind the spirit of Confucianism and practical concern for the improvement of the State.

Defends the novel's lack of a central plot by showing the superior excellence in this instance of a loose succession of 50-odd stories in as many chapters, likening the result to scrolls of ancient paintings presenting panoramas of the universe. Features an episode in which a young woman tricks a man into losing his money and a gallant man delights in accepting his punishment.

F2. Chang, H.C., tr. "Young Master Bountiful (Chapters 31-32)." CHINESE LITERATURE: POPULAR FICTION AND DRAMA. Chicago: Aldine Publishers, 1973. Pages 329-381.

Besides providing an annotated and accurate translation of two important chapters, interprets JU-LIN WAI-SHIH (AN UNOFFICIAL HISTORY OF THE WORLD OF LEARNING) as an apology for and a veiled representation of author Wu Ching-tzu's own life (1701-1754). Here also includes attention to Wu's cousin, Wu Ch'ing-tzu, strikingly different in temperament and attitude.

Depicts the poverty and neglect dogging author Wu through most of his 54 years as, while honoring social obligations, he steadfastly refuses to compete for property or a public career. Recalls Wu's contempt for those who vie for such honors in servile, ridiculous, and hypocritical ways, or wear them with hauteur and disregard for others. Rehearses Wu's judgment on these characteristics as incompatible with the disinterested and honorable pursuit of learning and morality, and the cultivation of friendship and conjugal affection constituting the author's *beau ideal*.

Marks the inflated and otherwise altered survival of an original JU-LIN in the 1803 56-chapter version and the 1888 60-chapter reading. Concludes that the original, substantially complete by 1736, consisted of 50 chapters only, these immortalizing real events and persons from the author's life. Highlights the basic question troubling men of Wu Ching-tzu's mentality: whether learning is to be pursued for its own sake (suggesting the fourth lecture of John H. Newman's

IDEA OF A UNIVERSITY) or as a road to public office, private wealth, and self-aggrandizement.

F3. Hsu Chen-ping, tr. "Four Eccentrics: The Epilogue to JU-LIN WAI-SHIH." TIEN HSIA MONTHLY 11 (1940-1941): 178-192. (Chapter 55.)

Introduces this new translation of JU-LIN WAI-SHIH's final chapter by comparing the novel with William M. Thackeray's THE BOOK OF SNOBS, calling the Chinese work more scathing and bitter, breathing the author's hatred of snobbery, convention, and hypocrisy.

F4. Kao, George, ed. "Two Scholars Who Passed the Examinations." CHINESE WIT AND HUMOR. New York: Sterling Publishing Company, 1974. Pages 189-208. (First published in 1946.)

Parallels the hsui-tsai of the Chinese examination attainment with the Western bachelor's degree; the chu-jen with the Master's degree; and the chin-shih and han-lin with the terminal doctoral degree. Shows the hilarity amid the bitterness of Wu Ching-tzu's satirical novel THE SCHOLARS.

F5. Tchang Fou-jouei, tr. CHRONIQUE INDISCRETE DES MANDARINS. Intr. Andre Levy. Paris: Gallimard Publishers, 1976.

Introduces this French translation of the 55-chapter THE SCHOLARS, each unit accompanied by end notes, with a Levy discussion of composition dates, authorship, manuscript history, cultural backgrounds, and critical assessments of content and style. Provides, in the appendix, a personae list and a bibliography of major French and English as well as Chinese studies.

F6. Yang Hsien-yi and Gladys Yang, trs. THE SCHOLARS. Peking: Foreign Languages Press, 1973. Earlier printings in 1957 and (in New York) 1972.

With Yangian sympathy, directness, and economy, offers a lively and abundantly illustrated translation of the 55-chapter THE SCHOLARS. Reviews social and political backgrounds, the life, character, and career of the author, and the work's chief satirical targets (the examination system, certain discriminations against women, and superstition). Praises the novel's dialogue, characterization, and simplicity of language. Appends a detailed and lucid explanation of the examination system and of official ranks represented in the work.

Studies

F7. Chang Chung-li. THE CHINESE GENTRY: STUDIES ON THEIR ROLE IN 19TH CENTURY CHINESE SOCIETY. Seattle: University of Washington Press, 1955.

After considering the components, privileges, and numerical constitution of nineteenth-century Chinese gentry, explores their "examination life." Includes the major role of examination preparation; the content of the exams and their relation to the selection of officials; the system's so-called "spirit of equality"; corruption; and the final collapse in late Ch'ing of the age-old testing institution. Because of the static nature of the system, sheds generous light on the eighteenth-century THE SCHOLARS.

F8. Coleman, John D. "With and Without a Compass: THE SCHOLARS, THE TRAVELS OF LAO TS'AN, and the Waning of Confucian Tradition During the Ch'ing Dynasty." TAMKANG REVIEW 7 (October 1976): 61-80.

Identifies as the major difference between the two often-compared episodic satires THE SCHOLARS (early Ch'ing) and THE TRAVELS OF LAO TS'AN (late Ch'ing) the presence or absence of a stable value system in both author and times. In THE SCHOLARS finds Confucianism the key ethic, an enduring moral and cultural ideal the more apparent for the charges made against its betrayers and the more hopeful as it can be revitalized. Calls this state of affairs consonance. By contrast finds in TRAVELS a basic spiritual wrenching between recognition of the need for change, brought about by contact with the West, and longing for the security of the old ideals and way of life. Calls this situation cultural dissonance.

F9. Franke, Wolfgang. THE REFORM AND ABOLITION OF THE TRADITIONAL CHINESE EXAMINATION SYSTEM. Cambridge: Harvard University Press, 1963.

Documents the Han Dynasty's original and admirable conceptions about the nature and functions of the examination system. Traces the deterioration of the institution into a tool for ambitious and unscrupulous men as it became the major road to power, status, and wealth. Quotes from Wang An-shih (1021-1081) and twelfth-century Neo-Confucianist Chu Hsi (1130-1200) about abuses, including stereotyped and formalistic structure, restrictions on development of talent, and inefficiency in providing able and virtuous officials. Traces such critiques through the nineteenth century, when reforms were earnestly sought. Makes no mention of the major vernacular novel to attack the system, Wu Ching-tzu's JU-LIN WAI-SHIH.

F10. Hightower, James R. TOPICS IN CHINESE LITERATURE. Cambridge: Harvard University Press, 1965. Page 106.

Offers few favorable comments on JLWS, perceiving its only unity as a social group and its marked weakness in praising upright but unambitious, bad-mannered, and self-righteous positive characters.

F11. Ho Ch'i-fang. "Wu Ching-tzu's SCHOLARS." PEOPLE'S CHINA 3 (March 1955): 17-20.

F12. Ho Ping-ti. THE LADDER OF SUCCESS IN IMPERIAL CHINA: ASPECTS OF SOCIAL MOBILITY 1368-1911. New York: Columbia University Press, 1962.

Offers invaluable data about Ming-Ch'ing social organization, attending particularly to the role of the examination system which lasted almost unaltered from A.D. 605 to 1904. Classifies the degrees from the chin-shih down, listing requirements for each and noting abrupt attitudinal social shifts when the scholar passed the examination and almost immediately was admitted to the bureaucracy, the ruling elite.

Contrasts, on the one hand, scholars and officials in the context of the imperial court; and, on the other, the commoners' milieu, with its peasants, artisans and craftsmen, and merchants and tradesmen. Calls JU-LIN WAI-SHIH "indispensable for the study of the key social classes in Ming-Ch'ing society," built as it is on episodes and personages from author Wu Ching-tzu's life. As second to JU-LIN in rich exposition of social life cites A MARRIAGE THAT AWAKENS THE WORLD by P'u Sung-ling (1640-1715).

F13. Ho Shih-chun. "JOU-LIN WAI-CHE": LE ROMAN DES LETTRES. Paris: L. Rodstein, 1933.

An early work seeking to promote appreciation in the West of a roman à lettres contemporaneous with HUNG-LOU MENG. Divides subject matter into Part I: author's biography, critical history of the work, bibliography, the author's "thought," and a plot summary; Part II: individual studies of outstanding characters; and Part III: translations into French of eight "des meilleurs passages."

F14. Hsia, C.T. "The Scholars." THE CLASSIC CHINESE NOVEL: A CRITICAL INTRODUCTION. New York: Columbia University Press, 1968. Pages 203-244.

Deplores misconception of the novel as merely a diatribe against the examination system and its stereotyped eight-legged essay. Views the work, rather, as a masterly panorama of eighteenth-century China, especially in its middle- and lower-class reality, with this intellectual commentary to match: Real and pseudo-scholars and bureaucrats derive their significance only from the comedy of environing social life. Attributes landmark importance to Wu's use of vernacular versus literary expression and other stylistic and technical innovations. Calls Wu the first true humanitarian among Chinese novelists.

F15. Idema, Wilt Lukas. CHINESE VERNACULAR FICTION: THE FORMATIVE PERIOD. Leiden: E.J. Brill Company, 1974. Pages 128-131.

Borrowing from Kral and Knoerle, delineates structural similarity between JU-LIN and HUNG-LOU MENG, both seen as centering on comparable but contrasting elements in action, character, and planes of existence. Distinguishes the pattern of continuing complementarity as a development from earlier novels with less sophisticated recurrent clashes between unequal powers.

F16. Kao, Yu-kung. "Lyric Vision in Chinese Narrative Tradition: A Reading of HUNG-LOU MENG and JU-LIN WAI-SHIH." CHINESE NARRATIVE: CRITICAL AND THEORETICAL ESSAYS. Ed. Andrew H. Plaks. Princeton: Princeton University Press, 1978. Pages 227-243.

See G56.

F17. Kral, Oldrich. "Several Artistic Methods in the Classic Chinese Novel JU-LIN WAI-SHIH." ARCHIV ORIENTALNI 32 (January 1964): 16-43.

In strictly aesthetic mode, explores Wu Ching-tzu's art of characterization, seen as the primary purpose and achievement of a work presenting "a whole social stratum." Differentiates Wu's method from that of the West, identifying JU-LIN's major techniques as description and narration rather than the probing of and into individual minds. Uses many passages from the novel to demonstrate the third-person mode of both description and narration in situations where Western writers were pioneering memoir and picaresque narrative to gain entree into inner feelings, reactions, and motivations.

In addition to its analyses of the literary function of details of physiognomy, clothing, bearing, and other-character reports, recognizes Wu's technical innovation in using nature and landscape as viewed by contrasting personalities to indicate moral, spiritual, intellectual, and aesthetic orientation. Stresses Wu's powers of evoking interest less by active conflict and clash than by tableaux of contrasting and confrontational personalities.

F18. Lai Ming. A HISTORY OF CHINESE LITERATURE. New York: Capricorn Books, 1966. Pages 327-332.

Praises Wu Ching-tzu's language as warm, humorous, and free from bitterness and abuse. Traces Wu's life, highlighting his detachment from wealth and fame, his gift for friendship, and his part in building Rainflower Hill Temple in memory of 230 ancient worthies, starting with Tai Po of the kingdom of Wu. Excerpts the story of tailor Chung Yuan.

F19. Leonard, Jane Kate. "Protest and the Ch'ing Intellectual." An undated, unpublished paper from Kean College of New Jersey.

Follows the mode of Chinese intellectuals' political protest from 1) the eighth century, exemplified by Li Yung and his withdrawal from public life; 2) through the middle eighteenth century, in which, through the k'ao chang, scholar-intellectuals with political patronage engaged in public debate about the ends and methods of statecraft; and 3) through the nineteenth century, in which, inspired by Kung Tzu-chen's denunciation of the official class, scholar-intellectuals increasingly exerted political power at provincial and local levels. Makes no mention of Wu Ching-tzu's JU-LIN WAI-SHIH, even while graphically describing the author's theme and milieu.

F20. Lin Shuan-fu. "Ritual and Narrative Structure in JU-LIN WAI-SHIH." CHINESE NARRATIVE: CRITICAL AND THEORETICAL ESSAYS. Ed. Andrew H. Plaks. Princeton University Press, 1978. Pages 244-265.

Points out the modernist critical error of judging JU-LIN a mere loose collection of stories without structural design. Declares li, the ritual ordering of human relationships rendering harmony possible, the integrative principle in a work of sophisticated design and demonstrable structural unity.

Describes the Western notion of structural unity as derived from a view of the world as created and governed by an external power on principles of hierarchical subordination and historical linearity. Contrasts this view with the Chinese idea, derived from a view of the world as self-contained and self-generating, with neither beginning nor end, in spatial, reticulated, and coordinated design and with synchronous rather than sequential emphasis. Likens Chinese novel structure to the handscroll, in which episodic durations succeed each other without climax or anticlimax, but leading coordinately to total vision, in this case a pageant of eighteenth-century Chinese society.

Marks 1) the prologue's initiation of the li ideal in the person of Wang Mien; 2) early-chapter presentations of pseudoscholars and pseudorecluses, ignorant or disdainful of true and sincere propriety (li), by which alone social harmony can be achieved; 3) middle-chapter culmination in the completion and ritual dedication of the temple of T'ai-po, ceremonials resplendently dramatizing the meaning of li; and 4) final-chapter exposure of the whole society, devastated by its neglect of the binding principle. Details that society, which ought to have been nurtured by true scholars in a noble officialdom, lying in disarray figured by the ruined temple and its forgotten teachings.

Concludes by considering the epilogue, in which four craftsmen a) courageously resist the temptation to withdraw to an eremetical existence, b) stoically endure derision--thereby refracting Wang Mien's perfections, and c) within a mundane environment and while precluded from public service, maintain li in their personal lives. Sees Wu Ching-tzu as despairing of society's ever achieving li-governed public life but insisting on this Confucian value as an irreplaceable ideal.

F21. Liu Ts'un-yan. CHINESE POPULAR FICTION IN TWO LONDON LIBRARIES. Hong Kong: Lung Men Bookstore, 1967. Pages 150-153.

In the light of manuscripts, editions, and documents held by the British Museum and the Royal Asiatic Society of London, explores the question of whether THE SCHOLARS originally consisted of 50 chapters only. Questions the validity of Hu Shih's judgment in the matter, preferring the 55-chapter version. See D41.

F22. Liu Wu-chi. "Great Novels by Obscure Writers." AN INTRODUCTION TO CHINESE LITERATURE. Bloomington: Indiana University Press, 1967. Pages 228-246.

Cites the more pronounced and intensive assault on social evils as the chief difference between satiric and realistic novels. Insists that, while specifically attacking literary pretensions and hypocrisy and official nepotism, graft, and corruption in the civil-service examinations, JU-LIN goes beyond this focus to expose human weakness in general, with emphasis on the ridiculous. Disdains the novel's "lack of organic structure," likening it to Thackeray's BOOK OF SNOBS as a series of loosely connected anecdotes. Argues that only under twentieth-century Western influence have Chinese writers learned the importance and the practice of effective plot construction.

F23. Lu Hsun. A BRIEF HISTORY OF CHINESE FICTION. Trs. Yang Hsien-yi and Gladys Yang. Peking: Foreign Languages Press, 1959. Pages 289-297.

Referring to its succession of stories only loosely connected, likens THE SCHOLARS to a patchwork quilt. Insists on the real-life origins of characters and events. Shows the author's psychological subtlety in, for example, dramatizing the clash between conscience and moral conventions. Identifies Wu with the character Tu Shao-ch'ing and his brother with Tu Shen-ch'ing and sees a major climax in the sacrifice at Tai-po's temple, though time quickly swallows the glorious affirmation and idealism of the occasion.

F24. Ropp, Paul Stanley. DISSENT IN EARLY MODERN CHINA: "JU-LIN WAI-SHIH" AND CH'ING SOCIAL CRITICISM. Ann Arbor: University of Michigan Press, 1981.

Seeks in this study, not a literary appraisal, but a sociological-intellectual assessment of the novel relative to its own time and to succeeding generations. In the first of four sections, describes the society and culture of early modern China (Ming and Ch'ing Dynasties). In the second, reviews the life and character of Wu Ching-tzu, reflected in the novel as Tu Shao-ch'ing, and of persons in his life who figure in the novel.

In the third section, develops three major objects of Wu's satire. First, considers the stultifying and morally subversive civil-service examinations. Shows, on the one hand, the over-stressing of the <u>pa-ka</u> (eight-legged essay) and a narrow Ch'eng-Chu Neo-Confucianism, both emphasizing form over content; rote memorization; subject-matters removed from reality; and usages which squelch originality, critical thought, true erudition, and a practical approach to public affairs. More importantly, exposes serious moral abuses induced by rabid pursuit of success in the examinations, notably the undermining of filiality, honesty, humility, and selflessness. Second, examines inequities between men and women, dramatically apparent in the cult of widow-suicide, concubinage, footbinding, female illiteracy perceived as a virtue, total female submission to the male, and physical restriction to the domestic sphere. Third, condemns superstitious and revolting practices of popular religions, notably those connected with astrology, fortune-telling, geomancy, and ghost-spirit agencies.

In the fourth and final chapter reviews interpretations of the novel by textualists and by ideologists ranging from Marxists with varying and conflicting views of the novel as centrally concerned with class-warfare and an attack on Manchu feudalism, to Conservatives who find in the book a defense of basic Confucianism sprinkled with strong Taoist elements.

Concludes that the work essentially reflects the early disintegration of traditional Chinese order and the beginning of modern Chinese culture. Identifies this change as one in which individualism, humanitarianism, and egalitarianism develop, not as new and Western imports, but as attitudes derived from an important minority tradition in Chinese intellectual life--notably in the work of Neo-Confucian Wang Yang-ming.

F25. Ropp, Paul Stanley. EARLY CH'ING SOCIETY AND ITS CRITICS: THE LIFE AND TIMES OF WU CHING-TZU (1701-1754). Ann Arbor: University of Michigan, 1974. An unpublished dissertation.

F26. Ropp, Paul Stanley. "The Seeds of Change: Reflections on the Condition of Women in the Early and Mid Ch'ing Societies." SIGNS: JOURNAL OF WOMEN IN CULTURE AND SOCIETY 2.1 (Autumn 1976): 5-23.

Explores Ch'ing (1644-1911) literature for early feminist writings attacking, among other oppressions, footbinding, concubinage, prostitution, and sanctions against widows and rape victims. Identifies notable male authors who challenged conventional understanding of li-chiao (female duties), which demanded of women gentle, yielding, totally submissive behavior and a sexuality enhanced by weakness, pliability, dependence, and a shy and bashful mien. Notes that three emperors unsuccessfully sought to curtail footbinding, the encouragement of widow suicide, and the cutting off of a wife's flesh to provide medicine for ill mothers-in-law.

Among male writings identifies P'u Sung-ling's STRANGE STORIES (1679) as the first fiction with feminist implications; poems of Yuan Mei (1716-1797) opposing encouragement of rape-victim suicide and discouragement of widow remarriage; and Li Ju-chen's eighteenth-century novel FLOWERS IN THE MIRROR, using T'ang Empress Wu's reign (625-705) to endorse female literacy and artistry (a work inviting collation with Alfred Tennyson's THE PRINCESS).

Above all, cites JU-LIN WAI-SHIH by Wu Ching-tzu (1701-1754) as the most effectual vernacular fiction attacking female oppression by exposing the system's contradictions and inhumane implications. Points to the novel's example of emancipation in Tu Shao-ch'ing's wife, regarded by him as an intellectual and artistic equal and a cherished friend, whose opinions he highly regards and who, to the scandal of Wu's peers, openly accompanies him to social gatherings usually reserved for men.

Traces geographic and socio-economic considerations relative to women's condition. Remarks that Manchu insecurity and conservatism led to a stiffening of upper-class restrictions, while emergent cultures in the lower classes subverted the conventions by disruptive practices and especially by a growing taste for vernacular literatures, notably the novel, which attacked social wrongs.

F27. Slupski, Zbigniew. "Literary and Ideological Responses to the [JU-LIN WAI-SHIH] in Modern Chinese Literature." MODERN CHINESE LITERATURE AND ITS SOCIAL CONTENT. Nobel Symposium 32. Ed. Goran Malmqvist. Stockholm: Nobel House, 1975. Pages 123-139.

Establishes the influence of the famous eighteenth-century novel on modern Chinese narrative. In composition finds contrast, parallel presentation, mosaic development of character, and hidden or oblique exposition the major structural models. In poetics insists that JU-LIN presents, not chiefly or purely satire, but, more importantly, non-judgmental realism. Shows the author's use of multi-leveled meanings in seeming farce as resulting in an array of various attitudes and views of life and a gallery of diverse characters only indirectly inviting moral evaluation. Notes Wu Ching-tzu's scorn for the examination system and its "stupifying" eight-legged essays, corruption-producing bureaucracy, and an institutionalized morality honoring ethically deficient and intellectually stunted pseudoscholars.

Considers the novel less Confucian, as conventional criticism would have it, than syncretic. Cites Wu's observation of weak spots in the praxis of all so-called noble teachings and the near impossibility of living without hypocrisy. Sees Wu as eventually finding recourse only in a comic spirit assessing life and society as ultimate absurdity. Notes Wu's method of first presenting a philosophic view and then calling it into doubt, only in the final chapter hinting at his personal belief that life is best lived, not by pursuit of learning and moral wisdom, but by individual cultivation of one's talents, regardless of the larger society (Voltairean?).

Discounts Lu Hsun's denial of borrowings from JU-LIN, noting his use of motifs, oblique presentation, and irony in the style of the earlier novel. Applies findings specifically to twentieth-century novelists Shi Tuo and Qian Zhong-shu.

F28. Tu Lin-che. "Wu Ching-tzu." EMINENT CHINESE OF THE CH'ING DYNASTY 1644-1912. Two volumes. Ed. Arthur W. Hummel. Ann Arbor: University of Michigan Press, 1981. II: 737-739.

Contrasts the intellectual and official distinction of Wu Ching-tzu's forbears with the author's growing disillusionment relative to official institutions, including, not only the examination system, but also concubinage, widow self-immolation, belief in fairies, and geomantic superstitions. Dates the original work between 1768 and 1779 and cites as the first extant printed version that of 1816.

F29. Wells, Henry W. "An Essay on the JU-LIN WAI-SHIH." TAMKANG REVIEW 2 (April 1917): 143-152.

Propounds the extraordinary ambivalence and eclecticism of Wu Ching-tzu's satire, wherein moral judgment and ideologic stance are generally left to readers. Likens JU-LIN's author to Sung scholastics who declared Confucianism, Taoism, and Buddhism to be substantially one--each valid in its own nobility and high realization, each susceptible to gross deterioration, none complete in itself.

Responding to charges of the novel's formlessness, points to the succession of minor characters growing into major ones, and thence fading back again into minor personae, and to a general movement from poor village life to thriving metropolises. Notes the first-chapter Scholar's retreat from public office to reclusive mountain life and the final-chapter's four Eccentrics' opting to remain in the city, to defy its temptations, and to retain their integrity amid its immoralities.

F30. Wong, Timothy Chung-tai. SATIRE AND THE POLEMICS OF CRITICISM OF CHINESE FICTION: A STUDY OF THE JU-LIN WAI-SHIH. Ann Arbor, Michigan: University Microfilms International, 1981.

Takes as its point of departure the 1960s' literary scuffle between Hsia, insisting that the same expressive and aesthetic critical standards be applied to all literature regardless of nation, period, or ideology, and Prusek, as fervidly avowing that literature primarily mirrors universal historical reality and subserves sociopolitical ends. Adopting Individualist and Socialist as identifying terms for the two postures, argues that a more valid theory accommodates both views and is seen with special advantage in satire, specifically in China's first novel of social criticism, JU-LIN WAI-SHIH.

Prefaces analysis of this work by reviews of a) dating, between 1736 and 1779; b) 19 major texts, beginning with the first extant, the 1803 publication; c) number of chapters, set at 50, 55, 56, and 60; d) and the author's life, carefully examined. After defining satire as morality (the Socialist stress) and wit (the Individualist stress), distinguishes it from humor, which does not attack; invective, which lacks wit and indirection; and lampoon, which focuses on the narrow and personal whereas satire strikes out against general vice and folly.

Identifies as the novel's basic ethos Confucianism in its ideal, eremitic phase, as against Prusek's and Mao's Communist readings and Inada Takashi's 1963 Nihilist interpretation. Contends that Wu battles against the prioritizing of career-fame-wealth-rank (kung-ming fu-kuei) promoted by the examination system; false propriety; injustice to women; and superstition. Points out his stress on Confucian values and choice of virtue and learning over practical and utilitarian concerns, notably in the behavior of "yielding" (jong).

In the realm of wit or the battle against dullness, as exemplified in Alexander Pope's DUNCIAD, identifies the JU-LIN author's skill in magnifying, diminishing, and jumbling details and episodes for sophisticated ironic effects. Describes the structure as advancing from the opposition of values (Chapter 1) to dullness described (Chapters 2-29) to virtue, learning, and talent intervening (Chapters 29-41) to dullness dominating again (Chapters 42-54) and, finally, to an affirmation of hope within a dunce-society (Chapter 55).

In characterization argues (against Kral [F17] and Hsia [F14]) that psychological insight is a cornerstone of Wu's art. Calls Wu's method objective and historical--without traditional poems or storytellers' descriptive markings, and without commentary, allegory, hyperbole, or litotes. Believes that this method produces immediacy and believability, the avoidance of sermonizing and the illusion of discovery, a seductive conversion to the narrator's moral view, and effective self-examination.

Concludes that the eclectic use of techniques drawn alike from traditional storytellers and classical literati enables Wu to effect both the morality of satire (the Socialist aim) and its wit (the Individualist demand).

F31. Wu Tsu-hsiang. "The Realism of Wu Ching-tzu." CHINESE LITERATURE 4 (April 1954): 155-165.

Reviews the cultural milieu and personal history of Wu Ching-tzu (1701-1754), author of the autobiographical and satirical novel JU-LIN WAI-SHIH, stressing the oppressive Manchu rule and failing family fortunes, both generating disillusionment with the examination system as the major consideration in appointment of public officials. Under the K'ang-hsi, Ying-chung, and Ch'ien-lung rules, finds Manchu political and thought control powerfully manipulating scholars, other intellectuals, and authors of vernacular fiction and "other licentious works."

Highlights the first-chapter presentation of Wang Mien, the historical ideal of scholarly wisdom and integrity, whose example becomes the referent by which other characters are judged. Cites several of the 30 or 40 major characters whose scholarly principles, personal integrity, and Confucian social ideals are lost or marred by obstructionist, stultifying examinations, marked by the hated pa-ka (eight-paragraph) essay, and by venal examiners. Calls attention to contrastive high-minded persons who, disdaining worldly success won by moral defection, prefer the old ways, and to humble characters of undisputed kindliness and decency.

Stresses Wu's realism and his compassion in delineating even negative characters as not essentially bad, but victims of an evil political and social system. Finally, cites the last chapter's four eccentrics as those who, though from lowly walks of life, without withdrawing from society altogether offer hope for China's moral and intellectual regeneration.

F32. Yang, Winston L.Y., Peter Li, and Nathan K. Mao. "THE SCHOLARS (JU-LIN WAI-SHIH)." CLASSICAL CHINESE FICTION: A GUIDE TO ITS STUDY AND APPRECIATION. ESSAYS AND BIBLIOGRAPHIES. Boston: G.K. Hall Publishers, 1978. Pages 85-93.

Assumes the autobiographical content of the novel, while focusing on six technical innovations or merits: 1) the use of an omniscient narrator, seen as a departure from early colloquial fiction; 2) the use of multiple differing and sometimes clashing reports on a character to give complexity, depth, and subtlety to the portrait; 3) a realistic approach to social realities which, in the midst of comedy, hints at the tragic or pathetic; 4) a structure which depends on a movable rather than a fixed focus and which, ignoring linear unity, opts rather for a vast network of coordinated relationships, a harmonious blending of many characters, events, and lines of action; 5) a vision, in Chapter 37's account of a temple dedication, of the true Confucian spirit, radiant with humanity and the harmony of humans with their environment; 6) a narrative style largely free from regional slang, gross supernaturalism, and reliance on conventional verse and song for fictional effects.

CHAPTER SEVEN

HUNG-LOU MENG (THE DREAM OF THE RED CHAMBER)

By whatever name it be called of the five names suggested by author Ts'ao Hsueh Ch'in (1715-1763), China's greatest novel, HUNG-LOU MENG (THE DREAM OF THE RED CHAMBER), excels in three particulars. It is, first, a work of art, a literary masterpiece of world interest and importance whose raison d'etre is richness and beauty of design. It is, second, a reflection of its national and historical backgrounds--social, political, economic, intellectual, and aesthetic. It is, third, a statement of the sublimity and pathos of the human condition, mirroring experiences and responses of men, women, and children everywhere and at all times as they struggle with forces natural, cosmic, human, and divine.

HUNG-LOU MENG (THE DREAM OF THE RED CHAMBER), also known as SHIH T'OU CHI (THE STORY OF THE STONE), written between 1744 and 1763, was first published in 1792. It emerged precisely in that period when Britain was producing four of her greatest novelists: Samuel Richardson (1689-1761), Henry Fielding (1707-1754), Lawrence Sterne (1713-1768), and Tobias Smollett (1721-1771). A fascinating concurrence this, at a time of almost total lack of East-West communication.

HLM's textual history extends from its earliest extant (and incomplete) manuscripts of 1754 and 1761 through others (all but one carrying only 80 chapters) until its first publication, in 1792, as a 120-chapter work, edited by Kao E and Ch'eng Wei-yuan. This first printing, besides its sudden accretion of 40 chapters (of disputed authorship), lacked valuable commentaries and marginalia of Ts'ao friends and relatives appearing in the earlier versions. The two most important of these commentators signed themselves, respectively, Red Inkstone Slab (Chih-yen Chai) and Odd Tablet (Chu-hu). Other pre-1792 commentators left no signature; these may include Ts'ao T'ang-ts'un, the author's younger brother, and Ts'ao T'ien-yu, a cousin.

While debate about the authorship of the last 40 chapters continues to rage, a tenable opinion, proffered by David Hawkes, places Ts'ao's drafted and partially written last chapters in the hands of his widow, perhaps an illiterate Manchu woman. She, Hawkes surmises, would have given them to a close friend or relative to complete. That some three decades passed without these chapters being known about is easily attributable to the Ch'ien-lung emperor's severe literary inquisition during the last half of his reign (1736-1796). This speculation helps explain the altering of perspective in the last chapters (when they finally appeared in 1792), so that they seem to compliment Manchu emperors' humanity and generosity rather than blame them for the suffering and impoverishment of the once favored family.

As a work of art THE DREAM OF THE RED CHAMBER offers its own theory of the novel, of its themes, tone, and perspective, its form and structure, its characterization, and its use of myth and imagery.

In his opening pages Ts'ao scorns run-of-the-mill romances, filled, he says, with stale conventions, characterizations of unbelievable moral grandeur, and artificial period settings. Disdaining such conventions, he will tell his story "exactly as it occurred," and in doing so, far from depriving it, will give it "a freshness ... other books don't have."

Concerned, moreover, with traditional Chinese moralism, he continues (as translated by David Hawkes): "Your so-called 'historical romances' ... scandalous anecdotes about statesmen and emperors of bygone days and scabrous attacks on the reputations of long dead gentlewomen, contain more wickedness and immorality than I care to mention. Still worse is the 'erotic novel,' by whose filthy obscenities our young folk are all too easily corrupted." As for boudoir romances, they offer dreary stereotypes "all pitched on the same note [with] characters undistinguished except by name [ideally beautiful young women and eligible young bachelors]...[who] seem unable to avoid descending sooner or later into indecency."

The psychological realism of Ts'ao thus espoused forbids his creating a narrative "just to show off his love poems" or to engage in stilted bombastic language "remote alike from nature and common sense." He will record faithfully "the meetings and partings, the joys and sorrows, the ups and downs of fortune ... exactly as they happened, not daring to add the tiniest bit of touching up, for fear of losing the true picture."

Ts'ao thus firmly founds his literary art on fidelity to human experience. His perspective or point of view is more difficult to define. Lucien Miller, for example, distinguishes six voices: the dogmatic-authority Buddhist monk, the naive-pedant Taoist priest, the objective-innovator Stone, the autobiographical-confessor Ts'ao, a faithful-scholar narrator, and hovering-commentator Chih-yen Chai. Other critics offer simpler judgments about this important matter.

The master theme of HLM is by some critics identified as the search for meaning in a world of suffering. Whether the narrative chiefly concerns an individual (Pao-yu) or a family (the Chias), or a culture (the early Manchu reign), that search remains the same, culminating in the tragic dissolution of things once beautiful, noble, and brave. Yet seeing the novel in this light does not cancel, rather enhances other thematic concerns.

HUNG-LOU MENG has been interpreted in many ways: 1) as a <u>roman à clef</u> about a Manchu emperor and a courtesan, or a Manchu poet and his favorite concubine, or the bad morals of the Manchu court; 2) as an attack on Chinese disciplines relative to the extended family, marriage, education, law, politics, and the examination system; 3) as an autobiography dealing with romantic love, or with the initiation of a youth into adulthood, or with a middle-aged man's lamenting his misspent youth or the passing of youth and innocence and the coming of sorrow, evil, and death; 4) as a reenactment of myths about creation, paradise, fall, and redemption, making of individual experience a symbol of the universal human condition and its ties with cosmic realities; 5) as an expose of the oppressions of the privileged against the poor and powerless.

Summing up Chinese critical reaction to the novel, Joey Bonner lists five phases: 1) In the pre-1792 period critics focused on the 80-chapter version and pursued largely intrinsic qualities rather than external concerns. 2) In the following century, 1792-1900, they sought for magical and hidden meanings, generally neglecting historical considerations, and, after 1875, used the term Redology (later identified as the Old Redology, chiu Hung-hsueh) for intensive studies of the work. 3) In the early twentieth century, 1900-1922, analysts turned to political interpretation, especially as a way of attacking the Manchu regime.

4) In the second quarter of this century, 1922-1953, theorists of the New Redology (hsin Hung-hsueh), led by Hu Shih (1891-1962), insisted on modern, scientific methods of study and relentless collection of documentary evidence for statements about authorship, dates, and texts. This pursuit quickly led to the conclusion that the novel is autobiographical, a fictionized account of a real individual's experiences and feelings. 5) In 1954 and thereafter Marxist critics have fiercely assaulted both Old and New Redologists, insisting on the triviality of such matters as autobiographical elements or textual studies beside the great issue, as they see it, of class warfare and HUNG-LOU MENG's correlative exposure of upper-class corruption and lower-class suffering.

A final consideration of HLM's interpretation is the propriety of calling the work, in the formal sense, a tragedy. Any attempt to answer this question evokes the dragon of definition. But if tragedy be defined as a final fall hastened by a protagonist's hubris and/or hamartia and occasioning grave human waste (as punishment exceeds the fault) resulting in a catharsis of the emotions--then a case can be made for this novel as tragedy. Several studies advert to this dimension of the work and some find it applicable on three levels: Pao (or Tai-yu), the family, and the dynasty.

Still, to call the novel only tragic is to miss its cosmic and human comedy. From the merry insouciance of the Buddhist and Taoist in the opening chapter and the echoes of their glee punctuating the narrative as it moves along, to the crazy laughter of Pao leaving home for good, HLM, declares C.T. Hsia, "is a Taoist or Zen Buddhist comedy." It moves "from low comedy to sheer pathos with the greatest of ease," as it lays open human "hopeless involvement in desire and pain and the liberation of [but a few] individuals besides the hero."

Yet the novel is not fully described even as tragicomedy. Many critics focus on it as primarily a novel of manners, a story of life styles both descriptive and normative. Liu Wu-chi calls it "one of the best documents for a study of the extended Chinese family: its structure, organization, and ideals such as clan solidarity and honor, respect for old age, parental authority, filial obedience, sex relationships, the position of women, concubines, maids, and other domestics."

HUNG-LOU MENG offers, in short, a faithful picture of an upper-class Chinese family of the late seventeenth- and the eighteenth-centuries. In this connection the vast network of relationships, with its incredibly detailed hierarchical protocol, provides endless material for study, especially on the three family levels: senior married adults, junior married adults, and unmarried children. The same patterns echo among the servants, with, however, job-function as an additional factor. One important study examines how Ts'ao depicts servants a) as individuals, b) as parts of the larger society, and c) as agencies for literary effects.

Scholars perceive the structure of HLM to be purposely episodic. It evolves into a great tapestrylike portrayal of the glory and decline of a powerful and wealthy seventeenth/eighteenth-century Chinese family. But beyond this elementary framework Andrew H. Plaks discerns other more sophisticated and subtle structural elements. The basic allegory of the novel (plenitude and emptiness endlessly transforming into each other) works, he believes, through archetypes. These are structurally knit by complementary bipolarity (yin/yang dynamics) and multiple periodicity (the five-elements theory and its system of correspondences). In such a reading the cyclical recurrence of sequential and contrastive patterns (of time, place, character, motif, or event) binds disparate entities into an intelligible whole, and that strikingly Chinese. Thus this chiefly relational, interstitial, spatial, horizontal composition (Lu Hsun [1881-1936] uses the figure of a patchwork quilt) strikingly contrasts with Western novel structures, seen as typically linear, hierarchical, and time-oriented.

Besides structural integrity, HLM offers a tone basically tragic, but not devoid of mirth gentle and nostalgic, whimsical and poetical, caustic or sardonic. Of the occasional negative tone, however, one critic remarks that it is aeons away from the hard cynicism and coarse dullness of CHIN P'ING MEI or the cool, critical expose of Wu Ching-tzu's THE SCHOLARS.

However great its themes, moving its tone, or unified its structure, an even more impressive aspect of Ts'ao's masterpiece is the characters' individualization. Of about 20 major and over 400 minor personae, many are unforgettable for their complexity; clashing ideas, desires, and attitudes; unexpected yet plausible behavior; and, if alive at book's end, potential for an interesting extended life.

Pao-yu, critics believe, is a composite creation, one based partly on the author's personality and experience, partly on those of cousins or other close relatives. By nature Taoist, with an appetency for Buddhism, Pao is trapped in a Confucian world demanding conformity which he must either yield or--at cost of beloved persons, places, and activities--abjure for a realm of detachment where feelings no longer count and all desire is dead. From stone he came; to stone he must, in this scenario, return.

Tai-yu, with her neurotic sensitivity, exacerbated by early loss of parents and home, her dazzling poetic and intellectual talent, her fragile, consumptive beauty, and her affinity for Pao-yu--as passionate, ragged, and reciprocal as Heathcliff and Catherine knew--is, in the eyes of critic Anthony C. Yu, the novel's real tragic center, more so than Pao. He (Pao) finds reconciliation and peace; she dies in a paroxysm of loneliness and pain--by the norms of her society unredeemed. Her counterpart, serene and gracious Pao-chai, flower of understanding and compassion, springs from the profoundest vision of Confucian sincerity, moderation, propriety, humanity, and family loyalty. Yet the doom of the one is as assured as that of the other; both belong to the Red-Dust World.

Attitudes toward these two heroines are a kind of touchstone for certain critical schools. Marxists, for example, read Pao-chai as an evil force and Tai-yu as a glorious revolutionary heroine. Those who favor a more Confucian interpretation see Tai-yu as a neurotic, self-centered eccentric far less admirable than her counterpart.

Other extraordinary portrayals include Chia Cheng, Pao's father, upright, honest, narrow, demanding Confucian patriarch, hurt and unhealed by the premature death of his favored, virtuous eldest son. Constitutionally unable to understand or to communicate meaningfully with Pao-yu, Chia Cheng evokes pity in his awkward yearning for intimacy with his family and in his pleas with that greater Confucian, his mother, to forgive his excessive zeal in beating almost to death his younger, incorrigible son.

Ts'ao Hsueh-Ch'in's ability to create complex characters is nowhere better observed, however, than in Hsi-feng, a daughter-in-law to stir feminists everywhere as she takes charge of her life and others' lives in household affairs entrusted to her. Generous and dutiful when these virtues work to her advantage, she rules rigorously over spoiled and venal servants and ruthlessly turns tables on flawed business men. Growing older in years and avarice, she turns to usury, deceit, forgery, and even graver sins. Yet Hsi-fen, too, loves and is loved and trusted, makes merry with her companions and sorrows with their griefs.

The high humor of the novel appears notable in episodes involving poor relations and old servants, both protected by Confucian protocol. Especially here characters are differentiated and individualized, whether Liu Lao-lao, unabashed by her rustic bumblings as she seeks aid for her son in the splendid Jungkuofu; or the lascivious Chia Jui, a poor tutor's son infatuated with the imperious Hsi-feng; or rambunctious Big Chiao Ta, the old servant whose sloth, stubbornness, and impudence must be tolerated in view of his age and of an ancient heroism on behalf of the family. Like Firs of Anton Chekhov's THE CHERRY ORCHARD, Chiao deeply understands and values traditional ideals and knows about and deplores family deviations. And so with Nannie Li, Pao's old wet nurse, and with others who figure in this panorama of eighteenth-century Chinese life and the extended family.

Of Ts'ao's skill in creating dialogue Yi-tse Feuerwerker writes that it ranges from the light and bantering to the romantic and poetical, to the businesslike and manipulative, to the profound and the probing, and the superficial and the trivial--all, by the special intonation, the revealing word choice, the accompanying gesture, meticulously adapted to character and situation. Written in colloquial Chinese, even today the language of Beijing, the conversations project nuances and ironies only much rereading can fully divulge.

Increasingly critics, notably Plaks, are realizing and writing about the central importance to the novel of Takuanyuan (Prospect) Garden, the earthly paradise contrived on the occasion of the Imperial Consort's visit and thereafter, at her request, given over to the young girls of the house and to Pao. As archetype the Garden exemplifies a time and place of unending love, joy, and beauty, of freedom from division, burdensome work, and pain. As a real place it must, like T'ai-po Temple of JU-LIN WAI-SHIH, fall to ruin, as will also the lives of all within. Whereas the introductory chapter presents the mythic Land of Detachment, where feelings and desires never mar the perfect serene; and whereas subsequent chapters limn the Red-Dust World of blood and pain and loss--only in the middle world of the Garden can, if briefly, love and desire coexist with edenic happiness. Nowhere more abundantly manifest is Ts'ao's genius than in the creation of Takuanyuan.

The major symbolism of the Garden, its image of plenitude here and implication of emptiness beyond, is reflected in countless other, smaller details. These include jade pins, china cups, handkerchiefs, not to mention the jade stone after which the book is named or Pao-chai's golden locket. Of special interest is the doublet purse-image, one of those recurrent details described by Plaks as integrating units. On the one hand Tai-yu knits a purse for Pao as token of their souls' affinity; on the other, a purse, lasciviously embroidered, finds its way, like the serpent, into the Garden, to break its integrity, occasion bitter quarreling, and bring about the death of a favorite maid.

While some scholars have tried exhaustively to locate the real-life site of the Garden, others deride such a search. The Garden is, these insist, quintessentially an ideal place, an imaginative creation. No English-language study has, however, to my knowledge, related the Garden to the extraordinary development of architecture and landscape gardening during the first hundred years of the Manchu reign. Not only did the K'ang-hsi, Yung-cheng, and Ch'ien-lung emperors restore and complete the Ming-planned Forbidden City. In addition they built, in the words of Rene Grousset, "a kind of Chinese Versailles known as the Summer Palace and several other groups of magnificent edifices." To read a description of the Forbidden City is, for example, to have an incredible preview of the idealized Garden of HLM.

Much of the English-language study of HLM has centered on the author's life and times, "the last days of glory and prosperity that China was to enjoy." The Ts'ao family had realized its glory days under the patronage of the K'ang-hsi emperor (r. 1662-1722), a sovereign often compared with Louis XIV for the length and brilliance of his reign. Though Ts'ao all his life remembered the dazzling days of royal patronage, he was only seven when the Yung-cheng emperor (r. 1722-1736) ascended the throne, and, under his less than favorable regard, family fortunes began to fail. Matters worsened in the Ch'ien-lung reign (1736-1796) so that Ts'ao (1715-1763) was, in the end, forced, for the last decades of his life, to struggle with poverty. For funds to support his family (and his drinking) he had to market his paintings.

But if political developments determined much of Ts'ao's experience, even more influential on his life and writing were the diverse strands of developing Chinese thought, and tensions arising from the clash of Confucian ideals and institutions with Taoist and Buddhist forces. The problem is even more complicated. Within Confucianism itself an inherent dualism had developed between the Chu Hsi (twelfth-century) and Wang Yang-ming (fifteenth- and sixteenth-centuries) schools of Neo-Confucianism. Chu Hsi's sanctioned a way of thought and conduct rationalist, mechanist, determinist, and materialist. Wang Yang-ming's as emphatically stressed the intuitive, subjective, and affective within the same basic system, that founded on the secondary Confucian Classics, i.e. the ANALECTS, MENCIUS, THE DOCTRINE OF THE MEAN, and, especially, THE GREAT LEARNING.

Within the novel, therefore, the tensions are not always Confucian versus Taoist-Buddhist. At times they suggest, rather, Chuist versus Wangian modes of Neo-Confucianism. A case may thus be made for Chia Cheng, Pao's father, as exhibiting a Chuist mentality, while his mother, Pao-yu's grandmother, the Matriarch, as clearly exemplifies the mind of Wang Yang-ming (as does also Pao-chai, a youthful version of the Matriarch).

Still, the major tensions of the novel wax between Confucian and Taoist components of Chinese thought. The complementarity (or dichotomy) parallels, not only yin/yang elements as set forth in the I CHING (THE BOOK OF CHANGES, a primary Confucian classic), but also Western polarities expressed as Apollonian and Dionysian. Against Confucianism's regularity and protocol, the Taoist-Buddhist alliance underscores freedom, naturalness, spontaneity, unconventionality, and, above all, that detachment necessary for absorption into the Absolute. There, differentiation and particularity vanish into the whole; there pain cannot be and pleasure is unknown. The novel makes no strong or clear distinction between Buddhist and Taoist modes.

As for the Confucian Classics, Chia Cheng reproaches Pao-yu for favoring the primary classic SHIH CHING (THE BOOK OF POETRY) over the secondary classics on which the examinations are based. In any case, Pao's preferences run to Laotse's TAO TE CHING and its companion BOOK OF CHUANG-TSE; even more passionately does he respond to romantic dramas like THE ROMANCE OF THE WESTERN CHAMBER and THE PEONY PAVILION.

Among the universally valid insights dramatized by the novel are 1) the experience of youth awakening to warmth, joy, creativity, and romantic dreams of lasting love and beauty; 2) the gradual realization that the ineluctable condition of human love and beauty is pain, suffering, tears, and death; 3) the rapturous, confounding initiation into sexuality; 4) the wrenching choices that must be made as prudence and natural appetency clash; 5) alienation from parents overzealous for order and respectability and strangely oblivious of deeper springs whence life and feeling flow; 6) a resorting to grandparents willing to overlook convention and rule by love; 7) the decay of a great family or culture, induced as much from inner as from outer ills; 8) nostalgia for the past, for golden days gone by, a mood which links the novel, not only to Marcel Proust, but, as well, to Murasaki Shikibu.

HUNG-LOU MENG (THE DREAM OF THE RED CHAMBER)   225

Murasaki Shikibu! The name conjures up links between Japan's eleventh-century masterpiece and China's of the eighteenth. In both, tragic tensions bind characters to a world of particularity and ecstatic beauty and to recognition that enjoying them brings sorrow, pain, decay, and death. Though, significantly, Genji dies before effecting his resolve, he proposes to become a Buddhist, to cut himself off finally from earthly desire and involvement. Pao-yu in fact leaves his family and friends to join the Taoist and Buddhist who had, in the first place and at his own request, initiated him into the Red-Dust Sphere.

World-literature students for years chafed at the lack of a good, complete, and accessible translation of HLM into English. As of the mid 1980s two such works are available: the Yang Hsien-yi and Gladys Yang three-volume DREAM OF RED MANSIONS (a more accurate rendering of the Chinese title, HUNG-LOU MENG) and the David Hawkes-John Minford five-volume THE STORY OF THE STONE (a restoration of an older title). While, to my knowledge, no English-language study of length has compared the two versions, comments here and there find both of high and equal merit. A student evaluation, however, on one occasion showed preference for the Yang translation as more moving, sympathetic and immediate.

English-language scholarship on HLM, besides a number of unpublished doctoral dissertations, has produced five notable book-length studies: Wu Shih-ch'ang's 1962 ON THE RED CHAMBER DREAM explores major eighteenth-century manuscripts for textual evidence relative to dating, authorship, drafts, revisions, and commentaries. Jonathan Spence's 1966 TS'AO YIN AND THE K'ANG-HSI EMPEROR: BONDSERVANT AND MASTER thoroughly studies the Ts'ao family's Manchu connections. Jeanne Knoerle's 1972 THE RED CHAMBER DREAM: A CRITICAL STUDY uses conventional Western norms of subject, story, plot, and character. Lucien Miller's 1975 THE MASKS OF FICTION: MYTH, MIMESIS, AND PERSONA applies to the novel the modal norms of allegory, realism, and perspective. Andrew H. Plaks' 1976 ARCHETYPE AND ALLEGORY IN THE DREAM OF THE RED CHAMBER probes the novel's deeper structures as a reflection of the traditional Chinese way of viewing the world and relating events, people, and places within the cosmic order.

Besides Hsia's "ground-breaking" analysis of HLM in his 1968 THE CLASSIC CHINESE NOVEL and Hawkes' comprehensive introduction to THE STORY OF THE STONE, eight articles particularly illuminate Ts'ao Hsueh Ch'in's achievement in HLM:

1) Francis Westbrook's 1971 comparison of Pao-yu with Prince Myshkin of Dostoyevsky's THE IDIOT; 2) James Fu's 1973 interpretation of crone Liu Lao-lao as both real and mythic; 3) Rudolph Chu's 1976 contrast, relative to HLM, of Western and Chinese modes of coping with suffering; 4) Joey Bonner's 1976 account of Marxist critics' war against traditional readings of Chinese classics; 5) John C.Y. Wang's study of Chih-yen Chai's commentary; 6) Lewis Robinson's 1979 paralleling of Pao-yu and Parsifal to show personal growth as a literary substructure; 7) Anthony Yu's view of Tai-yu as Schopenhaurian tragic heroine; and 8) Marsha Wagner's 1985 exposition of Chinese individualism as projected in HLM's minor characters.

The ultimate human relevance of THE DREAM OF THE RED CHAMBER is its projection of the dichotomy between the life force--insistent on freedom, creativity, spontaneity, intuition,. feeling, and becoming--and the controls of reason, law, art, restraint, and morality. For achieving insight into this tension no novel better serves. Only the poetry of John Keats can even challenge it.

Translations

G1. Birch, Cyril, tr. "How to Be Rid of a Rival." ANTHOLOGY OF CHINESE LITERATURE. Two volumes. New York: Grove Press, 1972. II: 203-258.

Extended extracts from Chapters 63-69, showing Hsi-feng's (Phoenix's) vengeance on Second-Sister Yu, who lacks the younger, Third-Sister Yu's courage and aggressiveness. Illustrates author Ts'ao's use of clothing for special (here ironic) effect, as, by her glittering white-and-silver mourning garb, Hsi-feng subtly reproaches her husband's new, gaudily-gowned favorite. Encourages debate on whether the work was written by a) a nostalgic middle-aged Bohemian, b) a merciless dissector of a family by its own moral failures fallen on evil times, or c) a Buddhist-Taoist contemplator of the ashes of human experience.

G2. Chai Ch'u and Winberg Chai, trs. and eds. "HUNG-LOU MENG (DREAM OF THE RED CHAMBER)." A TREASURY OF CHINESE LITERATURE: A NEW PROSE ANTHOLOGY INCLUDING FICTION AND DRAMA. New York: Appleton-Century Publishers, 1965. Pages 255-267.

Provides brief notes, outdated at times, on the novel's textual history, variant versions, and authorship theories, as well as a 10-page plot summary. Assumes as central theme the Pao-Tai love affair, while nodding at autobiographical content, Ming-Ch'ing political allegory, and novel-of-manners realism. Praises plot, characterization, portrayal of human emotions, and earnest philosophy of life. Calls attention to HUNG-LOU MENG's carrying on of "a splendid tradition of the Chinese novel ... the creation of numerous characters in one work." From Chapter 41 presents the story of Liu Lao-lao's touring of Takuanyuan, the fabled Chia garden.

G3. Chang, H.C., tr. "A Burial Mound for Flowers." CHINESE LITERATURE: POPULAR FICTION AND DRAMA. Chicago: Aldine Publishers, 1973. Pages 383-403.

Translates Chapter 23 of HUNG-LOU MENG, wherein Taiyu prepares a burial mound for fallen flowers, unconsciously anticipating her own early demise. In accompanying notes, identifies author Ts'ao as a Manchu aristocrat and his work as the only Chinese colloquial fiction in which feelings are paramount, utterly refined and precious, with no slightest vagary, blush, or caprice going unobserved. Points out Ts'ao's original purpose of writing a drama, the Taoist quality of Pao's strongest instincts, his aversion for Confucian norms of filial piety, family honor, and duty, and his frequent quotations from romantic dramas ROMANCE OF THE WESTERN CHAMBER and THE PEONY PAVILION.

G4. Giles, Herbert A. "The HUNG-LOU MENG Commonly Called THE DREAM OF THE RED CHAMBER." JOURNAL OF THE NORTH CHINA BRANCH OF THE ROYAL ASIATIC SOCIETY. New Series 20.1 (November 1, 1885): 1-23, 51-53.

A readable, condensed retelling of Pao-yu's story, accompanied by an extensive note calling attention to the "wholly inaccurate translation" of the title HUNG-LOU MENG as DREAM OF THE RED CHAMBER and considering the alternatives.

G5. Guerne, Armel, tr. LE REVE DANS LE PAVILLON ROUGE. Paris: Guy le Prat, 1964.

Based on Kuhn's 1932 German translation.

G6. Hawkes, David, and John Minford, trs. THE STORY OF THE STONE (SHIH T'OU CHI) by Ts'ao Hsueh-ch'in. Volumes I-III tr. by Hawkes; volumes IV and V by Minford. New York: Penguin Books, 1973-1986.

Shares honors with the Yang rendering as the best complete English translation of HUNG-LOU MENG (here called SHIH T'OU CHI, THE STORY OF THE STONE). Contributes, in the introduction, the soundest and most lucid presentation of Ts'ao Hsueh Ch'in's life and career and that of his immediate forbears, ethnic Chinese who, for a century, functioned as Manchu Bannermen. Provides tenable identifications, not only of Ts'ao's father and younger brother, but, as well, of the two commentators most important before the 1792 first printing of the 120-chapter novel, Red Inkstone and Odd Tablet. Speculates that Ts'ao completed the last 40 chapters of the book in a kind of rough draft, the manuscripts of which were entrusted by his widow to a still unidentified relative or friend.

Explains that the severe literary witchhunt of the Ch'ien-lung emperor, beginning in the 1760s and lasting until the mid 1790s, and Ts'ao's vulnerability as a possible critic of Manchu rulers responsible for his family's fall rendered advisable the withdrawal from public attention of the completed manuscript. Explains the role of Odd Tablet, following on the 1763 and 1764 deaths, respectively, of Ts'ao and of Red Inkstone, in assembling diverse manuscripts eventually to be submitted to editors Kao and Ch'eng for its January 1792 first publication (their prefaces appear in Volume Four's Appendix).

Suggests, further, that inconsistencies in the narrative sometimes arise from the necessity of disguising characters and merging fact and fiction so as to escape political censure. In addition to full identifications of characters at the end of each volume, contains, among other matters, explanations of games, music, rites, and celebrations.

G7. Hudson, E., tr. "An Old, Old Story." CHINA JOURNAL 8 (June 1928): 7-15.

A quaint retelling in 14 pages and fairy-tale language of Pao-yu's central narrative.

G8. Joly, Bancroft, tr. HUNG-LOU MENG or DREAM OF THE RED CHAMBER. Hong Kong: Kelly and Walsh, 1892.

A dated first translation into English of Chapters 1-23 of HUNG-LOU MENG in which antiquated diction, roundabout phraseology, and unexpected shifts of tense do not cancel the merit of a bold attempt to make the classic available to English readers unversed in Chinese.

G9. Kao, George, tr. and ed. "Liu Lao-lao." CHINESE WIT AND HUMOR. New York: Sterling Publishing Company, 1976. Pages 149-160. First published in 1946.

The irresistible antics of Liu Lao-lao, a world-class comic.

G10. Kuhn, Franz, tr. DER TRAUM DER ROTEN KAMMER. Leipzig: Insel-Verlag, 1932.

Has provided the base for many recensions into English.

G11. Li Tche-houa, and Jacqueline Alezais. LA REVE DANS LES PAVILLONS ROUGES (Revised by Andre D'Horman). [Paris]: Editions Gallimard, 1981.

A two-volume complete translation into French, subsidized by UNESCO and augmented by an extensive introduction, a map of seventeenth/eighteenth-century China, sketches of Ningkuofu and Yungkuofu compounds and Takuanyuan Garden, lists and locations of places and of characters by family and by personal names, genealogical tables, and identifications of historic editions from which the numerous illustrations have been taken.

G12. McHugh, Florence and Isabel McHugh, trs. DREAM OF THE RED CHAMBER BY TS'AO HSUEH-CH'IN. From the German text of Franz Kuhn. New York: Pantheon Press, 1958.

Described by Knoerle as a sometimes awkward but generally effective attempt to catch the spirit of the original, offers a translation of Kuhn's 1932 German rendering of HUNG-LOU MENG. In the Kuhn introduction, reviews Hu Shih's 1921 publication of pioneer research on the novel; Benjamin Joly's 1892-1893 Englishing of less than half the original; and Wang Chi-chen's even shorter 1929 version. Claims for the Kuhn work a five-sixths completeness and service in making available for the first time in a Western language an adequate translation, enabling the work to claim its place in world literature.

Considers the work as a) autobiography and b) as roman à clef, revolving about the Ch'ien-lung emperor (r. 1736-1796) and his father (a view Kuhn believes tenable). Notes the important array of secondary characters, specifically old servant Jiao, whose appearance at story's end confirms his role as unwanted and unheeded prophet. Proposes alternate answers to the question of the novel's core: 1) a Confucian story of a noble house, its destruction and rehabilitation, 2) a Taoist-Buddhist morality about spiritual awakening, 3) a Westernlike case history of a degenerate young aristocrat confronting reality and, in the end, slinking cravenly away.

G13. Wang Chi-chen, tr. DREAM OF THE RED CHAMBER. New York: Twayne Publishers, 1958. First edition New York: Doubleday, 1929.

Compresses the original 120 chapters into 60, including a seven-chapter recension of the concluding 40 units, while conveying the spirit of the original in attractive English. In the introduction calls HUNG-

LOU MENG first to break with early novel traditions (but CHIN P'ING MEI?) and unique among the classic novels in featuring autobiography (but JU-LIN WAI-SHIH?). Accepts the work as a novel of manners, but also as the story of a Chinese family whose survival precedes in urgency individual satisfaction or fulfillment. Looks on Pao-yu and Tai-yu as figures of high comedy à la Beatrice and Benedick or Millamant and Mirabell. Calls attention to Manchu connections of the Ts'ao family and their declining fortunes as sources for poignant, realistic detail.

G14. Yang Hsien-yi and Gladys Yang, trs. DREAM OF RED MANSIONS (HUNG LOU-MENG). Three volumes. Illus. Tai Tun-pang. Peking: Foreign Languages Press, 1978.

A complete and accurate translation, with special strength in renditions of poetry, in presentation of intimate dialogues, and in sadder, more moving episodes. Includes for each volume over a dozen full-page colored illustrations depicting characters and authentic background detail. Offers amenities by way of a cover depicting in full color the Garden of Takuanyuan, end-pages of choice material and delicate design, page markers, and a small brochure identifying characters and relationships.

Studies

G15. Alexander, Edwin. "China's 'Three Ways' as Reflected in DREAM OF THE RED CHAMBER." CHINESE CULTURE 17 (1976): 145-157.

Likens Chinese culture as reflected in its greatest novel to a three-legged stool (Confucianism, Taoism, and Buddhism) on which people rest comfortably without severe oppositions of one system to another. After capsulated descriptions of each belief, examines plot, style, character, and society to find in each the triple elements. Concludes that Hsia's view of the novel's theme as unresolved tension between compassion and detachment (Hsia would like more

compassion) and Knoerle's reading as a similar bind
between transcendence and immanence (she wishes for
more transcendence) both err, that Chinese culture
has never suffered from Western either-or, but ease-
fully resides on a triple-footed foundation.

G16. Berry, Margaret. "The Apprenticeship Novel in China:
HUNG-LOU MENG." PROCEEDINGS OF THE EIGHTH INTER-
NATIONAL SYMPOSIUM ON ASIAN STUDIES 8.1 (1986):
11-21. (Hong Kong: Asian Research Service.)

Following Plaks' suggestion that in HUNG-LOU MENG the
Bildungsroman form blossoms into an indisputable
masterpiece, analyzes the novel using norms suggested
by Suzanne Howe and articulated by William P. Shaffner in his 1983 THE APPRENTICESHIP NOVEL: The hero,
gifted, sensitive, perceptive, sets out, meets with
reverses due largely to his own temperament, falls in
with various guides and counselors, makes false
starts in choosing his friends, his wife, and his
work, and finally adjusts to the demands of his time
and environment by finding a sphere of action in
which he may work effectively.

Questions whether Chia Pao-yu masters the art of
living, and concludes that the answer is ambiguous
and contingent on one's perception of the ending as a
reprehensible withdrawal from adult responsibility or
a sublimation into a higher form of life. See G69
and G82.

G17. Berry, Margaret. "Heroes as Shining Princes." PEGA-
SUS OVER ASIA: VENTURES IN EAST-WEST LITERARY
ANALYSIS. Hong Kong: Asia Research Service, 1980.
Pages 45-52.

Collates Chinese, Japanese, and English protagonists
for what they may reveal of national identity. Finds
in Pao-yu of HUNG-LOU MENG a rebel against a) the
normal primacy of the Chinese social group; b) order-
ly, hierarchical, prescribed human relationships; and
c) structure, ceremony, and ritual.

In Genji of Murasaki's GENJI MONOGATARI, sees the
paragon of Japanese mono no aware, sensitivity to the
beauty and passingness of things by which emotions

are enriched, disciplined, and refined; and in Stephen Dedalus of Joyce's PORTRAIT OF THE ARTIST AS A YOUNG MAN a rage for order comprehensible to human reason and the experience of the Self as the center of the universe.

Finds all three protagonists strikingly talented, hypersensitive, aesthetically discriminating and sexually precocious; all, alienated from their societies, oblivious to or neglectful of social and political urgencies; all arriving by way of guilt, remorse, and anguish at separation from conventional life; all suffering from crucial relationships with their parents; all identifying with prototypes from older literatures; all finding the catalyst of their development in women or in the female principle.

G18. Bonner, Joey. "Yu P'ing-po and the Literary Dimension of the Controversy Over HUNG-LOU MENG." CHINA QUARTERLY 67 (September 1976): 546-581.

An indispensable article focusing on the critical history of HUNG-LOU MENG and its culmination in the 1954 Marxist campaign against Yu P'ing-po, distinguished New Redologist and Hu-Shih protege and disciple.

Lists as stages 1) 1754-1791, in which Chih-yen Chai annotations, mostly literary, dominated study of the 80-chapter manuscript SHIH T'OU CHI; 2) 1791-1900, in which the printed 120-chapter HUNG-LOU MENG led critics to question the authorship of the addendum and to speculate about magical and hidden meanings little related to historical and autobiographical backgrounds; 3) 1900-1922, in which the old (chiu) Redology (Hung-hsueh) explored the work's underlying dynamics, perhaps an attack on the Manchu government; 4) 1922-1953, in which, prompted by the pragmatic Hu Shih, the New Redologists (hsin Hung-hsueh) adopted "modern," "scientific" methods to identify texts, authorship, dating, authenticity, and related historical and especially autobiographical issues; and 5) 1954-   , in which Marxist-Leninist literary criticism prevails.

Summarizes the 1954 onslaught, spearheaded by Li Hsi-fan and Lan Ling, against Yu as, despite his recognized loyalty to Communism, a holder of bourgeois idealist literary views, user of "totally" erroneous critical methods, and substituter of trivial textual and historical data for the larger significance of the work [Yu recanted some of his views within the year. See G113].

Differentiates conflicting views in three areas: 1) Artistic style: Yu focuses on DRC as an impartial mirroring of the protagonist's own life and society without praise or blame; Marxists see it as a mirroring of that society so as to convey the author's condemnation of its failures. 2) General significance: Yu reads the work as an individual personal tragedy, in which the protagonist, convinced of the illusoriness of love, retires from the world without giving up his compulsion to immortalize his charming girl companions; Marxists read it as an expose of an unjust, corrupt, and decaying Ch'ing feudal society.

3) Interpretation of major characters: Yu interprets Pao-yu as a tragic individual drawn by regret and poverty into Buddhist-Taoist retirement from the world, and Pao-chai as a girl equally lovable and beautiful as Tai-yu, the two together representing Pao's ideal, each with her excellence, not to be subsumed by the other. In this view Yu diverges from the Old Redologists, who extolled Tai-yu's preeminent beauty and romantic desirability. Marxists interpret Pao as "the new man," the anti-feudal hero whose fate results from unheeded protest against social inequity, and Pao Chai as the negative, repulsive embodiment of essential feudal evil contrasted with the luminous beauty of rebel Tai-yu.

Recapitulates the aims of the anti-Yu campaign as 1) to discredit bourgeois hsin Hung-hsueh (New Redology) scholarship, 2) to educate people, especially students, in Marxist-Leninist literary theory, and 3) to recapture the classics, China's cultural heritage, not only for their aesthetic worth, but also for their service as weapons in ongoing class war.

Sees the 1954 campaign reenacted in 1960-61 debates. Recalls that the Party at this time sought, alternately by persuasion and penalty, to assure itself of the loyalty of intellectuals despite constant resurfacing of their questions. Lists these questions as about a) the dynamics of history (whether evolutionary or revolutionary), b) historical materialism (whether technical-economic or Promethean-willed), c) relations of social classes (whether harmonious or antagonistic), d) the peasant rebellion and mentality (whether conservative or revolutionary), e) certain personae (whether conservative or revolutionary), and f) the nature of consciousness (whether the spirit of the age or the expression of perennial class opposition).

Points out, finally, that in its insistence on "correct" intellectual and literary positions, the Communists urge discrimination in cultural objects between false passages and true, between negative and positive elements (HUNG-LOU MENG, for example, is said to hold certain undesirable tendencies toward nihilism and fatalism), between the elixir of the work and its dregs, and, finally, the identification of a two-fold enemy, the bourgeois West and the China of a bygone day. See G31, G51, and G113.

G19. Brandauer, Frederick P. "Review: Miller's MASKS OF FICTION IN DREAM OF THE RED CHAMBER and Plaks' ARCHETYPE AND ALLEGORY IN DREAM OF THE RED CHAMBER." JOURNAL OF ASIAN STUDIES 36.3 (1977): 554-557.

Praises both Miller's MASKS OF FICTION and Plaks' ARCHETYPE AND ALLEGORY for pioneering in literary, aesthetic, formal analysis of Chinese masterpieces as against authorship, dating, and textual studies.

After summarizing each book's argument, judges that 1) Miller's work makes the unexplained assumption that myth equals the allegorical mode; mimesis, the realistic; and persona, the narrative; and that 2) Plaks' work implies that his standards, structural patterns of complementary bipolarity and multiple periodicity, define all Chinese literature. Concludes that the Miller work provides the best available introduction to HUNG-LOU MENG and that the Plaks work must interest all students of Chinese literature, philosophy, and thought, and that his mastery of differences between Western and Chinese allegorical modes must benefit comparative-literature scholars.

G20. Brandauer, Frederick P. "Some Philosophical Implications of the HUNG-LOU MENG." CHING FENN 9 (1966): 14-23.

Distinguishes in the novel's mythical framework elements of Confucianism (propriety, the determining Will of Heaven), Taoism (popular superstitions), and Buddhism (incarnation and reincarnation). Sees this framework as an elusive model posing deep and subtle questions about the society and the individual's place in it. Observes, in the main narrative, the climactic enigma of the relation of Chia (false) Pao-yu to Chen (true) Pao-yu: With which, if either, are we to sympathize and/or identify?

G21. Brokaw, Cynthia J. "The Uses of Literature in Communist China: THE DREAM OF THE RED CHAMBER Campaign 1954-55." Unpublished paper (1971): 6-7.

G22. Brown, Carolyn T. "The 'Loss of Paradise' Myth in THE DREAM OF THE RED CHAMBER." CEA CRITIC 44 (May 1982): 12-19.

Discusses the novel's dual myth: 1) the explicit, begun in Chapter One and carried on by the jade, the priest, the monk, the Goddess of Disillusionment, and "the lost paradise," itself part of an ever-recurring cycle; and 2) the implicit, "the fall of man" of the main narrative, ending in defeat and despair, or at least caught agonizingly in an irresolvable conflict between compassion and detachment, a situation emotionally more powerful than its companion myth. Invokes Plaks' analysis of the novel's structure as a kind of interplay between opposites, a network of events and non-events in a temporal flux with little of Western linear thrust, but its own integrity.

G23. Chan Bing-cho. THE AUTHORSHIP OF "THE DREAM OF THE RED CHAMBER": A COMPUTERIZED STATISTICAL STUDY OF ITS VOCABULARY. Madison: University of Wisconsin, 1981. An unpublished dissertation.

Computerizes linguistic variables to explore the authorship of HUNG-LOU MENG, concluding that scientific, objective, quantitative data negate the dual-authorship theory for Chapters 1-80 and Chapters 81-120 and substantiate the one-author hypothesis. Reviews the manuscript history of the work, from the Gengchen version, hand-copied from another dated 1760, to the 120-chapter, first-printed publication of 1791. Argues from internal and external evidence against Ts'ao's authorship and identifies the several commentators responsible for marginalia and interlinear annotations of early manuscripts. Even to the generalist offers important materials for understanding and interpretation.

G24. Chan Ping-leung. "Myth and Psyche in HUNG-LOU MENG." CRITICAL ESSAYS ON CHINESE FICTION. Eds. Winston L.Y. Yang and Curtis P. Adkins. Hong Kong: Chinese University of Hong Kong, 1980. Pages 165-179.

Declaring HUNG-LOU MENG more than love story or Bildungsroman, calls on John H. Armstrong's study of the Paradise myth to elucidate the mystic import of Takuanyuan Garden within the Illusory Realm of the Great Void. Contrasts the carefree happiness of the young there with the sordid tumult in the adult society beyond. Joins with spatial symbolism of and within the Garden the ahistorical timelessness characteristic not only of the Garden and of the originating world of the Stone and Jade, but also of events like the Lantern Festival. For a study of the Lantern Festival's function in CHIN P'ING MEI see E15.

Associates the Festival with three crucial events and their mythic significance: the abduction of Chen Ying-lien (the loss of innocence), the homecoming of Cardinal Spring (the zenith of family fortunes), and the death of the royal concubine (the beginning of family decay). To time-space symbolism adds that of doublets, especially of characters, these functioning at three psychic levels: Chen Pao-yu as superego; Chia Pao-yu and Black Jade (Tai-yu) as ego; and Precious Clasp (Pao-chai) and Pervading Presence as libido or id. Defends the positive role of Precious Clasp, the affirming function of Pao's turn to Buddhism, and the complementary rather than hostile relationship of all the opposites.

G25.   Chang, H.C. "On THE RED CHAMBER DREAM." ANNUAL (China Society of Singapore) (1962-63): 1-6.

G26.   Ch'en Wen-hua. "Review of Wu Shih-ch'ang's ON THE RED CHAMBER DREAM." T'UNG-HAI HSUEH-PAO 7.1 (June 1965): 135-151.

Evaluates Wu Shih-ch'ang's 1961 study based on two annotated eighteenth-century manuscripts, acknowledging his discovery of prefaces written by Ts'ao's younger brother; a firming up of 1715 as Ts'ao's birth year and February 12, 1764, as his death date; the site of Takuanyuan Garden as a place formerly owned by Ts'ao's father and later acquired by Sui Ho-te; and especially Wu's reconstruction of episodes in the last 40 chapters to accord more closely with the author's plan and intent. Criticizes what is perceived as Wu's overemphasis on autobiographical detail as part of continuing New-Redology strategy.

G27.   Chow Tse-tsung. "Ts'ao Hsueh-ch'in." INDIANA COMPANION TO TRADITIONAL CHINESE LITERATURE. Eds. William H. Nienhauser, Jr., and others. Bloomington: Indiana University Press, 1986. Pages 791-793.

Traces Ts'ao's illustrious genealogy, starred with generals, officials, and familiars of emperors as far back as the Five Dynasties (907-959). Notes the Ts'aos' close association with Manchu rulers and their serving as Bannermen in an important military unit. Attends particularly to Ts'ao Yin, the author's grandfather, a learned scholar, poet, and official, who four times at his own residence entertained the K'ang-hsi emperor (r. 1661-1722) and who gave two of his daughters as brides to Manchu princes. Debates Ts'ao Hsueh Ch'in's paternity: whether he was the posthumous son of Ts'ao Yung (Yin's son-heir) or an adopted nephew.

Follows bloody political events after the K'ang-hsi emperor's death, including the Ts'aos' fall from favor and loss of properties and income during the Yung-cheng reign (1723-1735). Observes their partial retrieval during the Ch'ien-lung reign (1736-1796), but a final fall by 1740 and, after that, for Ts'ao Hsueh-Ch'in a life of struggle, poverty, and dependency. Places the writing of the novel between 1740 and 1750 despite Ts'ao's drinking problems, poor success in selling his paintings, and his first wife's untimely death. Speculates that his own 1763 (?) death was hastened by the loss of an infant son, possibly borne by his first wife.

Characterizes Ts'ao Hsueh-ch'in as unconventional in his thought and action and suggests the influence on him of the writings of Chuang-tse (second half of the fourth century B.C.) and of Neo-Taoists of the Wei-Chin period (A.D. 265-418). Remarks that Ts'ao's fame came only long after his death.

G28. Chu, Rudolph Y. "The Hermit and the Sufferer: Two Different Prototypes in Chinese and Western Literature." TAMKANG REVIEW 6 (October 1975/April 1976): 329-340.

Offers as literary evidence of a major difference in East-West psyches that "turbulent" Westerners (beginning with the Greeks) glory in defiant confrontations with their gods and with nature and portray literary heroes as chiefly Sufferers, as witness Achilles, Ulysses, Agamemnon, Medea, Dido, Christ, the martyrs, and, in modern times, the creations of Sartre, Kafka, Dreiser, Hemingway, and Faulkner.

By contrast, depicts the harmony-loving Chinese as, from the beginning, holding up moderation and adjustment (yielding) between humans, Nature, and the gods, as the desirable good. Notes that their typical hero, if unable to cope with one member of the triad (usually Society), has resorted to the other (Nature), and so has been identified, not as Sufferer, but as Recluse. Thus with Confucius, Mencius, Laotse, Chuang-tse, and myriad poets and other writers who, from the public fray, especially in times of failure, have fled for refuge to the mountains, forests, rivers, and rocks. Offers interesting implications for the study of HUNG-LOU MENG.

G29. Chuang Hsin-cheng. THEMES OF "DREAM OF THE RED CHAMBER": A COMPARATIVE INTERPRETATION. Bloomington: Indiana University, 1966. An unpublished dissertation.

An extraordinary gathering of eight East-West themes affording parallels with HUNG-LOU MENG: 1) portrait of the artist: Pao compared with Joyce's Stephen Dedalus, Lawrence's Paul Morel, Dostoyevsky's Dmitri, Proust's Marcel, Wolfe's Elmer Gant; 2) father and son relationship: Pao and his father, Chia Cheng, compared with similar duads in Fielding's TOM JONES, Smollett's TRISTRAM SHANDY, Dickens' HARD TIMES and GREAT EXPECTATIONS, Stendhal's LE ROUGE ET LE NOIR, Balzac's LA COMEDIE HUMAINE, Tolstoi's WAR AND PEACE, Turgenev's FATHERS AND SONS, Meredith's RICHARD FEVEREL, Mann's BUDDENBROOKS, Zola's ROUGON-MARQUART series;

3) victimized adolescents: Ts'ao's characters generally, contrasted with those of Dickens, Dostoyevsky, Nabokov, George Eliot, Proust, Colette, Moravia; 4) the little worlds of women: Jin-ling maids and matrons aligned with the feminine casts of Meredith, Proust, Dickens, Chekhov, Dostoyevsky, Thackeray; 5) sex repression: certain DREAM characters set alongside those of Boccaccio, Henry James, Charlotte Bronte: 6) love and frustration: cases from THE DREAM paralleled with selections from Dickens, Dostoyevsky, Goethe, Mann, Proust; 7) lust: examples from THE DREAM matched with analogues from Euripides, Racine, Stendhal, Wolfe, Colette, Proust, Gide; 8) the problem of time: the sense of stasis and passingness in THE DREAM matched with passages from Proust, Chekhov, and Mann.

G30. Cornaby, W. Arthur. "The Secret of the Red Chamber." NEW CHINA REVIEW 1 (August 1919): 329-339.

Makes a case for HUNG-LOU MENG as a roman à clef involving two Manchu stories: 1) Wu San-kuei, a Ming general, on hearing of his favorite concubine's abduction by an upstart Ming ruler, in reprisal joined the Manchus and helped them capture Peking; and 2) following the death by poisoning of the young Imperial Concubine Tung-O, daughter of a noble Ming family and favorite of Manchu emperor Shun-chih-ti, the young ruler, after attempting suicide, retired from the world. Finds both tragic women depicted by no less than seven girls in HUNG-LOU MENG, notably by Tai-yu. Attributes repeated Ch'ing suppression of the novel to a powerful family's determination to hide its identity, citing the author's opening statement about "concealing true matters."

G31. "The DREAM OF THE RED CHAMBER Case." CURRENT BACKGROUNDS 315 (March 4, 1955).

An indispensable collection of seven essays by Marxist scholars (notably Li Hsi-fan and Lan Ling) who, beginning in 1954, "recovered" for the masses China's classic novels, especially HUNG-LOU MENG. Performs this task by denigration of almost all preceding criticism, beginning with the work of Yu P'ing-po, for 30 years China's most respected authority on HLM. Accuses Yu of subjectivism, formalism, triviality, and bourgeois-idealism inimical to the State's historical materialism and socialist realism.

Attributes Yu's deviations to the pernicious influence of Hu Shih (1891-1962), leader of the May 4th Movement (1917-1923) and renowned pragmatist and Western-oriented intellectual of the twenties and thirties. Provides the basic materials for the "Redologist controversy of the fifties and sixties," one diminished by time and evolution as Chinese critics regain more balanced and comprehensive perspectives. Includes Yu's apology for errors, stupidity, and mistaken political views and his efforts at revision of former ideas and conformity with official policy in literary assessments. See G18, G51, and G113.

G32. Fang Chaoying. "Ts'ao Chan." EMINENT CHINESE OF THE CH'ING DYNASTY 1644-1912. Two volumes. Ed.

Arthur H. Hummel. Washington, D.C.: Library of Congress, 1943-1944. II: 737-739.

Identifies Ts'ao Chan (Ts'ao Hsueh Ch'in) as a member of the Bondservant Division of the Manchu Plain White Banners. Traces his family from days of glory as Manchu favorites to their 1728 fall, when the new emperor confiscated their property and forced them to struggle for survival. Affirms that by 1754 Ts'ao had completed, with Chih-yen Chai's commentary and glossing, 28 chapters, these copied several times (one such manuscript was in 1928 revealed to be in the possession of Hu Shih); and before 1769 had completed the 80-chapter version, this to be succeeded in 1792 by the first known printing, the 120-chapter version.

G33. Feuerwerker, Yi-tse Mei. "The Chinese Novel." APPROACHES TO THE ORIENTAL CLASSICS. Ed. William Theodore De Bary. New York: Columbia University Press, 1958. Pages 171-185.

Focuses on the novel as an embodiment of universal human realities in a peculiar culture, as the child-parent relationship, young love, or the status of the aged. Considers the dialogue--artfully revealing conflict and compromise, nuance and irony--as the author's forte. Denigrates the final chapter, even the scene of Tai-yu's death.

G34. Fitzgerald, C.P. "The Chinese Novel as a Subversive Force." MEANJIN QUARTERLY 10 (Spring 1951): 259-266.

Reads HUNG-LOU MENG as satire on officials and underlings of contemporary Chinese government, an idea not very developed.

G35. Fu, James S. "Liu Lao-lao and the Garden of Takuanyuan." LITERATURE EAST AND WEST 17 (1973): 305-314.

Studies the famous old woman who provides, not only laughter and sympathy, but wisdom and energy as well, to the Chia extended family. Presents Liu as a rejuvenating force in the Green World of Takuanyuan, as an embodiment, in Jung's terms, of the unconscious, the feminine component of the human psyche, who, among other benefits, provides antidotes for Tai-yu's narcissism and Hsi-feng's avarice. Differentiates Liu's roles in her four visits, especially as object of nun Miao's disdain and arrogance and as ever-reconciling agent between disparate social sectors.

G36. Giles, Herbert A. "HUNG-LOU MENG." HISTORY OF CHINESE LITERATURE. New York: Grove Press, 1901. Pages 355-384.

Rates HUNG-LOU MENG the Chinese novel's highest point of development, with a plot integration worthy of Fielding; characterization comparable with the best in Western novels; a vivid panorama of Chinese social life; a colloquial style rich in pathos and humor; and a close interrelation of spiritual and mundane worlds. Mistakenly attributes the time of composition to the last half of the seventeenth century.

G37. Grieder, Jerome B. "The Communist Critique of HUNG-LOU MENG." PAPERS ON CHINA 10 (1956): 142-168.

Literary, political, and ideological controversies over the interpretation of DREAM OF THE RED CHAMBER in China in the 1950s. See G18, G31, G51, and G113.

G38. Gutzlaff, Karl A.F. "HUNG-LOU MENG or DREAMS IN THE RED CHAMBER: A Novel." CHINESE REPOSITORY 5 (May 1842): 266-273.

A classic example of poor reading and critical ineptitude by "an unnamed correspondent," who, implying that he has read the work in the original, identifies Pao as a budding young lady whose callow romancing involves her in tedious misadventures.

G39. Hanan, Patrick. "The Development of Fiction and Drama." THE LEGACY OF CHINA. Ed. Raymond Dawson. London: Clarendon Press, 1964. Pages 135-136.

Finds the form and feeling of HUNG-LOU MENG reminiscent of Proust's LA RECHERCHE DU TEMPS PERDU. Points up the naturalness of the language, the truth to life of its story, and the merging of plot, character, and tone into an artistic whole.

Finds HLM's depth and range of sensibility unrivalled in Chinese fiction, not only by reason of the exchanges of highly articulate characters, but, as well, by the author's narrative style and subtly emotive symbols. Observes that Ts'ao brings to the story his own life experience and his family's decline from prosperity and imperial patronage.

G40. Hawkes, David. "Introduction." THE STORY OF THE STONE. Tr. David Hawkes and John Minford. Five volumes. New York: Penguin Books, 1973-1986. I: 15-46.

Includes discussions on the following matters: 1) the almost 30-year gap between the author's death and the publication of the completed novel; 2) the vindication of Kao E's integrity as editor, not author, of the final 40 chapters; 3) the five suggested titles (including THE PASSIONATE MONK'S TALE, A MIRROR FOR THE ROMANTIC, and THE TWELVE YOUNG LADIES OF JINLING); 4) the term "dream" as related to title and narrative; 5) the original plan of writing a drama, in emulation of sixteenth-century T'ang Hsien-tsu, noted for plays exploring dream and reality; 6) the "redness" of the novel as indicator of youth, spring, and prosperity in a sense close to the English "golden";

7) the career and character of the author's grandfather Ts'ao Yin, Bondservant-friend of the K'ang-hsi emperor (r. 1662-1722); 8) the author's paternity, here ascribed to Yin's nephew; 9) the identity of Red Inkstone (d. c1769), probably the author's cousin, and of his successor as close commentator on the early drafts, Odd Tablet (possibly the author's father), who prepared the first 80-chapters for publication; 10) Pao-yu as a composite of author, cousin, and brother-by-adoption; 11) the Ch'ien-lung emperor's literary inquisition in the decades following the author's death as reason for suppression of the last 40 chapters, originally describing harrowing scenes of persecution and poverty brought on by post-1722 Manchu emperors.

G41. Hawkes, David. "LE HONG-LEOU MONG, roman symboliste." MELANGE DE SINOLOGIE OFFERTES A MONSIEUR PAUL DEMIEVILLE. Two volumes. Paris: Presses Universitaires de France, 1974. II: 43-54.

Delays discussion of symbolism in HUNG-LOU MENG (DREAM OF THE RED CHAMBER) to review a) readings of the novel as a roman à clef, b) positive and negative characters (including a defense of Hsi-feng) and praise for "la subtilite de la psychologie ... [et] la complexite des personnages," c) Pao-yu's relation to the author, whether as alter ego or uncle.

Chooses as major symbols names, dream, the phoenix, the stone, tears, flowers, handkerchiefs, titles, mirrors, word games, the garden, and Chapter Five's Register. Believes that the girls cited in the Register represent diverse passions contemplated by Pao in his earthly odyssey, eventuating in "desillusion a la contemplation mystique et a la paix liberatrice."

G42. Hawkes, David. "The Translator, the Mirror, and the Dream: Some Observations on a New Theory." RENDITIONS 13 (Spring 1980): 5-20.

Argues that internal textual problems of HUNG-LOU MENG go deeper than an authorship rift between the first 80 and the last 40 chapters, that the earliest chapters are, in fact, "the disiecta membra of several different novels, notably MIRROR FOR THE ROMANTIC."

Calls on writings of Yuriri, an early nineteenth-century Ts'ao kinsman in possession of important documents, and the even more radical theories of today's Dai Bufan, who insists that the novel is "a greatly expanded and altered version of ... A MIRROR FOR THE ROMANTIC written, not by Ts'ao Hsueh-ch'in, but by an earlier author...who spent most of his life in the South."

Finds that such speculations explain many disjunctions of sequence and factual disparities, as for example, in Chapters 63-69, the stories of the sisters You-jie and You San-jie. Insists that such theories in no way alter the greatness of Ts'ao as a writer, the genius who could so meld intractable materials that the novel stands today among the world's greatest works of imaginative literature.

G43. Hegel, Robert E. "Heavens and Hells in Chinese Fictional Dreams." PSYCHOSINOLOGY: THE UNIVERSE OF DREAMS IN CHINESE CULTURE. Ed. Carolyn T. Brown. Washington, D.C.: Woodrow Wilson International Center for Scholars, 1987. Page 4.

Presents dreams in HUNG-LOU MENG as a means of communication between spiritual and mundane levels of existence, with realistic detail from actual life. Sets these images against the great cosmic order to which individual action must conform, always underscoring the emptiness of earthly attachment.

G44. Hightower, James R. TOPICS IN CHINESE LITERATURE: OUTLINES AND BIBLIOGRAPHIES. Cambridge, Massachusetts: Harvard University Press, 1965. Pages 105-106. (Originally published in 1949 and revised in 1952.)

Targets the love story as the real plot, based on the author's autobiography as member of a wealthy but declining family in a luxurious and extravagant milieu. Considers Pao a child throughout the novel's seven years, sentimental, effeminate, and greedy for affection, yet lauds the author's insight into the psychology of love as unique in Chinese literature. Accepts Kao E as author of the final 40 chapters.

G45. Ho Ch'i-fang. "On THE DREAM OF THE RED CHAMBER." CHINESE LITERATURE 1 (January 1963): 65-86.

Applauds Ts'ao Hsueh Ch'in's boldness and originality in championing women as men's equals and at times their superiors in purity, virtue, intelligence, sensitivity, courage, and even administrative skill. Expresses lavish appreciation for Tai-yu, contrary to Hsia's more negative evaluation (G47), but does less than justice to Pao-chai, tagged as ingratiating, heartless, hypocritical, and rigorous in maintaining feudal ideas. Praises Chinese novelists' ability to manipulate many characters in a unified narrative. Declares HUNG-LOU MENG superior to CHIN P'ING MEI in going beyond "darkness, vulgarity, and filth" to goodness, beauty, hope, and courage.

G46. Ho, Douglas I-ping. "Religious Figures in the DREAM OF THE RED CHAMBER." FU JEN STUDIES: LITERATURE AND LINGUISTICS 16 (1983): 1-32.

Explores the relation of HUNG-LOU MENG as a Taoist-Buddhist novel to the historical background of these religions and their proponents. Quotes government documents of the Manchu K'ang-hsi emperor's reign, citing certification and ordination of 300,000 priests and monks during four years. Cites, further, evidence of 300,000 more disciples or apprentice clerics, most of whom, according to miscellaneous official edicts, were ignorant and self-seeking, though a few monks and priests strictly followed religious practices, doctrines, and disciplines.

Analyzes numerous passages and characters in the novel, elucidating two basic attitudes of the author: respect for true religious figures and contempt for worldly and negative ones, especially older female religious figures.

G47. Hsia, C.T. "DREAM OF THE RED CHAMBER." THE CLASSIC CHINESE NOVEL: A CRITICAL INTRODUCTION. New York: Columbia University Press, 1968. Pages 245-297.

Reviews origins, textual complications, and artistic significance of China's greatest novel, especially as related to authorship of the last 40 chapters. Reads Lin Tai-yu as chiefly a neurotic, less tragic and complex than Pao-yu, a view discounted by Anthony Yu (G112). Compares the hero with Dostoyevsky's Prince Myshkin of THE IDIOT and speculates about Christian treatment of corresponding events as compared with Ts'ao's Taoist-Buddhist disposition of affairs. Frequently refers to Communist interpretations of the work as chiefly an attack on feudal and imperial institutions.

G48. Hsia, C.T. "Love and Compassion in DREAM OF THE RED CHAMBER." CRITICISMS 5 (Summer 1963): 261-271.

Concedes that autobiographical and sociopolitical readings have contributed much to RED CHAMBER studies, but charges that such readings miss the tragic essence of the novel: the irreconcilable conflict between compassion (caring involvement) and detachment (removal from all concern), the contrary pulls of disparate ideals, the struggle to maintain eros/agape despite intellectual preference for Taoist renunciation.

Discusses Ts'ao's understanding of love (ch'ing) and lust (yin), that love properly expands to include lust, whereas lust acts without love; that, in any case, love is inherently fragile and characteristically shattered by winds of the world, so that no alternate exists to counter Taoist insistence on a detachment excluding all care and love as well as hate. Warns against construal of the novel as chiefly a love tale, seeing Pao as remarkably free of concupiscence, resembling Holden Caulfield of THE CATCHER IN THE RYE in youth and sensitivity, disgust with cant and falsity, capacity for compassion, and desire to rescue innocent young girls.

Interprets Takuanyuan as a paradise in which frightened adolescents indulge dreams and aspirations, irretrievably disturbed when, by way of an erotica-embroidered purse, the serpent enters to scandalize prudish elders and occasion a destructive and fatal search into personal privacies. Identifies as Pao's spiritual awakening the moment of questioning: Is insensibility to joy and sorrow the price of liberation? Is it better to suffer and sympathize, knowing oneself powerless to alleviate pain? Or to pursue one's personal salvation regardless of others' agonized cries.

Sees Communist critics' blackening of Pao-chai and exaltation of Tai-yu as a serious distortion of text and author's intent. Cites a long passage omitted in the Wang translation and only passingly alluded to in McHugh-Kuhn, in which Pao-yu and Pao-chai debate the meaning of moral character as projected in the image of a newborn babe by both Mencius and Lao-tse. Likens Pao, not to Dostoyevsky's Dmitri (see G101), but rather to his Prince Myshkin of THE IDIOT, both loving innocently and compassionately in a depraved world.

Speculates about a "Christian" mode of resolving Pao's crisis, but concludes that the final irony may lie in the illusoriness of any escape, including the Taoist-Buddhist, leaving only human nostalgia for and need to be liberated from the World of the Red Dust.

G49. Hsia, C.T. "Review of Wu Shih-ch'ang's ON THE RED CHAMBER DREAM." ASIAN STUDIES 21.1 (November 1961): 78-81.

Calls Wu's book, covering the last four decades of HUNG-LOU MENG textual study, interesting and often valuable but outdated in its insistence that Kao E (c1740-c1815) authored the last 40 chapters. To illustrate, cites the reversed opinions of illustrious scholars like Yu P'ing-po, and, more importantly, evidence in recent manuscript findings negating the conventional view first promulgated by Hu Shih in 1928.

Compares two newly-found manuscripts supplementing the 1754 16-chapter manuscript annotated and glossed by Chih-yen Chai (the Chia-hsu pen) and the 1761 78-chapter manuscript with the same kind of additions (the K'eng-ch'en pen). Identifies the new findings as 1) an 80-chapter MS. dated 1784, like the 1791 publication lacking commentaries and exhibiting the same excisions; and 2) a 120-chapter MS. (with a superimposed date of 1855), discovered in 1959 and, like the 1784 version (and the 1791 printing), lacking commentary and showing the same deletions. Points out as the crucial point a notation found in the second MS. in Kao E's hand reading "Kao E has read it."

Reproaches Wu for disregarding Lin Yu-tang's "important" 1958 essay declaring, on the basis of internal literary evidence, Ts'ao Hsueh Ch'in author of the complete 120-chapter novel. Also, like Lin Yu-tang, defends the literary excellence of the last 40 chapters against conventional judgment that the chapters are "inferior ... dog's fur on sable." Blames general misjudgment here, not on bad will, but on the ideological assumptions of Wu and certain others.

Attributes the suppression of the 40 chapters following Ts'ao's 1763 death, and later serious alterations and suppressions of passages to the Ch'ien-lung emperor's literary inquisition at a time when the Ts'ao family's loyalty to the throne was under fire. Gives as one cause of imperial suspicion the Ts'aos' ownership of a gold lion-figure, formerly the property of a person regarded as the Emperor's mortal enemy.

G50. Hsia, C.T. "Yen Fu and Liang Chi-ch'ao as Advocates of the New Fiction." CHINESE APPROACHES TO LITERARY FORM. Ed. Adele Austin Rickett. Princeton, New Jersey: Princeton University Press, 1976. Pages 221-257.

Shows pioneers Yen and Liang as the first Chinese in modern times to proclaim fiction's power to educate the populace for political purposes. Notes these critics' scorn for what they perceive as HLM's projection of "lust" and its encouragement of readers to identify with "the weak and decadent Pao-yu." Registers Yen's and Liang's pleas for replacement of the classic novels, seen as seductive, unrealistic, and harmful, with modern political novels based on Western models and portraying heroes exemplifying the new political ideals.

G51. Hsu Min. "DREAM OF THE RED CHAMBER and Its Author-- Exhibition to Mark the 200th Anniversary of Death of Ts'ao Hsueh-ch'in." PEKING REVIEW 43 (October 1963): 25-28.

Purports to review the 1963 Peking-Palace Museum exhibit honoring the bicentennial of the death of Ts'ao Hsueh Ch'in, author of HUNG-LOU MENG. Always viewing the work as an expose of and attack on feudal China, rehearses a) the declining-family theme, accenting upper-class living gained by oppression of peasants and workers; b) individual characterizations as positive (rebels against the system) and negative (upholders of the traditional order and Confucian ideals of behavior); c) autobiographical evidence supporting Ts'ao's growing awareness of rottenness in the examination system and official venality and corruption.

Pays little attention to the exhibit as such, except to allude to land-leases drawn up by "debauched and extravagant nobles," and piles of high-interest loan receipts as proof of landlord oppression. Rehashes the fifties' critical revolution against bourgeois-idealist and autobiographical interpretations of the novel, concluding that "the proletariat has proved [itself] the only class that can critically inherit all that is best in the culture of mankind." See G18, G31, and G113.

G52. Hung Ming-shui. "Yuan Hung-tao (1568-1610)." THE INDIANA COMPANION TO TRADITIONAL CHINESE LITERATURE. Eds. William H. Nienhauser, Jr., and others. Bloomington: Indiana University Press, 1986. Pages 955-956.

Reviews the life and works of this second oldest of "the three Yuan brothers of Kung-an," literati-critics noted for their stress on originality and spontaneity and their early recognition of the vernacular novel, specifically SHUI-HU CHUAN and CHIN P'ING MEI, the latter, until Yuan Hung-tao's essay, publicly unnoticed.

G53. Hwang Mei-shu. "Chia Pao-yu: The Reluctant Quester." TAMKANG REVIEW 1 (April 1970): 211-22.

G54. Idema, Wilt Lukas. CHINESE VERNACULAR FICTION: THE FORMATIVE PERIOD. Leiden: E.J. Brill Company, 1974. Pages 128-131.

Contrasts HUNG-LOU MENG and JU-LIN WAI-SHIH. See F16.

G55. Kaltenmark, Odile. CHINESE LITERATURE. Tr. Anne-Marie Geoghegan. New York: Walker and Company, 1964 (revision of the 1948 original). Page 128.

Judges HUNG-LOU MENG sentimental, diffuse, and filled with unintelligible allusions, yet written with stylistic purity, poetic talent, and psychological understanding.

G56. Kao Yu-kung. "Lyric Vision in Chinese Narrative Tradition: A Reading of HUNG-LOU MENG and JU-LIN WAI-SHIH." CHINESE NARRATIVE: CRITICAL AND THEORETICAL ESSAYS. Ed. Andrew H. Plaks. Princeton: Princeton University Press, 1978. Pages 227-243.

Regards China's age-old esteem for lyric vision and accompanying distrust of discursiveness as basic to the development of autobiographical and romantic novels. In THE DREAM OF THE RED CHAMBER and THE SCHOLARS finds both the continuation of lyric complaint (conflict between the private and social selves, between poetic vision and philosophic thought) and modifications of its expression necessitated by extensive time/space narrative.

Illustrates the dilemma in the famous ENCOUNTERING SORROW (LI SAO), not epic or narrative, but lyric expression, and even in historical and religio-philosophical writings like those of Ssu-ma Ch'ien and Chuang-tse. Notes the development of the lyric novel at a time of lyric poetry's stagnation in presence of increasingly complex social realities demanding broader artistic forms. Contrasts the lyricism of THE SCHOLARS (the individual's response to more public, history-associated, and ritual-centered experience) with that of THE DREAM (the individual's response to more personal, myth-related, and dream-motivated presentation). Cautions against reading THE SCHOLARS as mere objective satire rather than as lyric anger at the individual's impotence in face of institutions obstructing personal self-fulfillment; and THE DREAM as mere love triangle rather than as a cry of despair at the impossibility of rendering love attachments permanent, or, for that matter, any private communication or commitment.

Structurally, proposes that episodes (groups of actions) function as basic building blocks, to be read as symbols, the totality of which represents the novel's lyric vision. Finds the key, accordingly, to

THE SCHOLARS' lyric vision in the prologue's idealized portrait of the distanced Wang Mien and in the epilogue's refraction of that ideal in four fame-and-riches-scorning craftsmen. In THE DREAM sees as "model story" the early chapters' account of the resplendent Goddess of Disillusionment and the austere monk and priest spelling out the philosophy at the heart of symbolic episodes. Delineates Pao's progression from an isolated, self-contained Self, through attachment and commitment to the Other, at first One and then the Many, and eventually his awakening to the conceptual ideal of the nothingness of earthly delight.

Regards the lyric vision of THE SCHOLARS as epitomized in the completion and ritual dedication of Temple T'ai-po and the ensuing reduction of its teachings to oblivion and the temple itself to ruins; that of THE DREAM, in the completion and dedication of Takuanyuan Garden, doomed, also, to ruin, with all its inhabitants, before many years have elapsed. Offers as alternative to bitterness a gallant (i.e. doomed) emphasis on "simple delight in the perceptual and imaginative world of individual experience."

G57. Kelleher, Teresa. "Comments on [Conference] Papers." CEA CRITIC 44 (1982): 26-28.

Responding to papers read in a world-literature panel of the College English Association, suggests that beyond the key issue of myth in HUNG-LOU MENG, the bright, human side of the novel, the typical Chinese zest for life and humor, for food and drink and conviviality, for intimate human relations should not be overlooked. Points out the fluid social situation in eighteenth-century China where, because of the examination system and bureaucratic organization, fame and fortune might rise and fall with devastating suddenness. Warns against overplaying Confucian stereotypes to the neglect of creative inner tensions abounding in the system, citing Precious Virtue's exhortations to Pao-yu and the dilemma which he faces about the "correct" way in which to act, whether to withdraw from or throw in his lot with the conventional world.

G58. Knoerle, Jeanne. THE DREAM OF THE RED CHAMBER: A CRITICAL STUDY. Foreword by Liu Wu-chi. Bloomington: Indiana University Press, 1972.

Pioneers a strictly aesthetic critique of THE DREAM, based on subject, story, plot, and character. In narrative style, finds that disjointedness and irregularity mar a surface of myriad finely-wrought characters and episodes. In the story of the Chia family's disgrace, seen as central, remarks the voracious inclusiveness and spreading detail never finely ordered to Jamesian unity, but satisfying Barbara Hardy's norms. Finds moral coherence in the triple vision of Confucian, Taoist, and Buddhist world views.

G59. Knoerle, Mary Gregory. A CRITICAL ANALYSIS OF THE DREAM OF THE RED CHAMBER IN TERMS OF WESTERN NOVELISTIC CRITERIA. Bloomington: Indiana University, 1965. An unpublished dissertation.

G60. Koepping, Klaus-Peter, and Lai Sing-lam. NEW INTERPRETATIONS OF THE "RED CHAMBER DREAM." Singapore: Public Press Company, 1973.

Explores, simplistically and superficially, HUNG-LOU MENG's sociological import, including, in the first essay, the artist's place in society, the censorship repeatedly imposed on his work, its descriptions of sexual techniques, and its attitude toward religion and morality. In the second, proclaims the novel centrally a condemnation of carnal lust, perceived as the ultimate evil, based on the author's misogyny, misanthropy, and loathing for himself.

G61. Kunst, Richard Alan. "The Beginning and the End of THE DREAM OF THE RED CHAMBER." Berkeley: University of California, 1969. An unpublished Master-of-Arts thesis.

Provides new insights into the structural unity of HUNG-LOU MENG by examining three discourse levels introduced in the opening chapter: mythic (signified by the Goddess Nigua's actions), descending into the mysterious (signified by Chen Shih-yin and his colloquy with the Buddhist monk and the Taoist priest), and then into the mundane (the Red-Dust empirical world into which the Stone will enter).

Traces the interweaving of the three levels throughout the novel, concluding with their reappearance, now in ascending order, at story's end. Finds the unifying entity in the Stone, identified as the author himself. Reinforces these views by detailed paralleling of author and novel with Luigi Pirandello and his play EACH IN HIS OWN WAY (1923). Correlates the two works, not only in the theme of reality and illusion, but also in technical devices productive in each case of extraordinary unity of effect.

G62. Lai Ming. A HISTORY OF CHINESE LITERATURE. New York: Capricorn Books, 1966. Pages 332-340.

Underscores the Manchu heritage of Ts'ao Hsueh Ch'in, author of the first great tragedy of Chinese literature, a story of unfulfilled, triangular love. Includes an extensive summary and a moving passage from the narrative.

G63. Langlois, Walter G. "THE DREAM OF THE RED CHAMBER, THE GOOD EARTH, and MAN'S FATE." LITERATURE EAST AND WEST 11 (1967): 1-10.

Looks at "the death of Confucian China," i.e. the idea of two classes (the rulers and the agricultural masses, the ruled), the basic importance of land, the ethic of unselfish public service, and the ideal of a leadership learned, wise, and non-violent.

Examines three novels to demonstrate the dissolution of Confucianism: a) THE DREAM OF THE RED CHAMBER, illustrating the old-order aristocracy trembling, by reason of its neglect of the old ideals, its self-serving corruption, and its loss of contact with the land, on the edge of collapse; b) Pearl Buck's THE GOOD EARTH, focusing on post-dynastic farmers forced off the land and into urban centers where dependency, begging, and welfare replace the old satisfaction in honest and self-reliant work, where violence achieves what virtue cannot, and where Christianity fails but Marxism takes hold; and c) Andre Malraux's MAN'S FATE, examining post-dynastic leadership roles in the new revolutionary society. Finds Chiang Kai-shek depicted as a bourgeois warlord not really interested in land and/or peasantry; Mao as a slow, but in the end successful, promoter of the peasant cause; other leaders as backward and reactionary deadweights, or decadent, violent, exclusive, or isolationist.

Concludes that in the revolutionary society certain Confucian values survive: the turning of energy and education toward social reform, reliance on social and human rather than religious dynamics, the ideal of sacrifice for the public good as a way of giving meaning to workers' and peasants' lives, and emphasis on action rather than speculation.

G64. Li Hsi-fan. "Restudying Chairman Mao's Letter Concerning the Study of THE DREAM OF THE RED CHAMBER." CHINESE LITERATURE 11 (1977): 108-113. Text of the letter, pages 3-10.

From Li Hsi-fan, <u>enfante terrible</u> of the fifties' New-Redologist attackers, a reaffirmation, 23 years later, of his original position, instigated by a rereading of Mao's October 16, 1954, letter. (See G18, G31, and G51.) Reiterates charges against the formerly prestigious critic Yu P'ing-po and his mentor, "comprador (foreign agent)"-scholar Hu Shih, of erroneous views, i.e., interpretation of the novel as chiefly a personal, idealist romance dramatized in a faithful, non-judgmental rendering of contemporary society.

Alleges that such views, besides being trivial, ignore the larger import of the novel and remain blind to "all the murders committed by the four big families, all the blood and tears shed by the people." Impugns the motives of such "reactionaries," who seek in fact "to lead young people astray and stop them from participating in the revolution": --in Mao's words, functioning as "willing captives of the bourgeoisie."

Although Mao has died at this writing, insists that "his glorious teachings still light our way." Now reorients the attack to focus on Chiang Ching and her "gang of four," who seek by false claims about literary reform "to mask their counterrevolutionary aims."

G65. Li, Peter. "Review Article: ARCHETYPE AND ALLEGORY IN THE DREAM OF THE RED CHAMBER by Andrew H. Plaks." JOURNAL OF THE CHINESE LANGUAGE TEACHERS ASSOCIATION 17.1 (February 1982): 101-108.

Judges the Plaks book most important for its philosophical and theoretical discussion of the problem of dualism in, respectively, Western and Chinese cultures, specifically as it affects understanding of literary terms. Declares the work a test case for Western literary concepts claiming universal validity.

Among other points notes Plaks' analyses of 1) Western stress on narrative as versus Chinese stress on lyric modality, 2) Nu-kua and Fu-hsi of the novel's opening chapter as archetypes of metaphysical opposites which, united, bring creation, harmony, and order, 3) complementary bipolarity (yin/yang) and multiple periodicity (five-elements correspondences) as structural components, 4) textual density as achieved by ceaseless alternations and constant overlappings of characters, episodes, settings, events, and tropes, 5) the function of allegory to render one plane of existence intelligible in terms of another, 6) the difference between Western bileveled (the heavenly and the earthly gardens are antithetical) and Chinese one-leveled (the gardens are complementary, are phases of the One) cosmologies, chiefly as this contrast affects interpretation of HLM's Garden of Total Vision (Takuanyuan). Interprets the garden's name as indicating, not panoramic view, but vision within an enclosed space.

G66. Liao Hsien-hao. "Tai-yu or Pao-chai: The Paradox of Existence as Manifested in Pao-yu's Existential Struggle." TAMKANG REVIEW 15 (Autumn 1984/Summer 1985): 485-494.

Studies choices as indicators of Pao-yu's character.

G67. Lin Yu-tang. "Appreciations of THE DREAM OF THE RED CHAMBER." RENDITIONS 2 (Spring 1974): 23-30.

Offers, not new data or even deepened insight, but warm and expressive appreciation of character, humanity, style, tragic elements, and themes of THE DREAM OF THE RED CHAMBER. Points out the wealth of cultural content set forth in the work: official corruption, court etiquette, religious and superstitious practices, divination, the planchette (ouija board), exorcising of evil spirits, poetry, food, wine games, card and dice competition, music, painting, medicine, school, state examinations, Ch'an Buddhism, Confucianism, and Taoism. Analyzes Pao-yu with depth and balance, stressing his attitude toward the feminine. Parallels Ts'ao Hsueh Ch'in's celebration in this novel of feminine inspiration with medieval Europe's Gothic cathedrals, inspired by devotion to Christ's virgin mother. In this connection likens the twelve beauties of Chin-ling to saints carved on cathedral facades.

G68. Liu Chun-jo. "Syllabicity and the Sentence: an Inquiry Into the Narative Style of the HUNG-LOU MENG." CRITICAL ESSAYS ON CHINESE FICTION. Eds. Curtis Peter Adkins and Winston L.Y. Yang. Hong Kong: Chinese University of Hong Kong, 1980. Pages 181-199.

Studies the sentence unit in THE DREAM as organic model, closed as well as generative, and, with its verbs, indicating specific narrative features, including hereditary process, oral delivery, and distancing from everyday speech. Interprets themes as derivative from collective formulae of vernacular narrative and their constant motifs of meetings and partings, joys and sorrows, and the ups and downs of fortune. Sees each episode as forming a loop in the deep structure, and the whole as a polyphonic narrative emerging from verb functions and marked by significant use of the caesura.

G69. Liu, Joyce Chi-hui. THEME OF RENUNCIATION IN DREAM OF THE RED CHAMBER, LE ROUGE ET LE NOIR, AND JUDE

THE OBSCURE: AN EAST-WEST COMPARISON OF THEMES AND TECHNIQUES. Urbana: University of Illinois at Urbana-Champaign, 1984. An unpublished dissertation.

Parallels three novels of diverse cultures to show a constant in human experience and art: an individual's choice of conforming to an order of conflicting values or renouncing it altogether. Tags the latter choice in its fictional representation as anti-Bildungsroman, rejection of the accommodating and optimistic German form (see G16).

Identifies the antitheses in DREAM OF THE RED CHAMBER as Taoism and Confucianism; in LE ROUGE ET LE NOIR as enlightenment and materialism; and in JUDE THE OBSCURE as Shelleyan modernism (free love) and Victorian convention. Finds each order epitomized in a) two contrasting women; b) symbol sets, as stone-jade, white-black, pigs-birds; and c) temporal-spatial sequences identifying stages in the protagonist's life-journey: Takuanyuan Garden and the Chia mansions; Vergy Garden and the homes of the de Renals and the de le Moles; and Marygreen and Christminster.

Offers the study as corrective to Western denigration of Chinese novel art, an attitude springing from ignorance of Chinese aesthetics and reliance on norms deriving exclusively from Western literary theory and experience.

G70. Liu Wu-chi. "Great Novels by Obscure Writers." AN INTRODUCTION TO CHINESE LITERATURE. Bloomington: Indiana University Press, 1967. Pages 228-246.

Equates the author's introductory remarks to a manifesto of realism in presentation of his central subject, Chinese family life in all its vast complexity: "structure, organization, ideals such as clan solidarity and honor, respect for old age, parental authority, filial obedience, sexual relationships, the position of women, and the role of concubines, maidservants, and other domestics"--all based on the author's own life and experience. Excerpts extensive passages to illustrate techniques of plot and characterization. Scans alternative allegorical, romantic, satiric, and political readings.

G71. Lu Hsun. A BRIEF HISTORY OF CHINESE FICTION. Trs. Yang Hsien-yi and Gladys Yang. Peking: Foreign Languages Press, 1959. Pages 298-316.

After an extended plot summary, discusses extremist theories about hidden meanings in HUNG-LOU MENG. Selects for special attention the novel as 1) a chronicle of the Na-lan Hsing-teh family, 2) the story of Emperor Shun Chih (1644-1661) and his lady Tung, and 3) an account of political events under the K'ang-hsi emperor (1662-1722), a view suggested by Hu Shih. Prefers the simpler reading of the novel as autobiography, "merely relating true incidents from life ... no sarcasm was intended, only regret over his [the author's] misspent life."

G72. Mao Tun [Shen Yen-ping]. "What We Know of Ts'ao Hsueh-ch'in." CHINESE LITERATURE 5 (May 1964): 85-104.

Makes five points about THE DREAM OF THE RED CHAMBER's influence: 1) the completion of the last 40 chapters by Kao Ngo, who, in basic respects, altered the original plan; 2) the creation of about 25 sequels in the century following the work's publication; 3) numerous imitations, all failing to see "the profound social significance of the original"; 4) beginning with the Chih-yen Chai commentary of Ts'ao's contemporary, development of hundreds of commentaries and annotations; 5) emergence of volumes of theories about and elucidations of HLM's hidden meanings and messages.

Highlights issues and conclusions of the fifties' debate about the narrative's bourgeois-idealist or historical-materialist content. Attributes the progressive element in Ts'ao's outlook to teachings of Li Cho-wu (1527-1602) and Wang Chuan-shan (1619-1692), and to rising urban-class views in eighteenth-century China detailing current economic abuses. Interprets Pao-yu's final withdrawal as an ideological negative, understandable as, at the time, a protester's only alternative. Calls attention to Ts'ao's lost painting and poetry.

Analyzes, perfunctorily, structure, characterization, and language, proclaiming HLM "the earliest masterpiece of critical realism, preceding [European] critical realist literature by more than a hundred years." Contains much useful material in extended footnotes treating, among other things, the Bacon-Jonson-Shakespeare controversy, Chih-yen Chai's identity, notable bibliographic and commentary items, pre-twentieth century interpretations, and debate about Ts'ao's birth and death dates.

G73. Miller, Lucien M. THE MASKS OF FICTION IN "HUNG-LOU MENG": MYTH, MIMESIS, AND PERSONA. Tucson: University of Arizona Press, 1975.

Seeks to provide a form of literary analysis (of style, structure, and organizing principle) mostly missing from the hundreds of DREAM books and articles which concentrate on authorship, dates, and texts. Reformulates the novel in terms of three primary literary modes--myth, mimesis, and persona--an approach anticipated by late nineteenth-century allegorists reading the novel variously as political satire, imperial love story, patriotic dirge for the fallen Ming dynasty, and autobiography.

Notes the tendency of modern Chinese social realists to debunk the novel's supernatural elements as vestiges of obsolete feudal, superstitious, and elitist worlds. Disputes the views of so-called realists, including Waley, who see the supernatural content as mere framework or casing rather than as an integral part of a vision of reality in which transcendent and immanent are unified. Insists, too, on the non-detrimental presence of a didacticism (not sententious moralizing) in part responsible for the novel's beauty and power.

In "Myth: the Allegoric Mode" reads Ts'ao's creation as essentially an ironic and painful vision of a heavenly, as well as an earthly, construction ultimately meaningless and absurd. In "Mimesis: the Realistic

Mode" finds in the stories of complementary opposites Chen (true) Shih-yen and Chia (false) Yu-ts'un, and Chen Pao-yu and Chia Pao-yu the means of inducing reader awareness that reality itself is an illusion. In "Persona: the Narrative Mode" identifies a dogmatic authority (the Buddhist monk), a naive pedant (the Taoist priest), an objective innovator (the Stone), an autobiographical confessor (Ts'ao), a faithful scholar (the anonymous narrator), and the hovering commentator (Chih-yen Chai), a combination leaving the reader free to choose his responses from alternative and opposing views.

Finds the term "realism" inappropriate for the novel's polysemous layers and varied styles and concludes that the real if elusive didactic points toward an enlightenment possible only for the open mind and forever unattainable to realists and literalists.

G74. Miller, Lucien M. "Naming the Whirlwind: Cao Xueqin and Heidegger." TAMKANG REVIEW 11 (1981): 143-163.

Avows that in THE DREAM OF THE RED CHAMBER Ts'ao Hsueh Ch'in seeks to answer the same anguished questions about mutability and suffering that tormented Job in the Hebrew Old Testament. Invokes Heidegger's terminologies--facticity, fallenness, thrownness, Being and Becoming, and others--to elucidate the mysteries wherein Pao-yu, brought by his own wish from Being to Becoming, so suffers from disillusionment that, unable longer to endure, he renounces attachment and desire and returns to the purity of Being.

G75. Miller, Lucien M. "Sequels to the RED CHAMBER DREAM: Observations on Plagiarism, Imitation, and Originality in Chinese Vernacular Literature." TAMKANG REVIEW 5 (1975): 187-215.

Of the 30 known sequels to DREAM OF THE RED CHAMBER written between 1798 and 1940, examines the first three, all written in the late eighteenth century: LATER RED CHAMBER DREAM, SEQUEL TO THE RED CHAMBER DREAM, and DREAMING AGAIN IN THE CRINOLINE CHAMBER.

Finds all deficient in creative imitation, the first being mere formulaic plagiarism and rhetorical imitation; the second, an entertaining ghost story, with sexual parody; the third, pornography admixed with warrior adventures, written to satirize a rival.

G76. Minford, John, and Robert E. Hegel. "HUNG-LOU MENG." INDIANA COMPANION TO TRADITIONAL CHINESE LITERATURE. Eds. William H. Nienhauser, Jr., and others. Bloomington: Indiana University Press, 1986. Pages 452-456.

Covers these aspects of HUNG-LOU MENG: textual history; genre, based on mythic and mundane levels of action with the Garden as intermediary; major individuals and relationships; the family and its relation to the outside world; the massive cast of characters; the encyclopedic covering of eighteenth-century China; Redology; and Marxist critiques.

G77. Na Tsung-shun. STUDIES ON DREAM OF THE RED CHAMBER: A SELECTED AND CLASSIFIED BIBLIOGRAPHY. Hong Kong: Lung Men, 1979. (Also in Taipei, 1982.)

Over 800 unannotated entries, chiefly from Chinese and Hong Kong publications, most in Chinese. No new materials in English.

G78. Palandai, Angela J. "Women in DREAM OF THE RED CHAMBER." LITERATURE EAST AND WEST 12 (1968): 226-238.

Considering the novel fundamentally about women, examines the unorthodoxy of the author's attitude toward them, their characterizations in the light of modern psychology, and their significance in the novel's structure. Uses yin/yang theory to rationalize traditional Chinese association of women with weakness, darkness, and evil. Cites the lower value set upon female children, and the pseudo-Confucian view that to be without intellectual attainment is for females a virtue, though exception is made for daughters of ducal families, as with the novel's Chias.

Calls on William Sheldon's personality theory to classify Hsi-feng (Phoenix) as a mesomorph (athletic, muscular, upright in posture, aggressive in action); Pao-chai (Precious Clasp) as an endomorph (soft, plump, relaxed, easygoing, sociable, popular); and Tai-yu (Black Jade) as an ectomorph (nervous, fragile, slender, intense, precise, melancholic).

Structurally, considers a) the love triangle of Pao-yu, Pao-chai, and Tai-yu; b) class commentary provided by comic Granny Liu; c) social irony implicit in the sadness of the Imperial Consort, deprived of the freedom even maids enjoy in her parental home; and d) the respective Confucian/Taoist and Apollonian/Dionysian contrasts in roles played by Pao-chai and Tai-yu in the Garden Takuanyuan.

G79. Plaks, Andrew H. "Allegory in HSI-YU CHI and HUNG-LOU MENG." CHINESE NARRATIVE: CRITICAL AND THEORETICAL ESSAYS. Princeton: Princeton University Press, 1977. Pages 163-202.

Reviews the nature and history of allegory as literary form and mode of composition (see D50). Based on criteria from traditional Chinese commentaries as well as from the West, declares that HUNG-LOU MENG's allegory centers on the complementarity of opposites, notably truth/falsity, reality/illusion, and other pairs including stillness/movement, emotion/social control, self/society, dream/waking, and, above all, plenitude/emptiness. Details the ways in which the author transmits his intent and directs his readers to meanings below the mimetic surface.

Proposes Takuanyuan Garden as the allegory's central figure, differing from the Western locus amoenus (earthly paradise) by proposing, instead of European insistence on the seductive oppositeness of the false earthly garden and the true heavenly garden of grace, the Chinese regard for the equal interfusion of particularity and universality in the self-contained ground of existence as a whole.

Recalls that the seeming plenitude of Takuanyuan and its inexorable dissolution into emptiness depicts the self-contained individual within the external world, subject to problems of adjustment that may mean tragedy. Calls the novel's story line, not a unilinear trajectory of a family's rise and fall or lovers' union and separation, but "a welter of overlapping cycles without any sense of direction."

Concludes that Dante and Spenser also dealt with the issue of Self against Society, and that elucidation of the differing solutions of Europe and of China may identify essential distinctions in their philosophic views and literary practice.

G80. Plaks, Andrew H. ARCHETYPE AND ALLEGORY IN "THE DREAM OF THE RED CHAMBER." Princeton: Princeton University Press, 1976.

Tests the universality of archetype and allegory as modes developed by but not restricted to the West, while observing that substantial cultural differences mark their use in the various national literatures.

Attributing these differences to basic world views, contrasts Western allegorical and archetypal expression--Christian-derived, dependent on transcendental reality, hierarchical, linear, and time-defined--with its Chinese counterpart, structured on principles of complementary bipolarity (yin/yang) and multiple periodicity (five-elements cosmology).

Believes that THE DREAM OF THE RED CHAMBER eminently illustrates this structuring, its events being less important than its patterns of interrelation and sequence, often figured in ritual rather than narration. Explores the novel's opening Nu-kua myth, with its implications of union with Fu-hsi, to illustrate the archetypal patterns and cyclical recurrences that define the novel's spatialized vision. Marks its tragic disjunction between "the time-based perspective of moral sensitivity and the detemporalized structure of intelligibility" beyond mimetic representation.

Contrasts the literary garden _topos_ in DRC with that in ROMANCE OF THE ROSE, THE FAERIE QUEENE, and PARADISE LOST as another example of culturally differentiated use of the two major literary modes of allegory and archetype.

G81. Rexroth, Kenneth. "DREAM OF THE RED CHAMBER." SATURDAY REVIEW (January 1, 1966): 19.

Offers shallow, distorted, and contradictory ideas on almost every aspect of the novel, while essaying a comparison with GENJI MONOGATARI.

G82. Robinson, Lewis S. "Pao-yu and Parsifal: Personal Growth as a Literary Substructure." TAMKANG REVIEW 9 (1979): 407-426.

A New-Criticism analysis worthy of Northrop Frye in his Jungian phase. Shows how Pao's psychological health, like Parsifal's, demands that his anima, the female side of him, be well integrated into while not dominating his male psyche. Equates female characters in the novel with the five Greek archetypes of ideal womanhood--Aphrodite, Hera, Demeter, Artemis, and Athena--each nurturing Pao's growth toward wholeness of personality. Observes that Parsifal's vision concerns Christian service of God; Pao's, the distinguishing of the Unreal from the Real.

Questions whether such studies of personal growth, equated with a literary form, the Bildungsroman, are as valid in the East as in the West? Answers yes, provided distinction be made between the Western ideal of wholeness as harmonious integration of all one's personal powers, and the Eastern idea of it as transcendence of ego into an eternal One. See G16.

G83. Shu Chin-ten. ALLEGORICAL STRUCTURE IN LITERARY DISCOURSE: WESTERN AND CHINESE. Madison: University of Wisconsin, 1981. An unpublished dissertation.

Following discussions of the nature of allegory and East-West differences in using it, focuses on HUNG-LOU MENG. Shows how, in the opening, the author combines supernatural myth pervaded by Buddhist-Taoist views with absurdity and fictionality. Understands this binary treatment as an important thematic statement about the equally illusory nature of the Land of the Void and the Red-Dust World.

G84. Soong, Stephen C. "Two Types of Misinterpretation--
Some Poems From the RED CHAMBER DREAM." RENDI-
TIONS 7 (1977): 73-92.

Examines English renderings of selected verses in
HUNG-LOU MENG, notably Pao's four seasonal or garden
poems in Chapter 23, here translated, respectively,
by David Hawkes and by H.C. Chang, both acknowledged
first-rate translators. Finds flaws in versions of
both Western and Chinese scholars.

G85. Spence, Jonathan. TS'AO YIN AND THE K'ANG HSI
EMPEROR: BONDSERVANT AND MASTER. New Haven: Yale
University Press, 1966.

Provides a detailed and colorful account of the early
Manchu (Ch'ing) Dynasty under the K'ang-hsi emperor
(r. 1662-1722), the milieu of HUNG-LOU MENG. Centers
on the life and career of Ts'ao Yin (1658-1705), the
novelist's grandfather, a trusted Manchu bondservant
and official, cherishing both his classical Chinese
education and the distinctive Manchu culture. Describes his delight in horsemanship and archery, as
well as poetry and intelligent conversation, and
observes that Yin's importance lies less in his deeds
than in what his life reveals about Manchu economic
and social institutions.

Considers HUNG-LOU MENG's Chapter 18 (the creation of
Takuanyuan, Prospect Garden, for the Imperial Concubine's visit) as, by its meticulous detail, lavish
preparation, and the brilliance of the arriving
guest's entourage, a fictional account of the K'ang-
hsi emperor's real-life visits to Ts'ao residences.

In an appendix concludes, arguably, 1) that the
author's birthdate is 1715; 2) that, born posthum-
ously, he was adopted, reluctantly and despite animadversion, by his father's stepbrother, Ts'ao Fu; and
3) that Takuanyuan is a composite of Ts'ao Yin's
garden in his Nanking textile-commissioner's yamen
and of a family residential garden in suburban Nanking hills. Uses the novel's alternate title SHIH

T'OU CHI (THE STORY OF THE STONE) to confirm as authentic the latter site.

G86. Spence, Jonathan. "Yuan Mei." THE INDIANA COMPANION TO TRADITIONAL CHINESE LITERATURE. Eds. William H. Nienhauser, Jr., and others. Bloomington: Indiana University Press, 1986. Pages 956-958.

Points out the relation of poet-critic-essayist Yuan Mei's family estate to Takuanyuan Garden of HUNG-LOU MENG. Notes that Yuan's garden, long the property of Ts'ao Hsueh Ch'in's grandfather or granduncle, was thought to be the model for the celebrated locale of HUNG-LOU MENG and was, for the last half of the eighteenth century, a noted gathering place for scholars.

G87. Sun Wen-kuang. "THE DREAM OF THE RED CHAMBER Must Be Studied From a Class Standpoint." CHINESE LITERATURE 5 (1974): 81-113.

With plentiful diatribe against Hu Shih "and his lackeys ... slaves of bourgeois idealism," analyzes HUNG-LOU MENG from a thoroughly Marxist perspective. Uses Mao Tse-tung's 1954 Letter to the Politburo of the Central Committee as takeoff for a study of the novel (see G64). Reiterates Mao's view that HLM is not centrally about romantic love or autobiographical retrospect or a naturalist's view of individual human nature, but about historical events whose "main theme is political and its content class struggle." Forces events and persons into the procrustean bed of Communist ideology in a classic application of Marxist literary theory.

G88. Sychov, L., and V. Sychov. "The Role of Costume in Cao Xue-qin's Novel DREAM OF THE RED CHAMBER." TAMKANG REVIEW 11 (Spring 1981): 287-305.

G89. Teng Shao-chi. "Ts'ao Hsueh-ch'in and his DREAM OF THE RED CHAMBER." CHINA RECONSTRUCTED 12 (December 1963): 30-34.

G90. Tso Hai. "Ts'ao Hsueh Ch'in and THE DREAM OF THE RED CHAMBER." CHINA PICTORIAL 10 (1963): 16-19.

G91. Tu Ching-i. "A Study of Wang Kuo-wei's Literary Criticism." Seattle: University of Washington, 1969. An unpublished dissertation.

Explores ways in which Western literary theory, notably Schopenhauer's views on art and tragedy, influenced the aesthetics of scholar-poet-teacher Wang Kuo-wei (1877-1927). Finds Wang's essay on HUNG-LOU MENG profoundly affected by Schopenhaurian concepts of the tragic conjunction of fatal elements issuing from a blind and insensitive Immanent Will governing the universe. Shows, further, that in later years Wang turned back increasingly to native philosophic views, especially as altered by Buddhism.

G92. U.S. Consulate in Hong Kong. "Can We Read Books Like DREAM OF THE RED CHAMBER?" SELECTIONS FROM CHINA MAINLAND MAGAZINES 498 (November 16, 1965): 29-30.

G93. Wagner, Marsha L. "Maids and Servants in DREAM OF THE RED CHAMBER: Individuality and Social Order." EXPRESSIONS OF THE SELF IN CHINESE LITERATURE. Eds. Robert E. Hegel and Richard C. Hessney. New York: Columbia University Press, 1985. Pages 251-281.

Offers a long, lucid, probing, important analysis of diversity, depth, and literary suppleness in Ts'ao Hsueh Ch'in's characterizations. Observes that personae are treated 1) as individuals, 2) as parts of the larger society, and 3) as functions in a literary design.

As individuals, studies cantankerous old nanny Li Ma; ambitious opportunist Crimson Flower; and faithful maids Precious Gem and Purple Cuckoo, showing in each an amazing and credible complexity, presented from multiple points of view and attentive to interior clashes between social role and personal self-esteem and fulfillment.

As literary functions, examines maids' roles in enriching portrayals of masters and mistresses, often by parallel character sets and always by showing that misunderstandings, altercations, and tensions invariably arise from concealment of true feelings. Summarizes servants' literary functions as facilitating, explicating, and mirroring central events and characters.

Interprets lower-class roles in highlighting extremes of laxity and rigor figuring in the breakdown of hierarchical Confucian relationships and in the emergence of isolated and deracinated individuals whose strong sense of Self develops against a background of social disruption and trauma.

G94. Wang, C.H. "Recognition in Wang Kuo-wei's Criticism of HUNG-LOU MENG." TSING HUA JOURNAL OF CHINESE STUDIES 10 (1974): 91-113.

G95. Wang Hsi-yen. "Characterization Through the Depiction of Externals." CHINESE LITERATURE 7 (July 1964): 85-93.

Proposes that characterization in Chinese novels relies on depiction of externals, often exaggerated, as appearance, conversation, action, and behavior in conflict and struggle. In HUNG-LOU MENG demonstrates the point 1) by the scene in which Tai-yu is introduced to the three Springs (daughters of the presiding families); 2) by conversations about the embroidered purse, culminating in Skybright's death; and 3) by reactions to Hsi-feng's machinations as she seeks to destroy Chia Lien's second wife, Yu Erh-chieh.

G96. Wang Jing. THE MYTHOLOGY OF STONE: A STUDY OF THE INTERTEXTUALITY OF ANCIENT CHINA STONELORE AND THREE CLASSIC NOVELS. Amherst: University of Massachusetts, 1985. An unpublished dissertation.

Uses the composite symbolism of the stone in Chinese folklore to explore its use in SHUI-HU CHUAN, HSI-YU CHI, and HUNG-LOU MENG. Notes how modifications and accretions mark the literary use of the stone symbol.

G97. Wang, John C.Y. "The Chih-yen Chai Commentary on THE DREAM OF THE RED CHAMBER: A Literary Study." CHINESE APPROACHES TO LITERATURE FROM CONFUCIUS TO

LIANG CH'I-CH'AO. Ed. Adele Rickett. Princeton, Princeton University Press, 1978.

Examines the Chih-yen Chai Commentary, a composite of criticisms and manuscript annotations by several unidentified critics, the author's friends, relatives, and acquaintances, who had read drafts of even unfinished parts of the novel. Shows that the comments are not primarily intent on illuminating date, authorship, and text, but on exploring literary, aesthetic content.

Calls attention to the Commentary's consistent praise of the novel's unconventionality and its truthfulness; to its characters, credible mixtures of virtue and defect; and, finally, to its warning that the book be not read allegorically (as roman à clef), but as a capturing of the illusory nature of life and its tragic passingness, a view reinforced by subtle juxtapositions of sorrowful elements next to moments of seeming happiness.

Observes that, as against 40 comments on theme and 90-odd on character, notes on technique number over 200. Cites 34 specific literary strategies used in HLM, often quoting their poetical Chinese epithets, as in the following:

1) "To write without writing" (using suggestiveness rather than factual detail).

2) "Clouds cutting the mountain in half" (interruption of events or dialogue).

3) "The grey line of a grass snake" (repeated use of a key image or symbol).

4) "The gold cicada shedding its shell" (clever and smooth moving from one topic to another).

G98. Wang, John C.Y. "The Cyclical View of Life and Meaning in a Traditional Chinese Novel." ETUDES D'HISTOIRE ET LE LITTERATURE CHINOISES OFFERTES AU PROFESSEUR JAROSLAV PRUSEK. Paris: Institut des Hautes Etudes Chinoises, 1976. Pages 275-301.

Reviews Hu Shih's famous 1928 study of an unfinished 1754 version of HUNG-LOU MENG (some nine years before Ts'ao's death) accompanied by a commentary signed Chih-yen Chai (Red Inkslab Studio). Accepts the composite authorship of the commentary and declares it important, not only for its illumination of the author's life and times and its bearing on the dating and relationships of different versions of the work, but also for its information about how THE DREAM was received by early critics and by what critical standards.

In this context selects several major points among some 200 in the commentaries on novel technique, notably those showing disdain for stereotyped romances of the time and for all-evil or all-virtuous characterizations. Insists, contrary to much critical judgment, that Chih perceives THE DREAM as, not primarily a romantic and tragic love story nor yet as anti-Manchu satire, but rather as a novel about life's illusory nature and the painful truth that good things do not last forever.

G99. Wang Yu-k'un. "Forever Inter [sic] the Exploitation System: After Reading the 53rd Chapter of DREAM OF THE RED CHAMBER." SURVEY OF THE PEOPLE'S REPUBLIC OF CHINA PRESS (July 14-18, 1975): 208-212.

G100. Werner, Edward Chalmers. "The Translation of Chinese: Notes on Joly's Translation of the HUNG-LOU MENG." CHINA JOURNAL 6 (1927): 125-127.

Adversely reviews the 1892 Joly translation of Book One of HUNG-LOU MENG, comparing it with William Wade's translation of the same chapters (1-28). Collates passages from the two versions to show the superiority of Wade's Englishing.

G101. West, Anthony. "Through a Glass Darkly." The NEW YORKER MAGAZINE (November 22, 1958): 223-232.

Caustically reviews two recent (1958) English translations of DREAM OF THE RED CHAMBER. Finds the McHugh recension of Kuhn's German version superior, despite labored, pedantic, and pedestrian English, to Wang

Chi-chen's charming and amiable rendering, "so wrapped up in the nitty-gritty of day-to-day management of a Chinese household" that larger issues slip by scarcely noticed. Quarrels with Wang's handling of names, his diminishing of episodes and themes powerful and moving in the original, and his omission of psychological details important to characterization.

Argues, on the other hand, that, however lacking in stylistic appeal, the Kuhn-McHugh translation gives profundity to its characterization. Cites, for example, how Pao-yu, "blood-brother of Dmitri Karamazov (see G48)," is pointedly shown in Kuhn-McHugh to mature steadily even as his cousin Phoenix as surely deteriorates. Believes that the Kuhn-McHugh translation integrates the controversial last 40 chapters into the novel as a whole, sustaining the work's inexorable chain of logic and unbroken emotional tension.

Concludes, arguably, that the Kuhn-McHugh version preserves the novel's central thrust, condemnation of the Confucian family system (a shadow play of the imperial court), and that it has grasped the truth of the novel while Wang's has failed.

G102. Westbrook, Francis A. "On Dreams, Saints, and Fallen Angels: Reality and Illusion in DREAM OF THE RED CHAMBER and THE IDIOT." LITERATURE EAST AND WEST 15 (1971): 371-391.

Parallels HUNG-LOU MENG and Dostoyevsky's THE IDIOT in a) their wealthy, aristocratic milieux, both disintegrating socially from inner corruption; b) their clashes between illusion and reality; c) their parallel characters; d) their subordination of plot to character; e) their focus on human relationships; and f) their intensive use of dreams to underscore and explicate human developments.

Differentiates THE IDIOT's probing into characters' minds as against HLM's more epic or dramatic method, inner realities externalized only through gesture, symbol, or dialogue; and the Russian characters' feverish and frustrated search for goals as against Chinese characters' suffering from suppressions mandated by Confucian ethics.

Details likenesses between Pao-yu and Prince Myshkin (not Dmitri of BROTHERS KARAMAZOV as Anthony West proposes in G101): their irremediable idealism; physical vulnerability, often marked by trances; frustration with the society; relations with the feminine sex; desperation at failure; and, in the end, withdrawal from the conventional world. Parallels Tai-yu, not with Sonia of CRIME AND PUNISHMENT, but with Natasya of THE IDIOT, calling attention to Hsia's unsympathetic and denigratory critique (G47 and G48). Attributes to both novels a bleakly pessimistic view of human society.

G103. Wong Kam-ming. "Point of View, Norms, and Structure: HUNG-LOU MENG and Lyrical Fiction." CHINESE NARRATIVE: CRITICAL AND THEORETICAL ESSAYS. Ed. Andrew H. Plaks. Princeton: Princeton University Press, 1978. Pages 203-226.

Attributing Western and even universal novel development to increasing sophistication in the use of point of view, declares HUNG-LOU MENG the first Chinese novel to present a fully realized third-person reflector.

Distinguishes in early chapters the voices of storyteller, memoirist (in both preincarnation and postincarnation phases), and editor, the blending of which enriches action, characterization, dialogue, and commentary with subtle ironies. Follows further merging of point of view in Pao's voice as reflector with (as his, Pao's, perception lapses or fails) the author's, again to powerful and nuanced ironic effect. Projects the contrasting voices of various personae on the axes of aesthetics, women, and officialdom as objects of social judgment.

Finally, in numerous passages, notes the use of things and images to establish meaningful patterns of episodic progression, always signaling the author's lyric intent.

G104. Wong, Y.W. "The Parallelism Between Aristotle's Theories and Two Chinese Novels: Principles of Catharsis." TAMKANG REVIEW 6 (October 1975/April 1976): 465-477.

Declares Aristotelian catharsis substantially identical with concepts in the Chinese seventeenth-century novel JOU P'U T'UAN (PRAYER MAT OF FLESH) and the eighteenth-century novel HUNG-LOU MENG (THE DREAM OF THE RED CHAMBER). Analyzes each work for its light on the healthful release of the emotions of pity and terror, and accompanying techniques of reversal (peripeteia), discovery (epiphaneia), and suffering (agon). Notes, nevertheless, that Western catharsis leads to a renewed facing of life and society, whereas Eastern catharsis leads to escape from conventional life and society and withdrawal into transcendental modes of existence. Omits, curiously, any reference to hubris and hamartia, ideas essential to Western understanding of catharsis.

G105. Wu Shih-ch'ang. "History of the RED CHAMBER DREAM." CHINESE LITERATURE 1 (January 1963): 87-100.

Mostly recapitulates matter from Wu's 1962 ON THE RED CHAMBER DREAM, a New-Redologist work. Mentions that Hu Shih, to maintain the materials for his exclusive personal research, for 30 years (until 1927) withheld from the public the 1754 16-chapter annotated manuscript considered the oldest extant copy of the original. Notes that the second-oldest copy, a similarly annotated 1761 78-chapter manuscript, became available to scholars only in 1954. Names Ts'ao Fu as the novelist's father, commentator Chih-yen Chai as his uncle, and Kao Ngo (E) as author of the final 40 chapters—all points disputed by subsequent critics.

Summarizes Chih-commentary information as including the inside story of the novel, actual episodes in the Ts'ao home, the proportion of true to fictitious stories, the original plan, the overall plot and fundamental theme, early drafts, titles, and revisions, the author's plans for the concluding section, original drafts and manuscripts for this part lost by borrowers, and the role of Ts'ao's younger brother, T'ang-ts'un.

Identifies the old Ts'ao garden in Nanking, later owned by poet Yuan Mei, as the original Takuanyuan. Declares Ts'ao's original plan for the novel's ending grander and more tragic than the existing version, a diminishment attributed to Kao E and his collaborator Ch'eng Wei-yuan. Charges them, also, with the altering of story line and characterization, the "improving" of the author's style to a "Peking dialect affected and artificial ... a text ungrammatical and illogical ... [and] wrong references to ancient classics [and] obscured [background passages]."

Partly excuses Kao's expunction of the author's "clearly intended satire against contemporary social institutions" by the Ch'ien-lung emperor's literary inquisitions allotting death to writers, readers, and sellers of works considered politically offensive.

G106. Wu Shih-ch'ang. ON THE RED CHAMBER DREAM: A CRITICAL STUDY OF TWO ANNOTATED MSS. OF THE XVIIIth CENTURY. Oxford: Clarendon Press, 1962.

Extracts passages from the famed 1754 16-chapter manuscript (chia-hsu pen, first published in 1927) and the equally famed 1761 78-chapter manuscript (ch'en pen, first published in 1933) of SHIH T'OU CHI (alternate title of HUNG-LOU MENG). From these concludes 1) that the chief contributor to the Chih-yen Chai Commentary in both manuscripts was the author's uncle, 2) that certain prefaces and poems were written by the author's younger brother, Ts'ao T'ang-ts'un, 3) that author Ts'ao's dates are 1715-1764, 4) that an author's draft and odd chapters for the last third of the novel have been lost, and 5) that Kao E in major ways revised the story's intended drift.

Supports the charge against Kao E of ignoring the novel's social import by omitting accounts of the feudal estate in ruins and of jail and brothel miseries; and of changing tragic endings planned for several characters so as to portray them as happily resorting to simpler, nobler ways of lifelike farming.

Finally, declares that Kao substituted for Ts'ao's tragic ending the restoration to the Chias of their properties and titles, the imperial pardoning of transgressions, and victims' promotion to places of honor and happiness. Decries the judgment of critics, including Kallgren and Lin Yutang, who insist on single authorship for the 120-chapter work.

G107. Wu Xiang-lin. "A Few Poems in RED-CHAMBER DREAM." EASTERN HORIZON 20 (January 1982): 10-14.

Rejoices that both David Hawkes' THE STORY OF THE STONE and Yang Hsien-yi and Gladys Yangs' DREAM OF RED MANSIONS present complete translations of China's greatest novel, especially with respect to the poetry, some 170 items in various classical Chinese verse forms. In particular praises Hawkes' rendering of Chapter Five's description of the Goddess of Disenchantment for its waltzing rhythms and resounding couplet rhymes. Finds equally beautiful the Yangs' Englishing of Lin Tai-yu's Chapter-27 lament on fallen blossoms for its fidelity to the original pathos, passion, and yearning in restrained but exquisite language and their Chapter-28 Courtesan's ditty for its light tempo and liveliness. Collates specific passages from the two works to show varying degrees of excellence in both.

G108. Yang, Gladys. "THE RED CHAMBER DREAM Today." ARTS AND SCIENCES IN CHINA 1 (October/December 1963): 31-34.

G109. Yang, James Parish. "Mythic and Mimetic Threads: Chih-yen Chai's Commentary as Guide to THE DREAM OF THE RED CHAMBER's Narrative Structure." An unpublished paper presented for the Middle-Atlantic Regional Association for Asian Studies at Princeton University, November 1984.

G110. Yang Jiang. "Art and the Overcoming of Difficulty— THE DREAM OF THE RED CHAMBER." COWRIE 1 (1983): 31-47.

Treats of difficulties encountered by HLM's characters in maintaining and developing love.

G111. Yang, Winston, L.Y., Peter Li, and Nathan K. Mao. "The Dream of the Red Chamber (HUNG-LOU MENG)." CLASSICAL CHINESE FICTION: A GUIDE TO ITS STUDY AND APPRECIATION. ESSAYS AND BIBLIOGRAPHIES. Boston: G.K. Hall Publishers, 1978. Pages 95-103.

Calls attention to early studies of the novel, to Hu Shih's twentieth-century pioneer research, and to floods of material from Chinese Redologists.

Reviews interpretations of HUNG-LOU MENG as a) a political allegory of Ming-Manchu conflict; b) a roman à clef based on the life and love of a Manchu emperor; c) a love story founded on the author's life; d) a political satire on the evils of feudalism (the Communist favorite); e) a version of Schopenhauer's theory of tragedy; f) a philosophic allegory of life's complementary opposites: innocence and experience, self and other, creation and dissolution, being and non-being, truth and illusion; and g) an amalgam of China's diverse religions.

Concludes that the richest and best appreciation of the work requires consideration of all tenable readings. Calls attention to the expressive colloquial style, dialogue, contrast, dream and poetry, subtlety of characterization, and psychological realism--all fully informed with the spirit of tragedy, more tightly knit than other Chinese novels, and relatively free of didacticism and authorial digression--a work for the world.

G112. Yu, Anthony C. "Self and Family in the HUNG-LOU MENG: A New Look at Lin Tai-yu as Tragic Heroine." CHINESE LITERATURE: ESSAYS, ARTICLES, REVIEWS 2 (1980): 199-223.

Refutes the notion that tragic vision is lacking in Chinese literature. Invokes Schopenhauer's theories to buttress the analysis of HUNG-LOU MENG as tragedy, notably in reference, not to Pao-yu, but to his beloved, Lin Tai-yu. Observes that not wickedness nor blind fate in this view brings on the wrenching, grave, and irretrievable waste of human potential, but life situations of ordinary characters so positioned that they are compelled knowingly to seriously injure one another, without anyone's being entirely to blame.

Reviews the circumstances of Tai-yu's orphaning, exile, ostracism, illness, and rejection even as, in her extraordinary intelligence, sensitivity, beauty, and talent, she aches for total acceptance and emotional security. Suggests that critics have overplayed the element of tragedy in Pao-yu's life, that in the end he achieves salvation, reconciliation, and peace, while Tai-yu expires convulsed in loneliness and pain.

G113. Yu P'ing-po. "The DREAM OF THE RED CHAMBER." PEOPLE'S CHINA 10 (October 1954): 32-35.

A Marxist reading of the novel as the "swan song" of feudal China, an expose of social and economic corruption. Concentrates on the arranged marriage as a typical destructive institution and, denigrating Pao-chai's character, exalts that of Tai-yu. Portrays Tai as, with Pao-yu, an uncompromising rebel against feudal oppressions [a position taken by Yu P'ing-po only after the organized attack against him earlier in the year by Marxist critics tutored by Mao-tse Tung]. See G18, G31, and G51.

G114. Yu Ying-shih. "The Two Worlds of HUNG-LOU MENG." Tr. Diana Yu. RENDITIONS 2 (1974): 5-21.

Reacts against the "excessive" stress of Redologists (HUNG-LOU MENG scholars, the term being first used about 1875) on historical criticism, especially its autobiographical phase, and its consistent denigration of the role of the ideal world, exemplified in the garden Takuanyuan, as an integral partner with the real world in the author's intent.

Reproves the efforts of autobiographical critics to locate a real prototype for Takuanyuan, arguing that it is essentially an imaginary world. Declares its intent to illuminate the purity, truth, and love of the Chia girls and to protect them from pollutions pervasive in the outer world of avarice, falsity, and lust.

Refutes autobiographical critics by demonstrating that Pao-yu's point of view differs from that of the author, the one believing in the separateness of the two worlds, the other in their tragic interrelatedness. Recalls that the new garden was produced by merging the old, sin-tainted gardens of East and West mansions, creating the greatest purity from the greatest impurity. Adds that, after a period of innocence exemplified in Chapter 23's flower-burial episode, the garden society is gradually invaded by old depravities, a development marked by Chapter 73's discovery of the obscenity-embroidered purse. Sees this reversion exemplified in the career of fastidious nun Miao.

Finds in the Garden's architecture an image of the inner structure of its society as symbolized by the position, fineness, and size of the four major structures. Notes that, among them, Pao's residence, reflecting his complexity, holds the only full-size mirror (image and reality) and the chief water supply (human-heartedness), which from that point flows in all directions and even, inevitably, into the polluted streams of the world beyond.

Reaffirms that, unlike Pao, the author perceives cleanness coming from squalor and squalor from cleanness in the eternal cycle of existence and therein beholds the ineffable tragedy of the human experience.

G115. Yuan Shui-lo. "THE DREAM OF THE RED CHAMBER." CHINA RECONSTRUCTS 4.5 (1955): 20-23.

INDEX OF AUTHORS

Abrams, M.H., 39, 58
Adkins, Curtis Peter, 11, 62, 81, 85, 88, 237, 258
Alber, Charles, J., 103
Aldridge, A. Owen, 12, 23, 36
Alexander, Edwin, 231
Alezais, Jacqueline, 229
Anderson, G.L., 46-47, 135
Apuleius, Lucius, 189
Aquinas, Thomas, 154
Aristotle, 12, 48, 52, 61, 275
Armstrong, John H., 237
Augustine (Saint), 154
Avenol, Louis, 134

Ba Jin (Pa Chin), 25
Bacon, Francis, 261
Balazs, Etienne, 74, 75
Balzac, Honore de, 240
Bartell, Shirley Miller, 96, 104
Bateson, F.W., 47
Bauer, Wolfgang, 13
Berdyaev, Nicholas, 58
Berry, Margaret, 13-14, 232-233
Birch, Cyril, 14, 135, 226
Bishop, John L., 15, 138, 152, 171
Boccaccio, Giovanni, 240
Boner, Georgette, 134
Bonner, Joey, 218, 226, 233
Brandauer, Frederick, 133, 137-138, 235-236
Brewitt-Taylor, C.H., 71, 85
Brokaw, Cynthia, J., 236
Bronte, Charlotte, 240
Brown, Carolyn Thompson, 29, 75, 109, 236, 246
Bryant, Daniel, 171
Buck, Pearl, 11, 15-16, 98, 100, 102, 104, 112, 114, 120-121, 122, 124-125, 255

Buote, Edward, 71, 76
Byron, George Gordon, 19

Campbell, Joseph, 12, 137-138, 146
Camus, Albert, 5
Capote, Truman, 85
Carlitz, Katherine, 168, 172-174, 177
Carlyle, Thomas, 193
Cass, Victoria Baldwin, 168, 174-176
Cervantes, Saavedra de, 142-143
Cevasco, G.A., 16
Cha Tsung, 152
Chai Ch'u (and Winberg Ch'u) 72, 100, 134, 169, 197, 227
Chan Bing-cho, 237
Chan, Christina, 134
Chan Ping-leung, 138, 237
Chan, Plato, 134
Chang Ching-erh, 139
Chang Chung-li, 200
Chang Chu-p'o, 68, 167-168, 170, 184, 186-187, 190
Chang, H.C., 17, 104, 198, 227, 238, 267
Chang Heng, 154
Chang Hen-shui, 40
Chang Hsueh-ch'ang, 65
Chang Su-lee, 176
Chang Ts'ai, 47
Chao Ching-shen, 105
Chaucer, Geoffrey, 152
Cheang Eng-chew, 105
Chekhov, Anton, 221, 240
Chen Chen-to, 115
Ch'en Ming-sheng, 76
Ch'en Shou-yi, 18, 20, 65, 72-73, 76, 83, 89
Ch'en Ssu-hsiang, 167
Ch'en Tu-hsiu, 28
Ch'en Wen-hua, 238

Ch'en Yu-chiao, 115
Cheng Gek-nai, 18
Ch'eng Wei-yuan, 207, 215, 228
Chesneauz, Jeane, 106
Cheung Yek-mau, 72
Chi Ch'ui-lang, 19, 176
Chia Chung-ming, 84, 88
Chih-yen Chai (Red Inkstone Slab), 68, 186, 216-217, 226, 228, 233, 242, 249, 260-261, 270-272, 275-277
Chin Sheng-t'an, 58, 67-68, 83, 93, 96, 100, 113, 116-117, 123-124, 186
Chin Shih-hsiang, 12
Chou T'an, 77
Chou Tso-jen, 47-48
Chou Ying-hsiung, 152
Chow Tse-tsung, 145, 238
Chu Hsi, 73, 201, 207, 223, 234
Chu-hu (Odd Tablet), 216, 228, 244
Chu, Rudolph Y., 139, 226, 239
Chu Shu-chen, 33
Chu Y.S., 72
Ch'u Yuan, 19, 31, 46, 75
Chuang Hsin-cheng, 240
Chuang-tze, 1, 46, 224, 239, 240, 252
Clark, Richard C., 20, 127
Coleman, John D., 200
Colette, Sidonie Gabrielle, 240
Conrad, Joseph, 95
Constant, Benjamin, 175
Cornaby, W. Arthur, 240
Crump, James I., Jr., 77
Csongor, B., 107-108, 140

D'Horman, Andre, 229
Dai Bufan, 245
Dante, Alighieri, 152, 160, 265
Dars, Jacques, 100, 102
Davidson, Martha, 9

Dawson, Raymond, 20, 28, 36, 78, 109, 144, 178, 243
De Bary, William Theodore, 9, 21, 26, 141, 177, 242
Deeney, John J., 8, 10, 21-23
Demieville, Paul, 245
Dickens, Charles, 240
Dignaga, 154
Dostoyevsky, Fyodor, 5, 48, 226, 240, 247, 249, 273-274
Dreiser, Theodore, 239
Duan-mu Hong-liang, vii, x, xi
Dudbridge, Glen, 133, 140, 150, 157, 159
Dunlop, Geoffrey, 101
Dye, Harriet, 140

Eberhard, Wolfram, 24
Egerton, Clement, 168-169
Ehrenstein, Albert, 101
Eide, Elisabeth, 24
Eliade, Mircea, 146, 174
Eliot, George, 240
Eoyang, Eugene, 25
Erickson, George, xiv-xv
Etiemble, Rene, 23
Euripides, 240

Falk, Eugene H., 47
Fan Hsi-che, 116
Fan Ning, 25
Fang, Achilles, 72
Fang Chaoying, 28, 88, 109, 148, 186, 188, 241
Fasteneau, Franke, 177
Faulkner, William, 239
Feng Meng-lung, 3, 58
Feng Yuan-chun, 26, 131
Feuerwerker, Mei Yi-tse, 26, 141, 177, 221, 242
Fielding, Henry, 189, 215, 240
Fitzgerald, C.P., 26, 77, 108, 141, 178, 221, 242
Fletcher, Angus, 47

INDEX OF AUTHORS

Forster, E.M., 154
Franke, Wolfgang, 201
Frankel, Hans H., 27, 103
Frazer, James George, 12, 143, 146
Frenz, Horst, 23, 46-47
Freud, Sigmund, 7, 146
Frye, Northrop, 12, 47, 130, 143, 146, 173-174, 266
Fu, James Shu-hsien, 133, 141-143, 226, 242

Geoghegan, Anne-Marie, 79, 114, 145, 182, 251
Gide, Andre, 240
Giles, Herbert A., 27, 178, 227, 243
Goethe, Johann Wolfgang von, ix, 240
Goodrich, L. Carrington, 28, 88, 109, 148, 185, 188
Gordon, Terence, 77, 144
Grieder, Jerome B., 243
Grousset, Rene, 77, 144, 223
Guerne, Armel, 228
Guillen, Claudio, 36
Gulik, Robert H. van, 178
Gutzlaff, Karl, A.F., 243

Han Fei-tse, 46
Han Pang-ch'ing, 40
Han, Sherman, 144
Han Yu, 46
Hanan, Patrick, 35, 78, 109, 115, 144, 168, 178-182, 243
Hardy, Barbara, 254
Hardy, Thomas, 48
Hawkes, David, 4, 28, 36, 216, 225-229, 244-246, 267, 277
Hegel, Georg H., 18, 84
Hegel, Robert E., 8, 14, 29, 30, 109, 246, 263, 269
Heidegger, Martin, 262
Hemingway, Ernest, ix, 239
Hennessey, William, 109

Herzfeldt, Johanna, 135
Hessney, Richard C., 30, 269
Hightower, James R., 30-32, 36, 78, 110, 133, 145, 181, 201, 246
Ho Ch'i-fang, 201, 246
Ho, Douglas I-ping, 247
Ho Ping-ti, 201
Ho Shih-chun, 202
Hobbes, Thomas, 165
Horace, 138
Hou, Sharon Shih-juian, 32
Howe, Suzanne, 232
Hsia, C.T., xiii, 5, 8, 21, 33-34, 41, 71-78, 95-96, 104, 110-114, 116, 133, 135, 145-146, 157, 168, 173, 181, 183, 187-188, 197, 202, 211-212, 218, 225, 231, 247-250
Hsia, T.A., 145
Hsiang Mo-hsi, 58
Hsu Chen-ping, 199
Hsu Min, 250
Hsu Tzu-ch'ang, 115
Hsuan-tsang, 144-145, 149, 151, 154-155
Hsun-tze, 165
Hu, John Y.H., 12
Hu Shih, 19, 28, 131, 137, 140, 147-148, 205, 218, 230, 233, 242, 249, 256, 260, 268, 272, 275
Hu Tseng, 77
Hudson, E., 229
Hui-li, 128, 149, 154-155
Hummel, Arthur W., 34, 112, 114, 210, 242
Hung Ming-shui, 113, 181, 251
Hwang Mei-shu, 34, 251

Ibsen, Henrik, 24-25, 48
Idema, Wilt Lukas, 35, 79, 202, 251
Inada Takashi, 211
Irving, Washington, ix

Irwin, Richard Gregg, 79, 98,
    108, 113, 115, 120

Jackson, J.H., 98, 101, 102
James, Henry, 140, 240, 254
Jenner, W., 133, 135
Joly, Bancroft, 229-230, 272
Jonson, Ben, 261
Jor Chi-keung, 35
Joyce, James, 233, 240
Jung, Carl Gustav, 12, 130,
    138, 142-143, 146, 243,
    266
Juvenal, xiii, 138

Kafka, Franz, 29
Kallgren, Joyce K., 277
Kaltenmark, Odile, 36, 79,
    114, 145, 182, 251
Kan Pao, 46
Kao E (Ngo), 215, 228, 244,
    246, 249, 260, 275-276
Kao, George, 36, 101, 171,
    199, 229
Kao, Karl S.Y., 133, 146
Kao Yu-kung, 203, 252
Kayser, Wolfgang, 27
Keats, John, 226
Kelleher, Teresa, 253
Klein, Donald W., 127
Knechtges, David R., 36, 37
Knoerle, Jeanne(Mary Gregory),
    202, 225, 230, 232, 254
Koepping, Klaus Peter, 254
Koss, Nicholas Andrew, 133,
    146-147
Kral, Oldrich, 202-203, 212
Krieger, Murray, 47
Kroll, Paul William, 71, 80
Kuhn, Franz, 73, 101, 114,
    120, 168, 170, 230, 249,
    272-273
Kung Tzu-chen, 254
Kunst, Richard Alan, 254
Kuo-hsun, 92
Kuo Mo-jo, xv, 127, 128

La Fayette, Madeleine de, 15
Lai Ming, 20, 37, 81, 114,
    147, 182, 203, 255
Lai Sing-lam, 254
Lai T.C., 159
Lan Ling, 234, 241
Langlois, Walter G., 255
Lao-tse, 224, 240, 249
Lawrence, David Herbert,
    176, 240
LeFevere, Andre, 37
Leonard, Jane Kate, 204
Lenin, Vladimir Ilich, 233-235
Levin, Harry, 23, 36
Levy, Andre, 41, 182, 199
Levy, Howard S., 182
Li Chih, 21, 58, 105-106,
    113, 123
Li Ch'ing-chao, 33
Li Cho-wu, 260
Li Hsi-fan, 114, 234, 241,
    256
Li Ju-chen, 33, 208
Li K'ai-hsien, 115, 165
Li, Peter, 10, 81, 89, 115,
    124, 156, 189, 213, 257,
    278
Li Po, 19, 31, 154
Li Po-yuan, 40
Li Tche-houa, 229
Li Tien-yi, 10-11
Li Tso-wu, 76
Li Yu, 12
Li Yung, 204
Liang Ch'i-ch'ao, 55, 58, 250
Liao Hsien-hao, 257
Liao Chaoyang, 182
Lidin, Olaf G., 38
Lin Shuan-fu, 196, 204
Lin Yu-tang, 36, 249, 258,
    277
Liu Ching-chih, 115
Liu Chun-jo, 258
Liu Hsieh, 19, 23, 38-39
Liu, James J.Y., 39, 116
Liu, Joyce Chi-hui, 258
Liu Ta-chieh, 19
Liu Ts'un-yan, 40, 81,
    147-148, 205

INDEX OF AUTHORS

Liu Wu-chi, 18, 40-41, 50, 82, 116, 131, 148, 183, 206, 219, 254, 259
Lo, Andrew Hing-bun, 71, 73, 82-83, 116
Lo Chin-t'ang, 41, 149
Lo Kuan-chung, 65, 72, 76, 78-79, 81, 84, 88-90, 95, 99-100, 104, 114
London, Jack, ix
Longinus, 48
Lu Erh-kang, 105, 117
Lu Hsun, 41, 47, 83, 117, 131, 137, 147, 149, 183, 196, 206, 209, 219
Lu Su-fu, 115-116
Lynn, R.J., 42

Mai Tai-loi, 117
Ma Wen-yee, xv, 128, 150
Ma Yau-woon, 8, 41-45, 71, 83-84, 117
Macaulay, Thomas Babington, 67
Machaut, Guillaume de, 152
Machiavelli, Niccolò, 43, 73, 78, 83
Mackerras, Alyce, 106
Maeno Naoaki, 45
Malinowski, Bronislav Kasper, 143
Malmqvist, Oran G., 24-25, 209
Malraux, Andre, 255-256
Mann, Thomas, 240
Mao Dun, 25
Mao Lun, 67, 82
Mao, Nathan K., 10, 89, 124, 156, 189, 213, 278
Mao Tse-tung, 38, 98, 106, 118, 127-128, 150, 211, 256-257, 268
Mao Tsung-kang, 67-68, 70, 73, 76, 81-83, 89-90
Mao Tun (Shen Yen-ping), 260
Margoulies, George, 20
Martinson, Paul V., 168, 183-184

Marx, Karl, 6, 53, 120, 128, 130, 142, 155, 207, 218, 220, 226, 233-235, 256, 268, 279
McHugh, Florence and Isabel, 230, 248, 272-273
McLaren, Anne Elizabeth, 84
McMahon, Robert K., 184
McNaughton, William, 85
Mei, Y.P., 46-47
Mencius, 1, 36, 46-47, 223, 240, 249
Meredith, George, 240
Miall, Bernard, 168, 170-171, 176
Miller, Lucien, 47, 217, 225, 235-236, 261-263
Miller, Roy Andrew, 72, 85, 89
Milton, John, 146
Min Ze, 49
Minford, John, 4, 225, 228, 244, 263
Moravia, Alberto, 240
Morris, Ivan, 154
Mozart, Wolfgang Amadeus, 129, 132
Munro, Donald, 49
Murasaki Shikibu, 13, 15, 164, 224-225, 232

Na Tsung-shun, 263
Nabakov, Vladimir, 240
Nagarjuna, 132
Newman, John Henry, 192, 198
Nghiem Toan, 73
Nienhauser, William H., Jr., 8, 25, 32, 43-44, 50, 82, 84, 109, 117, 171, 238, 251, 263, 268
Nils, Maria, 134
Novatna, Zdene, 135

Odd Tablet (see Chu-hu)
Ogawa Tanaki, 118
Ono Shinobu, 185
Ota Tatsuo, 150
Owen, Stephen, 36-37

Palandai, Angela J., 263
Parker, Z.Q., 73
Pater, Walter, 13
Peffer, Nathaniel, 112
P'ei Sung-chih, 65, 73, 76, 89
Pien-chi, 128, 149, 155
Pirandello, Luigi, 255
Plaks, Andrew, H., 5, 8, 50-53, 60, 62, 68, 71, 81, 85-86, 94-98, 115, 118, 132, 133, 150, 152, 166, 168, 183-185, 203-204, 219, 222, 225, 232, 235-236, 252, 257, 264-266, 274
Plato, 61
Po Chu-i, 154
Polo, Marco, ix, 154
Pope, Alexander, 19, 211
Porret, Jean-Pierre, 171
Pound, Ezra, 13
Propp, Vladimir, 130, 174
Proust, Marcel, 224, 240, 243
Prusek, Jaroslav, 8, 42, 53-55, 57, 77, 86-87, 120, 123, 155, 188, 211, 271
Pu Hsiao-huai, 103
P'u Sung-ling, 40, 202, 208

Qian Zhong-shu, 210

Rabelais, Francois, 141
Racine, Jean, 240
Raglan, Fitz Roy, 12
Red Inkstone Slab (see Chih-yen Chai)
Rexroth, Kenneth, 266
Ricaud, Louis, 73
Richardson, Samuel, 215
Rickett, Adele, 55-56, 250, 271
Roberts, Moss, 71, 74
Robinson, Lewis S., 226, 266
Ropp, Paul Stanley, 197, 206-209, 278
Roy, David T., 168, 186
Ruhlmann, Robert, 56, 73, 86

Rushton, Peter Halliday, 168, 187
Ruskin, John, 63

Sa Men-wu, 105
Sartre, Jean Paul, 239
Satyendra, Indira, 188
Schlegel (Brothers), 142
Schopenhauer, Arthur, 18, 48-49, 58, 226, 269, 278
Schultz, William, 57
Scott, Walter, 43, 66, 84, 111, 188
Scudery, Marie Madeleine, 15
Shaffner, Rudolph P., 232
Shakespeare, William, 43, 66, 71, 84, 111, 132, 145, 261
Shapiro, Sidney, 98, 102
Shaw, George Bernard, 13
Sheldon, William H., 264
Shelley, Percy Bysshe, 157, 259
Shen Ching, 115
Shen Yen-ping (see Mao Tun)
Shi Tuo, 210
Shih Hung, 103
Shih Nai-an, 95, 99-100, 104, 109, 114, 122
Shih Vincent Y.C., 38
Shu Chin-ten, 266
Slupski, Zbigniew, 209
Smollett, Tobias, 215, 240
So, Francis H.K., 133, 152
Soong, Stephen C., 267
Spence, Jonathan, 153, 225, 267-268
Spenser, Edmund, 13, 265
Ssu-ma Ch'ien, 1, 31, 46, 54, 73, 252
Ssu-ma T'an, 1
Ssu-ma Kuang, 72
Stein, Aurel, 1
Steinen, Diether von der, 86, 120
Steiner, George, 160
Stendhal (Marie Henri Beyle), 111

INDEX OF AUTHORS

Sterne, Lawrence, 215
Strachey, Joseph P., 154
Strelka, Joseph P., 47
Styron, William, 85
Sun K'ai-ti, 44, 84
Sun, Phillip S.Y., 120
Sun Wen-kuang, 268
Surh, Olga, 87, 121
Swift, Jonathan, 141, 177
Sychov, L. and V., 268

Tagore, Rabindranath, 48
T'ang Hsien-tsu, 21, 244
T'ang Shih-te, 129
Tay, William, 152, 188
Tchang Fou-jouei, 199
Teele, Roy E., 154
Teng Shao-chi, 268
Tennyson, Alfred, 208
Thackeray, William Makepeace, 199, 206, 240
Theiner, George, 135
Todorov, Tzvetan, 130
Tolstoi, Leo, 48, 111, 240
Trilling, Lionel, 180
Ts'ao Hsueh Ch'in, 215-280
Ts'ao Tang-ts'un, 216, 276
Ts'ao T'ien-yu, 216
Ts'ao Ts'ao, 75, 78, 80, 83, 86-89
Tseng H.P., 40
Tseng P'u, 40
Tso Hai, 268
Ts'ui Shih, 75
Tu Ching-i, 269
Tu Lin-che, 210
T'ung Chung-ch'ang, 75
Tung Shuo, 134
Tung Yueh, 133-134, 138, 146
Turgenev, Ivan, 240
Twain, Mark, ix, 121, 142, 143

Vambery, Arminius, 154
Vasubandhu, 154
Venne, Peter, 121
Virgil, 160

Voltaire, Francois Marie, 13, 209

Wade, William, 272
Wade-Giles, xiv, 10
Wagner, Marsha L., 226, 269
Waley, Arthur, 133, 135-136, 153-154, 170, 261
Wang An-shih, 201
Wang, C.H., 270
Wang Ch'en, 80
Wang Chi-chen, 136, 230, 248, 273
Wang Chuan-shan, 260
Wang Feng-chou, 169
Wang Fu, 74
Wang Hsi-yen, 57, 87, 122, 270
Wang Jing, 122, 155, 270
Wang, John C.Y., 8, 57, 58-60, 87, 123, 155, 188, 226, 270-271
Wang Kuo-wei, 47-49, 58, 269, 270
Wang Pi-tuan Huang, 60
Wang Shih-chen, 165, 170-171, 178, 190
Wang Wei, 19
Wang Yang-ming, 19, 120, 151, 176, 186, 207, 223-224
Wang Yu-k'un, 272
Warren, Robert Penn, 128
Watson, Burton, 54
Watson-Gandy, Anthony, 77, 144
Watters, Thomas, 155
Wellek, Rene, 138
Wells, Henry W., 210
Werner, Edward Chalmers, 272
West, Anthony, 272
Westbrook, Francis A., 226, 273
Widmer, Ellen Bradford, 123-124
Winters, Lily C., 13
Witke, Charles, 60
Wivell, Charles, 60
Wolfe, Thomas, 240
Wong Kam-ming, 274

Wong, Timothy Chung-tai, 57, 124, 197, 210
Wong Yoon-wah, 61, 275
Woolf, Virginia, 154
Wordsworth, William, 19, 197
Wrenn, James J., 168, 189
Wright, Arthur F., 61, 74, 86
Wright, H.M., 74-75
Wu Ch'eng-en, 21, 121, 128-129, 131-133, 137, 140, 144, 147-149, 157
Wu Ching-tzu, 33, 57, 191-198, 201, 203-204, 208, 210, 212, 220
Wu, Jack, 124
Wu Shih-ch'ang, 225, 238, 249-250, 275-277
Wu Tsu-hsiang, 155, 212
Wu Wo-yao, 40
Wu Xiang-lin, 277

Xiao Hong, xi

Yang Chen-hsin, 129
Yang Hsien-yi and Gladys, 26, 41, 74, 83, 117, 136-137, 147, 149, 183, 197, 199, 206, 225, 228, 231, 260, 277
Yang, James Parish, 277
Yang Jiang, 277
Yang, Robert Yi, 189
Yang Ting-chien, 113
Yang, Winston L.Y., 10, 11, 62, 71, 81, 85, 87-90, 124, 156, 189, 213, 237, 258, 278
Yeh, Alfred Kuang-yao, 133, 157
Yen, Alsace, 157
Yen Fu, 250
Yen-tsung, 154
Yeo Song-nian, 62
Yieh Ch'ing-ping, 63
Yoshida-Krafft, Barbara, 190
Yu, Anthony, 63, 71, 129, 133, 135, 137, 158-161, 220, 226, 234, 247, 278
Yu, Diana, 279
Yu P'ing-po, 233-235, 241, 249, 256, 279
Yu Ying-shih, 279
Yu Yuh-chao, 124
Yuan Heh-hsiang, 23, 152
Yuan Hung-tao, 123, 165, 181, 188, 251
Yuan Mei, 154, 208, 268
Yuan Shui-lo, 280
Yuan Tung-li, 11
Yuan Wu-yai, 113
Yuriri, 245

Zola, Emile, 240

INDEX OF TITLES

```
CPM     CHIN P'ING MEI
DRC     THE DREAM OF THE RED CHAMBER
RCD     THE RED CHAMBER DREAM
HLM     HUNG-LOU MENG
HYC     HSI-YU CHI
JLWS    JU-LIN WAI-SHIH
JW      JOURNEY TO THE WEST
RTK     THE ROMANCE OF THE THREE KINGDOMS
SHC     SHUI-HU CHUAN
SKCYI   SAN-KUO-CHIH YEN-I
```

(Articles appear in upper-lower cases, books in all caps.)

About the Date of the First Edition of CPM, 182
ADOLPHE, 175
ADVENTURES OF HSI-MEN CH'ING, 169
Adventures of the Tattooed Monk, The, 101
AENEID, THE, 159
AFTER BABEL, 160
AJAX, 34
ALL MEN ARE BROTHERS (see SHC), 16, 98, 100, 104, 114, 120, 122, 125
ALLEGORICAL STRUCTURE ... HLM, THE, 266
Allegory and Personality in Modern Chinese Literary Criticism, 47
Allegory in HYC and HLM, 150, 264
ANALECTS, THE, 1, 21, 154, 223
Anatomy of the Political Satire in HYC, An, 144
ANNA KARENINA, 48
ANTHOLOGY OF CHINESE LITERATURE, 100, 135, 226
ANTIGONE, 34
Appreciations of the DRC, 258
APPRENTICESHIP NOVEL, THE, 232

Apprenticeship Novel in China: HLM, The, 232
Approaches to a History of Chinese Literature: A Bibliographical Spectrum, 20
APPROACHES TO THE ORIENTAL CLASSICS, 10, 21, 26, 141, 177, 242
Archetypal Approach to HYC, An, 146
ARCHETYPE AND ALLEGORY IN DRC, 225, 235, 265
ART AND PROFESSION OF TRANSLATING, THE, 159
Art and the Overcoming of Difficulty ... DRC, 278
Arthur Waley (Teele), 154
AU BORD DE L'EAU (SHC), 100
Author of SHC, The, 118
AUTHORSHIP OF THE DRC, THE, 237
AUTHORSHIP OF THE FENG SHEN YEN-I, THE, 39

Battle of the Red Cliff, The, 74
Beginning and the End of the DRC, The, 254

Beginnings of Professional Storytelling in China, The, 42
BIOGRAPHIC DICTIONARY OF CHINESE COMMUNISM (1921-1965), 127
BIZARRE HAPPENINGS EYEWITNESSED IN TWO DECADES, 40
BONES OF CHUANG TZU, THE, 154
BOOK OF CHANGES, THE (see I CHING)
BOOK OF CHUANG-TSE, THE, 1, 224
BOOK OF HISTORY, THE (see SHU CHING)
BOOK OF MENCIUS, THE, 1, 223
BOOK OF POETRY, THE (see SHIH CHING)
BOOK OF SNOBS, THE, 199, 206
BOOK REVIEW DIGEST, 9
BOOK REVIEW INDEX, 9
BRIEF HISTORY OF CHINESE FICTION, A, 41, 83, 117, 149, 183, 206, 260
BROTHERS KARAMAZOV, THE, 274
BUDDENBROOKS, 240
BUDDHIST AND TAOIST INFLUENCES ON CHINESE NOVELS, 39
Burial Mound for Flowers, A, 227, 329

CAMBRIDGE HISTORY OF CHINA, THE, 36
Can We Read Books Like DRC?, 269
CANDIDE, 13
CATCHER IN THE RYE, THE, 248
CELEBRATIONS AT THE GATE OF DEATH: SYMBOL AND STRUCTURE IN CPM, 168, 174
Chang Chu-p'o's Commentary on CPM, 186
Changing Attitude Toward Chinese Fiction, The, 41
Chapter-opening Mottoes in CPM and in Scott's THE HEART OF MIDLOTHIAN, 188

Characterization Through the Depiction of Externals, 57, 87, 122, 270
CHERRY ORCHARD, THE 221
Chia Pao-yu: The Reluctant Questor, 251
Chih-yen Chai Commentary on the DRC, The, 271-272
CHIN P'ING MEI (see CPM)
CHIN SHENG-T'AN, 122
CHINA AND THE SEARCH FOR HAPPINESS, 13
CHINA AND THE WEST: COMPARATIVE LITERATURE STUDIES, 152
China in the Mirror of Her Fiction, 15
CHINA IN WESTERN LITERATURE ... CORDIER'S BIBLIOTECA SINICA, 9, 11
China's Three Ways ... DRC, 231
CHINESE APPROACHES TO LITERATURE, 55, 250
Chinese Bandit Novels and the American Gangster Film, The, 104
CHINESE CIVILIZATION AND BUREAUCRACY, 74-75
Chinese Classic (SHC), A, 112
CHINESE FICTION: A BIBLIOGRAPHY, 10
CHINESE GENTRY: ... IN NINETEENTH-CENTURY CHINESE SOCIETY, 200
Chinese Historical Novel, The, 42
Chinese Historical Novels, 83
CHINESE HISTORY AND LITERATURE, 53,120
Chinese Influences on Pearl Buck, 124
CHINESE KNIGHT-ERRANT, THE, 116
CHINESE LITERATURE: AN HISTORICAL INTRODUCTION, 18, 20
Chinese Literature and Twayne's World Authors Series, 57

INDEX OF TITLES

CHINESE LITERATURE (Chang), 17, 104, 198, 227
Chinese Literature in the Context of World Literature, 30
CHINESE LITERATURE (Kaltenmark), 36, 79, 114, 145, 182, 252
CHINESE LITERATURE (Lynn), 42
CHINESE MIDDLEBROW FICTION, 40
CHINESE NARRATIVE: CRITICAL AND THEORETICAL ESSAYS, 50, 53, 81, 115, 150, 186, 203-204, 252
CHINESE NOVEL, THE, 15
Chinese Novel, The, 26, 141, 177, 242
Chinese Novel: A Confrontation of Critical Approaches, The, 27
Chinese Novel and Modern Western Historismus, The, 85
Chinese Novel as a Subversive Form, The, 26, 77, 108, 141, 178, 242
CHINESE NOVEL, THE (NOBEL LECTURE), 16
CHINESE POPULAR FICTION ... IN LONDON LIBRARIES, 147, 205
Chinese Popular Water-god Legends and the HYC, 138
CHINESE THEORIES OF LITERATURE, 39
CHINESE VERNACULAR FICTION: THE FORMATIVE PERIOD, 35, 202, 251
CHINESE WIT AND HUMOR, 36, 171, 199, 229
Chinese-English Comparative Literature Bibliography, 10
Chinese-English Comparative Literature Studies: Historical Survey, 35
Chinese-English Literary Relations, 21
CHINESE-WESTERN COMPARATIVE LITERATURE: THEORY AND STRATEGY, 22
CHING-HUA YUAN (FLOWERS IN THE MIRROR), 11, 33, 208
CHRONICLE OF THE THREE KINGDOMS, THE, 72
CHRONIQUE INDISCRETE DES MANDARINS, 199
CH'U TZ'U, 19
CHUANG-TSE (see THE BOOK OF CHUANG-TSE)
CH'IU-HU (MULBERRY TREE IN THE BALK), 75
CHUKO-LIANG AND THE KINGDOM OF SHU-HAN, 76
CH'UN CH'IU (SPRING AND AUTUMN CHRONICLES), 1, 45
CHUNG YUNG (THE DOCTRINE OF THE MEAN), 223
CLASSIC CHINESE NOVEL: A CRITICAL INTRODUCTION, THE, 33, 145, 181, 202, 226
CLASSICAL CHINESE FICTION: A GUIDE, 10, 89, 124, 156, 189, 213, 278
Classical Chinese Fiction in the West 1960-1980, 62
Clues Leading to the Discovery of HYC P'ing-hua, 149
Colloquial Short Story in the Novel CPM, A, 171
COMEDIE HUMAINE, LA, 240
COMMEDIA, THE (Dante), 160, 161
Comments on [Conference] Papers, 253
Communist Critique of HLM, The, 243
Comparative Analysis of SHC and HYC, A, 107, 140
Comparative Approaches to WM, 110
Comparative Essay on Two Novels: CPM and ADOLPHE, A, 175
Comparative Literature and China: A Bibliographical Review, 10
Comparative Literature East and West, 12
Comparative Literature Studies in Taiwan, 22

Comparative Literature: West and/or East, 23
COMPREHENSIVE MIRROR FOR AID IN GOVERNMENT, A (see TZU CHIH T'UNG CHIEN)
CONCEPT OF MAN IN EARLY CHINA, THE, 49
Concepts of Classicism and Romanticism ... Chinese Literature. 19
CONFERENCE ON ORIENTAL-WESTERN LITERARY RELATIONS, 46, 49
CONFESSIONS OF NAT TURNER, THE, 85
CONFUCIAN PERSUASION, THE, 56, 61, 86
Conservatism and Originality in Chinese Literature, 63
CONTRADICTIONS, 106
CPM, 3, 11, 27, 57, 68, 85, 91, 111, 119, 163-190, 231, 237, 247, 251
CPM, THE, (Hsia), 179
CPM: A Critical Study, 185
CPM and THE PRAYER MAT OF FLESH, 189
CPM as Wisdom Literature, The, 183
CPM: THE ADVENTUROUS HISTORY OF HSI-MEN AND HIS SIX WIVES (Miall), 168
CRIME AND PUNISHMENT, 274
CRITICAL ANALYSIS OF THE DRC ... WESTERN CRITERIA, 254
Critical Essay on DRC, A, 48
CRITICAL ESSAYS ON CHINESE FICTION, 25, 62, 81, 85, 258
CRITICAL ESSAYS ON CHINESE LITERATURE, 11, 50, 237
CRITICAL STUDY OF HYC, A, 138
CRITICAL STUDY OF HSI-YU PU, A, 133, 137
Cyclic Quest, The, 141
Cyclical View of Life and Meaning in the Traditional Chinese Novel, The, 57, 87, 123, 155, 188, 271

Development of Fiction and Drama, The, 78, 109, 144, 178, 243
DICTIONARY OF MING BIOGRAPHY 1368-1644, 28, 88, 109, 148, 188
DISSENT IN EARLY MODERN CHINA ... JLWS, 206
DISSERTATION ABSTRACTS ONLINE, 9
DOLL'S HOUSE, A, 25, 48
DON QUIXOTE, 131, 142-143, 164
DRAGON SEED, 122
DREAM OF RED MANSIONS, A (Yangs), 225, 231
DREAM OF THE RED CHAMBER, THE, (see HLM)
DRC, The (Hsia), 247
DRC, The (Rexroth), 266
DRC, The (Wang), 230
DRC, The (Yuan Shui-lo), 280
DRC: A CRITICAL STUDY, THE, 254
DRC and Its Author, The, 250
DRC BY TS'AO HSUEH CH'IN, THE (McHugh), 230
DRC Case, The, 241
DRC Must Be Studied From the Class Standpoint, The, 268
DRC, THE GOOD EARTH, and MAN'S FATE, The, 255
DREAMING AGAIN IN THE CRINOLINE CHAMBER, 262
DUNCIAD, THE, 211

EACH IN HIS OWN WAY, 255
EARLY CH'ING SOCIETY AND ITS CRITICS ... WU CHING-TZU, 207
EAST AND WEST AND THE NOVEL, 16
EASTWIND-WESTWIND, 122
ELABORATION ON THE TREATISE OF THE THREE STATES, AN (SKCYI), 80
EMINENT CHINESE OF THE CH'ING DYNASTY 1644-1912, 34, 210, 242

INDEX OF TITLES

ENCOUNTERING SORROW (See LI SAO)
EROTIC COLOUR PRINTS OF THE MING PERIOD, 178
Essay on the JLWS, An, 210
ESSAYS IN CHINESE STUDIES PRESENTED TO ... LO HSIANG-LIN, 138-139
ESSENTIALS OF CHINESE LITERARY ART, 39
ETUDES HISTOIRE DE LITTERATURE CHINOISE ... JAROSLAV PRUSEK, 42, 57, 87, 123, 155, 188, 272
EVOLUTION OF A CHINESE NOVEL: SHC, THE, 79, 98, 113, 120
Evolution of a Rebel ... JW, The, 133, 157
Explorer Who Never Left Home--Arthur Waley, The, 153
EXPRESSIONS OF SELF IN CHINESE LITERATURE, 30, 269

FAERIE QUEENE, THE, 13, 265
Fair Needs Foul: Moral Ambiguity in CPM, 176
FAMILY, THE (see JIA)
FATE IN TEARS AND LAUGHTER, 40
FATHERS AND SONS, 240
FAUST, 157
FEATHERS OF THE FIREBIRD, xi
FENG-SHEN YEN-I (THE INVESTITURE OF THE GODS), 147
Few Poems in the RCD, A, 277
Fiction, 43
FIGUREN DES CPM UND DES YU HUAN-CHI, DIE, 177
FIRST WIFE, THE, 122
FLAMING MOUNTAIN, THE, 136
FLOWER IN A SINFUL SEA, A, 40
FLOWERS IN THE MIRROR (see CHING-HUA YUAN)
Forever Inter [sic] the Exploitation System ... DRC, 272
Four Eccentrics: The Epilogue to JLWS, 199
FOUR MASTERWORKS OF THE MING NOVEL, THE (SSU TA CH'I-SHU), 85, 98, 118, 152, 185
FOUR PILGRIMAGES, 148
Full-length Hsiao-shuo and the Western Novel, 51

GAP IN THE WALL: CONTAINMENT AND ABANDON, THE, 184
General Principles for a History of Chinese Literature, 36
GENJI MONOGATARI (THE TALE OF GENJI), 4, 8, 13, 164, 232, 266
GILGAMESH, 159
GOLDEN ASS, THE, 187
GOLDEN LOTUS, THE (see CPM), 169
GOOD EARTH, THE, 16, 122, 256
GREAT EXPECTATIONS, 240
GREAT WALL GLISTENS, THE (Mao's poetry), 128
GREAT LEARNING, THE (see TA HSUEH)
Great Novel of Peasant Revolt, A, 114
Great Novels by Obscure Writers, 148, 183, 206, 259
GUIDE TO ORIENTAL CLASSICS, A, 9
GUILT AND SIN IN TRADITIONAL CHINA, 24
GULLIVER'S TRAVELS, 177

HARD TIMES, 240
Harmony With Nature in Chinese ... [and] Western Theory, 38
HATRED, x
HEART OF DARKNESS, THE, 95
HEART OF MIDLOTHIAN, THE, 186
HEART SUTRA, THE, 132, 143, 151, 160
Heavens and Hells in Chinese Fictional Dreams, 29, 109, 246

294   THE CHINESE CLASSIC NOVELS

Hermit and the Sufferer: Two
  Different Prototypes, The,
  239
HERO WITH A THOUSAND FACES,
  THE, 137
Heroes as Shining Princes, 232
Heroic Verse and Heroic Mis-
  sion: ... HYC, 158
HISTOIRE DE LITTERATURE CHI-
  NOISE MODERNE, 20
History and Epics in China and
  in the West, 53, 86
HISTORY OF A CURIOUS EROTIC
  CUSTOM [FOOTBINDING], THE,
  122
HISTORY OF CHINESE LITERATURE
  A, (Giles), 27, 178, 243
HISTORY OF CHINESE LITERATURE,
  A, (Lai Ming), 37, 81, 114,
  147, 182, 203, 255
HISTORY OF CHINESE LITERATURE:
  A SELECTED BIBLIOGRAPHY,
  THE, 10
HISTORY OF ENGLAND 1685-1700,
  THE (Macaulay), 67
History of the RCD, The, 275
HLM (DRC) xiii, 4, 8, 11-12,
  15, 17, 25, 27, 29-31, 39,
  48, 58-61, 123, 138, 150,
  156, 177, 184-185, 202-204,
  215-280
HLM (Chai), 134, 227
HLM, Commonly Called DRC, 227
HLM or DRC (Joly), 229
HLM or DREAMS IN THE RED CHAM-
  BER: A Novel (Gutzlaff),
  243
HONG (THE RAINBOW), 25
HONG-LEOU MONG, Roman Symbol-
  iste, 245
How to Be Rid of a Rival, 226
How to Read the CPM, 167, 188
HSI-HSIANG CHI (THE ROMANCE OF
  THE WESTERN CHAMBER), 30,
  224
Hsi-men and the Golden Lotus,
  171
HSI-YU PU, 134, 138

HSI-YU PU as an Example of
  Mythmaking in Chinese
  Fiction, The, 138
HSUAN-HO I-SHIH (PAST EVENTS
  OF THE HSUAN-HO PERIOD),
  92, 109-110
HUCKLEBERRY FINN, 131, 142-143
Humane Literature, 48
HUMANITIES INDEX, THE, 9
Hundred-chapter HYC and its
  Early Versions, The, 140
HYC (MONKEY, or JOURNEY TO THE
  WEST), 3, 11, 17, 21, 25,
  28, 31, 39, 44, 48-49, 57,
  71, 85, 119, 123, 127-160,
  179, 270
HYC: A STUDY OF ANTECEDENTS OF
  THE SIXTEENTH-CENTURY
  NOVEL, THE, 133, 140
HYC IN ITS FORMATIVE STAGES,
  THE, 133, 146
HYC: Pilgrimage to the Western
  Regions
HYC P'ing-hua, 149

I CHING (THE BOOK OF CHANGES),
  38, 153, 224
Ibsen's Nora and Chinese Inter-
  pretation of Female Emanci-
  pation, 24
IDEA OF A UNIVERSITY, THE,
  192, 199
IDIOT, THE, 226, 247, 249,
  273-274
ILIAD, THE, 91, 153
Immediate Audience: Oral Narra-
  tion in Chinese Fiction,
  The, 25
Importance of Tradition in
  Chinese Literature, The, 54
IN COLD BLOOD, 85
In Reply to Mr. Franz Kuhn (re
  Buck's translation of SHC),
  120
INDIANA COMPANION TO TRADI-
  TIONAL CHINESE LITERATURE,
  THE, 32, 43, 50, 82, 84,
  117, 171, 238, 263, 268

INDEX OF TITLES

Individualism and Humanitarianism in Late Ming Thought, 21
Individualism in Chinese Literature, 30, 110
INTRODUCTION TO CHINESE LITERATURE, AN, 40, 116, 148, 181, 206
Introduction to RTK (Miller), 85
Introduction to THE STORY OF THE STONE (HLM), 244
Introductory Note, An, 28
Is There Tragedy in Chinese Drama?, 34
Issues in Chinese Narrative Theory ... [and] Western Tradition, 51

JADE NECKLACE, THE (YU HUAN-CHI), 179
JIA (THE FAMILY), 25
JLWS, 4, 11, 18, 31, 33, 50, 191-213, 220, 222, 231, 251-252
JLWS (THE UNOFFICIAL HISTORY OF OFFICIALDOM) (Chai), 197
JOU-LIN-WAI-CHE: LE ROMAN DES LETTRES, 202
JOU P'U T'UAN (THE PRAYER MAT OF FLESH), 11, 61, 187, 275
JOURNEY TO THE WEST (Hsia), 145
JOURNEY TO THE WEST (Yu), 137
JUDE THE OBSCURE, 259
JW and FLOWERS IN THE MIRROR, 156
JW (Hsia), 145
JW (Jenner), 135
JW (Yu), 137

KERQIN BANNER PRAIRIE, x
KIN PING MEH, DIE ABEUTERLICHE GESCHICHTE VON HSI-MEN ... SECHS FRAUEN, 170
K'IN P'ING MEI ... HSI-MEN AVEC SES SIX FEMMES, 171

KNOWLEDGE INDEX, THE, 9

LADDER OF SUCCESS IN IMPERIAL CHINA, THE, 201
LADY FROM THE SEA, THE, 25
Landmark of the Chinese Novel, A, 179
LATE CH'ING VIEWS ON FICTION, 18
LATER RED CHAMBER DREAM, THE, 262
LAZARILLO DE TORMES, 91
LEGACY OF CHINA, THE, 20, 28, 36, 78, 144, 176, 243
LEGACY OF GREECE, THE, 20
LI CHIH AS A CRITIC: A CHAPTER OF MING HISTORY, 105
LI SAO (ENCOUNTERING SORROW), 13, 31, 46, 252
LING PAO TAO (THE MARVELOUS SWORD), 115
LIST OF PUBLISHED TRANSLATIONS FROM CHINESE, A, 9
Literary and Ideological Responses to JLWS, 209
LITERARY MIND AND THE CARVING OF DRAGONS, THE, 23, 38
Literary Transformation of Historical Figures in the SKCYI, The, 87
LITTLE CAESAR, 104
Liu Lao-lao, 229
Liu Lao-lao and the Garden of Takuanyuan, 242
Lo Kuan-chung, 84, 88
Lo Kuan-chung and His Historical Romances, 81
Lo Kuan-chung (Yangs)
Loss-of-Paradise Myth in DRC, The, 236
LOTUS SUTRA, THE, 21
Love and Compassion in the DRC, 248
LUTE SONG, THE, 12
Lyric Vision in Chinese Narrative: HLM and JLWS, 252

M.H. Abrams' Four Artistic
  Coordinates and ... Tradi-
  tional China, 39
MAGIC MONKEY, THE, 134
MAHABHARATA, THE, 91
Maids and Servants in DRC:
  Individuality and Social
  Order, 269
Man and Nature in Chinese
  Literature, 46
Man and Nature in Chinese
  Philosophy, 47
MAN'S FATE, 255-256
MARGINS OF THOUGHT: SHC AND
  ... MING LOYALISM, THE, 123
MARIUS THE EPICUREAN, 13
MARRIAGE AS RETRIBUTION, 40
MARRIAGE THAT AWAKENS THE
  WORLD, A, 202
MASKS OF FICTION IN HLM, THE,
  225, 235, 261-262
MASTERPIECES OF THE ORIENT,
  135
MEDEA, 34
Meeting of the Twain: Japanese
  and Greek, The, 18
MELANGE DE SINOLOGIE OFFERTES
  A MONSIUR PAUL DEMIEVILLE,
  245
MENCIUS (see THE BOOK OF
  MENCIUS)
MIDDLEMARCH, 4
Military Romana: A Genre of
  Chinese Fiction, The, 33
MING BIOGRAPHICAL DICTIONARY,
  THE, 14
Ming Chantefable and the Early
  Chinese Novel, 84
Ming Dynasty Fiction, 25
MING STUDIES, 14
MIRROR AND THE LAMP, THE, 39
MIRROR FOR AID IN GOVERNMENT,
  A, 82
MIRROR FOR THE ROMANTIC, A,
  244, 295
MLA ONLINE, 9
MODERN CHINESE LITERATURE AND
  ITS SOCIAL CONTEXT, 24, 209

Modern Relevance of SHC: Its
  Influence on the Rebel Move-
  ment, The, 106
MODERN TIMES, 40
MONKEY (Waley), 136 (see HYC)
Monkey (Waley), 135
MONKEY KING, THE (Theiner),
  135
Monkey King, The (Chapters
  1-8) (Wang), 136
MONKEYE PILGERFAHRT: EINE
  CHINESISCHE LEGENDE, 134
MOON AND THE LEATHER SACK:
  PARODY IN CPM AND JOUPU-
  TUAN, THE, 189
Moral and Aesthetic Values in
  Chinese Literature, 41
Morals of ALL MEN ARE
  BROTHERS, THE (SHC), 124
MORTE D'ARTHUR, 111
MUCH ADO ABOUT NOTHING, 231
MY FATHER'S LITERARY JOURNEY,
  40
Myth and Psyche in HLM, 237
MYTHIC AND COMIC ASPECTS OF
  THE QUEST: HYC, 133, 142
Mythic and Mimetic Threads:
  Chih-yen Chai's Commentary,
  277
MYTHOLOGY OF STONE, THE, 122,
  155, 270

Naming the Whirlwind: Cao
  Queqin and Heidegger, 262
NARRATIVE FORM OF CPM, THE,
  187
Narrative Patterns in SKCYI
  and SHC, 81, 115
Narrative Structure and the
  Problem of Chapter 9 ...
  HYC, 159
Nature of Chinese Narrative,
  The, 59
NEW INTERPRETATIONS OF THE RED
  CHAMBER DREAM, 254
New Perspectives on Two Ming
  Novels: HYC and HSI-YU PU,
  145

New Study on the Formation of HYC, 150
NJAL'S SAGA, 111
Notes for a Comparison of the ODYSSEY and MONKEY, 140
Novel as Folk Epic, The, 12, 82, 116
NOVEL IN SEVENTEENTH-CENTURY CHINA, THE, 29

ODYSSEY, THE, 91, 131, 140-141, 159
OLD HISTORY OF T'ANG, THE, 149
Old, Old Story, An, 229
On Dreams, Saints, and Fallen Angels ... DRC, 273
On the DRC (Ho), 246
On the Mind of the Child, 58
On the Pilgrimage to the West, 155
On the Popularity of the SHC, 107
On the Pre-history of the SHC, 108
On the RCD: TWO ANNOTATED MANUSCRIPTS ... 225, 238, 249, 276-277
On the RTK, 76, 238
On Translating the HYC, 159
ON YUAN CHWANG'S TRAVELS IN INDIA, 155
ORDEAL OF RICHARD FEVEREL, THE, 242
Origin of Fiction in China, The, 45
ORPHAN OF CHAO, THE, 24
Other Values, Other Assumptions: the Self and Social Order in China, 49
OUTLAWS OF THE MARSH, 98, 102
OXFORD HISTORY OF ENGLISH LITERATURE, THE, 36

PAO CHIEN CHI (THE PRECIOUS SWORD), 115
PAO ORDER AND REDEMPTION: ... CHINESE RELIGION AND SOCIETY ... CPM, 184

Pao-yu and Parsifal: Personal Growth as a Literary Substructure, 266
PARADISE LOST, 132, 265
Parallelism Between Aristotle and Two Chinese Novelists, 61, 275
PARSIFAL, 266
PASSIONATE MONK'S TALE, THE, 244
PA-WAY AND HIS LADY, 34
PEACOCK FLIES SOUTHEAST, THE, 34
Pearl Buck and the Chinese Novel, 16
Pearl Buck's Literary Portrait of China and the Chinese, 121
PEGASUS OVER ASIA ... VENTURES IN EAST-WEST LITERARY ANALYSIS, 13-14, 232
PEONY PAVILION, THE (see FANG HSIEN-TSU)
Personality of the Chinese Critic, The, 55
PILGERFAHRT NACH DEM WESTEN, DIE, 135
Pilgrimage to the West: Chapter 27, 134, 137
PILGRIM'S PROGRESS, 131, 141, 145, 156
P'ing-hua and the Early History of SKCYI, 77
Plot Against the Birthday Convoy, The, 100
Plot and Style of the Quest, The, 143
Poems of Ts'ao Ts'ao, 86
Point of View, Norms, and Structure ... HLM, 274
Political Philosophy and Social Crisis at the End of the Han Dynasty, 74
PORTRAIT OF THE ARTIST AS A YOUNG MAN, 233
PORTRAITS OF TS'AO TS'AO: ... THE MAN AND THE MYTH, 80
PRAYER MAT OF FLESH, THE (see JOU P'U T'UAN)
PRINCESS, THE (Tennyson), 208

Problem of Sentimental Fallacy in Chinese Literary Criticism, The, 62
Problem of Structure in Chinese Narrative, The, 51
Problems and Prospects in Chinese-Western Literary Relations, 63
Problems of Teaching Chinese Literature in a Comparative Literature Program, 60
PROCEEDINGS OF THE SEVENTH CONGRESS OF THE ICLA, 62
PROMETHEUS BOUND, 132
PROMETHEUS UNBOUND, 132, 157
Protest and the Ch'ing Intellectual, 204
Prototypes of Monkey, 147
PSYCHOSINOLOGY: THE UNIVERSE OF DREAMS IN CHINESE CULTURE, 29, 109, 246
PUBLIC ENEMY, THE, 104
Puns and Puzzles in the CPM: Chapter 27, 172

QUING HUA WEEKLY, x

RAINBOW (see HONG)
RAMAYANA, 91, 140
RAUBER VOM LIANG SCHAN MOOR, DIE, 101
RCD: A CRITICAL STUDY, THE, 225
RCD Today, The, 277
REAL TRIPITAKA AND OTHER PIECES, THE, 133, 154
Realism in Chinese Classical Literature, 49
Realism of Wu Ching-tzu, The, 212
RECENT WORKS BY DUAN-MU HONG-LIANG, xi
RECHERCHE DU TEMPS PERDU (REMEMBRANCE OF THINGS PAST), 4, 243
Recognition in Wang Kuo-wei's Criticism of HLM, 270
RECORDS OF THE HISTORIAN (see SHIH CHI)
REFORM AND ABOLITION OF THE TRADITIONAL CHINESE EXAMINATION SYSTEM, THE, 201
REGISTRY, 84
Relationship of HYC and FENG-SHEN YEN-I, The, 147
Religious Figures in the DRC, 247
REMEMBRANCE OF THINGS PAST (see RECHERCHE DU TEMPS PERDU)
Restudying Chairman Mao's Letter ... [re] DRC, 256
REVE DANS LE PAVILLON ROUGE LE, (Guerne), 228
REVE DU LES PAVILLONS ROUGES LE, (Li Tche), 229
Revels of a Gaudy Night (CPM), 175
Review Article: ARCHETYPE AND ALLEGORY ... By Plaks, 257
Review: Miller's MASKS OF FICTION and Plaks' ARCHETYPE AND ALLEGORY, 235
Review of CPM Translated by Bernard Miall, 176
Review of Pearl Buck's ALL MEN ARE BROTHERS, 114
Review of Wu Shih-ch'ang's ON THE RED CHAMBER DREAM, 238, 249
RHETORIC OF CPM, THE, 168, 172
RISE AND SPLENDOUR OF THE CHINESE EMPIRE, THE, 77, 144
Ritual and Narrative Structure in JLWS, 204
RIVERSIDE PAVILION, THE, 13
ROBBERS AND BROTHERS, 101
Role of Costume in Cao Xueqin's Novel DRC, The, 268
ROLE OF DRAMA IN CPM, THE 168, 173
ROMANCE OF THE ROSE, THE, 265
ROMANCE OF THE THREE KINGDOMS, THE (see SKCYI)
ROMANCE OF THE WESTERN CHAMBER (see HSI-HSIANG)

INDEX OF TITLES

ROMEO AND JULIET, 34
ROUGE ET LE NOIR, LE, 240, 259
ROUGON-MARQUART, 240
RTK, THE, 78-79
RTK and the WATER MARGIN, 89, 124
RTK (Brewitt-Taylor), 71
RTK (Chai), 72
RTK (Cheung), 72
RTK (Chu), 72

SAN-KUO CHIH, 38
SAN-KUO-CHIH YEN-I (see SKCYI)
SAN-KUO CHIH P'ING HUA, 80
SATIRE AND THE POLEMICS OF CRITICISM OF CHINESE FICTION ... JLWS, 210-212
SCARFACE, 104
SCHOLARS, THE (Hsia), 202
SCHOLARS, THE (Yang), 199-200
SCHOLARS, THE (Yang-Li-Mao), 213
SCHWURBRUDER VAN PFIRSICHGARTEN, DIE, 73
SEA OF THE EARTH, THE, xi
Secret of the Red Chamber, The, 240
Seditious Art of WM, Misogynists or Desperadoes? The, 120
Seeds of Change ... Ch'ing Societies, 208
Self and Family in the HLM ... Lin Tai-yu as Tragic Heroine, The, 278
SELF AND SOCIETY IN MING THOUGHT, 21
SEQUEL TO THE RED CHAMBER DREAM, 202, 262
Sequels to the RCD, 262-263
Several Artistic Methods in the Classic Chinese Novel JLWS, 203
SEXUAL LIFE IN ANCIENT CHINA, 178
SHC, 3, 11, 16-17, 21, 29, 34, 39, 42, 44, 53, 57, 66, 68, 78, 81-86, 91-125, 128, 144, 147, 163-167, 177, 179, 181, 251, 270
SHC AND CHINESE SOCIETY, 105
SHC and the Hung, or Heaven-and-Earth League, 105-117
SHC and the Sixteenth-century Novel Form, 86, 118-120, 185
SHC et son auteur, 120
SHC (THE WATER MARGIN) (see SHC)
SHIH CHI (RECORDS OF THE HISTORIAN), 1
SHIH CHING (THE BOOK OF POETRY), 47, 81, 224
SHIH HUA, 157
Shih Nai-an, 109
SHIH-SHUO HSIN-YU (VERSIONS OF CURRENT STORIES), 31
SHIH T'OU CHI (THE STORY OF THE STONE), 4, 215, 228
SHORT HISTORY OF CLASSICAL CHINESE LITERATURE, A, 26
SHU CHING (THE BOOK OF HISTORY), 1, 153
SHUI-HU (see SHC)
SHUI-HU HOU-CHUAN IN ... SEVENTEENTH-CENTURY CHINESE LITERARY CRITICISM, 124
SI YEOU KI, OU, LE VOYAGE EN OCCIDENT, 134
SIDELIGHTS OF CHONQUING, xi
SINGSONG GIRLS OF SHANGHAI, 40
SKCYI (RTK), 3, 5, 11-13, 15, 17, 26-27, 31, 34, 39, 41, 43-44, 57, 65-90, 96-97, 111-113, 127, 150, 167, 179
SKCYI (RTK) (Lo), 82
SKCYI and SHC in the Context of Historiography, 83, 116
SNOW GLISTENS ON THE GREAT WALL, xv, 150
Some Limitations of Chinese Fiction, 15
Some Philosophical Implications of the HLM, 236
Some Recent Studies in SHC, 105

Some Reflections on ... Comparative Literature in China, 23
Some Rhetorical Conventions of the Verse Sections of HYC, 152
SONGS OF THE SOUTH, 75
SONS, 125
SONS, SHC, and SKCYI, 87, 121
Sources of the CPM, 180
SOURCES OF THE EARLY CHINESE NOVEL, 16
SOU-SHUN-CHI, 45-46
SPRING AND AUTUMN CHRONICLES (see CH'UN CH'IU)
SSU-MA CH'IEN, GRAND HISTORIAN OF CHINA, 54
STORIES OF SPIRITS AND DEITIES (see SOU-SHEN-CHI)
STORY OF THE STONE, THE (SHIH T'OU CHI), 215, 228
Story of the Three Kingdoms, The, 73
Story of THE WATER MARGIN, THE, 100
STRANGE HAPPENINGS IN THE LAST TWENTY YEARS, 11
STRANGE STORIES, 208
STRANGER, THE, 5
Structure and Themes of HYC, The, 139
STUDIES IN CHINESE LITERARY GENRES, 14, 33
STUDIES IN CHINESE LITERATURE, 15, 171
Studies of Ming Literature: Observations on the State of the Art, 14
STUDIES ON DRC ... BIBLIOGRAPHY, 263
STUDY OF WANG-KUO-WEI'S LITERARY CRITICISM, A, 269
SUI SHIH I-WEN, 12
SUI T'ANG YEN-I, 12
Survey of English-language Criticism of SHC, 103
Syllabicity and the Sentence ... HLM, 258

TA HSUEH (THE GREAT LEARNING), 165, 172, 184, 223
Tai-yu or Pao-chai: The Paradox of Existence, 257
TALE OF GENJI, THE (see GENJI MONOGATARI)
TAO TE CHING (CLASSIC OF THE WAY), 224
TATTOOED MONK RAISING HELL, THE, 101
Technical Terms in Chinese Literary Criticism, 56
Technique of Chinese Fiction ... HYC, The, 157
Temptation of Saint Pigsy, The, 135
TEN YUAN DRAMAS ON STORIES FROM THE WM, 115
TESS OF THE D'URBERVILLES, 48
Text of the CPM, The, 180
TEXTUAL METHOD ... CPM, A, 189
Textual Method in Chinese ... Examples, 189, 259
THEME OF RENUNCIATION IN DRC, LE ROUGE ET LE NOIR, AND JUDE THE OBSCURE, THE, 258
THEMES OF DRC ... A COMPARATIVE INTERPRETATION, 240
THREE CLASHES BETWEEN THE GOLDEN MONKEY AND THE WHITE-BONE DEMON, THE, 128
THREE KINGDOMS: CHINA'S EPIC DRAMA, THE, 71, 74
Three Kingdoms, The (Grousset), 77
Three Readings in Jinpingmei, 182
Through a Glass Darkly, 272
To KUO MO-JO, November 17, 1961, xv, 127
TOM JONES, 140
TOPICS IN CHINESE LITERATURE, 32, 78, 110, 145, 181, 201, 246
T'OU CHIA CHI, 116
TOU-O YUAN, 34
Towards a Critical Theory of Chinese Narrative, 53

INDEX OF TITLES

Traditional Heroes in Chinese Popular Fiction, 56, 86
Translation of Chinese ... Joly's HLM, The, 272
Translator, the Mirror, and the Dream, The, 245
TRAUM DER ROTEN KAMMER, DER, 229
TRAVELS OF LAU-TS'AN, THE, 11, 200
TREASURY OF CHINESE LITERATURE: A NEW PROSE ANTHOLOGY, A, 72, 100, 134, 169, 197, 227
TREATMENT OF TS'AO TS'AO IN CHINESE VERNACULAR LITERATURE, THE, 75
Tripitaka Master's Pilgrimage to the West, 147
TRISTRAM SHANDY, 240
TROIS ROYAUMES, LES, 73
Ts'ao Chan, 241
TS'AO HSUEH CH'IN, xi
Ts'ao Hsueh Chin, 238
Ts'ao Hsueh Ch'in and his DRC, 268-269
Ts'ao Hsueh Ch'in (INDIANA COMPANION), 238
TS'AO MAN CHUAN, 80
TS'AO YIN AND THE K'ANG-HSI EMPEROR, 225, 267
TSO-CHUAN COMMENTARY, 1
Tung Yueh's HSI-YU PU, 146
TWELVE YOUNG LADIES OF JINLING, 244
Two Literary Examples of Religious Pilgrimage: the COMMEDIA and JOURNEY TO THE WEST, 160
Two Scholars Who Passed the Examinations, 199
Two Songs by Ts'ao Ts'ao, 75
Two Types of Misinterpretation ... Poems From the RCD, 267
Poems From the RED CHAMBER DREAM, 279
Two Worlds of HLM, The, 279
TZU CHIH T'UNG CHIEN (COMPREHENSIVE MIRROR FOR AID IN GOVERNMENT), 72-73

UNDERGROUND MAN, THE, 5
UNOFFICIAL HISTORY OF THE LITERATI, AN (see JLWS)
USE OF THE SAN-KUO-CHIH AS A SOURCE FOR THE SKCYI, THE, 90
Uses of Literature in Communist China, The, 236
Utopian Imagination in Traditional Chinese Fiction, 60

VERSIONS OF CURRENT STORIES (see SHIH-SHUO HSIN-YU)
Virtue of Yi in WM, The, 124

Wang Shih-cheng, 169, 171, 190
WAR AND PEACE, 240
WATER MARGIN, THE (see SHC)
WATER MARGIN, THE (Hsia), 112
WATER MARGIN, THE (Jackson), 101
WATER MARGIN (THE) Revisited, 113, 155
WEI-SHU (CHRONICLES OF WEI), 80
WEN-SHIN, 23
Western Analogues to Chinese Literary Archetypes, 60
Western Critical and Comparative Approaches to ... Traditional China, 62
Western Hermeneutics and Concepts of Chinese Literary Theory, 37
WESTERN INSCRIPTION, THE, 47
What We Know of Ts'ao Hsueh Ch'in, 260
WILD BOAR FOREST, THE, 103
WILSONLINE, THE, 9
With and Without a Compass ... THE SCHOLARS and LAO TS'AN, 200

Women in DRC, 263
Women's Literature, 32
Wu Ch'eng-en, 148
Wu Ch'eng-en: His Life and
  Career, 148
WU CHING-TZU, 57
Wu Ching-tzu, 210
Wu Ching-tzu's SCHOLARS, 201
WU WO-YAO (BIZARRE HAPPENINGS
  EYEWITNESSED IN TWO DEC-
  ADES), 40

YANGTSE RIVER, THE, xi
Yen Fu and Ch'i Ch'ao as Advo-
  cates of the New Fiction,
  250
YEN LING CHIA (STEELING THE
  ARMOUR), 115
YEN TAN-TZU, 41
YI HSIA CHI (THE ALTRUISTIC
  KNIGHT), 115
Young Master Bountiful, 198
YU HUAN-CHI (THE JADE NECK-
  LACE), 177
Yu P'ing-po and the Literary
  Controversy Over HLM, 233
YUAN HSIAO NAO (THE LANTERN
  FESTIVAL), 116
Yuan Hung-tao, 188, 251
YUAN HUNG-TAO AND ... MING
  LITERARY AND INTELLECTUAL
  MOVEMENT, 113, 181, 251
Yuan Mei, 268

For Product Safety Concerns and Information please contact our EU representative GPSR@taylorandfrancis.com
Taylor & Francis Verlag GmbH, Kaufingerstraße 24, 80331 München, Germany

www.ingramcontent.com/pod-product-compliance
Lightning Source LLC
Chambersburg PA
CBHW060553230426
43670CB00011B/1803